# The Rules of Logic

# Letter from the General Editor

The Library of Arabic Literature makes available Arabic editions and English translations of significant works of Arabic literature, with an emphasis on the seventh to nineteenth centuries. The Library of Arabic Literature thus includes texts from the pre-Islamic era to the cusp of the modern period, and encompasses a wide range of genres, including poetry, poetics, fiction, religion, philosophy, law, science, travel writing, history, and historiography.

Books in the series are edited and translated by internationally recognized scholars. They are published in parallel-text and English-only editions in both print and electronic formats. PDFs of Arabic editions are available for free download. The Library of Arabic Literature also publishes distinct scholarly editions with critical apparatus.

The Library encourages scholars to produce authoritative Arabic editions, accompanied by modern, lucid English translations, with the ultimate goal of introducing Arabic's rich literary heritage to a general audience of readers as well as to scholars and students.

The publications of the Library of Arabic Literature are generously supported by Tamkeen under the NYU Abu Dhabi Research Institute Award G1003 and are published by NYU Press.

Philip F. Kennedy
*General Editor, Library of Arabic Literature*

# About this Paperback

This paperback edition differs in a few respects from its dual-language hardcover predecessor. Because of the compact trim size the pagination has changed. Material that referred to the Arabic edition has been updated to reflect the English-only format, and other material has been corrected and updated where appropriate. For information about the Arabic edition on which this English translation is based and about how the LAL Arabic text was established, readers are referred to the hardcover.

# The Rules of Logic

by

Najm al-Dīn al-Kātibī

translated and with commentary by

Tony Street

foreword by

Paul Thom

volume editor

Joseph E. Lowry

NEW YORK UNIVERSITY PRESS

*New York*

NEW YORK UNIVERSITY PRESS
New York



Please contact the Library of Congress for Cataloging-in-Publication data.

ISBN: 9781479840687 (paperback)
ISBN: 9781479840724 (library ebook)
ISBN: 9781479840700 (consumer ebook)

This book is printed on acid-free paper, and its binding materials are chosen for strength and durability. We strive to use environmentally responsible suppliers and materials to the greatest extent possible in publishing our books.

The manufacturer's authorized representative in the EU for product safety is Mare Nostrum Group B.V., Mauritskade 21D, 1091 GC Amsterdam, The Netherlands. Email: gpsr@mare-nostrum.co.uk.

Series design and composition by Nicole Hayward.

Typeset in Adobe Text

Manufactured in the United States of America

10 9 8 7 6 5 4 3 2 1

# Contents

# Abbreviations

| | |
|---|---|
| *AI* | Avicenna. *Kitāb al-Ishārāt wa-l-tanbīhāt.* |
| *AʿI* | Avicenna. *Al-Shifāʾ: al-Manṭiq: al-ʿIbārah.* |
| *AM* | Avicenna. *Al-Shifāʾ: al-Manṭiq: al-Madkhal.* |
| *AN* | Avicenna. *Al-Najāt min al-gharq fī baḥr al-ḍalālāt.* |
| *AQ* | Avicenna. *Al-Shifāʾ: al-Manṭiq: al-Qiyās.* |
| *ḤA* | al-Ḥillī. *Al-Asrār al-khafiyyah fī l-ʿulūm al-ʿaqliyyah.* |
| *ḤQ* | al-Ḥillī. *Al-Qawāʿid al-jaliyyah fī sharḥ al-Risālah al-Shamsiyyah.* |
| *ḪK* | al-Khūnajī. *Kashf al-asrār ʿan ghawāmiḍ al-afkār.* |
| *RM* | al-Rāzī. *Manṭiq al-mulakhkhaṣ.* |
| *SQ* | al-Samarqandī. *Qisṭās al-afkār fī l-manṭiq.* |
| *ṬḤ* | al-Ṭūsī. *Ḥall mushkilāt al-ishārāt.* |
| *TŠ* | al-Taftāzānī. *Sharḥ al-Risālah al-Shamsiyyah.* |
| *TT* | al-Taḥtānī. *Taḥrīr al-qawāʿid al-manṭiqiyyah fī sharḥ al-Risālah al-Shamsiyyah* (Qom, 2011). |

# Foreword

PAUL THOM

Of all the logic books inspired by Avicenna's *Pointers and Reminders,* Najm al-Dīn al-Kātibī's *al-Risālah al-Shamsiyyah* (*The Epistle for Shams al-Dīn*) stands out for how long it was in continuous use, as Tony Street explains in his Introduction to the present text. In it, al-Kātibī orders the Avicennian subject matter in new ways, and develops distinctive doctrines on many points, especially on the theory of the predicables and on modal syllogisms. Students of the history of logic will be struck by how thoroughly al-Kātibī has rethought Avicenna's system. Students of modern logic will be impressed by al-Kātibī's attention to matters passed over in modern logical systems, particularly in modal logic.

The book's opening page extols the preeminent value of scientific knowledge as humanity's highest goal and brightest virtue, a path to the divinely ordered system of quiddities that make up the created world, so that our souls rise to the level of the angelic intelligences (§0). Implicit in these remarks is a Neoplatonic world-picture where everything emanates successively from the primary source of all being: first come the angelic intelligences, then the celestial bodies, animate bodies including humans, and inanimate matter down to its most degraded form as prime matter. In return, humans have the possibility of reversing the order of this process, ascending through the pursuit of scientific knowledge to a state in which their souls are perfected by active intellection. The intellectual tradition in which al-Kātibī flourished deemed nothing more worthy of human aspiration than the possession of scientific knowledge.

Following Avicenna, al-Kātibī takes knowledge to exist in two forms: conceptions and assertions (§1). Conceptions include definitions and other explanatory phrases; assertions include demonstrations and other arguments. Each branch of knowledge has its own objects of study, whose essential attributes (apart from those that are part of its essence) it establishes as flowing with necessity from the essence (§5). For example, triangles are among the objects that geometry studies. A triangle is essentially a figure with three straight sides, and geometry teaches that the attribute of having angles equal to 180 degrees, while not part of the essence of a triangle, flows necessarily from it.

Some conceptions and some assertions are primitive; others are inferred. The primitive conceptions and assertions have no further foundation. All non-primitive knowledge can be inferred from the primitive conceptions and assertions in an orderly knowledge-expanding manner. At each step of this process, what is unknown is made known by virtue of its connection with what is already known (§3).

We can make mistakes about conceptions and assertions, so we need a canon that teaches the correct ordering of conceptions and assertions in the individual sciences. This canon is logic. Logic is a science; and, like other sciences, it is made up of conceptions and assertions ordered in a knowledge-expanding manner—conceptions and assertions determining the proper ordering of conceptions and assertions. The science of logic lays down the conditions under which conceptions are ordered as species and genera, and assertions are ordered as antecedents and consequents. We need to grasp the principles of proper ordering if we are to construct scientific definitions and demonstrations.

All this bespeaks a conception of logic different from the one that prevails today. We think of logic as the study of valid argument. An argument may be about anything at all. So there is no necessary connection between the idea of logic and the idea of science.

Validity is not necessarily connected to the expansion of knowledge; a valid argument may be composed of propositions none of which are known. And even arguments about scientific questions are not normally about the essences of things.

Yet for al-Kātibī and his contemporaries, the concept of essence is foundational to any body of knowledge, including knowledge of logic. The concept is central to the idea of science as knowledge concerning a given genus, since for al-Kātibī a genus is part of an essence/quiddity. The notion of essence also plays a substantial role in the logic of modal propositions and arguments. Every simple proposition attaches one term to another, but the sense of a simple proposition may be enlarged by the inclusion of a *modality* indicating that the predicate attaches to the subject with necessity or possibility, always or sometimes.

In al-Kātibī's logic, a modality can enter a proposition in two ways, depending on whether it relates to the subject's essence or to the way the subject is described. Someone who is writing is necessarily moving, so long as she falls under the description "writing"; this is a necessity that qualifies the predication only because the subject is described as writing, not by virtue of the subject's essence as a human being. By contrast, a human is necessarily an animal; and this necessity expresses part of the essence of human beings. In other necessity propositions, what is predicated is an implicate, rather than a part, of the subject's essence.

Avicenna had laid the foundations for this typology of modal proposition. Al-Kātibī turns Avicenna's remarks into a systematic study. He lists thirteen modally or temporally qualified propositional forms, distinguishing several ways in which temporal notions enter the sense of a proposition. The predicate may attach to the subject in perpetuity, or occasionally, or with different types of regularity. For example, to say that every human necessarily breathes is to imply that breathing occurs in humans in a certain regular way—a way that is different from the regularity involved in the eclipse of the moon. For each propositional form, al-Kātibī lays out truth-conditions, thus supplying a basic modal semantics. And he maps the ways all these propositional forms undergo logical transformations through processes of contradiction, conversion, and contradiction.

The semantics and logical syntax of modal propositions is a preliminary to al-Kātibī's theory of reasoning. Here he studies inferences that are built up from simple or modalized propositions, concentrating on syllogistic reasoning. A syllogism is an inference from two subject-predicate premises arranged so that: (1) the predicate of the first is the subject of the second, or (2) both have the same predicate, or (3) both have the same subject, or (4) the subject of the first is the predicate of the second. There are thus four ways in which the two subject-predicate propositions can share a term.

These are the four figures of the syllogism. Avicenna recognized only three, dismissing the fourth as removed from nature. In each figure al-Kātibī lays down the conditions under which premise-pairs are productive, and he explains why these conditions are necessary. Based on these general conditions, he draws a syllogistic conclusion from each productive premise-pair, proving the resulting syllogism's validity in one of three ways: by converting its terms, by showing that its invalidity would result in an impossibility, or by expanding a particular premise into a pair of universals ("ecthesis").

In the case of modal syllogisms, the discussion is sparser. There are general rules for productivity in each figure, and rules for what follows from the productive premise-pairs, depending on whether the modality concerns essences or descriptions. But there are no explanations of why these rules are necessary. Nor are there proofs of validity for individual syllogisms. The presentation of the modal syllogistic takes the form of a summary of results, rather than a body of demonstrative knowledge. The work's original readers must have found this part frustrating. Modern logicians will read it as a field ripe for creative interpretation.

In a major departure from Avicenna's modal logic, al-Kātibī declares that the ultimate subject of modal reasoning—the subject of the minor premise—must be something actual, not merely possible (§98). Avicenna had envisaged syllogisms about possibilities within possibilities. At the same time, al-Kātibī was aware of the power of counterfactual reasoning. In one passage (§§45-46) he allows that we can consider what a non-existent individual would be if it were to exist, noting that even if there were no squares in existence, we can say truly that all squares are figures.

The book concludes with a return to the theme of scientific knowledge. Demonstrative inferences are distinguished from four different types of non-demonstrative reasoning. Whereas a demonstrative syllogism shows with certainty that its conclusion is true, dialectical reasoning aims simply to persuade the addressee, rhetorical reasoning aims to exhort the listeners to accept something that is useful to them, sophistical reasoning aims to silence or deceive, and poetic reasoning elicits an image in the listener's soul.

Al-Kātibī presents all this material in prose of chiselled precision. His book displays a powerful sense of order. Al-Katibi's text presents a sophisticated recapitulation/reordering of Avicenna's logic, now made accessible through Tony Street's translation.

Paul Thom
*The University of Sydney*

# Acknowledgments

Warm thanks to James Montgomery for entrusting *al-Risālah al-Shamsiyyah* to me in the first place, and for keeping faith over the years as I allowed myself to be distracted by other things. Joe Lowry has been an ideal editor; he has saved me from countless mistakes, alerted me to glaring omissions, and rallied my spirits when they flagged. LAL's editorial director Dr Chip Rossetti has been supportive throughout, and LAL's digital production manager Stuart Brown went beyond the call of duty and made substantive improvements to the content. I am grateful to the editors of the Library of Arabic Literature for finding a place for this book as one of their scholarly editions. What follows is not a scholarly edition in any sense of the phrase, but it is long, and fits better alongside other long books.

Many other people have helped, often without knowing, and most in more ways than I can record. Thanks to Nicholas Rescher for having paved everyone's path to the study of Arabic logic, to Tony Johns for introducing me to Fakhr al-Dīn al-Rāzī, to Father Georges Anawati for confirming me as a follower of al-Rāzī, and to Richard Frank for insisting I look beyond al-Rāzī. A timely phone call from Dimitri Gutas was the only thing that kept me in Islamic studies. Paul Thom has generously helped over the years as I struggled with the material. Asad Ahmed, Ahmed Alwishah, Feriel Bouhafa, Reza Dadkhah, Silvia Di Vincenzo, Asad Fallahi, Pree Jareonsettasin, Jari Kaukua, Dustin Klinger, Harun Kuşlu, Joep Lameer, Stephen

Menn, Yoav Meyrav, Reza Pourjavady, Boaz Schuman, Ayman Shihadeh, Rob Wisnovsky, Walter Young, and Behnam Zolghadr have helped me obtain manuscripts or solve interpretive problems. Colleagues close by—John Marenbon, Catherine Pickstock, and Yasser Qureshy—have made medieval philosophy at Cambridge deeply congenial. Colleagues farther afield have had the kindness to involve me in projects from which I have learned things crucial to understanding *al-Risālah al-Shamsiyyah*: Peter Adamson, Leone Gazziero, Nadja Germann, Yehuda Halper, Charles Manekin, and Shahid Rahman. I have learned more from my (mostly former) students than they have from me: Suf Amichay, Amal Awad, Necmeddin Besikci, Zhenyu Cai, Daniel Davies, Tareq Moqbel, Mohammed Saleh Zarepour, and Tianyi Zhang.

I owe special thanks to three former colleagues at Cambridge. Khaled El-Rouayheb came more than twenty years ago; his extraordinary work since then has transformed the study of Arabic logic. He has always been generous to a fault in sharing manuscripts and insights. At roughly the same time, Cornelia Schöck also arrived; she made me aware of the huge importance of the connections between logic and the broader Islamic sciences. After leaving for Bochum, Cornelia was awarded a grant from the DFG (German Research Foundation) that employed Riccardo Strobino, and in an act of monumental kindness allowed him to base himself in Cambridge. Riccardo's time here was certainly the happiest period of my academic career. If my translation has any fidelity to the original, or clarity in expression, it is entirely due to watching Riccardo go about his work.

This book is the fulfillment of a promise made—first implicitly, later explicitly—in applications to the Arts and Humanities Research Council for two grants on which I was principal investigator (19484/1 and AH/I50060X/1). I am grateful to the AHRC for its support.

Above all, much love and many thanks to Ruth for putting up with it all.

# Introduction

Logic was revered in the thirteenth century, perhaps more highly than it has been revered before or since. This is as true of the Muslim East as it is of the Christian West. It has recently been said of Peter of Spain's *Summaries of Logic*, probably written in the 1230s, that no other book on logic prior to the twentieth century had such wide readership or, in consequence, did so much to shape Western ways of constructing well-formed sentences and putting them together in valid arguments.[1] But perhaps one other logic text has had just as many readers, and as profound an impact on ways of formal discourse and argument. In the Muslim East, *The Rules of Logic* (*al-Risalah al-Shamsiyyah*, literally *The Epistle [on Logical Rules] for Shams al-Dīn*, henceforth *"al-Risalah al-Shamsiyyah"* or *"the Risālah"*) was written some forty years after the *Summaries*, by someone who was Peter's exact contemporary: Najm al-Dīn al-Kātibī (d. 675/1276). *Al-Risālah al-Shamsiyyah* also came to figure in the education of nearly every aspiring young scholar, and is still read in traditional schools.

## Logic in the Muslim East

How did logic come to be so important in the syllabus of Muslim schools? From the moment the armies first came out of the Arabian Peninsula, Muslims found themselves in control of communities that had studied logic for centuries, and that—in the case of the Syriac Christians—had made it a central feature of religious education.

But it is not until late in the Umayyad period (ca. 44–132/661–750) that we have clear evidence of Muslim interest in logic, specifically among courtiers of the regime, one of whom translated an introductory text based on Porphyry's *Introduction*, and Aristotle's *Categories, De Interpretatione*, and the first seven chapters of the *Prior Analytics*.[2] This interest intensified dramatically with the Abbasids (ca. 132–656/750–1258), when the needs of propaganda—the need to be seen to adopt Sasanian cultural projects—led the dynasty to support networks of translators of scientific literature drawn from the various religious communities. From the early ninth century, Baghdad was home to a number of translation projects, increasingly devoted to producing full translations of the texts that make up the Aristotelian *Organon*. The culmination of the work of these translators was the emergence of a textual Aristotelianism in the first quarter of the tenth century, led by the Muslim Abū Naṣr al-Fārābī (d. 339/950) and the Christian Abū Bishr Mattā ibn Yūnus (d. 328/940). Much of their output can be seen as a continuation of the late antique commentators, producing careful and often critical analyses of the Aristotelian texts on logic.

The commentary work continued through the first half of the eleventh century in Baghdad's school of loosely affiliated scholars, only to be rudely interrupted by a letter from a rising young star, Avicenna (Ibn Sīnā; d. 428/1037), who was working at the time in Hamadhān, asking the Baghdadi scholars details about their doctrine on universals.[3] Here was a philosopher who, seemingly outside of any scholarly network, had come to his own quite radical take on Aristotelian logic, who could defend his views with crushingly cogent arguments, and who—at the time of the letter to the Baghdadis—was in the process of presenting his views in various genres designed to appeal to different audiences, and to students at different stages in their education. Early on there was resistance to Avicenna's logic,[4] but fairly rapidly it became the standard system against which an Arabic logician would define his own position. The Aristotelian *Organon* was effectively replaced by the Avicennian logical corpus; indeed, reference to the First Teacher (Aristotle) dwindled, only to be replaced by constant reference to Avicenna, the Leading Master (*al-shaykh al-raʾīs*).

Throughout this period, from the early third/ninth to the late fifth/eleventh century, logic was still confined to networks of scholars associated more with courts, or institutions like hospitals and observatories, than with any given religion. At the same time, there was some anxiety among pious believers—whether Muslims, Jews, or Christians—that by studying the methods by which Aristotle arrived at his heretical beliefs, the student could end up holding the same beliefs. Lawyers and theologians learned no logic in their studies, or at any rate, no logic derived from the Aristotelian *Organon.* Against this trend, al-Fārābī wrote a work in the early fourth/tenth century designed to show that Aristotelian logic could contribute to legal studies a deeper understanding of forensic argument techniques. It is difficult to assign a single reason behind the ultimate acceptance of logic in Muslim institutions of learning, but there can be no doubt that the utility of logic for analyzing and justifying legal reasoning was a major consideration. Among others, the renowned scholar Abū Ḥāmid al-Ghazālī (d. 505/1111) took up this line of defense, and even prefaced his summa of jurisprudence, the *Distillation of the Principles of Jurisprudence* (*al-Mustaṣfā min ʿilm al-uṣūl*), with an introduction on logic.[5]

## Al-Kātibī's Life, Logic, Works, and Significance

Due to Avicenna's victory over conservative Aristotelianism, al-Kātibī's *al-Risālah al-Shamsiyyah* presents a logic strongly marked by Avicenna, and divergent in many ways from the logic in Peter's *Summaries.* Due to widespread acceptance of the claim that logic was helpful for legal studies, the *Risālah*'s major reception was not among scholars working in courts and scientific institutions, but in the religious schools, among Muslim students of law and theology. It is ironic that a work commended so highly by the *fatāwā*, the legal opinions, was written by someone working in an observatory funded by monies usurped from religious trusts, but so it was: al-Kātibī was one of the founding members of the Īl-Khānid observatory at Marāghah, on which work began in 657/1259.[6] The Shams al-Dīn to whom al-Kātibī dedicated his *Risālah* was the regime's vizier, who had come to power in 661/1263. This means that the *Risālah*'s dedication, and probably its composition, post-date 1263.

Najm al-Dīn Abū l-Ḥasan ʿAlī ibn ʿUmar al-Kātibī was born in 600/1204 in Qazvīn, about a hundred miles west of modern Tehran. A member of the Shāfiʿī school of law, the "al-Kātibī" in his name may mean he had connections of some kind with the scribal class. He went off to study the rational sciences with Athīr al-Dīn al-Abharī (d. ca. 660/1261), and manuscripts from that period of study survive to this day in al-Kātibī's hand.[7] The most important political event that unfolded through al-Kātibī's lifetime was the Mongol invasion and the sack of Baghdad (656/1258), among other cities. Catastrophic as the event was for many, for al-Kātibī it seems mainly to have presented him with a golden opportunity. In the late 1250s, he was approached by the famous Shiʿi scholar Naṣīr al-Dīn al-Ṭūsī (d. 672/1274), and enlisted to help found the Īl-Khānid observatory at Marāghah, far to the west of Qazvīn. Al-Kātibī taught a number of students, among them the famous Shiʿi theologian al-ʿAllāmah al-Ḥillī (d. 726/1325); there were others, but al-Ḥillī was the one who mattered most for the reception of the *Risālah*. Al-Kātibī seems by and large to have remained teaching in Marāghah until shortly before his death, and probably died there in 675/1276; he was buried in Qazvīn.[8]

The fact that al-Kātibī studied with al-Abharī is extremely significant, because al-Abharī is said to have been a student of Fakhr al-Dīn al-Rāzī (d. 606/1210; more likely he was a student of one of al-Rāzī's students),[9] and al-Rāzī is one of the three most important intellectual coordinates for al-Kātibī's work, along with Avicenna and Afḍal al-Dīn al-Khūnajī (d. 646/1248). Indeed, al-Kātibī is described as one of the followers of Fakhr al-Dīn (*min atbāʿ Fakhr al-Dīn*) by al-Ḥillī, so al-Abharī must have managed to convey to al-Kātibī a vivid sense of al-Rāzī's intellectual project. Exactly what that project was in terms of logic will emerge through the course of the commentary that follows the translation, but—in broad terms—al-Rāzī's project was to recruit the philosophy of Avicenna for the service of Islamic theology. This involved commentary on one of Avicenna's major works, *Pointers and Reminders* (*Kitāb al-Ishārāt wa-l-tanbīhāt*), and criticism of many of the principles it invokes; it also involved the composition of independent works in which traditional theological topics were developed with heavy use of philosophical concepts.

Just as al-Rāzī mediated al-Kātibī's reception of Avicenna, al-Khūnajī mediated his reception of al-Rāzī, mainly of the logic. Al-Khūnajī had ceaselessly and critically evaluated al-Rāzī's logical work, and pushed it in an ever more formal direction. So, while al-Rāzī had set *Pointers and Reminders* as the focus for much later work on Avicenna's logic, and established a number of crucial research questions and distinctions with which to deal with these questions, al-Khūnajī critically evaluated both al-Rāzī's distinctions and his arguments. Al-Kātibī often took up al-Khūnajī's refinements and alternative arguments, but often also defended al-Rāzī or introduced further refinements. However well al-Kātibī got on with his colleague al-Ṭūsī at the observatory, over logic they must have argued endlessly: al-Ṭūsī would never have been prepared to treat al-Rāzī and al-Khūnajī as though their arguments were on par with Avicenna's.

Al-Kātibī is almost as famous for a work that covered metaphysics and physics, *Philosophy of the Source* (*Ḥikmat al-ʿayn*), as concise and beautifully structured as the *Risālah*, and consequently equally popular in the schoolroom. He wrote a companion text on logic for the *Philosophy of the Source*, the *Source of the Precepts* (*ʿAyn al-qawāʿid*), and he wrote the long *Compendium of Subtleties in the Disclosure of Truths* (*Jāmiʿ al-daqāʾiq fī kashf al-ḥaqāʾiq*). He wrote other short treatises and epistles, and a commentary on al-Rāzī's text on philosophical theology, the *Treatise on the Thoughts of Ancient and Recent Scholars* (*Muḥaṣṣal afkār al-mutaqaddimīn wa-l-muta'akhkhirīn*). He also wrote two massive commentaries, on al-Rāzī's *Epitome of Logic and Philosophy* (*al-Mulakhkhaṣ fī l-manṭiq wa-l-ḥikmah*; I only consult the logic volume, published under the title *Manṭiq al-Mulakhkhaṣ*) and al-Khūnajī's *Disclosure of Secrets from the Obscurities of Thought* (*Kashf al-asrār 'an ghawāmiḍ al-afkār*). Al-Kātibī was, in short, first and foremost a philosopher with a special interest in logic.

*Al-Risālah al-Shamsiyyah* is a text that was read by nearly every aspiring scholar in the central territories of the Islamic world, through what has been called the Late Middle Period, and—in traditional schools—it is still read today.[10] One measure of its extraordinary standing as a high-level introductory text for the study of logic is the number of manuscripts of it we find in libraries that hold Arabic collections. Likewise, when lithography and printing became common in the Muslim world, numerous versions of the *Risālah* were made available. Most of these manuscripts and printed versions give the text of the *Risālah*, along with one of the many commentaries written on it, especially the commentary of Quṭb al-Dīn al-Rāzī al-Taḥtānī (d. 766/1365). Even the British East India Company joined in, producing what is probably the first movable-type version of the text, along with al-Taḥtānī's commentary. Indeed, another way to gauge the scale of the *Risālah*'s impact is in terms of these commentaries; it is certainly among the texts most commented upon in Muslim scholarly circles. The focus of the commentators changed over time, and this was a factor in the *Risālah*'s continued recognition as a central teaching text. Commentaries would dwell on subjects touched on in the text, contingent on the central focus in approaching the discipline as that focus changed through the centuries and across regions. And, of course, the commentaries continued to be written because the *Risālah* had found a secure place in the syllabus of many religious colleges. For whatever reason, even those scholars who regarded the broader logical tradition with suspicion were prepared to include the *Risālah* among texts unobjectionable to pious concerns.[11]

## Reception of the *Risālah*

A text lives in readers' reception of it; the way readers through the ages have received the *Risālah* is set out for us in the many commentaries written on it. Before I say a few words about the commentators I have used to understand the *Risālah* and assess its reception, let me say something about the place Aristotle and Avicenna have among the authorities invoked by the *Risālah*.

Most notable by his absence is Aristotle. Al-Kātibī makes no reference to Aristotle, though admittedly he makes no direct reference to anyone at all. But if we fill out the authorities al-Kātibī is tacitly invoking by looking at what his commentators say (and in particular al-Ḥillī, who studied the text under his guidance), the point remains: neither Aristotle nor his work occupies al-Kātibī's attention. Before I turn to Avicenna, who does have that honor, I should note that this does not mean that Arabic logicians did not recognize Aristotle's ultimate primacy in the discipline. Al-Rāzī could think of no higher compliment to pay al-Shāfiʿī than that he was to jurisprudence what Aristotle was to logic.[12] The respected bibliographer Ibn al-Akfānī (d. 749/1348) says much the same (along with some questionable chronology):

> It is widely known that the person who originated and instituted logic is Aristotle, that he found no other book [on logic] by his predecessors other than a book on the categories, and that he was alerted to writing logic down and putting it in that order by the organization of Euclid's book on geometry.[13]

But respect did not mean a student should devote time to reading the translations of Aristotle's logic that were available. Ibn al-Akfānī went on to set out a syllabus for the student of logic, and it is noteworthy that even someone who is prepared to read "the vast ocean of the logic part" of Avicenna's *Cure* (*Kitāb al-Shifāʾ*) is not advised to read Aristotle's logical works. Even so, there was a continuing sense that it was valid to evaluate at least some aspects of what the Arabic logicians were doing in terms of what Aristotle had done. This is what the great intellectual historian Ibn Khaldūn (d. 784/1382) did (following al-Taftāzānī, see Text 0.1 in the commentary) in a much-quoted passage in which he criticizes post-Avicennian logic for failing to cover the valuable uses of logic set out in the books, the *Posterior Analytics*, the *Topics*, the *Rhetoric*, the *Poetics*, and the *Sophistical Refutations*.[14] But—to return to the primary point—we do not find the textual engagement with Aristotle that shapes so much Latin philosophy, nor any appeal to his authority on substantive matters.

It is Avicenna who towers over al-Kātibī's *Risālah*, who replaces Aristotle in every sense, whose presence is underlined at every turn by the commentators. But Avicenna is for al-Kātibī as old as Kant is for us, and the logicians mentioned earlier—al-Rāzī and al-Khūnajī—played a huge role in how al-Kātibī read Avicenna. Indeed, Ibn al-Akfānī recommends that the aspiring logician read al-Kātibī's commentaries on the logic texts of both of his great post-Avicennian mentors.[15] But rather than go back to the books that make up al-Kātibī's canon of authorities to try to work out how he is responding to his predecessors, I have turned to three of the earliest commentators on the *Risālah*: al-ʿAllāmah al-Ḥillī, Quṭb al-Dīn al-Rāzī al-Taḥtānī, and Saʿd al-Dīn al-Taftāzānī (d. 792/1390). In fact, I have relied on them so much that, if the commentary that follows the translation clarifies what al-Kātibī is doing in the *Risālah*, these three scholars must take the credit.

A few words on these early commentators are in order. Al-Ḥillī is a young man writing one of his earliest books when composing *Clear Precepts in Commentary on the Epistle for Shams al-Dīn* (*al-Qawāʿid al-jaliyyah fī sharḥ al-Risālah al-Shamsiyyah*); he intends to provide (so we are told) guidance for his young colleagues trying to read a difficult text. (I would note that, at first glance, the *Risālah* does not look so difficult, so al-Ḥillī's colleagues are at least advanced enough to resist being lulled into a false sense of security by the *Risālah*'s brisk and straightforward tone.) Al-Ḥillī's major point of difference from al-Taḥtānī and al-Taftāzānī is that he writes a second, deeper book in tandem with the *Clear Precepts*, *Hidden Secrets* (*al-Asrār al-khafiyyah fī l-ʿulūm al-ʿaqliyyah*), and thus feels able for the most part to leave disputed points up in the air. These are especially the points at which al-Kātibī departs from Avicenna and follows al-Rāzī.

Al-Taḥtānī is a more senior scholar than al-Ḥillī was when he writes his commentary, *Redaction of the Rules of Logic in Commentary on the Epistle for Shams al-Dīn* (*Taḥrīr al-qawāʿid al-manṭiqiyyah fī sharḥ al-Risālah al-Shamsiyyah*), and he settles to each point (especially early in the commentary) with thorough and slightly self-satisfied precision. The sense I have is that he is more aligned with al-Kātibī's views on the subject, and even though he corrects a number of claims in the *Risālah*, he rarely displays hostility toward al-Kātibī's broader program, or the authorities on which he draws for inspiration.

Al-Taftāzānī is engaged in a second-order commentary, *Commentary on the Epistle for Shams al-Dīn* (*Sharḥ al-Risālah al-Shamsiyyah*), correcting al-Taḥtānī. He has a reputation—probably undeserved—for plodding scholarship,[16] and writes his commentary to clarify and at points deepen al-Taḥtānī's *Taḥrīr*. I follow him with fervor through the modal syllogistic; he and I agree on a central issue that culminates in Text 98.2. Al-Taftāzānī was drawn into a debilitating enmity with a younger scholar, al-Sayyid al-Sharīf al-Jurjānī (d. 816/1413), who wrote marginal notes (a *ḥāshiyah*) on the *Taḥrīr*; the work by al-Jurjānī is much shorter than al-Taftāzānī's, and is printed in the margins or footnotes of many versions of the *Taḥrīr* (including the edition I use, by Bīdārfar). It has been helpful for a couple of matters, though I have not used it systematically.

My sense is that al-Ḥillī's commentary is the clearest of the three, but it is also the most hostile, and its charity grows thinner the more al-Kātibī diverges from Avicenna.[17] Further, although each commentary has its virtues, none covers every point that seems important to me. So al-Taḥtānī alone presents tables of the modal mixes (sadly garbled in the Bīdārfar printing), and these are too helpful to leave out of a commentary. At the same time, he often fails to give details for the scholars on whom al-Kātibī draws, or from whom he distances himself. For example, although al-Taḥtānī gives the different truth-conditions for the coincidental conditional al-Ḥillī sets out in Text 60.1 in the commentary below (in *TT* 301.6–u),[18] he fails to note which Avicenna prefers. Similarly, al-Ḥillī draws attention to—and deplores—the fact that al-Kātibī is following al-Rāzī in his taxonomy of definitions (Text 36.2 in the commentary below), whereas al-Taḥtānī simply delivers al-Kātibī's account without complaint (*TT* 314.1–12). Al-Taftāzānī's commentary stands as an independent work much more than we would expect given its declared intention—dealing with what al-Taḥtānī had neglected, resolving problems arising from his zeal for explanation, pinning down his loose phrasing (*TŠ* 88.1–2)—but nonetheless he assumes more advanced knowledge of the subject on the part of his readers than either of his predecessors.

In writing my own commentary under the spell of the great early commentaries on the *Risālah*, I encountered a number of surprises. On many occasions, I have read a lemma of the *Risālah* and thought it straightforward, only to discover from the commentators a tangle of difficulties I simply had not seen. Take, for the earliest example of this, the first lemma. The resolutions and refinements of the phrasing (how does al-Kātibī intend us to take the disjunctive?) and of the material being treated (if a conception is actually a component of an assertion, rather than merely a precondition for it, how can the two be opposed?) become so ramified that a pragmatic decision has to limit how far to follow the discussion. Nearly always, I go no further than al-Ḥillī; if he feels we have reached a provisional preliminary interpretation of the lemma, I let it go. I have also been surprised by the questions, both those addressed and those that are not raised, not just in the reception of the *Risālah*, but in its initial composition. Why dwell so long, for example, on the aspects of signification theory set out in §§7–14 (and especially those set out in the first three lemmata), and not—given that the *Risālah* is meant for students early in their logical studies—say something about how to define signification, and to distinguish in particular conventional signification? Again, I import material from the commentators (in this case, al-Ḥillī) to fill in these gaps. Looking back over the translations I have made of what strike me as especially illuminating insights from the commentators, al-Ḥillī is overwhelmingly the resource to which I have turned. And he has certainly provided me with my guiding principle, which is at most to introduce issues raised in the *Risālah*, rather than to explore and assess them.

At the end of reading the *Risālah*, one may wonder what students of the text would have gained from their efforts. Theories of signification and predication, obviously, along with analyses of quantified, modalized, and hypothetical propositions; procedures for checking inferences; and the outlines of a philosophy of science. But, in the most general terms, they would have come to realize with what indeterminate materials natural language operates—the shifting significations of expressions, the overtones of meanings, and the deep ambiguities hidden in seemingly clear sentences—and the lengths to which one must go to make these aspects of language determinate. I suspect that few of the *Risālah*'s readers went on to formulate knowledge-claims in the propositional forms listed in the *Risālah*, and still fewer went on to deduce new knowledge-claims using the inference-schemata al-Kātibī had proved to be valid. But all would have come away from their study with an appreciation of the many pitfalls of building an argument or setting out an unambiguous claim in a natural language.

They were also made aware of a culturally revered canon of philosophical authority, one that freed their own culture from adherence to strictly Aristotelian forms. Reading the commentaries showed that no reference needed to be made beyond Arabic texts, and "the ancients" (*al-qudamā'*) only rarely recall a logician more ancient than al-Fārābī. Learning how all important problems were generated and resolved within the *Risālah*'s canon drove home more memorably than anything else could the resources of Arabic philosophical culture. We need not wonder how logic fitted so snugly into a legal and theological education: it reasserted rather than unsettled the independence of Arabic scholarship.

# Note on the Translation and the Commentary

*Al-Risālah al-Shamsiyyah* was edited and translated into English by Aloys Sprenger and William Kay in the 1850s. Their translation is an extremely helpful point of reference, which guided me in my early encounter with the *Risālah*, and against which I have checked my work at the end. Sprenger left the section on the modal syllogistic out of the translation (§§98–104 in the following text), and provided few notes on the *Risālah* to help the reader. It was more than a hundred years later that Nicholas Rescher came back to translate the omitted section.[19] Even before I read Sprenger-Kay, I had read Rescher's introductions and analyses of al-Kātibī's logic, and the translation is guided by an interpretation of the syllogistic that owes its main lines to Rescher.[20] I have also followed Rescher in adopting Sprenger's translations of the names of the various modal propositions for my version of the *Risālah*; this decision has a few curious consequences (for example, the English "conditional" applies both to one kind of categorical proposition and to one kind of hypothetical), but will hopefully make it slightly easier to refer back to earlier work on the *Risālah*.

Given its debts to earlier work, it is fair to ask whether the translation offered here represents the original text more clearly or more faithfully than its predecessor. I hope it does; and if it does, it will be for two reasons. One lies in the field's increasing grip on Avicennian and post-Avicennian philosophy, and the increasing availability of texts from the community in which al-Kātibī worked. In particular, recent editions of the works of al-Rāzī and al-Khūnajī allow us to see al-Kātibī's work as the outcome of a century-long project of assimilating Avicennian logic. Well over half the works on which I call regularly in the commentary (those under Abbreviations) have been translated or edited for the first time in the last twenty years. The other reason is that, as noted above, I have decided to follow in the footsteps of al-Kātibī's main early commentators, al-Ḥillī, al-Taḥtānī, and al-Taftāzānī. I concede that they may be wrong on points in interpreting the *Risālah*, but they (especially al-Ḥillī) are closely acquainted with al-Kātibī's central concerns, and strive to order the text according to these concerns. For the future, the most important single resource for guiding a fresh translation of al-Kātibī will be al-Kātibī's other logical works, nearly all of which remain in manuscript as of the time of writing this introduction.[21]

There is a grand tradition of translating medieval Latin logic into English—one need only think of Brian P. Copenhaver and his team, of Paul Thom, and above all of Gyula Klima—and the resulting translations are readable in ways that reflect a consensus on how to approach the task.[22] There are certainly accurate translations of Arabic logic texts—F. W. Zimmermann's translation of al-Fārābī's commentary on *De Interpretatione* still deserves honorable mention, even though his work has now been joined by a number of other worthy efforts (see Further Reading)—but the results have yet to converge on an agreed way to translate the terms of art. More than any other work to which I refer, Riccardo Strobino's entry on Avicenna's logic in the Stanford Encyclopedia of Philosophy serves as a glossary for the vast majority of the terms translated in the text that follows;[23] I hope this makes the task of putting al-Kātibī's logic in the context of the most important authority from which it derives somewhat easier. I also believe Strobino's entry reflects an emerging consensus on how to translate the terms.

This is a translation of a text written within a group of scholars whose activities grew out of translations made long ago, but who, as a group, avoided working with translated texts, which they believed must be misleading. They were right. I have hesitated when choosing among possible translations for technical terms, and I refer here to a few of those hesitations, chosen to illustrate some of the considerations at play. The first is perhaps the most difficult to resolve. Like other premodern logicians, al-Kātibī presented his logic in a natural language or, more precisely, did not present his logic by translating arguments into a formal language. At the same time, the sentence forms into which he regiments his propositions for logical treatment are hardly idiomatic Arabic; aside from anything else, they can involve opaque hangovers from the translation movement. Take as an example the absolute proposition (*al-qaḍiyyah al-muṭlaqah*) as set out in §78; the Arabic for the a-proposition would read *bi-l-iṭlāq al-ʿāmm kull jīm bāʾ*. One way to render this is in parallel with the structurally similar necessity proposition (*al-qaḍiyyah al-ḍarūriyyah*), for which *bi-l-ḍarūrah kull jīm bāʾ* is clearly "by necessity, every C is B." With Strobino, I render *bi-l-iṭlāq al-ʿāmm* with the clumsy phrase "general absoluteness," but the origin of the Arabic is cloudy, and its earliest usage is at variance with al-Kātibī's.[24] We are told that the contradictory of "by general absoluteness, every C is B" (*bi-l-iṭlāq al-ʿāmm kull jīm bāʾ*) is "always, some C is not B" (*dāʾiman baʿḍ jīm laysa bāʾ*; §69.2), so, however it is expressed, the general absolute should be understood as "every C is at least once B." Given that no native speaker innocent of Avicenna's logic would take this understanding from *bi-l-iṭlāq al-ʿāmm kull jīm bāʾ*, the translator has to decide whether the English should make the reader face the same difficulty as a pre-philosophical reader of the Arabic, or over-translate. I have chosen the first path for the translation itself, and the path of over-translation for my commentary. I hope the awkward phrasing in the translation reflects what I take to be al-Kātibī's intention: to make the language of regimentation awkward enough to signal that those passages should be read in a different register.

The second problem is often noted by translators in the Library of Arabic Literature series: there are words that are productive in Arabic for which no equally productive English term can be found. Take the example of *ʿāmm*, "general." The general absolute (*al-muṭlaqah al-ʿāmmah*) such as "every C is at least once B" is combined to make a second, two-sided absolute (§56 below, the non-perpetual existential): "every C is at least once B and at least once not B," referred to by al-Kātibī's commentators (but not by al-Kātibī himself, at least in the *Risālah*) as the special absolute (*al-muṭlaqah al-khāṣṣah*). The general proposition (*ʿāmmah*) is implicationally weaker ("more general," *aʿamm*) than the special (*khāṣṣah*), in the sense that a two-sided absolute implies a one-sided one, but not the other way round. *ʿUmūm*, "generality," may also refer to the relative extension of terms; if between the two there is *ʿumūm muṭlaq* (§26 and following), the individuals under the more particular term are included in or form a subset of the individuals under the more general. Inconsistently, I translate "proper inclusion," not "absolute generality." In short, technical English obscures deeper links among the terms of art that are clear to the Arabic logicians.

Let me conclude with a couple of more minor worries. Ideally, the translation of a term should reflect its Greek provenance. Strictly, *qaḍiyyah ḥamliyyah* should be "predicative proposition," not "categorical proposition," but then it would no longer correspond to the common English rendition of the original phrase in Aristotle's logic; this consideration is generally decisive. On the other hand, once a term is translated into Arabic, its further development may depend on whether the productivity of the Arabic term is exploited. Take *lāzim* (literally "inseparable") as we find it in the translation of Porphyry's *Introduction* (the classical text introducing the material given in the first treatise of the *Risālah*); Barnes's translation gives its corresponding Greek as "concomitant," now the most common translation of *lāzim*. But once in Arabic, *lāzim* the active participle invokes its passive participle *malzūm* ("what is followed"); together, they are used in technical phrases like *lāzim al-lāzim lāzim al-malzūm* ("the implicate of the implicate is the implicate of the implicant"; not in the *Risālah*, but often called on by commentators when explaining later sections of the text). The English terms "implicate" and "implicant" may sound ugly and jar with modern logical usage, but unlike "concomitant" and its cognates, both at least appear in modern dictionaries (for example, the Oxford English Dictionary) with meanings that make sense of such technical phrases.

I close with one last consideration. Avicenna is the culmination of the late antique tradition of commentary on Aristotle, and it makes the most sense to translate him with words evocative of the Greek tradition in which he intervenes. But writers of the second wave of Avicennian philosophy, from the twelfth century on, are at best mediated in their reading of Aristotle, and indifferent to textual problems in the ancient tradition. Their concern is rather to contest the reading of Avicenna, and increasingly they contest that reading in theological venues. In this respect, the activities of later readers of Avicenna's logic among adherents of the Shāfiʿī school of legal thought and the Ashʿarī school of theology, like al-Kātibī, strongly resemble the activities of their contemporaries in the Latin West; ideally, a translation should be designed to recall these contemporaries more than al-Kātibī's discarded Greek predecessors.

# Notes to the Introduction

1 Copenhaver et al., *Peter of Spain: Summaries of Logic: Text, Translation, Introduction, and Notes*, ix. Most references I make to Peter's *Summaries* are through Buridan's commentary on them; see Klima, *John Buridan, Summulae de Dialectica: An Annotated Translation, with a Philosophical Introduction*. Peter was a contemporary of al-Kātibī, and Buridan, Peter's greatest commentator, was a contemporary of al-Kātibī's commentator al-Taḥtānī.

2 Some of the convolutions of the early transmission are recently traced in Hermans, "A Persian Origin of the Arabic Aristotle? The Debate on the Circumstantial Evidence of the Manteq Revisited."

3 See an account in broad terms in Michot, *Ibn Sīnā: Lettre au Vizir Abū Saʿd*, 10*–14*; reference to the edition used is given by Michot on p. 134.

4 The reaction of Avicenna's contemporaries in Shiraz to his logic is examined in Street, "Avicenna's Twenty Questions on Logic: Preliminary Notes for Further Work."

5 On al-Fārābī's project, see for example Sabra's notes in his review of Rescher's *Al-Fārābī's Short Commentary on Aristotle's Prior Analytics*, 242. For al-Ghazālī's contribution, see the short account of his detractor, Averroes, *Le Philosophe et la Loi*, 122–23.

6 The classic account of the founding of the observatory is Sayılı, *The Observatory in Islam and Its Place in the General History of the Observatory*, 205; the finances are noted in passing in al-Rahim, *The Creation of Philosophical Tradition: Biography and the Reception of Avicenna's Philosophy from the Eleventh to the Fourteenth Centuries A.D.*, 106.

7 For a reproduction, see Eichner, "The Post-Avicennian Philosophical Tradition and Islamic Orthodoxy: Philosophical and Theological Summae in Context," 536.

8 Al-Rahim, *The Creation of Philosophical Tradition*, 107; al-Rahim's account of al-Kātibī (106–117) is a full and critical treatment of his life and work. For an account focused on his work on logic, see El-Rouayheb, *The Development of Arabic Logic (1200–1800)*, 56–59; for a resolution of doubts about date and likely place of death, see El-Rouayheb, "Al-Kātibī al-Qazwīnī."

9 Barhebraeus, *Specimen Historiae Arabum, Sive, Gregorii Abul Farajii Malatiensis de Origine & Moribus Arabum Succincta Narratio*, 485.

10 I adopt the periodization of Islamic history in Hodgson; see his *The Venture of Islam: Conscience and History in a World Civilization*, 2:3.

11 The later fortunes of the *Risālah* and the studies devoted to their various aspects are noted in Street, "Kātibī (d. 1277), Taḥtānī (d. 1365), and the *Shamsiyya*," 365.

12 In Lowry's introduction, quoting Fakhr al-Dīn al-Rāzī's *Irshād al-ṭālibīn ilā l-minhaj al-qawīm fī bayān manāqib al-imām al-Shāfiʿī* (*Guiding Students on the Right Way to Set Out the Virtues of Imām al-Shāfiʿī*); al-Shāfiʿī, *The Epistle on Legal Theory*, xv.

13 Quoted in Gutas, "Aspects of Literary Form and Genre in Arabic Logical Works," 60.

14 Ibn Khaldūn, *The Muqaddimah: An Introduction to History*, 3:142–43.

15 Gutas, "Aspects of Literary Form," 61.

16 Smyth, "Controversy in a Tradition of Commentary: The Academic Legacy of al-Sakkākī's *Miftāḥ al-ʿUlūm*," 594. I take all my information about al-Taftāzānī's relationship with al-Jurjānī from this interesting account.

17 Especially in the modal propositions and the way they contribute to syllogistic inferences; see Street, "Al-ʿAllāma al-Ḥillī (d. 1325) and the Early Reception of Kātibī's *Shamsīya*: Notes towards a Study of the Dynamics of Post-Avicennan Logical Commentary."

18 That is, al-Taḥtānī, *Taḥrīr al-qawāʿid al-manṭiqiyyah fī sharḥ al-Risālah al-Shamsiyyah*; for these and other abbreviations, see Abbreviations.

19 Rescher, *Temporal Modalities in Arabic Logic*.

20 Rescher and vander Nat, "The Theory of Modal Syllogistic in Medieval Arabic Philosophy."

21 Khaled El-Rouayheb was in the process of preparing an edition of al-Kātibī's *Jāmiʿ al-daqā'iq*; he has kindly sent me some transcribed text. Qarāmalikī makes use of *al-Munaṣṣaṣ fī sharḥ al-Mulakhkhaṣ* (*The Precise Commentary on the Epitome*), al-Kātibī's commentary on al-Rāzī's *Mulakhkhaṣ* (still in manuscript), and Mohammad Saleh Zarepour transcribed a considerable portion of al-Kātibī's commentary on al-Khūnajī's *Kashf al-asrār* from MS Süleymaniya: Carullah 1417 for a 2018 Cambridge Humanities Research Grant. Since then, a preliminary edition has been given of the whole commentary by Enver Şahin, "Kâtibî'nin Şerhu Keşfi'l-Esrâr Adlı Eserinin Tahkîki ve Değerlendirmesi (Critical Edition and Analysis of Kātibī's Sharh Kashf al-asrâr)," see al-Kātibī, *Sharḥ Kashf al-asrār*.

22 Copenhaver et al., *Peter of Spain: Summaries*; Kilwardby, *Notule libri priorum*; Klima, *John Buridan, Summulae*.

23 Strobino, "Ibn Sina's Logic."

24 See Lameer, *Al-Fārābī and Aristotelian Syllogistics: Greek Theory and Islamic Practice*, 55–62; the story is even more complicated, involving as it does Avicenna's reception of post-Aristotelian commentary, but Lameer's comments are more than enough for present purposes.

# The Rules of Logic

Praise be to God, who created the system of existence, drew forth the quiddities of things in accordance with His generosity, established through His power the species of intellectual substances, and bestows through His mercy the movements of the celestial bodies. Let us offer prayers for those holy souls free of human stains, especially for Muḥammad, the bringer of signs and miracles, and for his family and companions who follow his arguments and proofs. 0

The intelligent and the virtuous agree that the sciences—especially the exact sciences—are the highest goal and brightest virtue, and that those proficient in them are the noblest humans, with souls most apt to contact the angelic intelligences. Knowing the subtleties of these sciences and comprehending the essence of the realities they deal with is only possible through the science designated as logic, for by way of it one knows what is correct from what is wrong, what is worthless from what is valuable; knowing this, someone assigned me to compose a book on logic, gathering its rules and containing its principles and guidelines. He who assigned me this task is one who flourishes by the grace of truth, distinguished from all others by its support. Both those close and those distant are drawn to his side, and both the compliant and the wayward thrive through following him, for he is the exalted Lord Master, preeminent, pleasing, beneficent, noble, patrician, possessed of virtue and glorious traits, Sun of the Community, Shams al-Dīn, splendor of Islam and Muslims, model for the great and the exemplary, king of the powerful and the virtuous, pillar of the high, orb of the excellent. He is the son of the exalted and most great Lord Master who governs distant lands, the Asaph of his age,[1] king of ministers from the east and the west, convenor of the imperial court, Splendor of Truth, Bahāʾ al-Dīn, support of the scholars of Islam and of Muslims, pillar of kings. May God lengthen the reach of the power and redouble the glory of both. Though young in years, Shams al-Dīn is crowned with eternal happiness and honor, and characterized by beautiful virtues and praiseworthy traits. He assigned me this task, and I set out to draft the book and write it up, bound by a commitment not to omit any rule or guideline of consequence (along with a few worthy additions and pleasing insights of my own), a commitment not to follow any other logician, but rather plain truth: «falsehood cannot come at it from before it or behind it».[2] I gave this book the title *The Epistle on Logical Rules for Shams al-Dīn*, and I structured it as an Introduction, three Treatises, and a Conclusion; clinging all the while to the lifeline given by the Giver of Intellect,[3] and relying on His generosity, which bestows goodness and justice. Indeed, He is the best of those who sustain and grant aid.

# The Introduction

## Containing two discussions

### The First Discussion: On the Quiddity of Logic, and Proof of the Need for It

Knowledge is either merely conception, which is the occurrence of the form of something in the intellect, or conception together with a judgment, which is the subordination of one thing to another affirmatively or negatively; such an aggregate of conception and judgment is called assertion. 1

It is not the case that the whole of each of the two divisions of knowledge is entirely primitive (otherwise there would be nothing we do not know) or entirely inferred (otherwise knowledge claims would form a vicious circle or regress). 2

Rather, part of each division of knowledge is primitive, and part inferred, obtained by thinking, which is the ordering of known things such that they lead to knowledge of the unknown. But this ordering is not always correct, given that some thinkers contradict others according to what they think and, indeed, the same person may contradict himself at different times. Thus, there is need for a canon that provides knowledge of the ways of acquiring inferred knowledge from necessary propositions, and that also provides the comprehension of sound and unsound thinking which arises in the 3 course of such acquisition—this is logic. It is delineated as a canonical instrument, which, if implemented, preserves our mind from error in thinking.

4 Logic is neither entirely primitive (otherwise we could dispense with learning it), nor is it entirely inferred (otherwise its claims would form a vicious circle or regress); but part of it is primitive, and part inferred from what is primitive.

## The Second Discussion: On the Subject of Logic

5 The subject of a science is that whose essential accidents are investigated in the science, accidents that attach to the subject due to what it is (that is, due to its essence), or due to what is coextensive with it, or a part of it. So the subject of logic is known conceptions and assertions, because the logician investigates them insofar as they conduce to a conception or an assertion. He also investigates them insofar as what conduces to conception depends on them, like their being universal, particular, essential, accidental, genus, or differentia; and insofar as what conduces to assertion depends on them, whether proximately (like their being a proposition, the converse of a proposition, the contradictory of a proposition) or remotely (like their being subject and predicate).

6 It is customary to call what conduces to conception an explanatory phrase, and to call what conduces to assertion an argument. The first must be put before the second in an exposition due to the priority by nature of conception over assertion. This is because every assertion must involve the conception of what is subject to judgment (whether in itself, or under a matter that happens to be true of it); then, likewise, of what is judged to belong to it; and, finally, of the judgment itself, because it is impossible for anyone who is ignorant of any of these things to make a judgment.

## There are three treatises:

# The First Treatise: On Simple Terms

## Containing four sections

### The First Section: On Expressions

The expression's signification of a meaning by way of its having been imposed on that meaning is correspondence; this is like "man" signifying rational animal. The expression's signifying by way of that imposition what is contained in its meaning by correspondence is containment; this is like "man" signifying animal or rational. The expression's signifying by way of that imposition what is extrinsic to its meaning by correspondence is implication; this is like "man" signifying receptive of skill in writing. 7

It is stipulated for implicational signification that the extrinsic implicate be such that its conception follow from the conception of the named; otherwise, its being understood from the expression would be impossible. It is not, however, stipulated that the implicate be such that its actual realization follow from the actual realization of the named. This is like the expression "blind," which signifies sight even though there is no implicational relation between the two in actual existence. 8

Correspondence does not entail containment, as emerges when considering the case of simple entities. Whether correspondence entails implication is not known for sure, because it is unknowable 9 whether there is a mental implicate belonging to every quiddity whose conception follows from the conception of that quiddity. We have ruled out what has been said, that the conception of every quiddity entails the conception that it is not other than itself. From this it would also be clear that containment does not entail implication. Containment and implication only come about with correspondence, due to the impossibility of a consequent—insofar as it is a consequent—without an antecedent.

10 If one intends to signify by part of what signifies through correspondence a part of its meaning, then it is a compound expression (like "stone-thrower"); otherwise, it is a simple expression.

11 If the expression is not fit to be a predicate, it is a particle, like "in" and "not." If it is fit to be a predicate, then if by its form it signifies one of the three tenses specifically, it is a verb. If it does not so signify, it is a name.

12.1 Thereupon, its meaning is either one or many. If it is the first, then if that meaning is for an individual, it is a proper name. Otherwise, if its members—both mental and actual—are equal under it, as with "man" and "sun," it is univocal. But if its occurrence in one is more eminent than, and prior to, the other—like existence in relation to the necessary and the contingent—then it is systematically ambiguous.

12.2 If it is the second, with many meanings, then if it is imposed equally on each of those meanings, it is equivocal, like *ʿayn*.[4] If that is not the case, but rather it has been imposed in the first place on one of the two meanings, and then transferred to the second such that its first imposition has been abandoned, then it is called a conventionally transferred expression if it is transferred by general convention, as in the case of the word *dābbah*, "animal," which has come to mean "mount"; it is called a legislatively transferred expression if it is transferred by revealed legislation, as in the case of the word *ṣalāt*, "prayer," which has come to mean "ritual prayer," and the word *ṣawm*, "fasting," which has come to mean "ritual fasting"; and it is called a technically transferred expression if it is transferred by special convention, as in the case of the technical usage of the grammarians and theorists.

If the primary imposition has not been abandoned, the expression is said to be literal in relation to what it was initially imposed upon, and figurative in relation to what it has been transferred to, like "lion" in relation to the wild animal and the courageous man. 12.3

Every expression, when taken in relation to another expression, is synonymous with it if the two agree in meaning, and distinct from it if they differ. 13

A compound expression is either complete (after which silence is appropriate) or incomplete (which is the opposite). 14.1

If a complete expression bears the valuations true and false, it is information. But if it does not, then, if as its primary (that is, its imposed) signification it signifies seeking that an action be undertaken, it is a command (like "Beat!") when said with haughtiness; with submissiveness, a petition and supplication; with equality, a request. If it does not signify any of these, it is a notification, under which are subsumed wishing, hoping, oath swearing, and calling. 14.2

An incomplete expression is either restrictive, like "rational animal," or nonrestrictive, like the compound of a name and a particle, or a verb with a particle. 14.3

## The Second Section: On Simple Meanings

Every concept is a real particular if the very conception of its meaning precludes sharing in the meaning, and universal if the conception of its meaning does not preclude such sharing. The expression signifying one or the other kind of meaning is said to be particular or universal per accidens. 15

The universal is either the whole quiddity of the particulars under it, or intrinsic to the quiddity, or extrinsic from it. 16.1

The first division—that is, the whole quiddity—is the real species, whether it has numerous individuals under it (and this universal is what is said in answer to the question "what is it?" in respect of 16.2

both sharing and specificity, like man) or does not have numerous individuals under it (and this universal is what is said in answer to the question "what is it?" in respect of pure specificity, like sun). Thus, the real species is a universal said of one or of many things, which agree in realities in answer to the question "what is it?"

17 If it is the second division—that is, something intrinsic to the quiddity—if it is the whole of the part shared between the quiddity and another species, then this is what is said in answer to the question "what is it?" in respect of pure sharing, and is called genus. They delineate this universal as a universal said of many, which differ in realities in answer to the question "what is it?"

18.1 The genus is proximate if the answer about the quiddity and about something that shares with the quiddity in the putatively proximate genus is the same as the answer about the quiddity and about whatever else shares with it in that genus, like animal in relation to man. The genus is remote if the answer about the quiddity and about something that shares with it in the putatively remote genus is not the same as the answer about the quiddity and something else under the genus.

18.2 There are two answers to "what is it?" if it is remote by one degree (like growing body in relation to man), three answers if it is remote by two degrees (like body), four answers if it is remote by three degrees, and so on like this.

19 If it is not the whole part that is shared between the quiddity and another species, then inevitably either it is not shared, or it is a part of the whole that is shared and coextensive with it. Otherwise, it would be shared between the quiddity and another species. Yet it cannot be the whole that is shared in relation to that species, because the hypothesis is to the contrary. Rather, it is part of what is shared. This does not regress ad infinitum, but rather terminates in what is coextensive with what is shared, so it is the differentia of a genus. No matter how it distinguishes the quiddity from what shares with it—whether in a genus or in existence—it is a differentia.

They delineate the differentia as a universal predicated of something in answer to the question "which thing is it?" with respect to its substance. On this account, were a reality compounded from two or more coextensive matters, then each one would be a differentia for the reality, because each would distinguish it from what shares with it in existence. 20

The differentia distinguishing the species from what shares with it in genus is proximate if it distinguishes the species from what shares with it in a proximate genus (like "rational" for man), and remote if it distinguishes the species from what shares with it in a remote genus (like "sensate" for man). 21

As for the third division (in which the universal is extrinsic from the quiddity of the particulars under it),[5] if it is impossible to separate it from its substrate then it is an implicate; otherwise, it is a separable accidental. 22.1

The implicate may be an implicate of the existence of something, like black for the Ethiopian, and it may be an implicate of the quiddity. It is either evident, such that its conception along with the conception of its implicant is sufficient for the mind to declare an implication between the two (like divisibility into two equal parts for four); or it is not evident, such that it needs a middle for the mind to declare that there is an implication between the two (like the three angles of triangle summing to two right angles). "Evident" may also be said of an implicate whose conception follows from the conception of its implicant; the first definition is the more general. 22.2

The separable accidental may disappear quickly, like the redness of a blush or the pallor of fear; or it may do so slowly, like the graying of hair or the passing of youth. 22.3

If either the implicate or the separable is possessed solely by the members of one reality, it is a proprium (like "laughing"); otherwise, it is a general accident (like "walking"). We delineate the proprium as a universal said in an accidental way of what is under a single reality only, and general accident as a universal said in an 23 accidental way of members of more than one reality. The universals are therefore five: species, genus, differentia, proprium, and general accident.

### The Third Section: On Universals and Particulars

#### Containing five discussions

24 *The First Discussion* It may be that the universal cannot possibly exist outside the mind, though not due to the meaning of the expression alone, like partner of the Creator; and it may possibly exist yet not actually exist, like phoenix; and it may be that the existent under it is only one, and no other is possible, like the Creator; or that the existent under it is only one, but it is possible for there to be another, like sun; and it may be that there are many existents under it, whether finite (like the seven planets) or infinite (like rational souls).

25 *The Second Discussion* If we say of animal, for example, that it is a universal, there are three aspects to this: animal insofar as it is what it is, its being a universal, and the compound of the two. The first is called a natural universal, the second a logical universal, and the third a mental universal. The natural universal exists outside the mind because it is a part of this actually existent animal, and a part of an existent is existent. There is dispute about whether the other two universals exist outside the mind, but investigation into them falls outside logic.

26 *The Third Discussion* Two universals are coextensive if each one is true of whatever the other is true of, like man and rational. One is included within the other if one is true of whatever the other is true of, without the converse being the case, like animal and man. The two overlap if each one is only true of part of what the other is true

of, like animal and white. And they are disjunct if neither is true of anything of which the other is true, like man and horse.

The contradictories of two coextensive universals are coextensive. Were that not the case, then one of the two contradictories would be true of what the other is false of, so one of the original coextensive universals would be true of what the other is false of, and that is inconceivable. 27.1

In the case of inclusion, the contradictory of the more general simpliciter is more specific than the contradictory of the more specific simpliciter, due to the fact that the contradictory of the more specific is true of everything of which the contradictory of the more general is true, though not the reverse. As for the first part of the claim, it is because, were that not the case, then the more specific itself would be true of some of what the contradictory of the more general is true of, and that entails the truth of the more specific without the more general, and that is inconceivable. As for the second part of the claim, it is because, were that not the case, the contradictory of the more general would be true of everything of which the contradictory of the more specific is true, and that entails that the more specific be true of all of the more general, and that is inconceivable. 27.2

As for universals that overlap, there is no fundamental reason their two contradictories should overlap, due to the verification of the like of this limited overlap between the more general simpliciter and the contradictory of the more specific, along with complete disjunction between the contradictory of the more general simpliciter and the more specific itself. 27.3

The two contradictories of two disjuncts are disjoined at least partly. This is because if the two taken together are not true of anything—like nonexistence and non-privation—there is a complete disjunction between the two. And if they can be true together—like not-man and not-horse—there is a partial disjunction between the two as a necessary consequence of the fact that one of the two 27.4

disjuncts is true only with the contradictory of the other. So partial disjunction is certainly an implicate in this case.

28 *The Fourth Discussion* Just as "particular" is said of the meaning mentioned above (what is termed the real particular),[6] it is likewise said of everything more specific under the more general. This is called the relative particular, and it is more general than the first, because every real particular is a relative particular, without the converse being the case. As for the first part of the claim, it is because every individual is subsumed by its quiddity stripped of whatever individuates it; as for the second, it is because the relative particular can be a universal, whereas the real particular cannot.

29 *The Fifth Discussion* Just as "species" is said of what we mentioned above (what is termed the real species),[7] it may likewise be said of every quiddity that, along with other quiddities, has a genus said of it as a primary response to the question "what is it?" This is called relative species.

30 The ranks of relative species come to four: it is either the most general of the species, which is the supreme species, like body; or the most specific of them, which is the inferior species, like man (and it is called the species of species); or more general than the inferior and more specific than the supreme, which is the intermediate species, like animal and growing body; or distinct from everything else, which is the isolated species, like intelligence (if it is said that substance is a genus for it).

31 The ranks of genera also come to these four, but the supreme rank of the ranks of genera (like substance)—and not the inferior (like animal)—is called the genus of genera; an example of an intermediate genus is growing body and body; and an example of the isolated is intelligence (if we say substance is not a genus for it).

32 We may find the relative species without the real species (as in the case of the intermediate species), and the real without the relative (as in the case of the simple realities). One is therefore not

included in the other; rather, the two overlap because both are true of the inferior species.

Part of what is said in answer to "what is it?," if it is said by correspondence, is called what arises on the way to "what is it?"; this is like animal and rational in relation to "rational animal" said in response to the question "what is it?" asked about man. If it is mentioned by containment, it is called intrinsic to the answer to "what is it?"; this is like body and growing and sensate and moving voluntarily, which "animal" signifies by containment. 33

The superior genus may have a differentia that constitutes it (because the genus may be compounded from two or more coextensive matters), and it must have a differentia that divides it. The inferior species must have a differentia that constitutes it, and cannot have a differentia that divides it. The intermediates must have differentiae that constitute them and differentiae that divide them. Every differentia that constitutes the superior constitutes the inferior, though this does not convert universally. Every differentia that divides the inferior divides the superior, though this does not convert universally. 34

## The Fourth Section: On Definitions

What defines a given thing is something that, when it is conceived, entails the conception of that thing, or that thing's distinction from everything else. The definition may not be the quiddity itself, because the definition is known prior to what is made known, and a thing is not known prior to itself; nor may it be more general than what is defined (otherwise it would fall short of conveying a definition); nor may it be more specific (otherwise it would be more obscure than what is to be defined). The definition must be coextensive with what is being defined. 35

It is called a complete definition if it is by way of the proximate genus and differentia, and an incomplete definition if it comes about through the proximate differentia alone, or through the proximate 36 differentia and the remote genus. It is called complete delineation if it comes about through the proximate genus and the proprium, and incomplete delineation if it comes about through the proprium alone, or through the proprium and the remote genus.

37.1 One must be careful not to define something by what is equally known or unknown, as in defining "motion" by "what is not at rest," or "even" by "what is not odd." Nor may one thing be defined by another that is known only through the first, whether at one remove (as in "Quality is that in which similarity occurs," then "Similarity is coincidence in quality"), or at several removes (as in, "2 is the first even," then "the even is divisible into two equal parts," then "two equal parts are two things neither of which exceeds the other," then "two things are 2").

37.2 One must be careful not to use strange and barbarous expressions, which will be—in relation to the questioner—unclear as to what they signify. This would be to miss the whole purpose of the exercise.

# The Second Treatise: On Propositions and Their Valuations

## Containing an introduction and three sections

### The Introduction: On Defining the Proposition and Its Primary Divisions

A proposition is a discourse such that it is correct to say of him who produces it that he is truthful or false in what he says. It is a categorical proposition if its two extremes may be analyzed into two simple terms, as in "Zayd is knowing," or "Zayd is not knowing"; it is hypothetical if it cannot be analyzed in such a way. 38

The hypothetical proposition is either conditional or disjunctive. A conditional is that in which one proposition is judged to be true or not on the assumption of another proposition. This is like "if this is a man, it is an animal," and "not, if this is a man, it is inanimate." A disjunctive is that in which two propositions are judged to be incompatible with each other, either when both are true or false, or one is true and the other false (as in "this number is either even or odd"), or when their incompatibility is denied (as in "not, either this man is an animal or black"). 39

## The First Section: On the Categorical Proposition

### Containing four discussions

40 *The First Discussion: On Its Parts and Divisions* The categorical proposition is only realized through three parts: that on which judgment is passed (which is called the subject), that which is judged of it (which is called the predicate), and the relation between the two by which the predicate is connected to the subject; the expression signifying this relation is called a copula, like "is" in "Zayd is knowing." In this case, the proposition is called three-part. The copula may be omitted in some languages because the mind is aware of its meaning; in this case, the proposition is called two-part.

41 If the relation is such that it is correct to say that the subject has a given predicate, the proposition is affirmative, like "man is an animal." If the relation is such that it is correct to say that the subject does not have a given predicate, it is negative, like "man is not a stone."

42 If the subject of a categorical proposition is a specified individual, the proposition is called singular. If the subject is universal, and if the quantity of the individuals of which the judgment is true is made clear in the proposition (the expression signifying the quantity being called "quantifier"), then the proposition is called quantified. There are four kinds of quantified proposition. If it is made clear that the judgment is on all the individuals, the proposition is universal. The universal is either affirmative, its quantifier being "every" (as in "every fire is hot"), or negative, its quantifier being "no" or "not one" (as in "no man is inanimate"). If it is made clear in the proposition that the judgment is on some of the individuals, it is particular. The particular is either affirmative, its quantifier being "some" or "one" (as in "some animal is a man"), or it is negative, its quantifier being "not every" or "some are not" (as in "not every animal is a man").

If the quantity of the individuals is not made clear in it, then—if it is not fit to be true as a universal or a particular—the proposition is called natural, like "animal is a genus" and "man is a species." On the other hand, if it is fit to be true as a universal or a particular it is called indefinite, as in "man is in loss" and "man is not in loss."[8] 43

Such a proposition has the force of a particular, for if "man is in loss" is true, "some man is in loss" is true, and vice versa. 44

*The Second Discussion: On Verifying the Four Quantified Propositions* "Every C is B" is used occasionally according to the essence, and its meaning is that every possible individual that, were it to exist, would be a C, would be a B under the same assumption (that is, that it were to exist); in other words, everything that is an implicant of C is an implicant of B. And occasionally it is used according to external existence, and its meaning is that every C in external existence, whether at the time of the judgment or before it or after it, is B in external existence. 45

The distinction between the two considerations is obvious. Were there no squares in external existence, it would be true to say "every square is a figure" under the first consideration but not the second; and were there no figures in external existence other than squares, it would be correct to say "every figure is a square" under the second consideration but not the first. 46

On this basis, work out the remaining quantified propositions. 47

*The Third Discussion: On the Indefinite and the Determinate* If the negative particle is part of the subject (as in "the not-living is inanimate") or of the predicate (as in "the inanimate is not-knowing"),[9] or of both, the proposition, whether affirmative or negative, is called metathetic. But if the negative particle is not part of either term, the proposition is called determinate if it is affirmative, and simple if it is negative. 48

The consideration with respect to whether a proposition is affirmative or negative goes to the affirming or negating relation, and 49 not to its two extremes. "Every not-living is not-knowing" is an affirmative even though both extremes are privatives; "no moving is at rest" is a negative even though both extremes are positive.

50.1 The simple negative proposition is weaker than the affirmative with an indefinite predicate, because the negative is true given the nonexistence of the subject, but the affirmative is not. This is because affirmation is only correct for a subject verified to exist (as in propositions whose subject is under an externalist reading) or assumed to exist (as in propositions whose subject is under an essentialist reading). If the subject does exist, the simple negative and affirmative with indefinite predicate imply each other.

50.2 The distinction between the two is in expression. In the three-part proposition, the proposition is affirmative if the copula comes before the negative particle, and negative if it comes after it. In the two-part proposition, the distinction comes down to intention, or technical usage specifying "non" for metathetic affirmation, and "not" for simple negation, or the reverse.

51 *The Fourth Discussion: On Modal Propositions* Inevitably, the relation of a predicate to its subject, whether affirmative or negative, has a certain quality like necessity, perpetuity, nonnecessity, or non-perpetuity. This quality is called the matter of the proposition, and the expression signifying it is called the mode of the proposition.

52.1 The modal propositions that are customarily investigated (along with their valuations) come to thirteen. Some are simple (those the essence of which is only affirmation or negation), and some are compound (those the essence of which is made up of both an affirmation and a negation). There are six simple propositions.

52.2 The first, the absolute necessary proposition, is that in which affirming or negating the predicate of the subject is judged to be necessary as long as the essence of the subject exists, as in "necessarily, every man is an animal" and "necessarily, no man is a stone."

The second, the absolute perpetual proposition, is that in which affirming or negating the predicate of the subject is judged to be perpetual as long as the essence of the subject exists. The affirmative and negative examples for the absolute necessary proposition apply here too. 52.3

The third, the general conditional proposition,[10] is that in which affirming or negating the predicate of the subject is judged to be necessary on condition the subject is under a description, as in "necessarily, everyone writing moves his fingers as long as he is writing," and "necessarily, no one writing keeps his fingers still as long as he is writing." 52.4

The fourth, the general conventional proposition, is that in which affirming or negating the predicate of the subject is judged to be perpetual on condition the subject is under a description. The affirmative and negative examples for the general conditional proposition apply here too. 52.5

The fifth, the general absolute proposition, is that in which affirming or negating the predicate of the subject is judged to be actual, as in "by general absoluteness, every man breathes" and "by general absoluteness, no man breathes." 52.6

The sixth, the general possible proposition, is that in which the opposing absolute necessity is judged to be removed, as in "by general possibility, every fire is hot" and "by general possibility, no fire is cold." 52.7

There are seven compound propositions: The first, the special conditional proposition, is the general conditional proposition with the restriction of non-perpetuity with respect to the essence. If it is affirmative (as in "necessarily, everyone writing moves his fingers as long as he is writing, not always"), it is made up of an affirmative general conditional and a negative general absolute. If it is negative (as in "necessarily, no one writing keeps his fingers still as long as he is writing, not always"), it is made up of a negative general conditional and an affirmative general absolute. 53

54 The second, the special conventional proposition, is the general conventional proposition with the restriction of non-perpetuity with respect to the essence. If it is affirmative, it is made up of an affirmative general conventional and a negative general absolute; if it is negative, it is made up of a negative general conventional and an affirmative general absolute. The affirmative and negative examples for the special conditional proposition apply here too.

55 The third, the nonnecessary existential proposition, is the general absolute with the restriction of nonnecessity with respect to the essence. If it is affirmative (as in "every man actually laughs, not necessarily"), it is made up of an affirmative general absolute and a negative general possible. If it is negative (as in "no man actually laughs, not necessarily"), it is made up of a negative general absolute and an affirmative general possible.

56 The fourth, the non-perpetual existential proposition, is the general absolute with the restriction of non-perpetuity with respect to the essence. Whether affirmative or negative, it is made up of two general absolute propositions, one of which is affirmative and the other negative. The affirmative and negative examples for the nonnecessary existential proposition apply here too.

57 The fifth, the temporal, is that in which affirming or negating the predicate of the subject is judged to be necessary at one specified moment during the existence of the subject, with the restriction of non-perpetuity with respect to the essence. If it is affirmative (as in "necessarily, every moon is eclipsed on the earth's coming between it and the sun, not always"), it is made up of an affirmative absolute temporal and a negative general absolute. If it is negative (as in "necessarily, no moon is eclipsed at the moment of quadrature, not always"), it is made up of a negative absolute temporal and an affirmative general absolute.

58 The sixth, the spread proposition, is that in which affirming or negating the predicate of the subject is judged to be necessary at an unspecified moment during the existence of the subject, restricted by non-perpetuity with respect to the essence. If it is affirmative (as

in "necessarily, every man breathes at a given time, not always"), it is made up of an affirmative absolute spread and a negative general absolute. If it is negative (as in "necessarily, no man is breathing at a given time, not always"), it is made up of a negative absolute spread and an affirmative general absolute.

The seventh, the special possible proposition, is that in which absolute necessity is judged to be removed, both as to the predicate's existence and its privation. Whether affirmative (as in "by special possibility, every man is a writer") or negative (as in "by special possibility, no man is a writer"), the special possible is made up of two general possible propositions, one affirmative and the other negative. 59.1

The guideline regarding these restrictions is that non-perpetuity points to a general absolute proposition, and nonnecessity to a general possible proposition, each disagreeing in quality but agreeing in quantity with the proposition it restricts. 59.2

## The Second Section: On the Divisions of the Hypothetical Proposition

The first part of a hypothetical proposition is called antecedent and the second consequent. It is either conditional or disjunctive. 60.1

The conditional is either implicative or coincidental. In the implicative, the consequent is true on the supposition that the antecedent is true due to a connection between the two which necessitates that (as in causality or correlation). In the coincidental, the consequent is true by virtue of the two parts simply coinciding in being true (as in, "if man is rational, the donkey brays"). 60.2

The disjunctive is either exclusive, in which it is judged that the two parts are mutually incompatible with each other if true together or false together, as in "this number is either even or odd"; or alternative denial, in which it is judged that the two parts are incompatible with each other only when both are true, as in "this thing is either a stone or a tree"; or inclusive, in which it is judged 60.3

that the two parts are incompatible with each other only when both are false, as in "either Zayd is in the water or else he will not be drowned."

61 Each of the three kinds of disjunction is either oppositional, in which the mutual exclusion is due to the two parts themselves, as in the examples above, or coincidental, in which the mutual exclusion just happens to be the case, as for example by positing someone who is black and not a writer, we have "this person is either black or a writer" as an exclusive disjunction, or "not-black or a writer" as an alternative denial, or "black or a not-writer" as an inclusive.

62 The negative of each of these eight propositions is that which removes what is judged to be in their affirmatives. So that which negates implication is called a negative implicative, that which negates opposition is called a negative oppositional, and that which negates what happens to be the case is called a negative coincidental.

63 The affirmative conditional may be true with two true and two false constituent propositions; and with two unknown as to truth and falsity; and with a false antecedent and true consequent (but not the reverse, because it is impossible that a true proposition entail a false one). The affirmative conditional may be false with two false parts; and with a false antecedent and true consequent, and the reverse; and with two true propositions (that is, if it is implicative; if it is coincidental, it is impossible for it to be false with two true propositions).

64 The affirmative exclusive disjunctive is true with one true and one false proposition; it is false with two true and two false propositions. Alternative denial is true with two false propositions, and with a true and a false; it is false with two true ones. The inclusive is true with two true propositions, and with a true one and a false one; it is false with two false ones. The negative is true of that of which the affirmative is false, and false of that of which the affirmative is true.

65.1 Universality for the hypothetical proposition is that the consequent be implied by or opposed to the antecedent under all situations in which the antecedent can occur—that is to say, the situations that may arise for the antecedent by reason of being connected with matters that are compatible with it. It is the same for the particular hypothetical proposition under some of these situations; likewise for the singular under a specified situation.

The quantifiers for the universal affirmative in the conditional are "whenever," "whatever," and "when"; in the disjunctive, "always." The quantifier for the universal negative is "never" in both conditional and disjunctive. The quantifier for the particular affirmative is "sometimes" in both, and for the particular negative "sometimes not" in both (and also for the particular negative by inserting the negative particle in the quantifier for the universal affirmative). The quantifier for the indefinite in the conditional is by attaching "were it" and "if," and in the disjunctive, "either." 65.2

The hypothetical may be made up of two categorical propositions, or two conditionals, or two disjunctives, or a categorical and a conditional, or a categorical and a disjunctive, or a conditional and a disjunctive. Each of the last three divides, if conditional, into two subdivisions, due to the distinction by nature between their antecedent and consequent. This is in contrast to the disjunctive, for its antecedent is distinguished from the consequent only by its placement. So there are nine divisions of conditionals, and six of disjunctives. You should extract their forms for yourself. 66

## The Third Section: On the Valuations of Propositions

### Containing four discussions

*The First Discussion: On Contradiction* Contradiction has been defined as a difference between two propositions in affirmation and negation such that it requires of itself that one is true and the other false. 67

The contradiction of two singular propositions is only realized when the subjects of both propositions are the same (under which must be considered unity of condition, and of part and whole), and 68 if the predicates in both propositions are the same (under which must be considered unity of time, place, relation, potentiality, and actuality). With respect to two quantified propositions, there must be, in addition to the above, a difference in quantity (because the two particulars are true and the two universals are false in every propositional matter in which the subject is more general than the predicate). In all propositions, there must also be a difference in modality (because the two possible propositions are true and the two necessary propositions are false in contingent matter).

69.1 The contradictory of the absolute necessary proposition is the general possible proposition, because the negation of necessity and necessity are certainly mutually contradictory.

69.2 The contradictory of the absolute perpetual proposition is the general absolute, because negation at every moment contradicts affirmation at some moment, and vice versa.

69.3 The contradictory of the general conditional is the possible continuing: I mean, that in which it is judged to remove the opposing necessity with respect to the description, as in "everyone afflicted with pleurisy may cough at times while afflicted."

69.4 The contradictory of the general conventional is the absolute continuing: I mean, that in which it is judged to affirm or negate the predicate of the subject at some of the moments the description of the subject holds; the preceding example serves here too.

70 Let us turn to compound propositions. If the compound is universal, its contradictory is one of the contradictories of its two parts. This is clear once you have understood the realities of compound propositions and the contradictories of simple propositions. So, if you have verified that the non-perpetual existential is made up of two general absolute propositions, one of which is affirmative and the other negative, and that the contradictory of the absolute is the perpetual proposition, then you have also verified that the contradictory of the compound is either the perpetual proposition that opposes the original in quantity and quality, or the perpetual proposition that agrees with the original.

If the compound proposition is particular, however, what we have mentioned will not be sufficient to find a contradictory for it, for "some bodies are animals, not always" is false, and so are both of the contradictories of its two parts. The truth in forming the contradictory is to flank a disjunctive with the contradictories of the two parts for every one of the subjects—that is, each taken one by one must have both contradictories, so "every body is either always an animal or always not an animal." 71

The contradictory of the universal hypothetical is the particular that agrees with it in genus and species, but that opposes it in quality and quantity, and vice versa. 72

*The Second Discussion: On Straight Conversion* Straight conversion consists of placing the first part of a proposition second and the second part first, with the truth and quality remaining in the converse as they were in the convertend. 73

Consider the negatives: If the negative is universal, there are seven modalities that cannot be converted—namely, the two temporals, the two existentials, the two possibles, and the general absolute. This is because of the impossibility of converting the strongest of them, the temporal, due to the truth of "necessarily, no moon is eclipsed at the time of quadrature, not always," and the falsity of "some of what is eclipsed is not a moon" by general possibility (which is the weakest of the modalities), because everything that is eclipsed is necessarily a moon. If the strongest does not convert, neither does the weaker; for were the weaker to convert, so would the stronger (because the implicate of the weaker is necessarily the implicate of the stronger). 74

The absolute necessary and absolute perpetual propositions convert as a universal perpetual, because if it is of necessity, or always, true that "no C is B," then always "no B is C"; were it not the case, then "some B is C" as a general absolute proposition, and this, together with the original proposition, would produce "some B is not B by necessity" for the necessary proposition, and 75 "some B is not B always" for the perpetual proposition; this is absurd.

76.1 The general conditional and the general conventional convert as a universal general conventional, because if it is of necessity, or always, true that "no C is B as long as it is C," then "always, no B is C as long as it is B"; were it not the case, then "some B is C while B," and this with the original proposition produces "some B is not B while B"; this is absurd.

76.2 The special conditional and special conventional convert as a general conventional, which is non-perpetual-for-some. The general conventional component of the converse follows because it is the implicate of both the general conditional and conventional propositions; the component that is non-perpetual-for-some follows because, were it false, "always, no B is C" would be true, which converts as "always, no C is B"; but it was the case that every C is B actually. This is absurd.

77.1 Turning to the particulars: Both the special conditional and conventional convert as a special conventional, because if it is of necessity, or always, true that "some C is not B as long as it is C, not always," then "some B is not C as long as it is B, not always" must be true, because we may expose what underlies the subject, C, as D; then D is C actually, and D is also B due to the non-perpetual rider relative to negating B of C; further, D is not C as long as it is B (otherwise, D would be C while B, and so B while C; yet it was the case C is not B as long as it is C; this is absurd). And if B and C are true of D and are incompatible with each other, it is true that "some B is not C as long as it is B, not always," which is what is sought.

77.2 The remaining particular propositions do not convert. This is because "necessarily, some animals are not human" and "necessarily, some moon is not eclipsed at the time of quadrature, not always" are true, while their converses as general possible propositions are false. But the necessary proposition is the strongest of the simple propositions, and the temporal the strongest of the remaining compound propositions. When they do not convert, neither does any other proposition, due to what you have learned: the conversion of the weak entails the conversion of the strong.

The affirmative, whether universal or particular, does not convert as a universal due to the possibility that the predicate is more general than the subject. Turning to modality, the necessary, the perpetual, the general conditional, and the general conventional convert as an absolute continuing. This is because if "every C is B" is true under any of the four modalities mentioned, "some B is C while B." Were this not the case, then "always, no B is C as long as it is B," which, with the original proposition, produces "always, no C is C" in the case of the necessary and the perpetual, and "always, no C is C as long as it is C" in the case of the two generals; these conclusions are absurd. 78.1

The two specials convert as absolute continuing restricted by non-perpetuity. The absolute continuing component is due to its being an implicate of the two generals. The non-perpetuity rider from the original universal proposition is there because, were it false that some B is not C actually, it would be true "always, every B is C"; we add this to the first part of the original proposition ("necessarily or always, every C is B as long as it is C"), which produces "always, every B is B." Now add it also to the second part ("no C is B" by a general absoluteness), which produces "no B is B" by a general absoluteness; so it follows that two contradictories are conjoined, and this is absurd. 78.2

To convert the particular of the special conditional and special conventional, expose from the subject C D such that it is actually not C, otherwise it would always be C, and thus always B due to B's perpetuity as a function of the perpetuity of C. But the implicate is false due to the restriction of the original proposition by non-perpetuity. 78.3

The two temporals, the two existentials, and the general absolute convert as a general absolute. This is because if "every C is B" is true under one of the five modalities mentioned, then "some B is C" by general absoluteness. Were this not the case, then "always, no 78.4

B is C" would be true and, with the original proposition, produces "always, no C is C"; this is absurd.

79 If you wish, you may when dealing with affirmative propositions convert the contradictory of the converse so that the contradictory of the original proposition (or what is stronger than it) would be true.

80 The status of the two possible propositions with respect to conversion or its failure is unknown due to the fact that the demonstration mentioned to prove their conversion depends on the conversion of the negative necessary proposition as itself, and on the productivity of a possible minor with a necessary major in the first figure, and neither of these can be verified. This in turn is due to lack of success in finding a proof that requires either that the possible converts or that it does not.

81 Affirmative conditional hypothetical propositions convert as particular affirmative, and the universal negative as universal negative; since were the contradictory of the converse true, it could be ordered with the original as a syllogism producing the absurd. The particular negative does not convert because "sometimes not, if this is an animal then this is a man" is true while the converse is false. Conversion in the disjunctive is inconceivable due to the lack of distinction between the two parts by nature.

82 *The Third Discussion: On Contraposition* Contraposition consists of making the contradictory of the second part of the original proposition the first part of the derived proposition, and leaving the first part of the original unchanged as the second part of the derived proposition; the derived proposition differs from the original in quality but agrees with it in truth.

83.1 Consider universal affirmative propositions. Seven of them do not contrapose—namely, those whose negatives do not convert by straight conversion. This is because "necessarily, every moon is not-eclipsed at the time of quadrature, not always" is true while its contrapositive is not, due to what you have learned.

The necessary proposition and the perpetual contrapose as perpetual universals because, if "necessarily, or always, every C is B" is true, then "always, nothing that is not-B is C." Were that not the case, then "some of what is not-B is C actually," and this with the original proposition produces "necessarily, some of what is not-B is B" (in the necessary proposition), or "always . . ." (in the perpetual proposition); this is absurd. 83.2

General conditional and conventional propositions contrapose as general conventional universals because, if "necessarily, or always, every C is B as long as it is C" is true, then "always, nothing that is not-B is C as long as it is not-B." Were that not so, then "some of what is not-B is C while not-B"; this with the original proposition produces "some of what is not-B is B while not-B," and this is absurd. 83.3

The special conditional and conventional propositions contrapose as general conventional non-perpetual-for-some. The general conventional part of the contrapositive follows because both general propositions entail it. The non-perpetual-for-some part follows because "some of what is not-B is C" is true as a general absolute, otherwise "always, no not-B is C," which converts as "always, no C is not-B"; yet it is the case that "no C is B actually" (as a result of the judgment of non-perpetuity), from which it follows that "every C is not-B actually" (due to the existence of the subject in the original proposition); this is absurd. 83.4

If the original proposition is particular, then both the special conditional and the special conventional contrapose as a special conventional. This is because if "necessarily, or always, some C is B as long as it is C, not always" is true, then let us expose part of the subject C as D; D is not-B actually due to the non-perpetuity of the affirmation of B of it, and is not C as long as it is not-B (otherwise it would be C while not-B, whereupon D would be not-B while it is C, yet it is B as long as it is C; this is absurd), and D is C actually; this is obvious. So "some of what is not-B is not C as long as it is not-B, not always," which is what is sought. 84.1

84.2 As for the rest, they do not contrapose. This is because "some animal is not-man" is true by absolute necessity, and "some moon is not-eclipsed" is true by temporal necessity, yet their contrapositives are not true; since these two do not contrapose, nor do any of the weaker modals, due to what you learned in the treatment of straight conversion.

85.1 Negatives, whether universal or particular, do not contrapose as universal due to the possibility that the contradictory of the predicate is more general than the subject. The two specials contrapose as absolute continuing because, if "necessarily, or always, no C is B as long as it is C, not always" is true, then let us expose part of the subject as D; D is not-B actually, and C at some times of its being not-B (because it is not-B at all times of its being C); so "some of what is not-B is C at some moments it is not-B." And that is what is claimed.

85.2 The two temporals and the two existentials all contrapose as a general absolute. This is because if "no C is B" is true by one of these modalities, we expose part of the subject as D. So D is not-B actually, and C actually; so "some of what is not-B is C actually," which is what is sought. So too we may prove the contrapositives of the particulars.

86 As for the rest of the negatives, and the affirmative and negative hypothetical propositions: their status with respect to contraposition is unknown, due to lack of success in finding a proof.

87.1 *The Fourth Discussion: On the Implicates of Hypothetical Propositions* The affirmative universal conditional entails an alternative denial consisting of the original antecedent and the contradictory of the consequent, and an inclusive disjunctive consisting of the contradictory of the antecedent and the original consequent. And they both convert back to the original conditional, otherwise implication and disjunction mean nothing.

87.2 The exclusive disjunctive entails four conditional propositions. The antecedent of two of them is one of the two parts of the original proposition unchanged, each with a consequent that is the contradictory of the other part. The antecedent of the other two conditionals is the contradictory of one of the two parts, each with a consequent that is the other part unchanged.

Each of the other two nonexclusive disjunctives entails the other 87.3
compounded of the contradictories of the two parts of the original proposition.

# The Third Treatise: On Syllogism

## Containing five sections

### The First Section: On Definition and Division of Syllogism

88 Syllogism is a discourse composed of propositions from which alone, if admitted, another discourse follows necessarily.

89.1 A syllogism is repetitive if the conclusion itself or its contradictory is actually mentioned in the syllogism, as in "if this is a body, it is mobile; but it is a body," which produces "it is mobile"; so the conclusion itself is mentioned in the syllogism. Were we to say "but it is not mobile," it would produce "it is not a body," the contradictory of which is actually mentioned in the syllogism.

89.2 If that is not the case, then the syllogism is connective, as in "every body is composite" and "every composite is produced in time," which produces "every body is produced in time"; neither the conclusion nor its contradictory is mentioned in the syllogism.

90 The subject of what is sought is called the minor term, and its predicate is called the major term. A proposition that is made part of a syllogism is called a premise. The premise that contains the minor term is called the minor premise, and the one that contains the major term is called the major premise. The term repeated in both is called the middle term. The connection between the minor and major premises is called the connection-form, or mood. The

form resulting from how the middle term is positioned relative to the other two terms is called a figure. There are four figures, because if the middle term is predicate in the minor premise and subject in the major, it is first figure; if it is predicate in both, it is second figure; if it is subject in both, it is third figure; and if it is subject in the minor premise and predicate in the major, it is fourth figure.

The conditions of productivity in the first figure are that the minor premise be affirmative (otherwise the minor term does not come under the middle term), and that the major premise be universal (otherwise it may be that the part of the middle of which the major term is predicated is not the part of the middle predicated of the minor term). This figure has four productive moods. 91.1

The first, with two universal affirmatives, produces a universal affirmative, as in "every C is B, every B is A, therefore every C is A." 91.2

The second, with two universals, the minor premise affirmative and the major negative, produces a universal negative, as in "every C is B, no B is A, therefore no C is A." 91.3

The third, with two affirmatives, the minor premise being a particular, produces a particular affirmative conclusion, as in "some C is B, every B is A, therefore some C is A." 91.4

The fourth, with a particular affirmative minor and a universal negative major, produces a particular negative, as in "some C is B, no B is A, therefore some C is not A." 91.5

The conclusions of this figure are self-evident. 91.6

The conditions of productivity in the second figure are that the two premises differ in quality, and that the major premise be universal; otherwise, we get discrepant conclusions revealing lack of productivity (which is a syllogism with true premises leading in some cases to an affirmative conclusion, and in others to a negative conclusion). 92

Its productive moods are also four. 93.1

The first, with two universals, the minor affirmative, produces a universal negative, as in "every C is B, no A is B; therefore, no C is A." This is proved by reductio, which involves joining the contradictory 93.2

of the conclusion to the major to produce the contradictory of the minor. It can also be proved by conversion of the major premise to reduce it to the first figure.

93.3 The second, with two universals, the major affirmative, produces a universal negative, as in "no C is B, and every A is B; therefore, no C is A." This is proved by reductio, or by converting the minor, placing it as major, and converting the conclusion.

93.4 The third, with a particular affirmative minor and a universal negative major, produces a particular negative, as in "some C is B, no A is B, therefore some C is not A." This is proved by reductio, or by conversion of the major to reduce it to the first figure. It can also be proved by ecthesis: expose the subject of the particular as D, then "every D is B, no A is B, therefore no D is A." But "some C is D, no D is A, therefore some C is not A."

93.5 The fourth, with a particular negative minor and a universal affirmative major, produces a particular negative, as in "some C is not B, and every A is B, therefore some C is not A." It is proved by reductio.

94.1 The conditions of productivity in the third figure are that the minor be affirmative (otherwise there will be discrepant conclusions), and that one of the premises be universal (otherwise the part of the middle of which the minor term is predicated may be different from the part of the middle of which the major is predicated, such that the judgment does not necessarily pass to the minor).

94.2 Its productive moods are six.

94.3 The first, with two universal affirmatives, produces a particular affirmative, as in "every B is C, and every B is A, therefore some C is A." It is proved by reductio (which involves conjoining the contradictory of the conclusion to the minor to produce the contradictory of the major), or by reduction to the first figure by converting the minor.

94.4 The second, with two universals, the major negative, produces a particular negative, as in "every B is C, and no B is A, therefore some C is not A." It is proved by reductio, or by converting the minor.

94.5 The third, with two affirmatives, the major universal, produces a particular affirmative, as in "some B is C, every B is A, therefore some

C is A." It is proved by reductio, or by converting the minor, or by ecthesis: expose the subject of the particular premise as D. Then "every D is B, every B is A, therefore every D is A." Then we have "every D is C, every D is A, therefore some C is A"; and this is what is sought.

The fourth, with a particular affirmative minor and a universal negative major, produces a particular negative, as in "some B is C, no B is A, therefore some C is not A." It is proved by reductio, or by converting the minor, or by ecthesis. 94.6

The fifth, with two affirmatives, the minor universal, produces a particular affirmative, as in "every B is C, and some B is A, therefore some C is A." It is proved by reductio, or by using the converted major as minor and then converting the conclusion, or by ecthesis. 94.7

The sixth, with a universal affirmative minor and a particular negative major, produces a particular negative conclusion, as in "every B is C, and some B is not A, therefore some C is not A." It is proved by reductio, or by ecthesis if the negative is compound. 94.8

The conditions for the fourth figure with respect to quantity and quality are that the two premises be affirmative and the minor a universal, or that the two premises differ from each other in quality and one of them be universal; otherwise, there will be discrepant conclusions, which reveal lack of productivity. 95.1

The productive moods in this figure come to eight. 95.2

The first, with two universal affirmatives, produces a particular affirmative, as in "every B is C, and every A is B, therefore some C is A." It is proved by reversing the order of the premises and converting the conclusion. 95.3

The second, with two affirmatives, the major being a particular, produces a particular affirmative, as in "every B is C, and some A is B, therefore some C is A." The proof is what preceded. 95.4

The third, with two universals, the minor being negative, produces a universal negative, as in "no B is C, and every A is B, therefore no C is A." The proof is what preceded. 95.5

The fourth, with two universals, the minor being affirmative, produces a particular negative, as in "every B is C, and no A 95.6

is B; therefore, some C is not A." It is proved by converting both premises.

95.7 The fifth, with a particular affirmative minor and a universal negative major, produces a particular negative, as in "some B is C, and no A is B, therefore some C is not A." The proof is what preceded.

95.8 The sixth, with a particular negative minor and a universal affirmative major, produces a particular negative, as in "some B is not C, and every A is B, therefore some C is not A." This is proved by converting the minor to reduce it to the second figure.

95.9 The seventh, with a universal affirmative minor and a particular negative major, produces a particular negative, as in "every B is C, and some A is not B, therefore some C is not A." This is proved by converting the major to reduce it to the third figure.

95.10 The eighth, with a universal negative minor and a particular affirmative major, produces a particular negative, as in "no B is C, and some A is B, therefore some C is not A." It is proved by reversing the order of the premises and converting the conclusion.

96 It is possible to prove the first five moods by reductio—that is to say, by joining the contradictory of the conclusion to one of the two premises to produce what converts to the contradictory of the other premise. The second and fifth moods can be proved by ecthesis. Let us prove this in the second; the fifth can be proved in the same way. Let the some that is A be D such that "every D is A" and "every D is B." Thus, "every B is C, every D is B, therefore some C is D" and "every D is A," so "some C is A"; this is what is sought.

97 The scholars who went before us limited the productive moods to the first five of this figure, and spoke of discrepant conclusions from a syllogism with two simple premises to show the lack of productivity of the last three. We, on the other hand, stipulate that the negative be one of the two specials, and then the problem they mention to do with discrepant conclusions falls away.

## The Second Section: On Mixes of Modalized Premises

The condition for the first figure with regard to modality is that the minor premise be an actuality proposition. 98

If the major premise is not one of the two conditional propositions or the two conventionals, the conclusion has the modality of the major. If, on the other hand, the major is one of these four propositions, then (1) if the major is one of the two generals, the modality of the conclusion is like the minor, though dropping any restriction of non-perpetuity and nonnecessity, and whatever necessity belongs only to the minor; and (2) if the major is one of the two specials, the modality of the conclusion is like the minor, though joining the restriction of non-perpetuity to it. 99

The condition for the second figure with regard to modality comes down to two matters. One of them is that the minor be true as a perpetual proposition, or that the major be one of the propositions with convertible negatives. The second is that the possible proposition is only used with an absolute necessary, or with either of the two conditional propositions as majors. 100

If one of the premises is true as a perpetual proposition, the conclusion is a perpetual proposition; otherwise, it is like the minor, but dropping its restriction of non-perpetuity or nonnecessity, and dropping whichever necessity the minor may have. 101

The condition for the third figure is that it have an actuality minor. The modality of the conclusion is like the major if the major is not one of the four descriptional propositions. Otherwise it is like the converse of the minor from which the restriction of non-perpetuity is dropped if the major is one of the two generals, and to which that restriction is added if the major is one of the two specials. 102

The condition for productivity with respect to modality in the fourth figure comes down to five matters. The first is that the syllogism in this figure have actuality premises. The second is that the negative proposition used in it be convertible. The third is that, for 103 the third mood, the minor be true as a perpetual proposition, or the major be true as a general conventional. The fourth is that the major in the sixth mood be a convertible negative. The fifth is that the minor of the eighth mood be one of the two specials, and the major be one of the propositions true as a general conventional.

104 The modality of the conclusion in the first two moods is that of the converse of the minor if (1) it is true as a perpetual proposition or (2) the syllogism is from the six propositions with convertible negatives; otherwise, it is a general absolute. In the third mood, the conclusion is a perpetual proposition if one of the premises is true as a perpetual proposition; otherwise, the modality is that of the converse of the minor. In the fourth and fifth moods, the conclusion is a perpetual proposition if the major is true as a perpetual proposition; otherwise, it is that of the converse of the minor, though dropping its restriction of non-perpetuity. In the sixth mood, it is like the second figure after converting the minor. In the seventh mood, it is like the third figure after converting the major. In the eighth mood, it is like the converse of the conclusion after reversing the order of the premises.

## The Third Section: On Connective Syllogisms with Hypothetical Premises

### Containing five divisions

105 *The First Kind* This kind is compounded of conditional premises. The norm in this class is that in which what is shared is a complete part of both premises. The four figures are formed in it because, if the consequent in the minor is antecedent in the major, the syllogism is first figure; if the middle is consequent in both, the syllogism is second figure; if it is antecedent in both, the syllogism is third figure; and if it is antecedent in the minor and consequent in the major, the syllogism is fourth figure. The conditions of productivity, the number of moods, and the quantity and quality of the

conclusion in every figure are exactly the same as in the categoricals, with no distinction. The form of the first mood is "whenever A is B, C is D, and whenever C is D, H is Z," which produces "whenever A is B, H is Z."

*The Second Kind* This kind is compounded of disjunctives. The norm in this class is that in which the two premises share an incomplete part, as in: "either every A is B or every C is D," and "either every D is H, or every W is Z," which produces "either every A is B or every C is H or every W is Z" (because of the inclusive disjunction arising from the two premises of the composition and one of the other two). The four figures are formed in this class, and the conditions taken into account between two categoricals are taken into account here between the two sharing a part. 106

*The Third Kind* This kind is compounded of a categorical and a conditional. The norm in this class is that in which the categorical is the major and the consequent of the conditional is shared. The conclusion is a conditional, the antecedent of which is the antecedent of the conditional premise, and the consequent is the conclusion of the composition between the consequent in the minor and the categorical, as in "whenever A is B, C is D," and "every D is H," which produces "whenever A is B, every C is H." So the four figures are formed in this class, and the conditions taken into account between two categoricals are taken into account here between the consequent and the categorical. 107

*The Fourth Kind* This kind is compounded of a categorical and a disjunctive, and forms two subcategories. In the first, the categorical propositions are the same in number as the parts of the disjunction, and each categorical proposition shares a term with one of the parts of the disjunction. Further, the compositions are either united in the conclusion, as in "every C is either B or D or H," and "every B is T and every D is T and every H is T," which produces "every C 108.1

is T," because one of the parts of the disjunction is true along with a categorical with which it shares a term; or the compositions differ in the conclusion, as in "every C is either B or D or H; but every B is C and every D is T and every H is Z," which produces "every C is either C or T or Z," for the reason just mentioned.

108.2 In the second, the categoricals are fewer than the parts of the disjunction. Let the categorical be one, and the disjunctive have two parts, and the sharing takes place with one of those two parts, as in "either every A is T or every C is B," but "every B is D," which produces "either every A is T or every C is D," because an inclusive disjunction arises from the two premises of the composition and the unshared part.

109.1 *The Fifth Kind* This kind is compounded of a conditional and a disjunctive, and what is shared is either a complete or an incomplete part of the premises. In either case, the norm is what has a conditional as minor and a disjunctive as affirmative major. An example of the first is "whenever A is B, C is D," but "always, either C is D or H is Z" (the disjunctive is an alternative denial), which produces "always, either A is B or H is Z" as an alternative denial, because the impossibility of conjunction with the implicate always or in general entails the impossibility of conjunction with the implicant always or in general. The disjunctive with an inclusive disjunction produces "sometimes, if A is not B then H is Z," due to the contradictory of the middle entailing the two extremes universally (and the inference of what is sought is by a third-figure syllogism). An example of the second kind—when the two premises have an incomplete part in common—is "whenever A is B, every C is D," and "always, either every D is H or W is Z" as an inclusive disjunction, which produces "whenever A is B, either every C is H or W is Z."

109.2 A full treatment of these divisions is given in the epistles we have written on the art of logic.

## The Fourth Section: On the Repetitive Syllogism

This is a compound of two premises, one a hypothetical, the other a proposition that either affirms or denies one of the two parts of the hypothetical premise, such that affirming or denying the other part follows from it. It is necessary that the hypothetical premise is affirmative, and that the conditional is implicative and universal; or that the affirmation of the antecedent or denial of the consequent are universal (unless the time of the condition or disjunction is exactly the time of the affirmation or denial). 110

If the hypothetical proposition that forms part of the repetitive syllogism is conditional, then the repetition of the antecedent produces exactly the consequent, and the repetition of the contradictory of the consequent produces the contradictory of the antecedent; otherwise, the implication would be void (though not in the reverse of either of the two cases above, due to the possibility that the consequent is more general than the antecedent). If the hypothetical is a disjunctive, then, if it is an exclusive disjunction, the repetition of either part produces the contradictory of the other due to the impossibility of conjunction; the repetition of the contradictory of either part produces the other, due to the impossibility of excluding both. If the disjunctive is alternative denial, it produces only in the first case (due to the impossibility of conjunction though not exclusion); and if the disjunctive is inclusive, it produces only in the second case (due to the impossibility of exclusion though not conjunction). 111

## The Fifth Section: On Matters Appended to the Syllogism

### Containing four topics

The first is the compound syllogism, which is compounded of several premises, some of which produce a conclusion, from which, along with another premise, follows another conclusion, and so on 112 until what is sought is determined. The compound syllogism has either explicit intermediate conclusions, as in "every C is B, and every B is D, therefore every C is D," then "every C is D and every D is A, therefore every C is A," then "every C is A and every A is H, therefore every C is H"; or elided intermediate conclusions, as in "every C is B and every B is D and every D is A and every A is H, therefore every C is H."

113 The second is the reductio syllogism. What is to be proved is affirmed by disproving its contradictory, as in: Were "not every C is B" false, then "every C is B" and "every B is A" (on the basis that it is a true premise). This produces: Were "not every C is B" false, then "every C is A"; but it is not the case that "every C is A" (on the basis that it is something impossible); so this produces "not every C is B," which is what is sought.

114 The third is induction, which is a judgment on a universal made on the basis that it belongs to most of the particulars, as in "all animals move the lower jaw in eating because men, oxen, lions . . . do so." Induction does not convey certainty, because of the possibility that not all are like the ones considered (as, in this case, with the crocodile).

115 The fourth is example, which is taking a judgment belonging to one particular and affirming it of another particular because of a meaning common to both, as in "the world is composed of parts, so it is produced in time, like a house." Proponents of this argument technique affirm the real causality of the common meaning by concomitance along with division (though this division is not the one that proceeds by opposing negation to affirmation), as in "the real cause of temporal production is either composition or this or that; yet the last two are false due to counterexample, so the first is specified." But this kind of argument is weak. The concomitance step in the argument is weak because the last part and the other conditions may be a presumed concomitant cause even though it is not a real cause. The division step in the argument is weak because its exhaustiveness may be rejected due to the possibility that the real causality

belongs to something that has not been mentioned. Even supposing we grant the real causality of the common meaning in the principal analogue, its having real causality in the derivative analogue does not follow, due to the possibility that the specificities of the principal analogue are a condition for the causality, or the specificities of the derivative analogue are an impediment to such causality.

# The Conclusion

## Containing two discussions

### The First Discussion: On Syllogistic Matters

116.1 These matters comprise what is certain and what is not. There are six propositions of certainty.

116.2 Primary propositions, which are propositions such that conceiving their two extremes is sufficient to be certain of the relation between the two, as in "the whole is greater than the part."

116.3 Observational propositions, which are propositions in which judgments are made by the external and internal faculties, like the judgment "the sun shines" and that we are subject to anger and fear.

116.4 Propositions based on experience, which are propositions in which judgments are made due to repeated observations conveying certainty, like "drinking scammony leads to diarrhea."

116.5 Intuited propositions, which are propositions in which judgments are made due to a strong intuition of the soul that conveys knowledge, like the judgment that the light of the moon is acquired from the sun. (Intuition is rapidity of transfer from principles to what is sought.)

116.6 Propositions based on sequential testimony, which are propositions in which judgments are made due to copious testimony, after it is known that the occurrence of what is claimed is not impossible, and they are trusted due to widespread agreement about them; this is like the existence of Mecca and Baghdad. There is no number set for the right level of testimony; rather, reaching certainty is what decides that the number is complete.

Knowledge available from the last three propositions (that is, those based on experience, intuition, or sequential testimony) does not constitute a proof that is compelling for someone else. 116.7

Implicitly syllogistic propositions, which are those in which judgment is made by an intermediary always present to the mind upon conceiving the terms, like the judgment that four is even due to its divisibility into two equal parts. 116.8

A syllogism composed of these six propositions of certainty is called a demonstration. It is either a demonstration of the reasoned fact, in which the middle term is a real cause for the relation between the terms of the conclusion in the mind and in concrete reality, as in "This person has putrid humors, everything with putrid humors is feverish, therefore this person is feverish"; or it is a demonstration of the fact, in which the middle term is a real cause for the relation in the mind alone, as in "This person is feverish, everything feverish has putrid humors, therefore this person has putrid humors." 117

Those that are not propositions of certainty are six. 118.1

Endoxic propositions, which are propositions in which the judgment is made because it is acknowledged by all people, whether on grounds of general utility, compassion, or fervor, or under the influence of customs or laws and manners. The distinction between these and primary propositions is that were a man taken out of a social context, ignoring everything that is not in the mind itself, he would not judge the endoxic to be true (in contrast to the primary); as in "injustice is evil," "justice is good," "uncovering the pudenda is blameworthy," "looking after the weak is praiseworthy." Some endoxic propositions are true, others not. Every nation has its own endoxic propositions, as do the exponents of every craft with respect to that craft. 118.2

118.3 Conceded propositions, which are propositions conceded by the opponent and upon which discourse is built to refute him, as in the way jurists concede questions in jurisprudence.

118.4 A syllogism composed of these last two kinds of premises is called dialectic. Its goal is to persuade someone who fails to grasp a demonstration, and to refute an opponent.

118.5 Received propositions, which are propositions taken up on the authority of someone credible, whether due to a heavenly matter or superior intellect or religiosity, as in what is taken from scholars and the pious.

118.6 Suppositional propositions, which are propositions in which judgments are made in accordance with a supposition, as in "so-and-so roams about at night, so he is a thief."

118.7 A syllogism composed of these last two kinds of premises is called rhetoric. Its goal is to exhort the hearer to things useful for him, such as the cultivation of morals and religion.

118.8 Image-eliciting propositions, which are propositions that come upon the soul and have on it a marvelous influence such as melancholy and joy, as in "wine is a fluid ruby," and "honey is bitter and nauseous."

118.9 A syllogism composed of such propositions is called poetry, and its goal is to impress upon the soul a desire or dislike; it is animated by meter and a sweet voice.

118.10 Estimative propositions, which are false propositions, judgments made by the estimative faculty with respect to imperceptible matters, as in "every existent may be pointed to," and "beyond the world is a limitless void." Were they not refuted by reason or revelation they would pass for primary propositions. Their falsity can, however, be recognized, in that the estimative premise may agree with the intellect in premises of a syllogism, which then leads to the contradictory of the estimative judgment; the estimative faculty repudiates itself on arriving at the conclusion.

118.11 A syllogism formed of these is called sophistry, and its goal is to silence or deceive the opponent.

A fallacy is a syllogism whose form is corrupt such that it is not productive on account of a violation of some important condition in quantity, quality, or mode; or whose matter is corrupt such that the premise and the question may be identical due to synonymous expressions (as in "every man is a person, and every person is risible, therefore every man is risible"). Or one of the premises may be false but seem true with respect to expression, as when it is said of a painted horse: "every horse neighs, this is a horse, therefore the painting neighs." Or again, the falsity of the premises may be with respect to meaning, by failing for example to take care that the subject exists in the affirmative, as in "everything that is man-and-horse is man, and everything that is man-and-horse is horse," which produces "some men are horses"; or by using a natural proposition instead of a universal, as in "man is an animal, animal is a genus," which produces "man is a genus"; or by taking what is merely mental to be real (or vice versa). You should watch out for all these things to avoid falling into error. One who makes use of fallacies is called sophistical if he confronts a philosopher with them, and eristic if he confronts a dialectician with them. 119

## The Second Discussion: On the Parts of the Sciences

The parts include the subjects (of which you have learned already); the principles, which include the definitions of the subjects and their parts and essential accidents, the premises that are not self-evident but accepted by way of being posited (as in "to connect any two points by a straight line" and "to produce a circle at any distance round any point"),[11] and the self-evident premises (as in "quantities equal to another quantity are equal to each other");[12] and the questions, which are propositions in which the relation of the predicates to their subjects in the respective science is sought. 120.1

The subjects of the questions are either identical with the subject of the science, as in "every magnitude is either commensurable or incommensurable with another magnitude"; or the subject with 120.2

an essential accident, as in "every mean proportional is a side contained by the other two extremes"; or a species under the generic subject, as in "every line may be bisected"; or a species under the generic subject with an essential accident, as in "if one line is set upon another, the angles on either side are either two right angles or sum to two right angles"; or an essential accident, as in "every triangle has angles that sum to two right angles."

120.3 The predicates of the questions must be extrinsic to their subjects because it is impossible in a demonstration to seek to prove that a part of a given thing belongs to that thing.

Let this be the end of what we have to say in this epistle.

Praise be to God, Lord of the Worlds.

## Commentary

§0[13] The exordium of *al-Risālah al-Shamsiyyah* exhibits al-Kātibī's broader theological positions. He affirms a commitment to creation ex nihilo ("creation is bringing something forth without it being preceded by matter or time" [*TŠ* 89.1]), though in emanationist terms ("the system of existence is the series of contingent entities, the first of which is the creative intellectual substance, the first intelligence;[14] there we find existence in utmost honor and perfection" [*TŠ* 89.3–4]). He presents himself as a Muslim believer faithful to the prophet's example, and a practitioner of logic for its necessary role in allowing humans to flourish (except for those holy souls free of human stains—the prophets—who can do without logic). Al-Kātibī is intellectualist in the way he envisages how humans flourish, taking it to be brought about through contact with the angelic intelligences. The exordium records deep gratitude to his patrons, and displays quiet confidence in the originality of aspects of the *Risālah*.

The *Risālah* gives us great insight into the religious culture of the time. It is noteworthy that a Muslim whose theological positions are so deeply inflected by Avicennian philosophy should have such a secure position in the syllabus of legal schools otherwise opposed to al-Kātibī's broader vision of what the subject could do for its practitioners.[15]

The exordium ends with a few words on the structure of the *Risālah*. After defining logic and defending our need to learn it, the presentation begins with the simplest elements of logic (terms or, more strictly, expressions and the simple meanings they signify), moves on to propositions constructed from terms, then to arguments constructed from propositions, and finally to sciences that develop sets of arguments dealing with specific subject matter. The order of treatment is defended by the commentators in terms of the final goal of logic as a science (see Introduction generally, but especially §§5 and 6). There are aspects of nostalgia about al-Taftāzānī's consideration of the *Risālah*'s coverage, which is limited in comparison with the range of subjects covered by al-Kātibī's distant predecessors (universals, definitions, propositions, syllogism, demonstration, dialectic, rhetoric, sophistical refutations, and poetry).

> **Text 0.1** But the later scholars omit the five arts, [that is, demonstration, dialectic, rhetoric, sophistical refutations, and poetry,] in spite of their great value; instead they go on at length about conversions, co-implication, and connective syllogisms, in spite of their low value. (*TŠ* 93.1–2)

The *Risālah* is, as al-Taftāzānī says, mainly devoted to the formal aspects of logic.

## The Introduction

The Introduction deals with matters preliminary to coming to grips with any science. The need we have for a science involves identifying its final cause and benefit; the quiddity of the science allows us to identify the questions it asks that distinguish it from other sciences, and its subject matter confers a unity on it (*TŠ* 95.5–13). The lemmata that make up the Introduction broach issues that show what it means for logic to be a science, and foreshadow issues touched on in the Conclusion. (That said, as al-Taftāzānī notes, students embark successfully on the study of an instrumental science such as grammar without any notion of its delineation[16] or final cause [*TŠ*

97.7–8]). The questions of a science (the theorems to be proved) are most important for understanding the unity of a given science:

> **Text 1.a** Here there is a lofty insight, which is that the true nature (*ḥaqīqah*) of each science is its questions, because these questions have first arisen, then a name is imposed on the science relative to [the questions]; [the science] has no quiddity or true nature beyond these questions. So knowledge [of the science] with respect to its definition and true nature only comes about through knowledge of all its questions. (*TT* 62.pu–63.2)

### *The first discussion, on the quiddity of logic and proof of the need for it*

The first four lemmata set out two divisions of knowledge: the first, knowledge divided into its broadest kinds; the second, knowledge divided with respect to its acquisition. The first two lemmata culminate in the argument of §3 that it is necessary for humans to learn logic; §4 goes on to argue that logic involves both primitive and inferred knowledge claims.

§1[17] The first division of knowledge al-Kātibī considers is into conception (*taṣawwur*) and assertion (*taṣdīq*).[18] Everything we know is either a conception or an assertion, though not every conception or assertion is knowledge. This is Avicenna's doctrine (for example, *Pointers* 1.4 [*AI* 3.15–4.11]), which is in turn a development from a division first put forward by al-Fārābī (*SQ* 97–100). The precise definition of these two divisions of knowledge varied according to the philosopher using the terms. Although the first of the definitions offered by al-Kātibī ("conception . . . is the occurrence of a form in the intellect") follows Avicenna, the second (assertion is "an aggregate of conception and judgment" or, more properly, an aggregate of conceptions and a judgment) does not; according to al-Ḥillī, the first sentence of the *Risālah* marks al-Kātibī out as one of the followers of Fakhr al-Dīn al-Rāzī (see *RM* 7).

> **Text 1.1** If you judge [a conception such as "man"] to be a certain matter (as in "man is an animal"), then the aggregate of the conception "man" and the conception "animal" and the judgment of the relation one has to the other is said to be an assertion. This is according to the custom of Fakhr al-Dīn and his followers, and it differs from what the ancients laid down in their terms of art; for the ancients considered the assertion to be the judgment itself alone, and the conception a condition for the assertion. (*ḤQ* 183.1–5)

Both al-Rāzī's and Avicenna's accounts face a common problem.

> **Text 1.2** Philosophers agree that assertion depends on conception, whether by the dependence of the whole on the part, or the dependence of what is subject to a condition on the condition (according to the difference between the two opinions here [which is to say, al-Rāzī's and Avicenna's]); so, were the conception to consist of the occurrence [of the form in the mind] devoid of the judgment, then a judgment would depend on its own absence; but this is absurd. The answer to this objection is that "conception" is an expression equivocal between two meanings, one of which is the mental occurrence without qualification (without the restriction of the presence or absence of a judgment), and the other the mental occurrence devoid of judgment. The first is the condition for assertion, and the second is the counterpart of assertion. (*ḤQ* 183.12–184.4)

So the solution to the problem turns on the fact that "conception" is imposed on two meanings. Al-Kātibī's statement of the aggregate account raises a further problem in taking conception as a component of, yet opposed to, assertion. The fact that "conception" is equivocal once again solves the problem:

> **Text 1.3** The upshot is that al-Kātibī's position—made clear elsewhere—is that mere conception (*al-taṣawwur faqaṭ*) is apprehension insofar as it is apprehension without considering judgment or anything else along with it (and it is synonymous with conception and knowledge).[19] It is not impossible to divide knowledge into apprehension insofar as it is what it is, and apprehension along with judgment, by inclusive disjunction (*ʿalā sabīl manʿ al-khulūw*),[20] whereupon "which" in "which is the occurrence of the form of something" would refer to mere conception; and it is correct to take into consideration with it the conception that is the opposite of assertion. (*TŠ* 100.7–12)

Many object to the division of a thing into itself and something else, and investigate more deeply the equivocation of *taṣawwur*, and the referent of the pronoun I have translated as "which" (*TŠ* 100.13–u); but Text 1.3 presents a respectable preliminary reading of §1.

**§2**[21] Al-Kātibī goes on to consider the ways we come to have knowledge. For this, he presents the second division of knowledge, this time into *badīhī* and *naẓarī*. I translate these terms as "primitive" and "inferred."[22]

> **Text 2.1** Know that the primitive conception consists of that whose occurrence does not depend on search and acquisition, like the conception of hot and cold. The primitive assertion consists of an assertion for which conceiving the two extremes is sufficient for asserting the relation of one extreme to the other, as in "the whole is greater than

> the part"; for whoever conceives "whole" and "part" and "being greater" asserts this judgment. The acquired conception (*al-taṣawwur al-muktasab*) is the opposite of the primitive, such that its occurrence in the mind depends on search and acquisition (like conceiving "angel" and "jinni"). And the acquired assertion is such that conceiving its two extremes is not sufficient for the judgment (like "the world came to exist in time"). (*ḤQ* 184.u–185.8)

In this context, al-Taftāzānī takes "primitive" as synonymous with "necessary" (*ḍarūrī*) in §3, and both as antonyms of "inferred" and its synonym, "acquired" (*kasbī, muktasab*) (*TŠ* 104.5–6, 104.u). Note that the necessity of a proposition that is necessary in respect of how we come to know it has to do with the fact that we cannot fail to see the proposition's truth once we understand its terms; it is not the necessity of a necessary proposition that has to do with the relation between the predicate and the subject (explored from §52 on), the truth of which we often fail to see.[23]

On al-Ḥillī's definition of assertion, a primitive assertion may depend on acquired conceptions. Further, the primitive assertion may include the relating of conceptions by an assertion not brought about by thinking (*fikr*) but by intuition (*ḥads*) or repeated observation (*tajribah*) (*TŠ* 104.11–apu) (see §116.4 and §116.5). The examples Avicenna gives of acquired conceptions in *Pointers* 1.4 include "binomial" (*AI* 3.u–4.2), the definition of which is given as Proposition 36 in Book 10 of Euclid's *Elements*: "If two rational straight lines commensurable in square only are added together, then the whole is irrational; let it be called binomial." The example illustrates how theory-laden a conception can be; no one learns the meaning of binomial without preceding geometrical instruction deploying both assertions and conceptions, whether primitive or acquired. But al-Taḥtānī claims that the acquisition of an unknown conception is through matters of which we do have conceptions (*al-umūr al-taṣawwuriyyah*), whereas the acquisition of an unknown assertion is through assertions we have already (*TT* 55.pu–u); as al-Sayyid al-Sharīf al-Jurjānī says, "it has not been verified that there is a way to acquire conception from assertions, or the reverse (even though no demonstration has been given that it is impossible)" (*TT* 55n2). Whatever way we come to a conception of "binomial," insofar as it is acquired, it is acquired through—which is to say, expressible as—two prior conceptions.

Al-Kātibī then considers first whether every conception and every assertion is primitive; were that the case, he claims, we would know everything (and al-Kātibī assumes without argument that we do not). He then considers whether every conception and every assertion is inferred; were that the case, he claims, we could never know anything (and yet we do know some things). Al-Kātibī seems to assume that we know all primitive knowledge, which is too strong an assumption if al-Ḥillī's hot and cold are good examples of the primitive; he also assumes that inferred knowledge falls into regress or circularity if it is not ultimately based on primitive knowledge. Al-Kātibī does not need to consider further possibilities that arise on his approach to the problem (among them, that every conception is primitive but every assertion is inferred, and that every conception is inferred but every assertion is primitive); conceptions are inferred from conceptions, assertions from assertions. Here is al-Ḥillī's expansion of the elided argument in the lemma to do with regress or circularity:

> Text 2.2 It is impossible for knowledge claims—both conceptions and assertions—to be as a whole primitive, otherwise we would not be ignorant of anything; and the consequent is necessarily false, so the antecedent must be too. And it is impossible for them to be as a whole inferred, otherwise one of two matters would follow—namely, either a circle or an infinite regress; and the consequent consisting of these two parts is false, so the antecedent must be too.

> The explanation of the implication [in the second argument] is this: Everything acquired inevitably has something that allows its acquisition; were what allows this acquisition (*al-kāsib*) itself acquired, it would need something else that acquires it. If that which acquires it is the first knowledge claim, we have a circle; if it is yet another thing that allows its acquisition, we have either an infinite regress, or we come to a primitive thing that allows its acquisition, and that is what we seek to prove. (*ḤQ* 184.8–pu)

One possible motivation for this lemma is that al-Kātibī's predecessor al-Rāzī argued in one of his works that no conception is acquired (*anna shay'an minhā ghayr muktasab*, glossed by al-Kātibī as *ay lā shay' wa-lā wāḥid minhā ka-dhālik* [al-Kātibī, *al-Mufaṣṣal fī sharḥ al-Muḥaṣṣal*, 54.3, 54.8–10]); rather, they are either primitive or innate (*ḥāṣil fī l-nafs*). The first argument al-Rāzī offers for the claim is that we cannot seek what we are unaware of (because we are not aware of it), and we cannot seek what we are aware of (because we have it already); al-Jurjānī in his gloss on the lemma explicitly mentions this position of al-Rāzī (*TT* 53n2). I note the position simply to provide context for al-Kātibī's decision to address these questions; he is faced with a distant echo of Aristotle's motivation for writing the *Posterior Analytics*.[24] However, in the early parts of the book al-Rāzī wrote that is most directly connected with the tradition of logic al-Kātibī is developing in the *Risālah*, he seems to fall in with the Avicennian majority and affirms that some conceptions and assertions must be acquired (*RM* 8.10–9.5).[25]

§3[26] At this point, al-Kātibī takes himself to have shown that some conceptions and assertions are primitive, and some inferred. To infer conceptions and assertions of the unknown, we have to order known things; the delineation of thinking al-Kātibī gives need not delay us, though note that thinking may order things that are in fact false (*ḤQ* 185.pu–u). The fact that thinkers contradict each other, and even—over time—themselves, proves that we stand in need of a set of rules for thinking to make sure that the ways we order primitive knowledge are sound (this argument is taken, often word for word, from Avicenna's *al-Madkhal* [*AM* 34.apu–38.u]); this is the business of logic.

Al-Kātibī gives in §3 a delineation of logic as a canonical instrument (often rendered "normative instrument"; "normative organon" is another possible translation, and would highlight the fact that the same word is used for instrument as is used to refer to the system of methods developed in Aristotle's corpus on logic), the implementation of which preserves us from error in thinking.[27] (What is offered is only a delineation because al-Kātibī uses accidental matters in his formulation, like being an instrument, which belongs to logic only in relation to other sciences [*TT* 61.apu–u]; see the conditions for delineation in §36.) In §§5 and 6, he goes on to argue that logic is also a science with a determinate subject matter. In taking logic to be both an instrument and a science with its own subject matter, he is adopting Avicenna's position, which agrees with the Peripatetics that logic is an instrument for the other sciences, while at the same time agreeing with the Platonists that logic is a science in itself.[28] Al-Kātibī in §5, however, will differ from Avicenna as to what the subject matter of the science of logic is.

§4[29] Al-Kātibī goes on to make two claims specifically about how we come to know logic. As in the argument in §2, its knowledge claims cannot be entirely primitive or we would know logic without learning it (which clearly we do not); nor are they entirely inferred, otherwise they would form either a regress or a vicious circle. The lemma is taken to be an answer to an elided problem (*ḤQ* 188.1, TT 64.apu–u), treated by (among others) his colleague at Marāghah, Naṣīr al-Dīn al-Ṭūsī: if in logic we need to infer some of the knowledge logic contains, what are we using to protect ourselves from incorrect thinking in making those inferences? The logic that is not yet fully achieved? Or another logic?

> **Text 4.1** The greater part of logic consists of technical terms to which one needs to be alerted, of primary propositions that one needs to have brought to mind and that prepare for others, and of inferred knowledge claims that are such that one does not fall into error concerning them (the like of which geometry uses in its demonstrations). None of these stands in need of logic. Should any of these need logical canons (and that will be rarely), that need will only be for the first kind [that is, the technical terms]; there is therefore no circularity of need at all. (*ṬḤ* 118.18–apu)

*The second discussion, on the subject of logic*

§5[30] The lemma preempts the discussion of the structure of a science in §120 (the last lemma of the treatise) by assuming we know why it matters that we identify the subject of an Aristotelian science,[31] and what studying a science involves. A subject has to be assumed to exist, or be proved to exist outside the science itself; and the scientist tries to prove a number of essential accidents of the subject or its parts. So geometry has as its subject matter extended magnitude, which has subjects under it like line and plane figure. In this context, "essential accident" is used in a technical sense,[32] different from "essential" (*dhātī*) when used by Avicenna to mean "constituent" (*muqawwim*) in discussing the material covered by al-Kātibī in Section 2 of the first treatise (from §15 on, though note that al-Kātibī does not himself use the term "essential" in the *Risālah* until §120, where it quite clearly has the second sense, of essential accident). For present purposes, an essential accident is one that belongs to its subject in virtue of what the subject is (like capacity for astonishment belongs to man, *ḤQ* 189.15–16), or what constitutes the subject ("a part of it," like walking belongs to man because he is an animal, *ḤQ* 189.pu), or what is implied by the subject alone ("coextensive with it," like laughing belongs to man because he has a capacity for astonishment, *ḤQ* 189.u). Having internal angles that sum to two right angles belongs to triangle alone, and belongs to triangle necessarily. A science is developed by proving that (and why) essential accidents belong to the science's subjects; the questions as to whether or not they do are the questions spoken of in Text 1.a.

It is therefore crucial for the purposes of the Aristotelian theory of science to identify the subject matter of a science.

> **Text 5.1** The sciences are only distinguished among themselves by the distinction of their subjects; by reason of not knowing the subject of the science, one fumbles with its questions. For example, the parts of the cosmos with respect to form (*al-shakl*) are the subject of astronomy, and with respect to nature the subject of *On the Heavens*. Were we not to take notice of these two lines of approach, the investigation would sometimes be about astronomy, sometimes about physics; we need therefore to state the subject of a science. (*ḤQ* 189.7–11)

Avicenna had identified secondary intelligibles as the subject matter of logic (Avicenna, *Metaphysics*, 7), and al-Rāzī agreed with him on this point.

> **Text 5.2** The subject matter of logic is the secondary intelligibles insofar as it is possible to pass by means of them from the known (*al-maʿlūmāt*) to the unknown (*al-majhūlāt*).[33] The explanation of "secondary intelligibles" is that man conceives the realities of things (*ḥaqāʾiq al-ashyāʾ*) in the first place, then judges some with others either restrictively or predicatively (*ḥukman taqyīdiyyan aw khabariyyan*). The quiddity's being judged in this way is something that only attaches to the quiddity after it has

become known in the first place, so it is a second-order [consideration] (*fī l-darajah al-thāniyah*). If these considerations are investigated—not absolutely, but rather with respect to how it is possible to pass correctly by means of them from the known to the unknown—that is logic. So its subject matter is certainly the secondary intelligibles under the consideration mentioned above. (*RM* 10.1–8)

Against these two authorities whom he respects so highly, al-Kātibī follows Afḍal al-Dīn al-Khūnajī and takes the subject matter of logic to be more general than secondary intelligibles—namely, conceptions and assertions, investigated insofar as they lead to further conceptions or assertions. Being a differentia of human, for example, is somehow an essential accident of the primary intelligible rational, and since notions like differentia are part of the logician's brief, the logician is investigating essential accidents of primary intelligibles.[34] Al-Taftāzānī among others notes the dispute (*TŠ* 114.15–u), but defers its fuller treatment to a more advanced text (*TŠ* 117.9).[35]

§6[36] It is customary for logicians in the Avicennian tradition to structure their treatises to deal with definition (which leads to a conception) and proof (which leads to an assertion). So it is that §6 evokes the two terms introduced in the opening lemma of the treatise in promising to deal first with explanatory phrases and then with proofs. The exposition is linked directly to the logical priority of the components, the simple before the complex. This principle of ordering becomes ever more rigorously applied by post-Avicennian logicians (*mukhālafat al-waḍʿ al-ṭabīʿ fī quwwat al-khaṭaʾ ʿinda l-muḥaṣṣilīn*, *TT* 98.7), and is clearly a great concern for al-Kātibī. Al-Taḥtānī offers a detailed account of the reasoning behind the structure of the *Risālah*.

**Text 6.1** Al-Kātibī only ordered [*al-Risālah al-Shamsiyyah*] in this way because, of that which must be known in logic, it is either crucial for making a start in the discipline, or it is not. If it is crucial for making a start, it forms the Introduction. If it is not, then investigation of it either has to do with simple terms (the First Treatise), or with combinations. Investigation into combinations must either be concerned with those that are not the ultimate goal of the investigation (the Second Treatise), or with those that are. Reflection about the latter must either be relative to form alone (the Third Treatise), or relative to matter (the Conclusion). (*TT* 23.pu–25.1)

## The First Treatise, on Simple Terms

The first treatise of the *Risālah* is on the simple elements (*al-mufradāt*) that make up logical constructions; al-Kātibī does not limit his treatment to either simple expressions or simple meanings. The treatise is made up of four sections. In the first, al-Kātibī deals with simple expressions, which are defined negatively as not being compound expressions (*murakkabāt*; see §10 and commentary below). The section also offers definitions for complete and incomplete compound expressions (§14). Two compound constructions are of logical interest: the definition and the proposition. The treatment of definition is deferred to the fourth and final section of the first treatise (so the first treatise stretches to include compound expressions that convey simple meanings), and the other logically interesting compound expression—the proposition, or truth-apt sentence—and its role in inference occupy al-Kātibī for the remaining two Treatises and the Conclusion.

The first section presents material considered by Avicenna in his response, on the one hand, to Aristotle's *De Interpretatione*, the *ʿIbārah*, and on the other, to Porphyry's *Introduction*, the *Madkhal*. In between the first section on expressions and the last section on definition, al-Kātibī deals with simple meanings (which are what simple expressions are imposed on, and what definitions are both made up of, and define), and the five kinds of predicates used in logic, referred to as the five predicables, or the five universals. In the third section of the first treatise, al-Kātibī deals with five more profound discussions that affect how any universal should be used in logical investigations.

*The first section, on expressions*

These eight lemmata deal with the relation between expressions and meanings; given that the logician is not primarily interested in expressions (*ḤQ* 194.apu), subsequent lemmata nearly all concern the relation of one meaning to another meaning. There are a number of discrete discussions underway in this part of the *Risālah*. Lemmata 7–9 deal with a development on the theory of signification first set out by Avicenna in the *Madkhal* (*AM* 92.1–3); al-Kātibī is clearly following the version Avicenna put forward in *Pointers* 1.6 (*AI* 4.apu–5.7), emending it in light of criticisms advanced by al-Rāzī. Lemma 10 distinguishes simple from compound expressions, §§11–13 develop a division of simple terms in competition with grammar and—among other things—identify the name (or noun; see comments on §11 below for why I prefer the less technical term) as the expression imposed on the simple universal meaning. Lemma 14 offers distinctions relative to compound expressions. The distinctions developed in the first discussion isolate the expressions to be investigated through the rest of the treatise.

The *Risālah* was intended for teaching, and the teacher was meant to supply background for its treatment of signification. In broad terms, the problem of signification deals with the way meanings are conveyed. As treated by Avicenna and his followers, the discussion focuses above all on the way meanings are conveyed by someone uttering an expression to someone else familiar with the conventions of the language; it does not deal with the institution or acquisition of language. One way to introduce the topic—taken from al-Ḥillī (*ḤQ* 195.1–9)—was to say that the signification (*dalālah*) of a meaning may be by a gesture or by a verbal expression. Some expressions signify meanings without being imposed to signify those meanings, whether naturally (*bi-l-ṭabʿ*) like "ouch!" for pain, or intellectually (*bi-l-ʿaql*); that is, by mediation of inference: an articulated sound signifies a voice, in that even from a word we do not understand, we grasp a meaning—that someone has pronounced the word. As noted, most philosophical discussion is directed to the case in which an expression (*lafẓ*) has been imposed (*mawḍūʿ*) on a given meaning (*maʿnan*); in this case, the sense of "an expression's signifying a meaning" is "the meaning understood by one who is conversant with the imposition from the expression when it is uttered or brought to mind" (*fahm al-maʿnā min al-lafẓ ʿinda iṭlāqihi aw takhayyulihi bi-l-nisbah ilā man huwa ʿālim bi-l-waḍʿ*). A problem arises at this point due to the structure of meanings themselves: the containment (*taḍammun*) of one meaning in another, or the implication (*iltizām*) of one meaning by another (without the implicate meaning being contained in the implicant meaning).[37] An expression imposed to signify one meaning also signifies necessarily on being uttered (*ʿinda iṭlāqihi*) meanings contained in or inseparable from that meaning. The definition of signification was therefore refined by Avicenna, and this is where al-Kātibī takes up his discussion from §7. Such refinement is necessary if an account—at any rate, an Avicennian account—is to be given of what signifies the quiddity, or, in other words, what signifies what the thing is. Other problems come about because expressions can be imposed on more than a single meaning, either by the original imposition (*waḍʿ*) of the first Positor (*wāḍiʿ*), or by the later technical convention (*iṣṭilāḥ*) of a group of language users; this is the problem addressed in §12.

§7[38] To repeat: The theory of signification set out here starts with the assumption that an act of imposition has related an expression with a meaning. It is this relation that determines that the expression signifies the meaning by signification of correspondence; the meaning necessarily comes to mind for those familiar with the imposition on the utterance of the expression. But because of the necessary interconnections among meanings—and "necessary" here excludes purely cultural and personal associations, like the laurel with heroic deeds, and the rose with love—in most cases, other meanings beyond the one signified by correspondence are also signified on the utterance of the expression. These meanings beyond the one on which the expression is imposed are signified through a relation combining the first element, the imposition, and a second element, the relation the first meaning has to the other meaning. The relevant relations between meanings are containment (in which the second meaning is contained in the first, as ANIMAL and RATIONAL are contained in MAN), and implication (in which a meaning extrinsic to the first meaning follows it necessarily, as LAUGHING follows MAN, and 2R follows TRIANGLE).[39] The two further kinds of signification are named after these second elements that constitute them. (See Figure 1, where the broken line from "Expression" to "Meaning" represents imposition, the double line the containment of one meaning in another, the single line the implication of one meaning by another, the heavy dotted line the expression's signification of meaning by containment, and the light dotted line the expression's signification of meaning by implication.)

The definitions of the three kinds of signification al-Kātibī offers are highly compressed, and the translation is guided by al-Taftāzānī's expansion of §7, here given with subscripted numbers to make it clear which of the meanings is spoken of.

> **TEXT 7.1** The expression's signification of meaning$_1$ by way of that expression being imposed on that meaning$_1$ (like the signification by "man" of RATIONAL ANIMAL) is called correspondence (*dalālat al-lafẓ ʿalā l-maʿnā bi-tawassuṭ waḍʿ dhālika l-lafẓ li-dhālika l-maʿnā . . . tusammā muṭābaqah*), due to the expression matching the meaning$_1$ because it is imposed as its counterpart. The expression's

signification of meaning$_2$ by way of the expression being imposed on something$_1$ in which that meaning$_2$ is included (like signification by "man" of ANIMAL by way of its being imposed on that in which ANIMAL is intrinsic; namely, RATIONAL ANIMAL) is called signification by containment (*dalālat al-lafẓ ʿalā l-maʿnā bi-tawassuṭ waḍʿ al-lafẓ li-shayʾ dakhala fīhi dhālika l-maʿnā . . . tusammā dalālat al-taḍammun*), due to the signified meaning$_2$ being within the meaning$_1$ on which it is imposed. The expression's signification of meaning$_3$ by way of the expression being imposed on something$_1$ to which the meaning$_3$ signified is extrinsic (like signification by "man" of RECEPTIVE OF KNOWLEDGE, which is extrinsic to RATIONAL ANIMAL) is called signification by implication (*dalālat al-lafẓ ʿalā l-maʿnā bi-tawassuṭ waḍʿihi li-shayʾ kharaja ʿanhu dhālika l-maʿnā al-madlūl . . . tusammā dalālat al-iltizām*), due to the signified meaning$_3$ being an implicate of the meaning$_1$ on which it is imposed. (*TŠ* 121.4–12)

Al-Kātibī is stipulating, roughly, that if expression E signifies meaning X by containment, then there is a second meaning, Y, on which E is imposed, X is a part of Y, and is taken to be signified by E only in virtue of E's being imposed on Y. And if expression E signifies meaning X by implication, then there is a second meaning, Y, on which E is imposed, X follows Y as an implicate, and is signified by E only in virtue of E's being imposed on Y. These ponderous definitions are the outcome of a dialectical process (which I here pass over) from Avicenna's definitions in *Pointers* 1.6 (*AI* 4.apu–5.7), through their critical reception by al-Rāzī, and their final refinement at the hands of al-Khūnajī.[40] Among the commentators, al-Taftāzānī in particular dwells on the motivation for modifying Avicenna's definitions in *Pointers*; I do not intend to go into the details, but the modification eliminates problems for the definitions when dealing with particular kinds of equivocation (*ḤQ* 196.2–3) (among others, the kind of equivocation that arises in cases of conventionally and legislatively transferred expressions in §12.2 if the primary imposition is not abandoned).

§8[41] "Understood" in al-Kātibī's phrase "otherwise its being understood from the expression would be impossible" is glossed by al-Ḥillī as "always understood" (*ḤQ* 197.9); even the possibility of failure in following voids the implication. Signification by implication raises further questions as to how strong the relation should be between the implied meaning and the implicant meaning. To use the example given in §7, how should the meaning RECEPTIVE OF KNOWLEDGE follow from MAN? First, the relation between the meaning on which the expression is imposed and its implicate is specified as a relation at the conceptual level rather than one in existence; al-Kātibī's example of BLIND and HAVING VISION makes the distinction clear. Second, the implicate meaning (*al-lāzim*) must also be extrinsic to the implicant meaning (*al-malzūm*), which is to say, it cannot be part of the implicant meaning (in the way that ANIMAL is part of both the definition RATIONAL ANIMAL and the quiddity it defines, MAN); this is why it is referred to as extrinsic (*al-khārij*) in §8. (Recall that Avicenna reserves *lāzim* for meanings extrinsic to the implicant meaning [*AI* 8.pu–9.1].) Third, the implicate meaning involved in signification theory need not be predicable of the implicant meaning (as in the case of al-Kātibī's example of BLIND and SIGHT), whereas the implicate meanings dealt with in the next section (on the predicables; see §22) must be predicable of the implicant meaning. Finally, as al-Kātibī puts it, the implicate must "be such that its conception follows from the conception of the named"; this is formulated in a way that—set against al-Khūnajī's treatment of the matter—highlights an important distinction. (Al-Taftāzānī follows al-Kātibī's formulation most closely [*TŠ* 123.3–4].)

> **TEXT 8.1** Two notions are intended by mental implication, the first of which is that whenever there is an awareness of

> the implicant there is an awareness of the implicate (*kullamā ḥaṣala l-shuʿūr bi-l-malzūm ḥaṣala l-shuʿūr bi-l-lāzim*); the second, that whenever there is an awareness of both there is an awareness of the implication between the two (*kullamā ḥaṣala l-shuʿūr bi-himā ḥaṣala l-shuʿūr bi-l-luzūm*). The first is stronger than the second, and it is what is taken into account according to [the argument] just rehearsed. Nothing can have infinite implicates according to this sense, whether with a middle or without. (*ḤK* 13.1–5)

It is the stronger sense that is involved in signification by implication. In §22.2 below, when dealing with inseparable implicates,[42] al-Kātibī makes the same distinction (though in reverse order, weaker first). The two strengths of implication are used at different philosophical moments; the stronger is used in signification theory, the weaker for the immediate and evident implicates of a quiddity that give a demonstrative science its proper principles (on which see commentary on §22 and §120).

Looking into why it is the strong implication that is considered in signification reveals what is at stake; I consider two criticisms of the theory.[43] First, a meaning on which an expression is imposed might have infinitely many implicates; for example, from TWO follows HALF OF FOUR, THIRD OF SIX, and so forth. This is true, but according to al-Khūnajī these implicates follow only on the weak account of evident implication, and are only acknowledged when TWO is considered along with the putative implicate. Another objection is that implication is different for different people, and therefore signification by implication is not a determinate or necessary signification. Al-Khūnajī again disagrees: The implicate meaning is strongly implied, as in the case of one correlative with another. One simply does not understand the meaning of "father" unless one also understands the meaning of "child," nor does one understand the meaning of the privation "blind" unless one understands that of which it is a privation.

§9[44] Al-Kātibī goes on to consider whether, given the presence of one of the three significations, we may infer that one or both of the other two must also be present. Avicenna had made the claim that correspondence is necessarily entailed by containment and implication (Avicenna, *Manṭiq al-mashriqiyyīn*, 15.5–6). What he meant is: If expression E signifies X by containment, there must be a meaning Y of which X is a proper part and which is signified by E by correspondence. Similarly, if expression E signifies X by implication, there must be a meaning Y of which X is an implicate and which is signified by E by correspondence. The post-Avicennian logicians comprehensively explored the relations among significations, and investigated the remaining four possible entailments (correspondence-containment, correspondence-implication, containment-implication, implication-containment).

To take the claims in the order that we find them in the *Risālah*: Al-Kātibī considers but rules out the entailment of containment by correspondence (so he is ruling out what would amount to the claim: if expression E signifies meaning X by correspondence, there must be a meaning Y that is part of X and that E will signify by containment). He rejects this claim because there may be simple quiddities that are not constituted by a genus and differentia, or other parts; he gives what may be a relevant example in §31: "an example of the simple is intelligence (if we say substance is not a genus for it)." He also rejected al-Rāzī's argument for the entailment of implication by correspondence ("we have ruled out what has been said, that the conception of every quiddity entails the conception that it is not other than itself"). This is how al-Rāzī sets out his claim:

> **Text 9.1** Signification by imposition is correspondence, and the remaining two [kinds of signification] are consequences, not absolutely but rather on the condition that the quiddity is a compound for the first and an implicant for the second. Since the part does not necessarily belong to every quiddity, but an implicate has to belong to

every quiddity—at the least, that it is not other than itself (*wa-aqalluhu annahu laysa ghayrahu*)—containment does not have to follow correspondence, but implication does. Neither is found without correspondence because it is inconceivable that the consequent occur insofar as it is a consequent without an antecedent. (*RM* 19.pu–20.3)

It is difficult to know precisely what al-Rāzī means by the claim that any signification by correspondence implies that "it is not other than itself"; perhaps that DOG implies NOT-CAT, NOT-HORSE, and so forth, or perhaps that DOG is self-identical. Whatever al-Rāzī's precise claim, al-Khūnajī rejected it using the distinction in Text 8.1:

**TEXT 9.2** In response to the claim that everything has an evident implicate, we say that on the stronger understanding [of implication] this is rejected, and the consideration [al-Rāzī] mentions as inevitable and that follows everything is on the weaker sense not the stronger, due to the possibility of conceiving something while not paying attention to its being not other than itself (*li-imkān taṣawwur al-shay' ma'a l-dhuhūl 'an kawnihi laysa ghayrahu*). (*ḪK* 13.8–10)

As noted above, only the stronger sense of implication plays a role in signification theory. If I understand the root of al-Khūnajī's objection to al-Rāzī's claim, it lies in the distinction between an implicate of FATHER like NOT-ROCK and the implicate CHILD, a distinction that matters because the meaning of "father" cannot be understood without simultaneously understanding what a child is, whereas it can be understood without even adverting to a rock.

Al-Kātibī in the *Risālah* extends the last conclusion (that correspondence does not entail containment) to rule out the entailment of implication by containment. I cannot see how this stronger conclusion would follow from the weaker one, though I think he is right to rule it out. By contrast, al-Kātibī had accepted in *Jāmi' al-daqā'iq* that containment entails implication. In any event, here in the *Risālah* he is rejecting the claim that if expression E signifies meaning X by containment, there must be a meaning Z signified by E by correspondence of which X is a proper part, and further, there must be a meaning Y that is an implicate of meaning Z, and E signifies Y by implication. Al-Taftāzānī thinks al-Kātibī is right in the *Risālah* to reject containment-entails-implication:

> Text 9.3 From what we have mentioned, that correspondence does not decisively and certainly entail implication, it is apparent that containment does not decisively and certainly entail implication, because there may be a compound quiddity that has no evident implicate, and the expression would signify its part by containment but without implication. What al-Kātibī said in the *Jāmiʿ* (*mā dhakarahu l-muṣannif fī l-Jāmiʿ*)—containment entails implication because the conception of a compound quiddity definitely entails the conception that it is compound, thus verifying implication necessarily—is to be rejected (*fa-mamnūʿ*). Rather, the conception of the quiddity does not even entail that it is a quiddity, let alone its being simple or compound; otherwise, correspondence would also entail implication. If you were to argue: Containment is the understanding of the proper part insofar as it is a proper part, and the qualification being a part (*al-juz'iyyah*) is an extrinsic implicate meaning that entails the conception being a whole (*al-kulliyyah*) as a necessary consequence of the correlation between being a part and being a whole, so containment without implication is impossible, we would respond: The meaning of their claim "containment is understanding the part insofar as it is a part" is not that containment consists of understanding the part along with the qualification of being a part, but rather that it is understanding the part by way of its being a part and by

> reason of that; that is, the reason for understanding it from the expression is its being a part of what is understood from the expression (*mafhūm al-lafẓ*), whether or not the qualification of being a part is noticed in that state.
>
> Implication does not entail containment due to the possibility that there may be a simple quiddity that entails an evident implicate; this is something they ignore in spite of it being obvious. (*TŠ* 124.11–125.8)

On this last point al-Taftāzānī makes, note that al-Kātibī in the *Risālah* in fact fails to consider whether implication might entail containment. Al-Kātibī concludes §9 by accepting only Avicenna's initial claim, that signification by containment and signification by implication both entail signification by correspondence "due to the impossibility of a consequent—insofar as it is a consequent —without an antecedent." Another way to consider these cases is that both signification by containment and signification by implication are relative products, and are defined as having signification by correspondence as part of that product.

§10[45] Al-Kātibī needs to isolate simple expressions that signify simple meanings for the purposes of the discussion in the following two sections of the first treatise, and to distinguish them from compound expressions (see §14 below, where he gets his distinctions in order for the fourth section, and for the remainder of the treatise). Al-Kātibī adopts Avicenna's criterion for distinguishing simple from compound (in *Pointers* 1.8 [*AI* 5.13–6.1]), and al-Ḥillī, in his commentary, even brings in one of Avicenna's examples of a proper name composed of two significant expressions, ʿAbdallāh. The test consists of considering the expression's signification by correspondence. Is it intended that any part of the expression signify part of the meaning? If so, the expression is compound (*murakkab*). It may be that *insān* ("man") breaks down into elements which include *in* ("if"); but IF is no part of the meaning of "man." We must also ignore compounds used as a proper name, like ʿAbdallāh; as a name, neither part is intended to follow the intention of the first Positor (by which it would be the compound "slave of God"), because that intention has been overridden by a secondary intention, to use the two words as a single proper name for a given man.

> **Text 10.1** Some people divide the expression into three. First, the simple, no part of which signifies anything at all, like "man" (*insān*); second, the compound (*al-murakkab*), part of which signifies something that is not part of the meaning, like ʿAbdallāh (when it is used as a proper name); and third, the composite (*al-muʾallaf*), part of which signifies part of the meaning, like "stone-thrower."[46] (*ḤQ* 200.3–8)

The second division (here called *murakkab*) is of no logical interest, concerning as it does expression only insofar as it does not contribute to the signification of the relevant meaning. Note that the interpretation of Aristotle by al-Fārābī and the Baghdad school is the target of Text 10.1.[47]

It does not come up in the *Risālah*, but al-Khūnajī mentions a worry some have about compound expressions; I record it because it gives a deeper insight into the full range of the role imposition plays in language.

> **Text 10.2** It is not to be said that the compound expression's signification of its meaning (*dalālah . . . ʿalā mafhūmihi*) lies beyond the three [kinds of signification], since the Positor did not impose it for that meaning, nor [did the Positor impose it] for what is intrinsic to or follows from that meaning. Because we answer: The meaning of "the expression's signification of what it is imposed on" is that this exact expression is imposed on this exact meaning,

> or [the expression's] parts for [the meaning's] parts (such that the aggregate of the expression corresponds with the aggregate of the meaning). There is no harm in the variation that attaches to the complex (*al-jumlah*) through the form of the compound—among other examples, like the genitive term going second in Arabic and first in other languages—because the form of compounding simple expressions is imposed in each language as a function of the form of compounding those simple meanings; so the whole is by imposition. (*Ḫ̮K* 11.9–pu)

§11[48] The simple expression divides into the parts of speech: name, verb (*kalimah*), and particle. I adopt the convention of translating *ism* as "name" because it is not merely noun, but also adjective; on Avicenna's division in the *ʿIbārah*, it even applies to particles. Note too that most logicians use a calque from the Greek (*kalimah*, "word") for verb, departing from the usage of the Arabic grammarians, who use *fiʿl*.[49]

Avicenna had defined the name as "an expression signifying by convention a meaning abstracted from time, not one of whose parts is significant taken in isolation" (*lafẓ dāll bi-l-tawāṭuʾ ʿalā maʿnan mujarrad min al-zamān wa-lā yakūnu wāḥid min ajzāʾihi dalīlan bi-nfirādihi*), and a verb as "what signifies time along with other things, not one of whose parts is significant taken in isolation, and always signifies what is said of something else" (*yadullu maʿa mā yadullu ʿalayhi ʿalā l-zamān wa-lā yakūnu wāḥid min ajzāʾihi dalīlan bi-nfirādihi wa-yakūnu abadan dalīlan ʿalā mā yuqālu ʿalā ghayrihi*).[50] On this definition, the particle falls under name. Al-Kātibī has, however, chosen a different principle of division (used by al-Rāzī in *RM* 23.9–11; see Figure 2). An expression is either fit to be predicated, or is not (if not, it is a particle);[51] and a predicable expression either signifies by its form (*bi-hayʾatihi*) one of the three tenses (a verb), or does not (a name). (Names like "morning" that signify time are not verbs because they do not signify it by their form [*ḤQ* 201.3–4].) For the next two lemmata, al-Kātibī focuses on names and how they signify meanings by correspondence.

§12[52] The manuscripts I have looked at all divide §13 from §12, and that is how I present the two lemmata; that said, the commentators offer an analysis that runs them together, based on a division that in turn has been seen to lie at the heart of Aristotle's presentation of synonyms and homonyms at the beginning of the *Categories*. Philoponus, for example, fills it out by saying that some things "share with one another a name but differ in definition and these are called homonyms, while those things that have in common a definition but differ in name are called polynyms. Those things that have in common both a name and a definition are called synonyms, while those that differ both in name and in definition are called heteronyms."[53] I translate *mushtarak* as "equivocal" instead of "homonymous," *mutawāṭi'* as "univocal" instead of "synonymous," *mutarādif* as "synonymous" instead of "polynymous," *mutabāyin* as "distinct" instead of "heteronymous," and *mushtaqq* as "denominative" instead of "paronymous" (not given in the text quoted).

It should be noted that, even though al-Kātibī never uses the term *mushtaqq*, denominative, throughout the *Risālah*, his commentators do, and many of the example sentences in the *Risālah* have denominative predicates (among others, "rational" and "black"). Avicenna places the denominative and the abstract noun from which it is denominated under distinct (or heteronymous) terms—"neither their name nor meaning is one"—they are, however, linked "by a certain conformity (*mushākalah*) between the two names and the two meanings, not enough to make them a single name and a single meaning," and this is what makes the concrete term denominative. Avicenna's own examples include "eloquent" from "eloquence," "monied" from "money," and "ironsmith" from "iron" (Avicenna, *Al-Shifā': al-Manṭiq: al-Maqūlāt*, 16.12–17.4).[54]

Here is al-Ḥillī's partial division, one which could be extended to include the material in Text 13.1; see Figure 3 for a diagram.

**Text 12.1** This is a division of the simple name according to its relation to its meaning. Its meaning is either one or many. The first [1, simple name with one meaning] subdivides so that [1.a] the meaning is individual, the very conception of the meaning of which makes impossible sharing in the meaning; the expression signifying it is called a proper name, like "Zayd." Or [1.b.i] [the expression's] meaning is universal and its relation to its meanings is identical; the expression signifying [this meaning] is called univocal, like "animal," for its meaning is a universal true of many. Its relation to the many that are under it is one; none of them is more eminent than or prior to the others. No actually existing many is stipulated, for the sun is one actually, but what is understood from ["sun"] is a universal matter, which is true of many in the mind. Or [1.b.ii] the meaning is universal, but its relation to the items [under it] differs, so some of them are more eminent than others in that universal meaning, like existence; for its meaning is universal and its relation to the items under it differs, for the cause is more eminent in existence than the effect; or some are prior, again as existence is for the cause; or some are more intense, like white, for it is more intense in snow than it is in ivory. The expression signifying like this is called systematically ambiguous (*mushakkik*), and it is so called because the items under it differ in one respect and are united in another, so that the investigator doubts (*yushakkiku*) whether they are equivocal or univocal.[55]

The second [2] is that the meaning is many, and it also subdivides. The first [2.a, simple expression with more than one meaning] is equivocal (*al-mushtarak*), when

> the expression has been imposed on two different realities in a primary way, like *ʿayn,* for it is imposed on the kneecap (*ʿayn al-rukbah*) and the eye. The second [2.b] is what is transferred, which [in the first case, 2.b.i] is when the expression is first imposed on one of a number of meanings, and then is transferred from that meaning to another, leaving behind the first meaning. (*ḤQ* 202.6–203.12)
>
> Third [2.c] is that the expression is first imposed on one of a number of meanings, then is transferred to a second without leaving behind its first imposition. Then the expression is called literal in view of its use for the first meaning, and metaphorical in relation to its use for the second meaning; this is like "lion." (*ḤQ* 204.7–10)

§13[56] The second of the divisions given in §12 defines the terms I translate as "synonymous" (*murādif*) (2.a.ii) and "distinct" (*mubāyin*) (2.a.I). Here is al-Ḥillī, with examples (the last of which is of a denominative):

> **Text 13.1** Any two expressions either have a meaning that is one, and the expressions are called synonymous, like "man" (*insān*) and "man" (*bashar*); or they have meanings that are multiple as a function of the number of expressions, and the expressions are called distinct, like "man" and "horse," whether they are distinct in essence as in the example, or whether one of them signifies the essence and the other signifies the description (*al-waṣf*), like "man" and "laughing." (*ḤQ* 205.1–6)

Al-Rāzī offers a slightly different division, which shows more clearly how the material presented in §12 can fit with material presented in §13 (as 2.a in what follows [*RM* 22.3–23.5]; see Figure 4). Either (1) expression and meaning are each one; if (1.a) it is not possible for the meaning to have more than one instance—that is, it is a proper name—but if (1.b) it is possible, then the items under it (1.b.i) all equally instantiate the meaning, and it is univocal, or (1.b.ii) instantiate the meaning in differing degrees, and it is systematically ambiguous; or (2) expression or meaning are more than one; if (2.a) the expressions are more than one, then (2.a.i) the meanings may also not be one, whereupon they are distinct expressions for distinct meanings, but if (2.a.ii) the meaning is one, then the two expressions are synonymous (*mutarādifān*). If (2.b) the expression is one but the meaning is more than one, the expression is equivocal (or transferred; I have elided part of al-Rāzī's division both here and in Figure 4).

§14[57] This is the first lemma in the *Risālah* to deal with compound expressions, defined in §10. There is again a dichotomous division presented: compound expressions may be (1) complete (*tāmm*) or (2) incomplete (*ghayr tāmm*). The criterion for completeness is whether silence is appropriate after the expression is uttered. The complete subdivides into (1.a) the truth-apt (*muḥtamil al-ṣidq wa-l-kidhb*) and (1.b) what is not truth-apt (*insha'*), which further subdivides but holds no interest for the logician. The incomplete subdivides into (2.a) the restrictive (*taqyīdī*), for which al-Kātibī gives as an example two names (a noun and an adjective), "rational animal," and (2.b) the nonrestrictive, for which al-Kātibī gives fragments formed of a verb and a particle and a name and a particle; neither of these fragments could be either (1) complete or (2.a) incomplete restrictive.

In §38, at the beginning of the Second Treatise, on propositions, al-Kātibī comes back to (1.a), the truth-apt complete compound expression; it is the proposition (*qaḍiyyah*). There, however, he uses a different distinction to come to a definition of proposition.

*The second section, on simple meanings*

The following nine lemmata (§§15–23) introduce the doctrine of the predicables. As noted above, they correspond to material first gathered as a treatise by Porphyry in the *Introduction*, and then vastly changed in presentation and content in Avicenna's *Madkhal*. Al-Kātibī does not follow Avicenna slavishly here, but does adopt all the modifications Avicenna insisted were necessary to correct Porphyry's errors. Unlike Avicenna, al-Kātibī does not use the term "essential" (*dhātī*) in developing his account, though all his commentators use the term when expanding on the lemmata (see comments on §16). Al-Kātibī presents the material according to a division of the predicables set out in Figure 5, and defers a number of general questions about universals to the following section of the treatise.

A passage from Porphyry may help orient the reader in the material covered. I follow it with a warning sounded by al-Taftāzānī in comment on §16. Porphyry says toward the end of his treatment of genus that "animal, for example, is a genus; man a species; rational a difference; laughing a property; and white, black, sitting are accidents" (Barnes, *Porphyry: Introduction*, 4). It is tempting to think that any given meaning comes under one and only one kind of predicable; for example, that ANIMAL is always a genus, and MAN is always a species. Al-Taftāzānī corrects this misconception, saying that the predicables

> TEXT 15.A are relational matters that differ according to the consideration [at issue]. For color is a genus for black, a differentia for quality, a species for what is qualified, a proprium of body, and a general accident of animal. (*TŠ* 142.u–143.1)

Al-Ṭūsī notes that there are some problems with this example, but nonetheless agrees with the general point being made (*ṬḤ* 244.20–245.6).

§15[58] The particular is defined first by al-Kātibī. Al-Taftāzānī's definition differs slightly from al-Kātibī's, as that "whose very conception precludes the occurrence of sharing by a multiplicity," and that of universal as obtaining when the conditions for the particular are not met.[59] (Al-Taftāzānī clarifies the definition in Text 24.1.) The sciences are directed only to the study of the universal. Al-Taḥtānī says:

> **Text 15.1** You have come to know that the goal in composing this treatise is knowledge of the method of acquiring things unknown conceptually (*iqtināṣ al-majhūlāt al-taṣawwuriyyah*) from things which are known conceptually. These are not acquired through particulars (for these, rather, are not investigated in the sciences because they are transient and defy precise analysis (*li-taghayyurihā wa-ʿadam inḍibāṭihā*)). For this reason, the logician's investigations are limited to explaining universals and making precise their divisions (*bayān al-kulliyyāt wa-ḍabṭ aqsāmihā*). (*TT* 129.pu–130.2)

This is where al-Kātibī begins his investigation of semantic matters (*ḤQ* 207.u). A meaning (*maʿnan*) is "the form obtaining in the intellect insofar as it is intended by the expression; insofar as it is obtained in the intellect from the expression it is called an understanding (*mafhūm*)" (*TŠ* 139.3–4). Universality turns on what is meant by "the occurrence of sharing in it" (*wuqūʿ al-sharikah fīhi*). What is meant is that it is possible for the intellect to posit the putative universal as true of many and corresponding to them, whether or not it corresponds to them in fact (*fī nafs al-amr*). Thus merely posited universals (*al-kulliyāt al-farḍiyyah*) come under the definition, like the inconceivable (*al-lā-mumkin al-taṣawwur*). Al-Kātibī comes back to underline the fact that a universal need have no instantiations in his five discussions directed to the universal in the third section of the first treatise (specifically in §24), though he seems to expect—inconsistently—that the universal be instantiated in the delineation he offers of species in §16.

The term "quiddity" (*māhiyyah*) has been used often up to this point. Through the treatment of the predicables, however, al-Kātibī relies on the notion much more intensively, and a few words here and in the next section may help pin down how he uses it.[60] The expression for the quiddity of something—its *mā hiya*—is what is said in answer to "what is it?" (*mā huwa?*). A quiddity is, in most cases, a meaning made up of two component meanings, one of which is also a quiddity, the other of which, while not a quiddity, is denominated from a quiddity (for example, "rational" from "rationality"); a term derived (*mushtaqq*) in this way must have a quiddity as its substrate (see comments below on §19). So the quiddity MAN is made up of (has as proper parts) the quiddity ANIMAL and the differentia RATIONAL. Al-Kātibī seems to assume that even before philosophical study, we are aware that the answer to the question "what is it?" should be a quiddity.[61]

§16[62] Al-Kātibī divides the universal into that which is said of the whole of the quiddity of the particulars under it or at most a part of the quiddity, and that which is said either of what is intrinsic to the quiddity (a proper part of the quiddity) or of what is extrinsic to the quiddity (see Figure 5).[63] The first two (the quiddity, and what is intrinsic to, or a part of, the quiddity) are essential (*dhātī*) in the sense of constituent (*muqawwim*); the third (extrinsic to the quiddity) is accidental (*ʿaraḍī*). As mentioned before, al-Kātibī himself does not use "essential" in this sense anywhere in the *Risālah* (he uses it in a second sense in §120), though all his commentators do. "Extrinsic" (*khārijī* or *khārij*) is used to characterize the implicate (*lāzim*) introduced in §22; I come back to this specific usage in commentary on that lemma. Al-Taftāzānī comments on previous use of the criteria for the division.

> **TEXT 16.1** The ancients mentioned that the universal is related to something else, being either the whole of its reality (*tamām ḥaqīqatihi*), or intrinsic to it, or extrinsic to it. The first—what is said in answer to "what is it?"—is either said purely in respect of being specific [to the

> thing] (*bi-ḥasab al-khuṣūṣiyyah al-maḥḍah*), as the definition in relation to what is defined; or purely in respect of being shared [with other things] (*bi-ḥasab al-sharikah al-maḥḍah*), as the genus in relation to its species; or in respect of being both specific and shared, like the species in relation to its members. Since there are problems (*ishkālāt*) with this division, al-Kātibī used another consideration to divide [the universal]; he thereby dropped the definition in relation to what is defined because it is compound and the discussion concerns the simple.[64] (*TŠ* 141.10–16)

I believe that al-Kātibī assumes that an understanding of real species is common to speakers of a natural language. If I ask the question "what is it?" of a real particular, I can expect an answer that tells me what it is (its quiddity, its *mā hiya*), something that can be said of other particulars differentiated from the first particular only by accidental features such as color, position, age, and so forth; the phrase used by al-Ḥillī for these features is "accidental individuating factors" (*umūr mushakhkhiṣah ʿāriḍah*; [*ḤQ* 209.2]). I have a right to be answered with the most complete quiddity common to what I am asking about (the consequences of this expectation are further explored in Texts 17.1 and 17.3). So al-Kātibī assumes that "man" is the right answer to "what is it?" asked of a man. It would also be true to say "animal" in response, but it would not be as informative as "man" because there are quiddities such as horses that are also animals. And—to give examples of the considerations at play in the division of the predicables—a quiddity like MAN is a meaning that is made up of other, intrinsic meanings ("part of the quiddity," like ANIMAL), and that implies other, extrinsic meanings ("external to the quiddity," like LAUGHTER).

Al-Kātibī comes under fire from all of his commentators in his delineation of species in §16. He takes the whole quiddity insofar as it has many under it, or only one; as he puts it, whether the quiddity is said in respect both of being shared and being specific ("man" said of Zayd and ʿAmr in answer to "what are they?"; "man" said of Zayd in answer to "what is it?"), or whether it is said only in respect of being specific ("sun" said in respect of the contingently unique sun). So the delineation of species al-Kātibī offers is "universal said of one or many things in answer to the question 'what is it?'" Al-Ḥillī (for example) says that "thus we interpret 'many' as the externally existent many; were we to take it in the delineation as 'many' without restriction, we would say that it is the universal that may be said of many agreeing in reality in answer to 'what is it?'" (*ḤQ* 209.16–apu). Al-Ḥillī's modified delineation would then conform to the definition of universal given in §15.[65]

All the predicables are given by delineation, and the commentators offer fairly predictable comments on each delineation. Here is al-Ḥillī—whom I quote on each predicable as it comes up—on this one:

> **Text 16.2** So "universal" is like a genus for the five universals. By saying "said of many which agree in realities," genus, general accident, and differentia of the genus are excluded; by saying "in answer to 'what is it?,'" differentia and proprium are excluded. (*ḤQ* 209.pu–210.2)

Later on (in §29), al-Kātibī brings up the relative species (*al-nawʿ al-iḍāfī*), the species whose delineation includes coming under a genus. Al-Kātibī's division of the predicables only works with real species (*al-nawʿ al-ḥaqīqī*), which is what is presented in this section; many relative species can be a part of the whole of the meaning shared among quiddities.

§17[66] Al-Kātibī now turns to intrinsic components of the meaning (more specifically, of the quiddity). These are constituents (*muqawwimāt*, sing. *muqawwim*) of the quiddity, essential (*dhātī*) to the quiddity in the sense that its definition includes them.[67]

Genus is presented by al-Kātibī as a part of the meaning of the species. He does not speak of a genus including a species, but of two quiddities (or a quiddity and another species) sharing a genus. He is taking the meaning (the quiddity) of the genus to be a part of the meaning (the quiddity) of the species. Here is how al-Ḥillī introduces his commentary on the section, at the end of which he sets out the protocol of answering "what is it?":

> TEXT 17.1 This is the second division of the essentials [in §16.1], and it is that which is a part of those items under it. It further divides into two subdivisions, the first of which is the whole of what is shared between the quiddity and another species, the second of which is not [the whole of what is shared].
>
> The first is called genus, like ANIMAL; for it is the whole of what is shared between the quiddity of the particulars of a species under it like MAN, and another species like HORSE. It is also like BODY, for [BODY] is the whole of what is shared between the quiddity MAN and the quiddity STONE.
>
> It is said in answer to "what is it?" in respect of just being shared (*al-sharikah al-maḥḍah*); if you ask about man and horse, the answer is "animal," but were you to ask about man alone, "animal" alone would not be fitting as a response, because someone asking "what is it?" is simply seeking the whole of the reality of the thing, and the whole of the reality of the thing is not [given] by genus alone, but rather by [genus] and differentia. So genus is only said in response to "what is it?" if it is asked of the quiddity of a species and of something else under [the genus] that is different. (*ḤQ* 210.7–211.3)

This is Avicenna's delineation of genus, and al-Ḥillī analyzes the contributions of its components as follows:

**Text 17.2** So what is "said . . . of many" is a genus, and by the restriction "which differ in realities," species and differentia and proprium are excluded; and by saying "in answer to the question 'what is it?,'" the remaining [universal, accident] is excluded. (*ḤQ* 211.4–8)

The commentators after al-Ḥillī worry about just what it is to be "the whole of the part shared," and about whether a part can be predicated of the whole, which seems to be implicit in al-Kātibī's account. Al-Taftāzānī deals with the first question by examples:

**Text 17.3** What is meant by "the whole of the part shared" is the part shared for which there is nothing more than it (*warā'ahu*) that is intrinsic to the quiddity and the [other] species. This is like ANIMAL for MAN and HORSE, and LIVING BODY for MAN and TREE; and unlike LIVING BODY in relation to MAN and HORSE—for LIVING BODY is not the whole of what is shared between MAN and HORSE, because the whole of what is shared between them is LIVING BODY and SENSATE and MOVING BY VOLITION.[68] (*TŠ* 143.15–u)

Take the quiddity MAN; the whole of the part shared is relative to MAN and another quiddity, and changes as we have to go higher in the Porphyrian tree (see Figure 8, and commentary on the following lemma) to find that shared part. So MAN and HORSE share ANIMAL, whereas MAN and TREE share LIVING BODY; all of them share LIVING BODY, but in the case of MAN and HORSE, LIVING BODY is no longer the whole of the part shared, and only becomes that whole when taken along with the differentiae (there are arguably two in this case), SENSATE and MOVING BY VOLITION. This is the first condition on the whole of the part shared: it must be as proximate as possible to at least one of the two quiddities. The second condition is that it cannot be a denominative (*mushtaqq*, like SENSATE and MOVING BY VOLITION); that is, it cannot be a meaning that implies but does not contain its substrate (see Text 40.1).

Second, how can a part be predicated of a whole? It is easy to think of parts that cannot be predicated of the whole to which they contribute (think of a wheel and the car of which it is a part). The question is taken up by al-Taftāzānī, presenting a distinction from Avicenna's *Cure* (*Metaphysics* 5, 3:164.5–15).

> TEXT 17.4 If someone objects: It is unintelligible that the genus should be part of the quiddity and yet be said of it, because the part precedes the whole in the two [modes of] existence (*fī l-wujūdayn*), whereas the predicate is united in existence with the subject actually.
>
> We answer: It is not intended by the part being predicated that it is predicated insofar as it is a part; rather, what is meant is that the substrate of being a part is the substrate of being predicated. So, for example, ANIMAL taken on condition that RATIONAL enter it is a species, but taken on condition that RATIONAL does not enter it is a part. What is taken insofar as it is possible for it to be a substrate for being a part and for being a species is a genus and a predicate. (*TŠ* 145.9–u)

§18[69] Nearly everyone who writes on the predicables, whether inside or outside the Arabic tradition, follows Porphyry in giving an example of a quiddity—a species—with what may be taken to be all the genera above it, divided by what may be taken to be the differentiae that constitute the lower species down to what al-Kātibī has referred to as the real species (see Figure 8). MAN, at the bottom of the Porphyrian tree, is an animal differentiated by being rational. "What is man?" is answered with the genus "animal"; "which (*ayyu shay'*) [animal] is man?" is answered with the differentia "rational." Because it is the answer to the first "what is it?" question, ANIMAL is the proximate genus. The answer to a further "what is animal?" is with its proximate genus, "living body" (*al-jism al-nāmī*). So asking "what is it?" twice has given us the genus remote from MAN by one degree; asking it three times will give us the answer "body," remote from MAN by two degrees; asking it four times will give us the answer "substance," remote from MAN by three degrees.

We are obliged by philosophical convention to give the largest whole part shared between two quiddities if we are asked "what are they?" (*mā humā*), as noted in Texts 17.1 and 17.3. Of course MAN and HORSE share the ultimate genus SUBSTANCE, and the intermediate genera BODY and LIVING BODY, but none of these is the largest whole part that they share; "animal" is the proper response to "what is it?"; the proper answer is the most proximate genus shared by both quiddities. This means that for "what are they?" asked of a man and a tree, the proper answer will be "living body," one degree remote from MAN; asked of a man and a stone, the proper answer will be "body," two degrees remote from MAN. As will emerge in §30, there is no agreement as to where INTELLIGENCE falls in the tree, but many take it to be incorporeal substance. In that case, were "what are they?" asked of a man and a celestial intelligence, the proper answer would be "substance," three degrees remote from MAN.

In §21, al-Kātibī broaches degrees of remoteness when talking about the differentia; I return to the tree briefly in comment on that lemma.

§19[70] First, some context for this difficult lemma. The genus is taken to be a whole part (a quiddity) shared between two more complex quiddities. By contrast, the differentia is an essential part coextensive with the whole that is shared. A differentia is signified by a denominative (*mushtaqqah*); that is, denominated from a quiddity. The form of the denominative leaves a space for its substrate, such that, for example, we take *nāṭiq* (rational) actually to be *dhū nuṭq* (possessor of rationality); the form implies that there is a substrate—a quiddity—that is qualified by the denominative (the *dhū* to be filled in, so to speak), though it does not specify what that substrate is (see Text 40.1).[71]

This part that is possessed by its substrate—which is to say, has a gap for a quiddity—can either be shared by more than one species (the generic differentia, *faṣl al-jins*), or only by individuals under a single species (the specific differentia, *faṣl al-nawʿ*). An example of the first is SENSATE (*ḥassās*), which along with the quiddity, LIVING BODY, constitutes ANIMAL; this generic differentia is shared by all quiddities that share the quiddity it is a part of (so, since the quiddity ANIMAL is shared by all species of animal, so too is SENSATE). An example of the second is RATIONAL (*nāṭiq*), which is shared only by the individuals under the species, MAN, which RATIONAL along with ANIMAL constitutes.

Al-Kātibī claims in this lemma that a differentia as defined is either not shared (*intifāʾ al-ishtirāk*) with another species, or—if it is—it is not the whole of the part that is shared (*intifāʾ al-tamāmiyyah*), although the differentia is nonetheless coextensive with that whole shared part. Al-Kātibī is claiming that a meaning like SENSATE must be (1) only a part of the whole that is shared, and (2) coextensive with that whole. As stated above, there must be something—ANIMAL—that is sensate; it must always be possible to rephrase a denominative such that it have a *dhū* that possesses the quality. So the differentia qualifies the quiddity it constitutes, the whole of what is shared. The constitutive differentiae in a given quiddity must be finite, and part of such a whole, "otherwise a regress follows, that is, the composition of the quiddity from infinite parts (and that is what is meant by 'regress' here); that is absurd because it would entail enumerating the innumerable, so it would be impossible to understand [the quiddity] (*yamtaniʿ taʿaqquluhā*) even though we are concerned with an intelligible quiddity" (*TŠ* 148.8–10).

Part of the key to filling out the argument alluded to here is in §26, where al-Kātibī defines "coextensive," along with three other ways one universal meaning can relate to another; namely, as a subset of, having an overlap with, and being disjoined from. If al-Kātibī can show that the last three relations are excluded, then the differentia must be coextensive with the whole of the part that is shared. The commentators take it as obvious (*ẓāhir*) that al-Kātibī is entitled to exclude the possibility that the differentia is disjoined from the whole of the part that is shared. Al-Taftāzānī tells us that the differentia cannot be a proper subset or merely overlap the whole of the part shared (*lā akhaṣṣa minhu muṭlaqan aw min wajh*) "due to the impossibility of the whole being realized without the part" (*TŠ* 148.2–3); roughly, I think, that the whole of the part shared cannot be constituted unless the differentia is present for all of it. This means that the only real alternatives are that the differentia is coextensive with the whole of the part that is shared, or is more general than it.

This, roughly, is how the commentators take him to proceed: Let us refer to the whole of the part that is shared as Q1, the differentia as D. Suppose that D is more general than Q1; then (by the definition of more general given in §26) it must be true of what Q1 is true of, and of a species (S1) disjoined from Q1. So D is either the whole of what is shared (call it Q2) between Q1 and S1 (but this is against the hypothesis), or part of what is shared. If D is coextensive with Q2, this is what is sought; if it is not, then D is more general than Q2, and it must be true of what Q2 is true of, and of a species (S2) disjoined from Q2. And so forth. So D is coextensive with some Q, or we face an infinite regress.

In reading the compressed argument in §19 in this way, I follow al-Ḥillī, though the other commentators explain what al-Kātibī is doing in broadly similar terms. Considering the differentia, al-Ḥillī fills in al-Kātibī's lemma thus:

> **Text 19.1** Were it not coextensive with [that whole that is shared], it would be more general, so it would be shared between the quiddity and another species that does not come under the whole of what is shared. So it must either

> be the whole of what is shared between the quiddity and the posited species, or not. But the first is false because it is contrary to the [initial] hypothesis. And the second—[namely,] when it is coextensive with the whole of what is shared between the quiddity and this species—is what is sought. If it is more general than [that whole], then either it concludes in what is coextensive with the whole of what is shared between the quiddity and a given species, or not; the first is what is sought, and the second leads to regress, and is absurd. (*ḤQ* 214.11–pu)

With this argument, al-Kātibī reassures his students that any constitutive differentia of a quiddity is coextensive with either the whole quiddity, or with a whole part of the quiddity. A definition (say, for MAN as represented in Figure 8) given such that every part of it signifies by correspondence (as opposed to "rational animal," in which "animal" signifies a number of meanings by containment; see Text 33.1 below) will set out the highest genus and every constitutive differentia ("rational sensate animate corporeal substance"); each differentia is coextensive with the quiddities that are the genera of MAN. If the highest genus (SUBSTANCE) cannot be analyzed into more primitive components, he has also shown that every quiddity must either contain a quiddity or be a simple quiddity. Finally, he has set out his conviction that every composite quiddity must contain at least one differentia (but only a finite number). I take it that these are the questions al-Kātibī is addressing.[72] In the next lemma, he will allude to, rather than deliver, an argument aimed at undermining the claim that every quiddity must either contain a quiddity or be a simple quiddity.

Al-Kātibī concludes the lemma by saying that what distinguishes the quiddity from what shares with it, "whether in a genus or in existence," is a differentia. The discussion to this point seems to me to have presupposed that differentiae are essential to what they qualify, but the claim is not made explicit until §20, with the phrase "with respect to its substance." But the force of "in a genus or in existence" as against "in a genus" is made clear in a passage by al-Ṭūsī commenting on the discussion of differentia in *Pointers* 2.3.1 (*AI* 15.3–6).

> **Text 19.2** Thus, every essential that is not fit to be an answer to "what is it?" is fit to make an essential distinction, and is a differentia. The differentia may be proper to the genus and not present in another, for example like SENSATE for LIVING BODY; or it may not be proper [to a genus], like RATIONAL for ANIMAL, according to one who takes it to be said of the non-animal, like some angels, for example . . . In the first case, [SENSATE distinguishes ANIMAL] from everything else in existence, whereas in the second case, [RATIONAL distinguishes MAN] only from everything else that shares with it in the genus ANIMAL.[73] (*ṬḤ* 193.1–8)

§20[74] Al-Kātibī only now gives a delineation of differentia, a delineation from which he may intend to distance himself with the phrase "they delineate" (though see §34). Here is al-Ḥillī's analysis of the delineation and the way each of its elements contributes to its meaning.

> **Text 20.1** This is the delineation of the differentia. So universal is the genus, and by saying "predicated of something in answer to the question 'which thing is it?,'" those universals other than the proprium are excluded; because the differentia occurs in the question about the distinguishing factor, so it occurs in the answer to "which thing is it?," so the one who poses a question [in these terms] asks about the distinguishing portion (*al-qadr al-mumayyiz*). And by saying "with respect to its substance (*jawhar*)" the proprium is excluded, because although it occurs in answer

to "which thing is it?," it does not convey the substantial distinction (*al-tamyīz al-jawharī*)—that is, essential [distinction] (*al-dhātī*)—rather, it conveys an accidental distinction. (*ḤQ* 215.7–apu)

Al-Taftāzānī notes that this is the only delineation al-Kātibī gives of a predicable in which it is delineated as being something that is predicated of (*yuḥmalu*) something rather than said of (*maqūl*) something.

**Text 20.2** Al-Kātibī says "predicated" rather than "said" as, for the rest of the universals, just because people have noted that the differentia is a cause for the species' share of the genus (*ḥiṣṣat al-nawʿ min al-jins*),[75] so it was thought this might give the impression that the differentia is not predicated of it due to the impossibility of predicating the cause of the effect. (*TŠ* 150.apu–u)

Al Kātibī goes on straight after giving the delineation of differentia to set out one of the points on which it has been attacked. In doing so, he retraces—in highly compressed form—Avicenna's two attempts to delineate the differentia. Here is al-Khūnajī on Avicenna's change of heart:

**Text 20.3** Moreover, Avicenna delineated [differentia in the *Cure*] as "the universal said of species in answer to 'which thing is it?' under its genus essentially."[76] And he delineated it in *Pointers* as "the universal that is predicated of the thing in answer to 'which thing is it?' in its substance."[77] This [second delineation] is broader (*aʿamm*) than the first, and with it one has to add some clarification (*wa-bi-hi yajibu an yufassara*); otherwise, the proof that the essentials are limited (*inḥiṣār*) to genus and differentia does not go through. (*ḪK* 45.14–u)

So al-Kātibī has presented the definition from Avicenna's *Pointers* in this lemma. What is at issue between the two definitions? And how does the problem with two coextensive matters (for which the supreme genus is given as an example) highlight the issue? Al-Sharīf al-Jurjānī gives the clearest short account of what is involved in the example of something composed of two coextensive matters (though see also *ḤQ* 216.1–9 and, especially, *SQ* 183–84).

> **Text 20.4** They gave as examples these two [that is, the supreme genus and the ultimate differentia], due to the impossibility that they be compounded from both a genus and a differentia (otherwise the supreme genus would not be supreme, nor would the ultimate differentia be ultimate); if it is supposed that they might be compounded from parts, those parts would have to be coextensive. (*TT* 150n1)

Unless there is a proof that the supreme genus must be simple, or a similar proof in respect of the ultimate differentia, there are logically possible counterexamples to the notion that compound quiddities must be compounds of a genus and a differentia. Consider the case of the supreme genus. If the supreme genus is a compound, it cannot be—as al-Jurjānī says, and for the reason he gives—a compound of a genus with something else. Further, both meanings must be coextensive; were the second meaning broader in extension, it would be the genus, which has been ruled out. So both meanings serve equally to distinguish the supreme genus from other things in existence, and both meanings are essential to it; but neither is under a genus. On the *Cure* definition (*taʿrīf*), by which differentia involves the differentia coming under a genus, neither component is a differentia; on the *Pointers* definition (entertained but not endorsed by al-Kātibī in §20), both are. Any attempt to limit essentials (in the sense of constituents) of compound quiddities to differentiae and a quiddity is subject to modification (*wa-bi-hi yajibu an yufassara*) in light of this counterexample: all parts of a compound quiddity would ultimately be differentiae, and there would be no simple quiddity. Al-Ṭūsī notes that al-Rāzī and his intellectual forebears were, by reason of their account of differentia, associated with a claim like the one al-Kātibī describes; they were, according to al-Ṭūsī, "compelled by this to declare it permissible to compose the most general of the essentials (which is the supreme genus) from two matters coextensive with it, neither of which is a genus, but rather both of which are differentiae" (*ṬḤ* 193.20–apu).[78]

§21[79] The discussion of the degrees of differentiae harks back to §18 (see Figure 8), and a differentia's degree of remoteness will be a function of the quiddity it constitutes. If a differentia constitutes quiddity A itself, it is the proximate differentia of quiddity A, whereas if it constitutes quiddity A's proximate genus, it is remote from quiddity A by one degree, and so forth. Al-Taftāzānī notes (*TŠ* 151.12–u) that the *Pointers* definition of differentia—which has the component "in its genus or in existence," and which al-Kātibī tested in §20—is not appropriate for the discussion in §21. This is because §21 is assuming the old *Cure*-style definition in which every differentia distinguishes a quiddity under a genus.

§22[80] Al-Ḥillī says of this lemma that it begins investigation of "the third of the divisions of the universal" set out in §16.1, "that which is neither the quiddity itself nor intrinsic to it" (*ḤQ* 217.7), the accidental (*ʿaraḍī*). That is true, but it seems to me that al-Kātibī is pausing in his exposition of the predicables to examine aspects of a distinction between, on the one hand, a meaning that is extrinsic to a quiddity but inseparable from it and, on the other hand, separable extrinsic meanings. In doing this, he is laying the groundwork for his theory of science, which is more or less Avicenna's theory of science.[81] The distinction alluded to here is the one that matters most in identifying a science's principles and the predicates for the theorems it must demonstrate. The distinction is developed so that it also applies to meanings that cannot be predicated of a subject; these meanings are not taken into account in al-Kātibī's theory of science, though they figure in his theory of signification.

In his definition of inseparability, al-Kātibī—at least as he is interpreted by his commentators—is following Avicenna's response to a problem about the test to decide if something is essential (in the second of the senses set out in commentary on §16 above). Like his predecessors, al-Kātibī distinguishes between meanings whose inseparability from another meaning is immediately apparent when one is subject and the other predicate in a proposition, and those whose inseparability is only made apparent by finding a middle term that relates the subject to the predicate. Further—following al-Khūnajī (see Text 8.1)—he distinguishes different strengths of immediacy within those meanings whose inseparability is immediately apparent. Finally, in §22.3, he sketches some distinctions to do with separability, effectively to show that they are immaterial to logical discussions.

None of this lemma is continuous with the discussion of predicables up to now; the distinctions it develops are not used to distinguish among the five kinds of predicable. Since only proprium and general accident can be extrinsic to the quiddity, they are the only candidates to be inseparable in the sense developed here. But different features are used in §23 to delineate proprium and general accident—namely, extrinsic meaning possessed solely by members of one reality, or extrinsic meaning possessed by more than one reality.

Al-Kātibī opens the lemma by distinguishing between that which is inseparable from its substrate (that which "it is impossible to separate . . . from its substrate": *imtanaʿa nfikākuhu ʿan maʿrūḍihi*)—an implicate (*lāzim*)—from that which is separable (*mufāriq*). Note that by this definition, what is perpetually associated with a substrate but possibly separated from it is nonetheless separable.

The first section of the lemma sidesteps difficult aspects of the distinction. Al-Kātibī elides an Avicennian distinction between inseparability in conception (*fī l-taṣawwur*) and in estimation (*fī l-tawahhum*), and between both and inseparability in existence (*fī l-wujūd*).[82] The first is true of the relation between a constituent and the quiddity it constitutes (the relation the genus and the differentia have to the species they constitute); the second is true of the relation between a property that necessarily belongs to a quiddity but does not actually constitute it. 2R said of triangle is a common example of the second (al-Taftāzānī uses this as his prime example in commentary on the lemma). Although one can conceive a triangle and not advert to whether 2R belongs to it, one cannot imagine a triangle without 2R; as Avicenna puts it in *Pointers* 1.12.5, "it is impossible to remove [the property] in the estimation even though it is not a constituent" (*kānat mumtaniʿat al-rafʿ fī l-wahm maʿa kawnihā ghayr muqawwimah*) (*AI* 9.6–7). The claim is that what is posterior to the constitution of a quiddity but inseparable from it can be separated when conceiving the quiddity, whereas what is prior to that constitution (that is, the constituents) cannot be so separated. Those properties that are separable in conception but not in estimation are the implicates (what al-Kātibī calls the "implicate of the quiddity": *lāzim li-l-māhiyyah*); the further claim is that—if they do not evidently belong to the quiddity—they are exactly the predicates (the essential accidents) to be proved to belong to the subjects in the theorems of a given science. Those properties that are inseparable from a quiddity in existence (the dark skin color of someone from Ethiopia) but separable in both conception and estimation are of no scientific interest.

The second section of §22 passes over the problems involved in distinguishing the implicates of the quiddity from logically prior components of the quiddity (the constituents), and from scientifically uninteresting entailments of an actually existing quiddity (the implicates of existence), but then goes on to deliver two further crucial distinctions. The implicate of the quiddity may be evident (*bayyin*, often *bayyin bi-dhātihi*, "evident in itself") in that it is affirmed to belong to the quiddity without recourse to another term—a middle (*wasaṭ*)—that would make its belonging evident; it is, in short, immediate. At least some of the principles of a science must be such that the subjects of those principles have as their predicates implicates that are evident and not constituents of the subject. The reason for the second condition is that scientific theorems must have predicates extrinsic to the subject (see §120.3), so there must be such a predicate in the original premise-set. When the implicate is not evident, like 2R for triangle, proof is needed; the remaining two sections and the conclusion of the *Risālah* present what is needed to construct such proofs.

The third of the substantive points made in §22.2 (and this is, I believe, the only distinction that Avicenna does not himself make) is that "evident" is said of implicates in two different ways. The first and weaker (*aʿamm*) way is that, given a conception of the implicant and a conception of the implicate, we affirm that one is an implicate of the other. This is the definition of evident relevant for demonstration theory. The second and stronger (*akhaṣṣ*) way is that, given only a conception of the implicant, we both acquire a conception of the implicate and affirm that it is an implicate of the implicant. This is the definition of evident relevant for signification theory (see Text 8.1). These distinctions are laid out schematically in Figure 9.

§23[83] Al-Kātibī returns to an exposition directly related to the predicables. A second criterion over and above being extrinsic is added: single-reality instantiation. Given this extra criterion, both implicate and separable may be counted as propria. Attributes essential in the second sense (essential accidents, *ʿawāriḍ dhātiyyah*) are implicates, inseparable and extrinsic. If an accidental feature is shared across two or more realities, relative to those realities, it is a general accident. But every general accident will be a proprium of a genus higher than the reality under consideration (*TŠ* 161.1–4). Al-Ḥillī's meditation on the definition of proprium calls on the notion of intermediate species and genera set out in §§30 and 31 below.

Text 23.1 The proprium is delineated as "a universal said in an accidental way of what is under a single reality." By the first, ["what is under a single reality,"] genus and general accident are excluded, and by the second, ["in an accidental way,"] species and differentia are excluded.

This reality may be the reality of the supreme genus, and it may be an intermediate genus, and it may be the reality of the lowest species; the delineation of proprium covers them all. But if we delineate proprium as "universal said of members of the reality of a single species in an accidental way," as Avicenna delineated it in the *Cure* [*AM* 182.8], the proprium of the highest genus is excluded from this definition.[84] (*Ḥ Q* 220.5–11)

The division of the predicables is claimed to be exhaustive; see also Figures 6 and 7.

Text 23.2 The universals are therefore limited to these five, because the universal is either just what the individuals under it are, and it is the species; or is intrinsic to them, so if it is the whole that is shared between them and another given species, it is the genus, or if not [the whole], it is the differentia; or it is extrinsic to them, so if it is proper to a single reality it is a proprium; otherwise, it is a general accident. (*ḤQ* 220.14–apu)

*The third section, on discussions about universals and particulars*

The next eleven lemmata go more deeply into five topics to do with universals. The topics dealt with are: the relation between a universal and the existence of the particulars under it (§24); the existence of the natural, logical, and mental universal (§25); the relative generality of universals and their contradictories (§§26 and 27); the relative particular as opposed to the particular strictly so called introduced in §15 (§28); and a series of discussions coordinated around the notions of relative species and genera (§§29–34).

§24[85] A universal is a meaning such that it is not impossible to predicate it of more than one thing. As was noted in comment on §16, al-Kātibī uses a form of words that appears to take a universal as a meaning actually predicated of something. By the definition in §15, however, a universal need have no instantiations under it, and in this lemma, al-Kātibī gives examples of universals with no particulars under them, with unique instantiations, and with many instantiations. In this, he changes the criteria for the division and extends the examples given by Avicenna in *Pointers* 1.9 (*AI* 6.10–7.4). Al-Kātibī's examples, given by dichotomous division, are summarized in Figure 10.

Al-Taftāzānī provides a reformulation of the phrase "conception of its meaning does not preclude sharing" in addressing the lemma:

> **Text 24.1** This is an allusion to the fact that what is considered in universality is the possibility of supposing [the universal] true of many (*imkān farḍ ṣidqihi ʿalā kathīrīn*), and not its truth of them in respect of [actual] existence. (*TŠ* 163.3–4)

What kind of possibility is involved in this reformulation ("possibly supposed true of many")?

> **Text 24.2** What is meant by it is what is possible of existence as a one-sided possibility restricted to the side of existence (*al-imkān al-ʿāmm al-muqayyad bi-jānib al-wujūd*), which is to say, it negates the necessity of nonexistence. (*TŠ* 163.u–164.2)

§25[86] Al-Kātibī tackles the question of whether or not universals exist outside the mind, at least in part. He begins his treatment of the issue by first distinguishing among the kinds of universal. Here is a fuller statement of the distinctions al-Kātibī borrows from Avicenna:[87]

**Text 25.1** For example, if we say "animal is a universal," we have three matters: animal insofar as it is animal, the meaning of "universal" without alluding to any given matter, and the universal ANIMAL (being the compound aggregate of the two; namely, of ANIMAL and UNIVERSAL).

The difference between these meanings is clear, for were the meaning of ["animal" or "universal"] the meaning of the other, then bringing one to mind would follow necessarily from bringing the other to mind, but that is not the case. For the meaning of "universal" is "that the conception of which does not preclude the occurrence of sharing in it," and the meaning of "animal" is "sensate and moving-by-volition living body," and it is evident that it is possible to bring each one of these to mind without attending to the other.

The first is called "natural universal" because it is one of the natures, or because it exists naturally; that is, in extramental existence (*fī l-khārij*). The second is called "logical universal" because the logician investigates it. When al-Kātibī says "logical universal" it is only loosely speaking universal; universality is simply the basis for it. The third is called "mental universal" because it is only realized in the intellect. (*TT* 168.1–169.u)

Al-Khūnajī presents an argument for the actual existence of natural universals:

**Text 25.2** That which points to the existence of the universal inside actually existent particulars is that there is no doubting the existence of ANIMAL (for example) because

> it is a part of this actually existent animal (*hādhā l-ḥayawān al-khārijī*), so ANIMAL that is part of this animal is ANIMAL itself insofar as it is what it is, either without further restriction or with further restriction. If it is the second [with further restriction], it contains ANIMAL (*ishtamala ʿalā l-ḥayawān*) and the division occurs again; it only ends with the first division [that is, without further restriction]. Thus, ANIMAL is unconditionally and actually an existent thing, and is so insofar as its very conception does not preclude being shared; so that whose very conception does not preclude its being shared actually exists. So the universal actually exists. (*Ḫ̮K* 35.15–36.2)

The existence of the logical and mental universals is disputed.[88] They are in any event posterior to the natural universal.

> **TEXT 25.3** Universality and particularity are among the secondary intelligibles that occur to the primary intelligibles; for were universality the quiddity itself, or part of it, the quiddity would not be true of the particular falling under it. Further, universality is a relational matter that is only determined after the determination of the two relata. (*ḤQ* 221.u–222.3)

Al-Ḥillī records the basis for a dispute about the existence of the second and third kinds of universal, one that centers on the logical universal, which infects the mental universal of which it is a part.

> **TEXT 25.4** There is dispute among philosophers about the existence of logical and mental universals. This is because the logical is a kind of relation, and the arguments about the existence or otherwise of the relative is in metaphysics and not logic; and because part of the mental [universal] is relative, its existence is also disputed. (*ḤQ* 222.12–15)

§26[89] I do not offer shorthand versions of the proofs given by al-Kātibī in the next lemma, proofs that work with the definitions given in this lemma; however, diagrams of the cases he has in mind, with letters assigned to the terms he gives as examples, may be helpful (see Figures 11–19). There are a number of ways to set these relations out as diagrams, and I have chosen those that struck me as the clearest, Euler diagrams as set out by Keynes.[90] It will be clear on consulting Keynes that the diagrams needed to illustrate the points al-Kātibī is making do not exhaust all possible relations among two terms and their contradictories; I put this down to al-Kātibī's focus on natural language. Four of the diagrams are given twice, the first time in commentary on §26 with only positive terms (A, B) and—in all save one case (Figure 18)—a large empty circle that contains all the other things that are neither A nor B (what Keynes, but not al-Kātibī, calls the universe of discourse). On their second appearance, in commentary on §27, the empty circle in the diagrams has been allocated to indefinite terms (not-A, not-B, covered further in §48 and following) in the hope that this makes clear the relation between these terms, and between both these terms and the original terms. One last preliminary note: Keynes refers to not-A in relation to A as its complement, the common English term. Al-Kātibī, however, uses the Arabic *naqīḍ*, "contradictory," when used of a proposition. Since Joseph acknowledges the use of "contradictory term" in the sense that Keynes uses complement,[91] and it directly translates al-Kātibī's preference, that is the translation I adopt.

The diagrams for §26 are straightforward. There are four cases, each with examples that correspond with A and B in the respective diagrams. The first case (Figure 11) is when each term is true of whatever the other is true of; these terms are called coextensive (*mutasāwiyān*), and al-Kātibī's examples are "man" (A) and "rational" (B). Everything beyond the circle that bounds A and B are the things that are neither man nor rational. The second case (Figure 12) is when one term is true of whatever the other is true of, but the reverse does not hold; the relation between the two terms is called absolute generality (*ʿumūm muṭlaq*)—which I refer to as inclusion—and al-Kātibī's examples are "animal" (A) and "man" (B). Again, the circle bounding A marks the point beyond which are things neither animal nor man. The third case (one example of which is given in Figure 13) is when one term is true of part of what the other is true of; the relation between the two terms is generality in one respect (*ʿumūm min wajh*)—which I refer to as overlap—and al-Kātibī's examples are "animal" (A) and "white" (B). The last case (Figure 14) is when neither term is true of anything of which the other is true; the two terms are disjoined (*mutabāyinān*), and the examples are "man" (A) and "horse" (B). It will become obvious in §27 that al-Kātibī recognizes a second case of disjunction, in which the two terms together exhaust the whole universe of discourse (see Figure 18); the examples in this case are existence and privation.

§27[92] This lemma and the one before are linked by Asad Fallahi to Avicenna's response in the *ʿIbārah* to the tenth chapter of Aristotle's *De Interpretatione*, and—if I understand correctly—to the discussions taken up in §§48–50 and from §82. In the *ʿIbārah*, Avicenna argues for the claim that "whatever is narrower in truth than another thing has a contradictory that is broader in truth than the contradictory of that other thing" (*AʿI* 85.5). The complex of related problems, both historical and philosophical, has been investigated by Fallahi to a depth far beyond the aspirations of my commentary;[93] I hope only to make clear the outline of al-Kātibī's discussion here.

The first claim is that the contradictories of coextensive terms are coextensive. Figure 15 exhibits the claim. The proof is, roughly, if not-A and not-B were not coextensive, then one of them (say, not-A) must be true of something that not-B is not true of—namely, B; but then A would not have been true of everything of which B is true; this is contrary to the initial hypothesis.

The second claim is that in the case in which one term, B (the more specific), is contained within the other, A (the more general), then their contradictories are related such that not-A is contained within not-B (see Figure 16). For this claim to be true (drawing on the relevant definition set down in §26), not-B must be true of everything that not-A is true of, but not the reverse (that is, there must be something not-B is true of that not-A is not true of). Al-Kātibī takes the proof in two steps. First, were not-B not true of everything that not-A is true of, then B would be true of some of what not-A is true of. In that case, however, the more specific (B) would be true of something that the more general (A) is not true of; but the hypothesis was that B is contained in A. Second, were it not the case that there is something that not-B is true of that not-A is not true of, then not-A would be true of everything that not-B is true of; but this, along with the claim that not-B is true of everything that not-A is true of, would mean that they are coextensive, which—as shown in the preceding proof—means that their contradictories are coextensive. But the hypothesis was that one was contained in the other.

The third and fourth cases considered are not proofs for a given conclusion in the sense that the first two cases are, but rather counterexamples ruling out broad claims. So the third case exhibits the claim that contradictories of overlapping terms do not necessarily overlap. Figure 17 gives one example of overlapping terms (in al-Kātibī's example, "animal" and "white"), which have contradictories ("not-animal," "not-white") that overlap. But there are other ways for terms to overlap, and al-Kātibī refers back to the claim he has investigated immediately before, in §27.2. In Figure 16, note that not-B overlaps with A, but B is disjoined from not-A. It is therefore not necessarily the case that overlapping terms will have contradictories that overlap. There is another case of overlap that al-Kātibī does not consider, and I leave it to one side.

In the case of disjoined terms, al-Kātibī considers two subcases. First, it may be impossible for the two contradictories to be jointly true of anything (Figure 18); al-Kātibī's example of the two original terms is "existence" (A) and "privation" (B); in this case, the contradictories are completely disjoined. But in the second case (Figure

19), the contradictories overlap (in al-Kātibī's example, "not-man" and "not-horse") but must be partly disjoined. Given these examples, the most general conclusion is that contradictories of disjoined terms are at least partly disjoined.

§28[94] The fourth discussion is on the relative particular and its logical relation to the real particular, corresponding to Avicenna's *Pointers* 1.9 (*AI* 6.10–7.4). The real particular (which was used to define the universal in §15, the particular such that it can be pointed to as a "this") is now distinguished from the relative particular (of which it is a subset), which is either a real particular or a universal term that comes under a more general universal. On this understanding, HORSE would be a particular relative to ANIMAL. Al-Khūnajī uses the notion of the relative particular to identify natural subjects for logical propositions:

> **Text 28.1** Every universal is by nature a predicate, because it is, insofar as it is a universal, predicable of what is below it. Similarly, every relative particular is by nature a subject. (*Ḫ̮K* 36.3–4)

§29[95] This lemma is the first of a long discussion—the fifth—which runs for six lemmata to §34, a discussion of species, both real or relative; genus; matters to do with the ordering of species and genera; the scientific question that invites them as answers; and the role they play in those answers, and in constituting and dividing quiddities. To some extent, the material gathers reflections on a number of mistakes Avicenna had found in the work of his predecessors, and innovations in terms of art that post-Avicennian logicians like al-Rāzī had introduced.

This lemma compares the real species delineated in §16 with the relative species, delineated here as "every quiddity that, along with other quiddities, has a genus said of it as a primary response to the question 'what is it?' . . . is called relative species." This is the way

Porphyry tended to take species—namely, as a correlative of genus; Avicenna tended to take species as real species, thereby avoiding the circularity in defining technical terms that dogs Porphyry's account. Relative species as delineated by al-Kātibī corresponds to the second of the delineations Avicenna speaks of in *Pointers* 2.1 (*AI* 13.u–14.10). The last phrase in the delineation ("primary response") distinguishes the relative species from a nonessential type (*ṣinf*) such as we have with "Turk"; a species may be relative but it is nonetheless an essential division.[96] There is—so al-Ḥillī tells us—an alternative delineation of relative species: "the more special of two universals said in answer to 'what is it?'" (*ḤQ* 229.3 et seq.). Some divisions of the predicables take species as relative (for example, Figure 7).

§30[97] In this lemma, al-Kātibī considers the ranking of relative species; in the next lemma, he will consider the ranking of relative genera. Lemmata 30 and 31 correspond roughly to *Pointers* 2.2 (*AI* 14.10–15.2). It will be more efficient to deal with the issues common to both lemmata together. Al-Kātibī is effectively analyzing the structured hierarchy implicit in the Porphyrian tree first introduced in §§18 and 21 (see Figure 8). To consider this hierarchy as it moves up to the highest quiddity is to consider the ranking of genera, and to consider its downward movement to instantiated quiddities is to consider the ranking of relative species. In each of these two rankings, there are extremes: a highest species (under a genus that is not itself a species) and a lowest species (under a genus and directly above instantiations that only differ from each other numerically); or a highest genus (with nothing above it) and a lowest genus (under which are a number of lowest species). In the hierarchy of quiddities, the remaining quiddities will be intermediate genera if one is having regard to what is beneath them, and intermediate species if one is having regard to what is above them.

In this context, someone generated a question as to whether there can be an isolated species or an isolated genus (*al-nawʿ*

*al-mufrad, al-jins al-mufrad*).[98] In both lemmata, the question arises by applying the criteria of dividing species and genera given in the last paragraph, and asking, first, whether there can be a species with no species above it or below it, and second, whether there can be a genus with no genus above it or below it. For both questions, the disputed candidate answer is intelligence (in the sense that includes the first emanations from God, the celestial intelligences).[99] Intelligence may be a species of the ultimate genus, substance, and have only particular instantiations of intelligence below it, whereupon it would serve as an instance of an isolated species. Alternatively, intelligence may itself be an ultimate genus, and have species of intelligence below it, whereupon it would serve as an instance of an isolated genus. What we have, then, is candidate models to show the possibility of each isolated quiddity.

Al-Ḥillī sets out the dispute behind whether intelligence can be an example of an isolated species thus:

> **Text 30.1** What is disjoined from species is the isolated [species] like intelligence, if we say that substance (*jawhar*) is a genus [for intelligence]. That is because there is dispute among philosophers about substance being a genus (*jinsiyyat al-jawhar*). Some say that [substance] is a supreme genus, others that it is a general accident (*ʿaraḍ ʿāmm*); this is not the place to verify [the answer to the question]. On the hypothesis that substance is a genus, intelligence—which is substance both essentially and in action separated from bodies—is a species for it, yet there is no species above it, because substance—a supreme genus—is above it; and there is no species below it. So it is an isolated species. On the hypothesis that substance is not a genus, however, intelligence does not have a genus, and so is not a relative species. (*ḤQ* 230.7–14)

§31[100] I have covered the four kinds of genus in commentary on the last lemma. In this comment, I simply reiterate one consequence of using intelligence as an example of both an isolated genus and an isolated species. Genus is defined as what is said of many differing in species in response to "what is it?," or as a whole part of a quiddity that is shared with another quiddity. In using intelligence as the candidate model for an isolated species, al-Kātibī is assuming that what comes under it differs only numerically; but as a model for isolated genus, it must have species under it that differ from each other in their quiddities. So it is not simply the first assumption that changes (that intelligence is a species), but also the second (that under intelligence there are things which differ only numerically). Al-Taftāzānī makes both assumptions clear for the isolated species:

> Text 31.1 The second [case] is the distinct species (*al-nawʿ al-mubāyin*) like intelligence, on the assumption that substance is a genus for it such that it is said of [intelligence] and of other things in answer to "what is it?," and that the ten intelligences are instantiations of it and not species (*afrād lahu lā anwāʿ*), so that no other species is realized under it. (*TŠ* 183.10–12)

And for the isolated genus, which is

> Text 31.2 distinct from everything, being the isolated [genus] like intelligence, on the assumption that substance is not a genus for it but a general accident (so there will not be a genus more general than it), whereupon the ten intelligences will be different species and not genera (so there is no genus more particular than it) or individuals (so that its being a genus can be realized). So intelligence is an example for the isolated genus on one assumption, and for isolated

species on another assumption; this is enough about the example given. (*TŠ* 183.apu–184.2)

§32[101] Tempted by the terminology, some ancients have concluded that real species are a proper subset of relative species, in the same way that real particulars are a subset of relative particulars (see §28).[102] But in fact relative and real species only overlap (see the distinctions made in §26 above); neither wholly contains the other, nor are they coextensive. Relative species that are not real species are obviously distinct, and real species that are simple realities are not relative species.

> **Text 32.1** Know that a group of the ancients supposed that the relative species is more general absolutely than [that is, contains] the real species. The author refutes the view of such people by citing the presence of each without its counterpart. (*ḤQ* 232.11–13)
>
> The presence of the real species without the relative is as in simple realities; for the simple that has no part cannot be a relative species, due to the necessity that the relative species comes under a genus that constitutes it, so it will be a compound of genus and differentia; but we have already supposed it to be simple, so this is absurd. (*ḤQ* 232.pu–233.2)

§33[103] This lemma deals with how essentials are deployed in answer to "what is it?"; it is continuous with the discussion since §30 because it concerns how we signify the higher genera in the series we have been considering. This is a theme to which Avicenna returns from time to time in *Pointers*, starting at 1.16 and going through 2.3 (*AI* 11.16–15.14). He deals with two confusions to which his interlocutors are prone. The first is taking the essential to be what should be said in answer to "what is it?"; the second—on having it pointed out that the differentia is an essential but cannot be said in answer to "what is it?"—is that the answer to "what is it?" is the more general essential. The terms and phrases Avicenna deploys as he formulates his position on the matter are not as clearly defined as perhaps they could be; al-Rāzī gave the terms quite precise clarification, and al-Kātibī adopts these modified terms as his own. So for him, if "what is it?" is asked of a man, "animal" and "rational" are given by correspondence and therefore occur on the way to what is it (*fī ṭarīq mā huwa*), but the components of ANIMAL (such as LIVING BODY and SENSATE and MOVING BY VOLITION, which are signified by "animal" by containment) are given implicitly in the answer to "what is it?" (*dākhilan fī jawāb mā huwa*). Al-Rāzī and his followers are, however, not primarily concerned to provide a way to interpret Avicenna's texts, and al-Ṭūsī and his followers (among them al-Ḥillī) both object to their clarification of the terms, and offer an alternative clarification, which also provides a way to understand Avicenna's texts.

Since it is both important for understanding Rāzian logicians, and helpful in providing one way to understand Avicenna's texts, here is the full story, told by al-Taftāzānī.

> **TEXT 33.1** The goal in this discussion is that the notion had cropped up in the usage of literalist logicians that what is said in answer to "what is it?" is the essential (*al-dhātī*), and when they were reminded that the differentia is an essential, yet not said in answer to "what is it?," some of them shifted to the position that what is said in answer to "what is it?" is the more general essential (*al-dhātī al-aʿamm*). Avicenna responded to them that the generic differentia like, for example, SENSATE is a more general essential, yet not said in answer to "what is it?" For he claimed that "what is it?" is a question about the quiddity, so the answer must be a quiddity. Further, he distinguished between what is said in answer to "what is it?," what is intrinsic to the answer to "what is it?," and what occurs on the way to "what is it?";

[he made these distinctions by saying] that the answer itself is the quiddity, and what is intrinsic to it and occurs on its way is the essential—that is, part of the quiddity.

Al-Rāzī interpreted what is intrinsic in the answer to "what is it?" as the part signified by containment, and what occurs on its way the part signified by correspondence; the later scholars followed him in this [interpretation], and al-Kātibī alludes to it here. The verification of [this interpretation] is that the answer to "what is it?" is only given by correspondence, and part of it is either given by correspondence or by containment. This is because signification by implication is entirely avoided in answering "what is it?," such that it is inappropriate to signify a quiddity or even its parts by implication; and containment (aside from [signifying] a part) is avoided in answer [to the same question]. So if the part is given by correspondence, like "animal" or "rational" in "rational animal" said in response to "what is man?," we refer to it as having occurred on the way to "what is it?," and having been said in [the answer], because it occurs in [the process of] answering "what is it?" (which is the way to "what is it?"); if it is given by containment, like BODY and SENSATE in the example just offered, it is referred to as intrinsic in the answer to "what is it?"

Since there was nothing in their discussion [from Avicenna's works] that points to this interpretation, al-Ṭūsī interpreted what is intrinsic to the answer to "what is it?" as the essential which is part of the quiddity, whether more general or coextensive, and that which occurs on the way to "what is it?" as the more general essential. This means that he who interprets what is said in answer to "what is it?" as the essential [in *Pointers* 1.16, *AI* 10.apu–11.14] does not distinguish between what is said in answer to "what is it?" and what is intrinsic to it; and he who interprets it as the more general essential does not distinguish between what is said in answer to "what is it?" and that which occurs on its way. (*TŠ* 186.7–188.1)

§34[104] A final note, dealing with divisive and constitutive differentiae as they relate to the three levels of genera and species: Al-Kātibī begins with the hypothesis advanced in §20 and expanded in Text 20.4 that the highest genus might be compounded from two coextensive matters, which means—on the *Pointers* definition for differentia presented in §20—that both will be differentiae for the genus, and therefore constitutive (*muqawwim*) of it. Every genus must have more than one species below it. So every superior genus may have a differentia that constitutes it, and must have more than one divisive (*muqassim*) differentia. At the other end, the lowest species must have a differentia that constitutes it, but cannot have a differentia that divides it. In between, the intermediate genera and species must have both divisive and constitutive differentiae.

Traditionally, further relations are inferred from these claims. The first part of the first claim that al-Kātibī makes, that what constitutes the higher constitutes the lower, is proved as follows:

Text 34.1 The differentia that constitutes the higher is a part of it, and the higher is a part of the lower, and the part of the part is a part [of the whole] (*juz' al-juz' juz'*), so [the differentia] is also constitutive of the lower. (*ḤQ* 235.apu–pu)

This does not convert universally (that is, it is not true that what constitutes the lower necessarily constitutes the higher), and this is shown by counterexample. So RATIONAL constitutes MAN, but is only adventitiously a property of ANIMAL. At the same time, the constitutive of the lower may be constitutive of the higher, as is shown by the example of SENSATE, which constitutes MAN and ANIMAL.

The second claim mirrors the first: what divides the lower divides the higher, but again, it is not necessarily the case that what divides the higher divides the lower. The first part of the second claim (as when RATIONAL divides ANIMAL and BODY) is true

> **TEXT 34.2** because the meaning of the division of the lower is its presence in two natures (*wujūduhu fī ṭabīʿa-tayn*), and the presence of the lower entails the presence of the higher in the two [natures]. (*ḤQ* 236.7–8)

Examples are given to show that the reverse (that what divides the higher divides the lower) is not necessarily the case, but may be the case. So SENSATE divides BODY but not ANIMAL, but RATIONAL divides BODY and ANIMAL.

*The fourth section, on definitions*

This section deals with definitions in the broad sense (*taʿrīfāt*), both real or essential definitions in the Aristotelian sense, and delineations that simply differentiate the thing being defined (the definiendum, *muʿarraf*, or—in the case of real definition—*maḥdūd*) from other things. This is one of the parts of logic that al-Taftāzānī noted, with some regret, was treated superficially by post-Avicennian logicians. The *Risālah* has three lemmata on definition (corresponding to *Pointers* 2.7–2.11 [*AI* 17.3–21.u]), though of course the material leading up to this section goes to issues central to the topic. Lemma 35 first states the two goals that can motivate the search for a definition, and then stipulates two conditions that apply to all definitions, whether real or less-than-real (whether nominal or deficient definition, or delineation). Lemma 36 sketches a taxonomy of definitions based on the elements from which definitions are constructed; al-Ḥillī criticizes this taxonomy, relying on the Avicennian alternative that works from the effectiveness of a definition. Lemma 37 examines some defects that afflict definitions, dividing them into defects arising from the component meanings chosen for the construction of the definition, and into defects—in some cases relative to one of the parties to a debate—arising from poorly chosen expressions. Here again, al-Ḥillī finds fault with al-Kātibī for leaving material out of the section that should have been included. By contrast, Avicenna goes on to consider the acquisition of definitions even in an introductory exposition like the *Najāt* (*AN* §§139–144).[105]

Let me pause here to look back to the theory of signification, which matters a great deal in this section. Avicenna and his followers—and in this respect, al-Kātibī is one of those followers—stipulate that to define a quiddity (say, MAN), the highest quiddity that is part of its meaning (in this case, SUBSTANCE) must be given along with all differentiae that constitute the quiddity being defined. So MAN will be defined as "substance that is corporeal, living, sensate, and rational" (see the tree given in Figure 8).[106] Everyone is, however, prepared to proceed by abbreviation, giving the proximate genus of the quiddity followed by its specific differentia (as in §36, foreshadowed in §33). Although the expression signifying the specific differentia signifies it by correspondence, in this case the expression for the proximate genus is taken insofar as it signifies by containment the meaning of "substance that is corporeal, living, and sensate." These strict definitions do not call on signification by implication at all. In delineations—useful to distinguish the quiddity from other quiddities, but not to bring all components of its meaning to mind—signification by implication can be used (§36; al-Kātibī is prepared to call definition through the specific differentia alone deficient definition, though it is a kind of delineation).

§35[107] A definition is formulated with one of two goals in mind. The first is to find a compound meaning "the conception of which entails the conception of that thing" (*yastalzimu taṣawwuruhu taṣawwur dhālika l-shay'*); this is the essential definition (*ḥadd*). The second is to find a meaning that serves merely to distinguish (*imtiyāz*) the reality from other realities (whether—as al-Ḥillī notes on §36—absolutely or within a given subset of realities). Al-Kātibī returns to the formulations that fulfill these different functions in §36; these formulations deploy the predicables examined in §§15–23 in various ways.

Al-Kātibī gives two conditions for a successful definition, whether real or for the purposes of distinguishing something within a broader class. The first is that the definiens (*al-muʿarrif*) must be distinct from the definiendum; the second is that it must be equal (*musāwin*) to the definiendum, in the sense that it must be fit to serve as a substitute for the definiendum with no loss of truth or—specifically in the case of essential definition—meaning.[108] The argument that the first condition must be adopted is given with al-Kātibī's trademark concision—that is, that the definiens is known prior to the definiendum. A slightly less compressed version of the argument goes like this:

> TEXT 35.1 The definiens (*al-muʿarrif*) is a cause in the definition of the definiendum, so it must be distinct (*mughāyir*). [This is] because the cause is prior and what is prior is distinct [from what is posterior], due to the impossibility that something is prior to itself in any respect (*bi-ʿtibār wāḥid*). (*ḤQ* 237.8–10)

The second condition, that the definiens is equal to the definiendum in the sense set out above, works by excluding the other ways that the first could relate to the second. It cannot be overly broad (*aʿamm*) in the sense of being true of a wider group of realities, or overly narrow (*akhaṣṣ*) in the sense being true of a subset of the reality being defined; nor—and this is so obvious that al-Kātibī does not even advert to it—can it be entirely distinct (*mubāyin*) from the reality being defined. So the definiens must be equal to the definiendum,

> TEXT 35.2 because, were it overly broad, it would fall short of conveying the definition, for what is conveyed by a

definition is either the conception of the reality (*taṣawwur al-ḥaqīqah*), and the general does not entail the specific, or differentiation, and the general does not differentiate. And were it overly narrow, it would be more obscure, because it would be less available (*aqall wujūdan*), yet the definiens is more known [than the definiendum]. So it must be equal with [what is being defined]. (*ḤQ* 237.12–u)

§36[109] In this lemma, al-Kātibī orders definitions according to their component meanings, using the distinctions given in treatment of the predicables in §§15–23. Although al-Kātibī only uses the term "constitutes" (*yuqawwimu*) in dealing with differentia, and has not used the term "essential" (*dhātī*) at all, the use of genus and differentia—introduced in §16 as being intrinsic to the quiddity—in characterizing the components of definitions amounts to the same thing. His ordering of real and working definitions (respectively, *ḥudūd* and *taʿrīfāt*) is vulnerable to an objection arising from consideration of the goal of definitions stated in §35 (see Texts 36.2 and 36.3 below).

Al-Kātibī works with what is effectively another dichotomous division (see Figure 20). If an expository phrase (*qawl shāriḥ*) has (1) as one of its components the reality's proximate differentia, then it is a definition; otherwise, it is at best a delineation. Given that it has a proximate differentia, if it also has (1a) the proximate genus it is a complete definition (*ḥadd tāmm*), and if (1b) it has a remote genus, or no genus, or a genus in the wrong order relative to the differentia (cf. *ḤQ* 238.10), then it is a deficient definition (*ḥadd nāqiṣ*). If, on the other hand, the component of the definition is not the quiddity's differentia but (2) its proximate proprium, the expository phrase will be a delineation; if joined to (2a) the proximate genus, it will be a complete delineation (*rasm tāmm*), but if it is joined to (2b) a remote genus or no genus, it will be a deficient delineation (*rasm nāqiṣ*).

**Text 36.1** If the definition (*ḥadd*) includes the sum of constituents (*majmūʿ al-muqawwimāt*), then it is called a complete definition, like the definition of man as rational animal (*al-ḥayawān al-nāṭiq*); for the proximate genus is animal, and the proximate differentia is rational. If it does not include all [constituents] it would be deficient, whether with the differentia alone or with it and a remote genus, like "man is rational" or "man is rational body." If the specified order is abandoned in the definition, such that the differentia comes before the genus, it too will be deficient.

The complete delineation is that in which the proximate genus and a coextensive proprium are given, as in "man is a risible animal." The deficient [delineation] is that in which the proprium alone is given, as in defining [man] as "the risible"; or that in which the remote genus and the proprium are given, as in defining [man] as "the risible body." (*ḤQ* 238.5–u)

The attack al-Ḥillī launches against this division is historically informative and helpful in what it tells us about the definition theory of his time.[110] First, the accounts of incomplete definition and delineation fail to satisfy the conditions laid down in §35.

**Text 36.2** Know that in this discussion [of definitions], the author has followed Fakhr al-Dīn al-Rāzī, but it differs from what scholars who verify their work (*al-muḥaqqiqūn*) hold. First, in [claiming that] the differentia alone, or the proprium alone, conveys the differentiation of the quiddity from everything else (*ʿammā ʿadāhā*), this is a mistake, for "the risible" and "the rational" only signify a thing that possesses risibility or rationality without [further] restriction, so here there is scope (*tajwīz*) for the thing to be more general or more specific than man, or coextensive or distinct. Thus, without [further] restriction that signifies their being proper (*takhṣīṣ*) to man, these two [terms] convey neither differentiation nor the conception of the reality. (*ḤQ* 239.1–9)

So al-Kātibī's accounts of deficient definition and deficient delineation are wrong as they stand. So too, according to al-Ḥillī, his account of complete delineation:

> TEXT 36.3 Second, with respect to the complete delineation being a compound of genus and proprium, and the deficient being what dispenses with the genus: the common doctrine (*al-mashhūr*) among logicians is that the delineation only conveys differentiation, so if it conveys differentiation from everything else then it is a complete delineation, and if it conveys differentiation from some things apart from it, then it is deficient, and would be a delineation in relation to [those things]. (*ḤQ* 239.12–16)

For one of his commentators at least, al-Kātibī's presentation of the kinds of definition can stand only insofar as it treats complete definition.

§37[111] Al-Kātibī presents the defects that afflict definitions in two divisions, the first of which arises from matters relating to meaning, the second from matters relating to expression. Again, al-Ḥillī upbraids al-Kātibī for giving the wrong example to illustrate the definition of something by what is equally known or unknown, and for omitting altogether from the list of defects the definition of something by what is more obscure. By contrast, he seems to be content with al-Kātibī's account of defects arising from expression. On the first defect, al-Ḥillī noted:

> TEXT 37.1 Semantic mistakes include defining something with what is just as known or unknown [as the

> definiendum], like someone who defines movement as lack of stillness, and even as not odd; for lack of stillness is equally known as movement, and not odd as even. This [account of the defect] is according to widely accepted opinion (*al-mashhūr*), which holds that both movement and stillness, and even and odd, are opposed as contraries (*al-aḍdād*). But if we verify this matter, the opposition in these pairs is the opposition of privation and capacity; for stillness is lack of movement from what is prone to move, and odd is not even. So the definition with these terms is [in fact] defining something with that on which it depends to be known. The correct example [for the defect] is like the definition of one of two correlatives with the other, like defining "father" as "he who has a son." (*ḤQ* 240.9–u)

Then, on a defect al-Kātibī omits:

> **Text 37.2** Beyond this degree of outraging [good definition technique] (*al-radā'ah*) is defining something with what is more obscure (*al-akhfā*); this is more of an outrage than definition with the equally [unknown]. It is like defining fire as an element like soul, for soul is more obscure than fire. The author failed to mention this degree [of error]. (*ḤQ* 241.1–3)

Circular definitions are an even worse outrage, especially when the circularity works in a way that conceals itself.

> **Text 37.3** Beyond this degree [of error] is defining something with what is only known through [that thing] at one remove (*bi-martabah wāḥidah*), for this is clearly circular. It is like defining quality as a form through which similarity and dissimilarity occur, then defining similarity as agreement in quality.

And beyond this degree [of error] is defining something with what is only known through [that thing] at a number of removes (*bi-marātib*), like defining 2 as the first even, then defining even as the number divisible into two equal parts, then defining two equals as two things neither of which exceeds the other, then—in defining two things—that they are 2. This is a hidden circle, and it is more reprehensible (*aqbaḥ*) than the first because it involves making the knowledge of a thing prior to itself by a number of degrees. (*ḤQ* 241.4–12)

The problems that arise from expression are relative to the person who is being instructed by the definition; if expressions are strange for the auditor, the goal of definition is lost.

Text 37.4 For one who seeks a meaning [of an otherwise unknown expression] thereupon abandons what he seeks, and seeks rather to understand the expression, and thus he misses his goal. (*ḤQ* 241.pu–u)

## The Second Treatise, on Propositions and Their Valuations

The Second Treatise runs from §38 to §87.

Text 38.a Al-Kātibī ordered [this Treatise] as an Introduction (to define "proposition" and its primary divisions) and three sections. This is because the discussion either concerns the categorical specifically, or the hypothetical specifically, or both. What is meant by "its primary divisions" is the divisions that arise in considering the first division of the proposition, as in "the proposition is either categorical or hypothetical," in contrast with ". . . is necessary" and so forth, for the proposition only divides into these after being divided into categorical and hypothetical. (*TŠ* 201.3–7)

So the two lemmata of the Introduction (§§38 and 39) deal with the definition and primary divisions of the proposition. The first of the three sections, On the Categorical (§§40–59), covers four topics: the parts and divisions of the categorical proposition (§§40–44), the truth-conditions for the four quantified propositions (§§45–47), the relation between propositions with determinate and indefinite terms (§§48–50), and modal propositions (§§51–59). The second section, On the Divisions of the Hypothetical (§§60–66), sketches consequence and disjunction, their modal and non-modal variants, and their negation, truth-conditions, and quantification. The third section, Valuations of Propositions (§§67–87), deals with four topics, three of which relate to both categorical and hypothetical propositions: contradiction (§§67–72), conversion (§§73–81), contraposition (§§82–86), and—dealing with immediate inferences with no parallels in the categoricals—the implicates of hypothetical propositions (§87).

### *The Introduction, on defining the proposition and its primary divisions*

§38[112] Having finished with the First Treatise and its treatment of simple terms, al-Kātibī moves on to compound expressions that are complete—that is to say, after which silence is appropriate—and informative (both defined in §14): an informative expression (*khabar*) is a complete compound expression that is either true or false. In this lemma, al-Kātibī takes a slightly different tack in defining truth-apt discourse. Details of what he says are more easily appreciated by comparing §38 with the sentence with which Avicenna begins the third Path of the Logic of *Pointers and Reminders* (3.1.1):

> **Text 38.1** This kind of composition, which we all agree should be mentioned, is informative composition (*al-tarkīb*

> *al-khabarī*); he who produces it is said to be truthful or false in what he says (*huwa lladhī yuqālu li-qā'ilihi innahu ṣādiq fīmā qālahu aw kādhib*). (*AI* 22.2–4)

Al-Kātibī does not refer back to what he has said about informative expression in §14. Instead, he defines a proposition as "discourse such that it is correct to say of him who produces it that he is truthful or false in what he says." (The translation hides an ambiguity in the Arabic, the nominal clause of which could also be understood as "that it—what is said—is true or false"; whatever al-Kātibī really intended, he was understood by his commentators to be saying something similar to Avicenna in Text 38.1.)

> **Text 38.2** So discourse—which is the compound expression in the proposition as uttered (*al-qaḍiyyah al-malfūẓah*), or the compound intellectual meaning (*al-mafhūm al-ʿaqlī l-murakkab*) in the proposition as understood (*al-qaḍiyyah al-maʿqūlah*)—is a genus that includes complete and defective discourse, and "such that it is correct to say of him who produces it that he is truthful or false in what he says" is a differentia that excludes incomplete discourse and [complete discourse, which is] nonpropositional (*al-inshā'āt*). (*TT* 221.6–u)

Some raise the concern that the definitions (in fact, delineations) of "proposition" and "truth" might be circular. "Someone might object that it is only possible to define truth through 'information corresponding [to the actual],' so defining information through truth is circular" (*RM* 124.1–2), to which al-Rāzī responds that knowledge of the reality of information, and its distinction from other kinds of discourse, is necessary and primitive (*badīhī*) (*RM* 124.5).[113] Al-Taftāzānī takes truth to belong to a spoken discourse by virtue of the fact that the intelligible content signified by that discourse corresponds to what is actual.

**Text 38.3** "Discourse" (*al-qawl*) is synonymous with "compound [expression]" (*al-murakkab*). It is said of what is intelligible (*al-maʿqūl*) and of what is audible (*al-masmūʿ*); the first is what is considered in the intelligible proposition, and the second in the expressed proposition (*fī l-malfūẓah*). Just as "true" (*al-ṣādiq*) is used of discourse whose judgment corresponds with the actual (*al-qawl al-muṭābiq ḥukmuhu li-l-wāqiʿ*), it is also used of someone who makes the statement; this is what is meant here. (*TŠ* 202.1–3)

The proposition divides into the categorical and the hypothetical. This first division, and the one below it of the hypothetical into conditional and disjunctive (see Figure 21), are taken to be deeper and more natural than subsequent divisions into propositions under different readings, or different modalizations. (The commentators make use of these different kinds of division, for example, in discussion of §72.)

**Text 38.4** For the proposition at times divides into species (*aqsām nawʿiyyah*), and at others into types (*aqsām ṣinfiyyah*). The first is a primary division (like the division of the proposition into categorical and hypothetical, for these are two different species), whereas the division [of the proposition] into, for example, necessary, referential, and other modalizations is a division into types because the differences involved are only through adventitious considerations (*lā khtilāf fīhā illā bi-l-ʿawāriḍ*).[114] (*ḤQ* 242.8–apu)

The test for making the primary division of propositions into categorical and hypothetical turns on whether "its two extremes may be analyzed into two simple terms." As for the meaning of analysis:

**Text 38.5** The meaning of analysis (*al-inḥilāl*) is dropping the syncategorematic terms (*al-adawāt*) signifying the judgment through which that proposition is a proposition. So, if we have "Zayd is knowing" (*Zayd huwa ʿālim*) or "Zayd is not knowing" (*Zayd laysa huwa bi-ʿālim*), and we drop "is" (*huwa*) signifying affirmation, and "is not" (*huwa laysa*) signifying negation, then "Zayd" and "knowing" remain, and they are two simple terms (*mufradān*). And if we have "if the sun is up then it is day" and "number is either even or odd," and we drop the expressions "if" and "then" signifying conditional connection (*al-ittiṣāl*), and the expressions "either" and "or" signifying disjunction, "the sun is up" and "it is day" remain (and they are propositions not simple terms), and similarly for "the number is even" and "the number is odd." (*TŠ* 202.6–11)

Note that the phrase is "may be analyzed into two simple terms"; the phrase allows for compound expressions that amount to simple terms, which are "potentially simple" (*mufrad bi-l-quwwah*).

Text 38.6 We mean by "potentially simple" what is possibly expressed by a simple expression while being a part of that proposition and on conveying its judgment; so a proposition like "Zayd's father is standing" (*Zayd abūhu qāʾim*) is included under the categorical . . . [This is] because [such propositions] resolve to two things that can be expressed as two simple expressions taken respectively as that on which judgment is passed and that which is judged of it (*maḥkūman ʿalayhi wa-maḥkūman bi-hi*). This is contrary to the hypothetical, for in [the hypothetical] it is not correct to say "this is that." (*TŠ* 202.12–apu, 203.1–3)

Lemma 38 is the first mention of the hypothetical in the *Risālah*. All the examples al-Kātibī gives in the next lemma are of simple hypothetical propositions, though in §66 he encourages his readers to compose examples of the various kinds of more complex hypotheticals, and I have given there the examples al-Taftāzānī offers in comment on the lemma.

§39[115] Al-Kātibī carries on with the hypothetical propositions (*al-sharṭiyyāt*) in §39 (see again Figure 21). Although the treatment of hypotheticals in the *Risālah* is sparse relative to the treatment of categorical propositions, it nonetheless provides a solid introduction to the material. The treatment makes up 19 of the *Risālah*'s 120 lemmata on the division of the text I use (§38: definition against the categorical; §39: informal division into kinds with examples; §§60–67: more rigorous division into kinds of hypotheticals with their truth-conditions, their meaning when quantified and the terms expressing quantification, and their various compositions; §72: squares of opposition; §81: conversion; §86: contraposition; §87: co-implication of hypotheticals; §§105–109: some of the kinds of syllogistic inferences with hypothetical propositions). I cross-reference my comments on these passages to form a treatment of the subject that may be read as a single unit.

Al-Kātibī departs from Avicenna's foundational treatment of hypothetical propositions on a number of points, mostly minor. In the 250 years between Avicenna and al-Kātibī, Fakhr al-Dīn al-Rāzī had reordered the treatment (and indeed questioned the utility of covering the finer points in the exposition), and Afḍal al-Dīn al-Khūnajī had—with a number of remarks critical of the rigor of Avicenna's treatment—reworked the entire exposition and reaffirmed its centrality as a topic for logicians.[116] Al-Kātibī adopts the broad ordering of the material introduced by al-Rāzī, though he divides the various compositions of more complex hypothetical propositions in §67 as Avicenna does.[117] He differs slightly in dividing the various kinds of arguments built up using hypothetical propositions (§105 and following), however, and allows their limited utility in argument to shape his exposition (if we are to believe al-Taftāzānī, Text 105.a). He also differs in the truth-conditions he stipulates for a number of operators; his versions are stronger than Avicenna's (see §60 below, and especially comments I translate from al-Ḥillī's commentary). Other points—such as a square of opposition omitting some oppositions (see §72)—may indicate that al-Kātibī is seeking to provide a simplified account rather than a revision of the system.

Back to §39, in which al-Kātibī introduces the two kinds (later, in §72 on the squares of opposition, they will be referred to by the expression "species") of hypothetical propositions: the division is secondary relative to the division presented in §38. Obviously, the tradition is conscious of the fact that it is using terms—above all, "hypothetical" (*sharṭiyyah*)—which are among the terms of art of Arabic grammar. Al-Ḥillī explains:

> **Text 39.1** Know that calling the conditional (*muttaṣilah*) a hypothetical (*sharṭiyyah*) corresponds with linguistic custom, whereas calling the disjunctive (*munfaṣilah*) a hypothetical is metaphorical; similarly, calling the affirmatives conditionals or disjunctives is literal, whereas calling the negatives [by the same terms] is metaphorical. (*ḤQ* 245.15–apu)

That in which "one proposition is judged to be true or not on the assumption of another proposition" is called a *muttaṣilah*, which I have translated as "conditional"; the term is from the same root as Avicenna's *ittiṣāl*, contact with the Active Intellect, and the core idea may be of a productive contact between one proposition and another. Avicenna associates this with the form of words for the conditional of natural language (using "if-then"). The other hypothetical is that in which "two propositions are judged to be incompatible with each other"; this is a *munfaṣilah*, which uses the form of words for the disjunctive of natural language (using "either-or"). Al-Kātibī indicates how each kind of proposition will be negated: "not, if this is a man, it is inanimate," and "not, either this man is an animal or black" (more on negation in comment on §§62 and 72).

**The first discussion, on its parts and divisions**

The categorical proposition is in one view the simple element (*mufrad*) that makes up the hypothetical proposition, so it comes first in al-Kātibī's exposition of propositions. Of five lemmata, the first two go to aspects of the relation between the subject and the predicate (Is there a copula? Does the copula signify everything in the proposition other than the subject and the predicate? How do affirmation and negation relate to the copula?), and the next three go to aspects of quantification, which are taken to belong to the subject.

§40[118] The main points made explicitly in §40 are, first, that the proposition has three parts (the subject, the predicate, and the copula); second, that the copula (*rābiṭah*) can be omitted in Arabic; and finally, that as a function of including or omitting the copula in the expressed proposition, the proposition is called either two-part or three-part.

First, on the subject and the predicate taken together, al-Ḥillī notes that the subject and the predicate are the same in at least one respect (both true of certain things; I assume he has an affirmative proposition in mind), but must differ in some other respect. He is explicit that synonyms (in the sense specified in §13) cannot fulfill the roles of subject and predicate (*lam yakun al-waḍʿ wa-l-ḥaml fī l-alfāẓ al-mutarādifah*) (*ḤQ* 246.13–14). His discussion then moves beyond al-Kātibī's lemma to touch on univocal and denominative predication. I mention again the denominative,[119] though here as it has to do with predication. (I take it that because denominative predication has no impact on the valid inferences al-Kātibī presents in the *Risālah*, he has not defined it.) Speaking of univocal predication (*ḥaml huwa huwa l-musammā bi-ḥaml al-muwāṭaʾah*), al-Ṭūsī says it "invokes the unification of the subject and the predicate in one respect, and their differentiation in another." For example, in "triangle is figure," "the predicate alone is that through which there is unification, abstracted from that through which there is differentiation" (whatever specific properties make a figure a triangle).

**Text 40.1** There is another species of predication called denominative predication (*ḥaml al-ishtiqāq*), and it is the predication this-is-possessor-of-that (*ḥaml huwa dhū huwa*). It is like "whiteness" said of "body"; the predicate in this predication is not predicated by itself of the subject univocally, but rather is predicated with the expression "possessor of," as in "the body is possessor of whiteness" (*al-jism dhū bayāḍ*). Alternatively, an adjective like "white" is derived from it (*yushtaqqu minhu*), so it may be predicated univocally of [the subject], as in "the body is white" (*al-jism abyaḍ*); strictly speaking, the predicate is the first. (*ṬḤ* 142.7–u)

I come back to one aspect to do with the denominative predicate (in Texts 40.3 and 40.4) after briefly considering the second item on al-Kātibī's list of propositional components, the copula. Nothing is needed in Arabic to make *Zaydun kātibun* ("Zayd is a writer") a grammatical sentence (other than, strictly speaking, the case endings to show the syntactic function of the component words, and the awareness that "Zayd" is definite), but then there is no separate expression that signifies the connection the subject has to the predicate. There are expressions in Arabic for the tensed copula, but—as al-Taftāzānī tells us he learned from al-Fārābī's account of the reception of logic—an expression must be transferred to fill the need for an atemporal copula.

**Text 40.2** So they used *huwa* in Arabic in place of *hast* in Persian, and they made its gerund *huwiyyah*, like *insāniyyah* from *insān*. Some of them chose instead of *huwa* the expression *al-mawjūd*, and they set *wujūd* in place of *huwiyyah*; and in place of *kāna* and *yakūnu* and *sa-yakūnu* [, respectively,] *wujida* and *yūjad* and *sa-yūjad*. This is what al-Fārābī said.[120] (*TŠ* 209.9–12)

The *Risālah* has no example propositions with a tensed copula (except in the analysis of the essentialist proposition in §45, with the phrase *law wujida*, where the perfective is required by the conditional particle), and uses *huwa* throughout as atemporal copula. It follows from the differing preferences expressed in Text 40.2 that the copula seems to be in the form of a verb (*kalimah*) in the case of *kāna*, or of a name (*ism*) in the case of *huwa* (*ḤQ* 247.5–6). In fact, according to al-Ḥillī, the copula is a particle, a syncategorematic term (*adāt*) (see §11), as emerges in the following discussion involving denominative predicates.

> **Text 40.3** Know that denominative predicates and verbs may need no mention of the copula in [the proposition] because they connect of themselves (*li-dhawātihā*) with a given subject. Fakhr al-Dīn claimed that [verbs and denominatives] do [indeed] connect of themselves (*li-dhātihā*) with the subject in the proposition, but this is an error. (*ḤQ* 247.12–u)

The reason al-Rāzī's claim is an error—as we find in al-Ḥillī's *Asrār*—is that the relation an agent has to its verb is not the relation that is signified by the copula:

> **Text 40.4** Whether the predicate is a name or a verb or denominative, it requires that the copula be stated; for the verb in itself (*bi-dhātihā*) only connects to its agent, as in the form of "Zayd stood" (*qāma Zayd*). Know that the copula is not the pronoun implicit in the verb and the denominative name, for that pronoun is a name, and [the copula] is a particle (*adāt*). (*ḤA* 56.20–apu)

In any event, it may be that the verb or denominative as predicate needs a copula no less than univocal predicates,[121] but al-Kātibī is taken to make the claim that in all cases in Arabic it is open to the speaker to omit the expression for the copula.

TEXT 40.5 This is the case in Arabic, and therefore al-Kātibī restricted the omission to "some languages," because in Persian it is not omitted. (*ḤQ* 247.10–11)

Al-Taftāzānī goes on to show how a verbal predicate (as in the example in Text 40.4) is to be regimented for logical treatment:

TEXT 40.6 Know that the rules of logic taken literally do not include the proposition whose predicate is a verb—and it is that which is called by grammarians a verbal sentence—like "Zayd stood" (*qāma Zayd*); at best it is construed as "Zayd is an individual to whom standing belongs" (*Zayd shakhṣ la-hu l-qiyām*). (*TŠ* 210.8–10)

Let me now return to the first of the points raised by al-Kātibī in the lemma. He identifies the three parts of the categorical as the *maḥkūm ʿalayhi*—that on which judgment is made—for the subject; *maḥkūm bi-hi*—the judgment made—for the predicate; and the *nisbah*—relation—for the copula. The expressed proposition (*al-qaḍiyyah al-malfūẓah*) may omit the copula, but its meaning is still present in the intelligible proposition (*al-qaḍiyyah al-maʿqūlah*).

TEXT 40.7 In respect of the copula, the categorical proposition is either two-part or three-part, because if the copula is stated in [the proposition] it is three-part due to its including three expressions for three meanings; if it is omitted—because the mind is aware of the meaning of [the copula]—it is two-part because it only includes two parts as counterparts for two meanings. (*TT* 234.3–6)

The meaning of the copula is in respect of the judgment-relation (*al-nisbah al-ḥukmiyyah*); what is signified by the copula is affirmation or negation (*TT* 235.9–10).

> **Text 40.8** The correct thing is to say, the judgment in the proposition is either that the subject is the predicate or that the subject is not the predicate; or to say, the judgment in [the proposition] is either to put the relation forward (*bi-īqāʿ al-nisbah*) or to retract it (*bi-ntizāʿihā*). (*TT* 236.6–8)

Finally, al-Taftāzānī in commentary on this lemma notes a dispute about al-Kātibī's doctrine that the proposition has only three parts; it has been argued that in fact it has four parts. Speaking of the proposition "Zayd is the writer," he says:

> **Text 40.9** So if we understand "Zayd," and "the writer" and the relation (which is to say, the understanding that [the second] is affirmed or not affirmed of [the first]), the proposition will not obtain, as is the situation for those who doubt or merely entertain [a proposition] (*al-shākkīn wa-l-mutawahhimīn*). For these understand the two extremes and the relation between them without any judgment; until doubt ceases and the mind comes to believe that the relation is or is not actual (I mean that the predicate is affirmed or not affirmed of the subject), [only] then the proposition obtains.[122] (*TŠ* 204.15–pu)

§41[123] The negation toward which al-Kātibī gestures in this lemma—which is on affirmation and negation—is a propositional negation. Propositional negation (what Buridan calls negating negation), dealt with in this lemma, will be distinguished from nominal negation (what Buridan, for example, calls infinitizing negation; see §§26 and 27) in §§48–50.[124] As noted in Text 40.8, this negation relates above all to the connection (*al-nisbah al-ḥukmiyyah*) signified by the copula: "the judgment in [the proposition] is either to put the relation forward (*bi-īqāʿ al-nisbah*) or to retract it (*bi-ntizāʿihā*)" (*TT* 236.6–8). The effect of what al-Kātibī says in §50.2 is that the negative particle is distinct from the copula, and should be placed in the expressed proposition before the copula to signify that it is the proposition which is negated.

The test for the affirmative is whether it is correct to say that the subject has a given predicate; the test for the negative is whether it is correct to say that the subject does not have a given predicate. When a subject is under the predication of a determinate name, the result is an affirmative. Al-Taftāzānī reaches out to Persian to help the reader. When we can say that the subject has a given predicate, "it is the projective relation that is understood from (*al-nisbah al-īqāʿiyyah al-mafhūmah min*) a word like *hast*"; if we can say that the subject does not have a given predicate, "it is the retractive relation that is understood from (*al-nisbah al-intizāʿiyyah al-mafhūmah min*) the word *nīst*" (*TŠ* 210.apu–u). He goes on to stress that both affirmation and negation relate to formal aspects of the proposition; it may be that it is false to say that "man is a stone," but the question of the proposition's falsity is entirely different from the question of its being an affirmation or a negation (*TŠ* 211.1–4).

§42[125] In this lemma, al-Kātibī turns to the division of the categorical into propositions with singular terms as subjects, and quantified propositions, which have universal terms as subjects. He settles his focus immediately on quantified propositions, "because scientific discussions are only conducted using one of these" (*ḤQ* 249.6–7). As in the case of negation, al-Kātibī refrains from defining quantification, and is content merely to give examples. I have translated *maḥṣūrah wa-musawwarah* with the single English word "quantified," but al-Kātibī's commentators make it clear that *maḥṣūrah* signifies that the propositional meaning specifies the quantity of the subject, whereas *musawwarah* signifies that the expression for the proposition includes the particle (the *sūr*, the "wall"), which signifies the quantity of the subject ("every," "no," and so forth).

In this commentary, I adopt the Western convention of referring to the four quantified propositions using the letters A, E, I, and O in the following way:

A: Every C is B (universal affirmative, *kulliyyah mūjibah*);
E: No C is B (universal negative, *kulliyyah sālibah*);
I: Some C is B (particular affirmative, *juz'iyyah mūjibah*);
O: Some C is not B (particular negative, *juz'iyyah sālibah*).

The letters are used in the Western names for the syllogistic moods, so it is worth learning them. In the comments that follow, I often use, for example, "a-proposition" to translate *al-kulliyyah al-mūjibah*.

Most of what is given in §42 is simply a list of quantifiers with examples, and variant expressions that are synonymous with each other. This is true at least for the first three quantified propositions, but not for the last quantified proposition, the o-proposition. Al-Kātibī gives three variants (I have only translated two): *laysa kull*, *laysa baʿḍ*, and *baʿḍ laysa*.

> **Text 42.1** The difference between the first and the other two is that the first signifies by correspondence the negation of the judgment from all, and by implication its negation from some, while the other two are the reverse; they signify negation of the judgment from some by correspondence, and from all by implication. The difference between the second and the third is that the second may be used in universal negation as in "not, some stone is a man" (*laysa baʿḍ al-ḥajar bi-insān*), and by it one means to negate humanity of every stone taken one at a time; the third cannot be used like this. Further, the third may be used in the metathetic affirmation, such as "some animal is not-man" (*baʿḍ*

*al-ḥayawān huwa laysa bi-insān*), in contrast to the second, which simply cannot be used in affirmation. (*ḤQ* 250.6–13)

Al-Kātibī often uses the third form in the *Risālah*, though in §93.4 (for example) he uses the second and third forms one after the other, and in §113 (on the reductio) he uses the first form.

§43[126] The singular and the quantified propositions set out explicitly the quantity of the items under the subject, whereas the natural proposition (*qaḍiyyah ṭabīʿiyyah*) and the indefinite proposition (*qaḍiyyah muhmalah*) do not. In this lemma, al-Kātibī sets out the criterion to distinguish between these two—whether or not the proposition is apt to be true with a universal or particular quantifier added to it—and considers first the natural proposition (which is not apt to be true as a universal or particular proposition). It "is a judgment on the quiddity with respect to the universality attaching to it (*bi-ʿtibār ʿurūḍ al-kulliyyah la-hā*)" (*ḤQ* 251.9–10). Al-Ḥillī goes on to criticize al-Kātibī for neglecting a third kind of proposition, which also has no quantifier:

> **Text 43.1** The author has neglected another division of propositions: that in which judgment is made on the quiddity insofar as it is what it is; we call this proposition the natural proposition, and that which the author calls the natural we call the general proposition. (*ḤQ* 251.u–252.2)

Al-Taḥtānī pauses briefly to consider the division of propositions to this point, which is effectively quadripartite.

> **Text 43.2** Avicenna in the *Cure* gave a three-fold division, saying that if the subject is particular [the proposition] is singular; if it is universal, then if the quantity of items is made clear it is a quantified proposition; otherwise, it is indefinite.[127] The later logicians denounced this

> as incomplete, excluding [as it does] the natural proposition. The answer [to them] is that the discussion is focused on propositions taken into account in the sciences, and no account is taken [in the sciences] of the natural proposition. (*TT* 243.7–u)

Once again, the range of components of logic necessary for its use in the sciences determines how far al-Kātibī is prepared to diverge from his narrow path through the *Risālah*. The natural proposition does not, however, contribute to syllogistic inferences; neglecting that limitation can lead to fallacious reasoning (see Text 119.4).[128]

§44[129] Indefinite propositions have the logical status of i-propositions according to philosophers, in the sense that both an indefinite affirmative (say) and a particular affirmative are mutually implicative (*mutalāzimān*) (*TT* 244.79). Those who are not philosophers may worry that "man is a writer" is true whether taken as a universal or a particular, and "some man is a writer" can be heard as implicitly denying that all men are writers. The philosophers insist that when used in the context of logic, the i-proposition does not have this further implicit meaning (see also Avicenna *Pointers* 3.4 [*AI* 25.apu–26.9]).

### The second discussion, on verifying the four quantified propositions

From §45 on, al-Kātibī begins to focus on a set of issues that affect how he understands modalized propositions and their contribution to inferences. In §§45–47, he examines different ways to interpret the subject term of a proposition; some of his post-Avicennian colleagues held that these differing interpretations played a decisive role in determining which inferences were valid. In §51, he introduces the notion of matter (*māddah*) as the underlying relation between two terms that is expressed by the mode of a true modal proposition. In §52, he sets out the simple modalized propositions, along with the distinction between referential (*dhātī*) and descriptional (*waṣfī*) readings, and in §§53–59, the compound modalized propositions. He expands on his understanding of these propositions by specifying their contradictories in §§67–71. Using these contradictories, he proves the converses (§§73–80) and contrapositives (§§82–86) that may be inferred from each modalized proposition. Finally, in §§98–104, he examines which modalized propositions can be used in a productive syllogism, and what modal strength the conclusion will have. In short, al-Kātibī devotes nearly a third of the *Risālah* to modal logic. One goal of this short introductory passage is to identify the relevant lemmata. The other is to give the reader notice of themes the lemmata develop, and methods they deploy. Further, al-Kātibī and his Rāzian colleagues differ at certain points from Avicenna's account of modal logic, and I hope that by drawing attention to a number of texts translated from the commentators, I help clarify what post-Avicennian logicians thought Avicenna was doing, why some of them (let us call them the revisionist Avicennian logicians) wanted to do something different, and, finally, how the purists defended Avicenna's choices.

Since the substance in these reflections derives from texts I take from commentators for my own commentary, I should note again that the earliest of the commentators on the *Risālah*, al-Ḥillī, presents himself at the time of writing his commentary as a committed Avicennian purist, along with al-Ṭūsī; they both strain against the tendency among the Rāzians to reform Avicenna's modal logic. Whether al-Ḥillī's understanding of Avicenna is right or wrong, it represents the most hospitable reception of that logic in the late thirteenth century.

Al-Ḥillī criticizes al-Kātibī's account of inferences involving modal propositions, claiming that his own more faithfully reflects Avicenna's original account. His opponents (whether dead, like al-Khūnajī, or as yet unborn, like al-Taftāzānī) offer counterexamples to Avicenna's inferences (see for example Text 76.4, which spawned a family of counterexamples). Some acknowledge that the counterexamples do not touch Avicenna because of the truth-conditions he stipulates for his propositions (see al-Taftāzānī in Text 98.2); according to al-Taftāzānī, these truth-conditions include understanding the subject term ("every C") to include the possible as well as the actual, in the way al-Fārābī understood the subject term (see Text 45.3). Some, including al-Khūnajī, even accuse Avicenna of sliding between different readings of the subject term so that some of his inferences from modalized propositions cannot be treated systematically (see Text 45.10). Avicenna's doctrine on the subject term is given as al-Ḥillī understands it in Text 45.12; the Rāzian logicians put forward an alternative doctrine, which among other things determines what the relata are in a proposition (see Text 45.1). Their alternative doctrine rules out the relata that interest Avicenna (for example, Text 101.2, rejected in Text 101.3). The discussion in §§45–47 goes primarily to these matters.

The inferences al-Kātibī defends, both immediate (§§73–80, §§82–86) and syllogistic (§§98–104), differ from those defended by the Avicennian purists in respect of syllogisms with a possibility proposition as minor premise; such syllogisms are, according to the Rāzians, unproductive. One way these syllogisms could be made productive is by taking the subject term as understood by al-Fārābī (and, according to al-Taftāzānī, by Avicenna). Another way is presented by al-Ḥillī (see for example Text 98.1, first used though not named in Text 76.1), and works by supposing a possible actual (*ʿalā taqdīr wuqūʿ al-mumkin*; his teacher al-Ṭūsī used to refer to the method with phrases like "supposing the possible actual," *farḍ al-mumkin mawjūdan*; for example, *ṬḤ* 391.22). For example, the Avicennian purists want to defend Barbara LML ("every C is possibly B, every B is necessarily A, therefore every C is necessarily A"); as al-Ḥillī puts it in the first of the inferences in Text 98.1, assume the minor ("every C is possibly B") to be actual ("every C is B"), and the mix self-evidently concludes in a necessity proposition. But since the conclusion must be necessary given the way things really are (*fī nafs al-amr*), and since assuming what is possibly the case to be the case cannot lead to the impossible, the necessity proposition is the true conclusion.

Al-Khūnajī's student Ibn Wāṣil al-Ḥamawī (d. 697/1298) relays al-Khūnajī's complaint against this move: "We do not concede that on the supposition of the truth of the minor *actually* [and not merely possibly] the universal major remains true. Rather, it is true that on this supposition the middle term will include what the major term is not true of necessarily."[130] So take a typical counterexample against Barbara LML, framed on the assumption that Zayd only ever rides horses: "every donkey is possibly a mount for Zayd, every mount for Zayd is necessarily a horse, therefore every donkey is necessarily a horse." By supposing the minor actual, as "every donkey is a mount for Zayd," the middle term ("mount for Zayd") includes things of which the major is no longer true. As al-Khūnajī himself puts it, we cannot make the supposition "because the individuals under [the major's] subject term might at that point increase (*li-jawāz izdiyād afrād mawḍūʿihā ḥīnaʾidhin*)" (*ḪK* 136.13). Al-Ḥillī does what he can to fight against this criticism at the end of Text 98.1. In fact, al-Khūnajī has a second, more substantial criticism of the method.

> **Text 45.a** Know that some people interpret "the necessary" as that in which the separation of the predicate from the subject is impossible in itself, and as that in which the subject requires the predicate. Our own technical convention is that the necessary is weaker than this; it is that for which the separation of the predicate from the subject is impossible whether in itself or due to a matter independent [of the meanings of the extremes] (*aw li-amr munfaṣil*). We do not want to dispute with anyone who interprets it in the stricter sense, since there is no point arguing about expressions. Their further claims about the valuations of propositions, however, cannot stand, because they have interpreted the possible as the contradictory of the necessary, and use it in reductio proofs such that the possible is

> that from the supposition of which no impossibility follows (*anna l-mumkin lā yalzam min farḍihi muḥāl*). But it is not impossible that from the supposition of the possible—on the interpretation they propose—a number of impossibilities may follow, due to the possibility that the essence of the subject may not require the predicate, nor separation from it be impossible in itself, yet its separation from it may be impossible due to an external factor. (*ḤK* 109.5–apu)

The Avicennian purists are using too strong a definition of necessity; in consequence, its dual, possibility, is too weak, at least to be consistent with the method of supposing a possible actual.

Two reflections in concluding this short overview. The first is that the Rāzians accuse Avicenna, or at any rate his thirteenth-century devotees, of using definitions of modal notions that will not work with some of the methods and conclusions they seek to prove. The second—and I think this is the more significant—is that the Rāzians put forward misdirected counterexamples that do not touch Avicenna (as al-Taftāzānī acknowledges in Text 98.2). This is not a sign that they do not understand what Avicenna is doing; rather, it is a sign that they want to replace the program he follows in regimenting natural language for logical treatment with their own program. That program begins to crystallize in Text 45.1.

§45[131] This is the lemma in which al-Kātibī sets out the truth-conditions for the quantified propositions, and he does so under two "considerations," or readings of the subject, the essentialist (*bi-ḥasab al-ḥaqīqah*) and the externalist (*bi-ḥasab al-khārij*). Before considering the distinction between these two readings, al-Taḥtānī offers a number of preliminary reflections on the quantified propositions for which al-Kātibī is presenting truth-conditions; I summarize here some fundamental aspects of these reflections. One aspect is that presentations of this material customarily use dummy terms ("C," "B") rather than concrete terms like "man" or "animal"; this is because, first, it shortens the presentation and, second, if concrete terms were used, "one might imagine that these valuations occur only in this matter (*fī hādhihi l-māddah*),[132] and not in other a-propositions (*dūna l-mūjibāt al-kulliyyāt al-ukhar*)" (*TT* 245.apu–246.2). Another aspect is that the subject and predicate cannot be synonyms (see §13, and commentary on §40); the relation between the subject and the predicate is more complex:

> TEXT 45.1 If we have "every C is B," there are two aspects to consider (*amrān*), one of which is the meaning of C and its reality (*mafhūm jīm wa-ḥaqīqatihi*), the other the individual items (*al-afrād*) of which C is true. [The proposition's] meaning is not that the meaning of C is the meaning of B, otherwise C and B would be two synonymous expressions, so there would be no predication in meaning, but rather [a connection of some kind] in respect of expression. The meaning of [the proposition] is rather that every individual item of which C is true is B. (*TT* 246.pu–247.pu)

Identifying the individual items (*afrād*) of which the meaning C is true involves a number of considerations.

> TEXT 45.2 It is possible that aspects (*al-umūr*) that differ according to meaning may be true of a single essence; so what C is true of is called the essence of the subject (*dhāt al-mawḍūʿ*), and the meaning of C is called the description of the subject and its title (*ʿunwānuhu*) (because the essence of C—that which is judged—is made known as a reality through it just as a book is made known through its title). The title may be the essence itself, as in "every man is an animal" (for the reality of man is exactly the quiddity of Zayd and ʿAmr and Bakr and other individuals); it may be a part of it, as in "every animal is sensate" (for the judgment on ["animal"] is also on Zayd and ʿAmr and other

individuals, and the reality of animal is only a part of [the essence of these things]); and it may be extrinsic to it, as in "every walker is an animal" (for the judgment on it is also on Zayd and ʿAmr and other individuals, and the meaning of "walker" is extrinsic to their quiddities). (*TT* 250.7–251.4)

It is with these considerations in mind that Strobino has coined the term "referential" for the *dhātī* proposition: the subject term is taken insofar as it refers to an essence, whether it is necessarily or only momentarily true of it.[133] Is the subject term taken to refer to that of which it is merely possibly true? According to al-Fārābī, it is, whereas Avicenna insists that the subject term must have been actually true of the things it refers to at least once, "so that what is never C does not enter under [the subject term]."

**Text 45.3** If we say "every black is such and such," the judgment covers everything that is possibly black (even Greeks, for example), according to the view of al-Fārābī, due to the possibility of their being described by blackness; whereas in the view of Avicenna, the judgment does not cover them due to their never having been described by blackness at any time. The view of Avicenna is closer to customary usage (*aqrab ilā l-ʿurf*).[134] (*TT* 253.3–253.7)

The predicate may relate in a number of ways to the essence of which the subject is the title:

**Text 45.4** The description of the predicate may be true of the essence of the subject by necessity, or possibly, or actually, or always, according to what will follow in the investigation of the modal propositions. (*TT* 253.8–9)

With these points in hand, al-Taḥtānī begins his exposition of the essentialist and externalist readings. Before setting out his exposition, let me take a historical detour and say a few words about how the distinction seems to have first come about. The distinction first appears in the work of Fakhr al-Dīn al-Rāzī (*RM* 141.6–10, 142.13–143.1);[135] he used it to distinguish the propositions he wanted to investigate—and which, for the most part, are suitable for interpreting Avicenna's syllogistic (the essentialist reading)—from those he seems to have viewed as logically uninteresting or useless for interpreting Avicenna (the externalist reading). Al-Khūnajī adopted al-Rāzī's distinction, and used almost the same words to describe the essentialist reading (*Ḫ K* 84.14–84.15). But—and this is the important point—al-Khūnajī took the essentialist reading to refer not only to nonexistent things (as al-Rāzī, the first legislator of the reading, intended), but also to the impossible. So "every C—were it to exist—would be insofar as it were to exist a B" includes C of which, for example, a constituent part is denied ("not-animal man"). I am not going to rehearse the arguments for or against this specific interpretation of al-Khūnajī, but it is the reason that al-Kātibī stresses in §45—against al-Khūnajī—that the subject only has to do with "every possible individual" (*jīm min al-afrād al-mumkinah*) (*TT* 254.3–11, 255.12–16). Finally, and here I speculate, it is with al-Khūnajī that the main focus of texts came to settle on propositions under the externalist reading. I take it that the *Risālah* from §48 on is best read using the externalist reading.

What is the utility of these readings, and why are they referred to by the names they have?

> Text 45.5 "Every C is B" is considered at times according to the essence (*bi-ḥasab al-ḥaqīqah*) (whereupon it is called "essentialist," as though the subject is an essence in a proposition used in the sciences), and at other times according to external reality (whereupon it is called "externalist," and what is meant by "external" is what is external to the senses). (*TT* 253.10–13)

Note the common shorthand for the readings used in §50: *al-khārijiyyat al-mawḍūʿ*, *al-ḥaqīqiyyat al-mawḍūʿ*. And here is al-Taḥtānī's exposition of the reading:

> **Text 45.6** We mean by the first everything that, were it to exist, would be C (*law wujida kāna jīm*)[136] among possible individuals (*al-afrād al-mumkinah*), and so would be B, insofar as it were to exist. So the judgment on it[137] is not limited only to what has existence extramentally, but rather to everything whose existence is hypothesized (*quddira*), whether it does or does not exist extramentally. So, if C does not exist, the judgment on it is on its individuals assumed to exist, as in "every phoenix flies." If it does exist, the judgment is not only on its existent individuals, but rather is on them and on its individual items assumed to exist as well, as in "every man is an animal." (*TT* 253.14–254.2)

Al-Kātibī may have decided to reject al-Khūnajī's stipulation that the essentialist reading cover the impossible, but he nonetheless adopted important aspects of al-Khūnajī's further interpretation of the essentialist reading, which is to cast the reading into a form using implicative conditionals (see §60). Al-Kātibī adopts this interpretation in setting out the alternative "the implicant of C is the implicant of B." Here is al-Taḥtānī's account of al-Khūnajī's interpretation, followed by what seems to me a decisive criticism.

> **Text 45.7** Since connection [in the sense of a conditional] (*al-ittiṣāl*) is taken into account in the stipulation [relating to] the subject (*fī ʿaqd al-waḍʿ*)—that is, [with the expression] "were it to exist it would be C" (*law wujida kāna jīm*)—and so too in the stipulation [relating to] the predicate (*fī ʿaqd al-ḥaml*)—that is, "were it to exist it would be B" (*law wujida kāna bāʾ*)—and since connection may be by way of implication (*al-luzūm*), as in "if the sun is up, then it is day,"

and it may be by way of coincidence, as in "if man is rational, then donkeys bray," al-Khūnajī and those who follow him interpret [the subjunctive phrases] as implication. And so they say that "everything such that were it to exist it would be C, is such that were it to exist it would be B" amounts to "everything that is an implicant of C is an implicant of B."

I wish I could understand why they are not content with simple connection (*muṭlaq al-ittiṣāl*), since it follows from their position that most propositions are excluded from their interpretation; because [the implication interpretation] only applies (*lā yanṭabiqu illā*) to a proposition whose subject-description and predicate-description are implicates of the essence under the subject (*lāzimayn li-dhāt al-mawḍūʿ*). A proposition with one or both descriptions not implied [by the essence in this way], however, falls outside [their interpretation]. Further, they are forced to limit propositions to the necessary—since there is no sense to the necessary proposition other than the implication of the predicate description by the essence—indeed, to [propositions] stronger than the necessary, due to the consideration on this understanding of the proposition that the subject description must also be implied by the essence, and its not being taken into account in understanding the necessary proposition. (*TT* 256.1–257.9)

With that, we come to the second of the readings, the externalist (*al-iʿtibār al-khārijī*). For various reasons, it is easier to come to an unproblematically consistent account of syllogistic inferences using propositions under the externalist reading, and—although al-Kātibī never states this explicitly—it is the reading used for the rest of the *Risālah*.

**Text 45.8** What is meant by the second [interpretation of the proposition, the externalist reading,] is every C in extramental reality is B in extramental reality; and the judgment in it is on what exists in extramental reality, whether it is described as C at the time of the judgment or before it or after it (because what never exists extramentally cannot be B extramentally).

He only says "whether at the time of the judgment or before it or after it" to prevent one imagining (*dafʿan li-tawahhum*) that the meaning of "C is B" is describing C with B-ness at the time of its being described with C-ness. For the judgment on it is not upon the description of C such that it is necessary that it be realized extramentally at the same time the judgment is realized. Rather [it should be realized] for the essence of C, so the judgment only claims that it belongs [to that essence]. It is not necessary that describing [the essence of C] (*ittiṣāfuhu*) with C-ness be realized at the time of the realization of the judgment (*fa-lā yajibu taḥaqququhu ḥāl taḥaqquq al-ḥukm*). So if we say "every writer laughs," it is not among the conditions on the essence under "writer" as subject that it be writing at the time of its being described as laughing; rather, it is sufficient for [the truth of the proposition] that it be described with being-a-writer (*bi-l-kātibiyyah*) at a certain time. Thus, our statement "every sleeper wakes" is true; if the sleeper is described with the two descriptions, it is only at two [different] times. (*TT* 257.16–258.pu)

Let me underline the last stipulation. It is true to say "every sleeper is awake" because the things described at some moment by "sleeper" are at another moment awake.

One objection raised against these two accounts of the subject term is that they fail to deal with every proposition used in philosophical discourse. Consider the proposition—true as far as the participants in this debate are concerned—that "the cocreator is impossible."[138] This proposition cannot be expressed under the essentialist reading as al-Kātibī stipulates it, because "cocreator" is not among items that are possible (*min al-afrād al-mumkinah*); nor can it be expressed under the externalist reading because it has at no time existed extramentally.

> **Text 45.9** It is not to be said here [that these are] propositions which cannot be taken in either of the two ways, and they are those whose subjects are impossible, like "the partner of the Creator is impossible" and "every impossible is nonexistent"; and the art [of logic] (*al-fann*) should have general rules (*qawāʿid ʿāmmah*). Because we say: People do not claim all propositions are limited to either the externalist or the essentialist, but rather claim that the propositions used in the sciences are taken for the most part under one of the two considerations. Therefore, people set them down and extract their rules (*aḥkāmahumā*) that these propositions may thereby be of benefit in the sciences. The rules (*aḥkām*) for the propositions that cannot be taken under one these two considerations are not yet known; generalization of rules (*taʿmīm al-qawāʿid*) is only according to human capacity. (*TT* 258.u–260.1)

Some of the arguments about one- and two-premise modal inferences come down to how the subject term is understood, others to whether there is a real distinction between a perpetuity proposition and a necessity. By and large, from the time of al-Rāzī, a critique had developed against inconsistencies in Avicenna's account of the subject term, perhaps best summarized by al-Khūnajī, basing his criticism on inferences Avicenna is—or should be—committed to in his modal syllogistic, which are, however, inconsistent:

> **Text 45.10** Perhaps Avicenna hesitated over the conversion of actuality propositions (*al-fiʿliyyāt*) as either possible or

absolute propositions just because of his hesitation over technical usage. And so, when he says that they convert as possible propositions, he does not consider affirmation in actuality with respect to the subject; and when he says that they convert as absolute propositions, he does.[139] (*ḪK* 145.11–pu)

Much of al-Ḥillī's commentary on syllogistic inferences is directed to showing that there is no such inconsistency, and moreover that the later scholars fail to understand the argument, which works on the hypothesis that the possible occurs (*ʿalā taqdīr wuqūʿ al-mumkin*). For the moment, let me draw attention to the arguments al-Ḥillī advances for an alternative account of the subject term. Al-Ḥillī attacks shortcomings in al-Kātibī's account of the essentialist reading in dealing with the mental proposition (see Text 45.9 above); he also agrees with al-Taḥtānī that the alternative interpretation ("every implicant of C is an implicant of B") is vulnerable. He notes, further, that Avicenna has already rejected the externalist reading, presumably expecting his reader to find Avicenna's argument cogent:

**Text 45.11** The externalist proposition is the doctrine of a certain ancient scholar, and Avicenna in the *Cure* rejected it as folly (*nasabahu ilā l-sakhāfah*); he explained its falsity (*buṭlānahu*) by arguing that if we mean by "every C" what is C among the individuals that occur at a given time, it is only some of C, not all of it. (*ḤQ* 254.16–pu)

Al-Ḥillī concludes by restating Avicenna's position as he understands it:

**Text 45.12** Know that the meaning common among most people for "every C is B" is that every single thing of which C is said—whether verified or posited (*immā taḥqīqan wa-immā farḍan*), whether the C-ness is its essence (*dhātahu*) or its attribute (*ṣifatahu*), whether perpetually or not, whether existent externally or in the intellect or in mental supposition, and given that it is not impossible of existence in itself (*li-dhātihi*)—is a B. On this understanding, impossibilities do not enter under the subject, nor does what is only potentially C (unless it is assumed to be C). If the subject is impossible of existence, as for example the void and the atom (*al-jawhar*), it may be understood according to the opinion of someone who holds that it is not impossible; on being described as actually existing externally, as a vacuum and an atom, judgment is made of it insofar as what would be judged of it if it were like that.

This is a verification of this subject (*taḥqīq hādhā l-mawḍūʿ*), and we have gone on at length here due to the error of the author and a group of later scholars with respect to it. (*ḤQ* 254.u–255.9)

§46[140] This lemma and the next are devoted entirely to the implicational relations among the different quantified propositions under the two readings. This lemma deals with a-propositions under the two different readings. There are situations in which both propositions—the essentialist and the externalist—are true, but there are also situations in which one is true and the other is not. It is not possible to assume that one is true (or false) on the basis that the other is true (or false). Note that al-Ḥillī makes these implicational relations specific to al-Kātibī's usage.

Text 46.1 On al-Kātibī's technical usage, what distinguishes the absolute essentialist from the absolute externalist is that each one may be true while the other is not.

The essentialist may be true without the externalist because, were we to suppose there were never any squares in external existence, "every square is a figure" would be true [as an essentialist]. This is because were a square to exist it would be a figure (and you know that no existence is stipulated for this [to be true]); but the externalist would be false, due to the stipulation that its subject exist externally. The externalist may be true without the essentialist because, were we to suppose that the figures in external existence were limited to squares, "every figure is a square" would be true as an externalist proposition, because every figure externally would be a square externally. But the essentialist proposition would be false, because the triangle, were it to exist, would be, insofar as it were to exist, a figure, yet insofar as it were to exist, it would not be a square.

Neither of the two a-propositions is implicationally weaker (*aʿamm*) than the other; rather, they overlap in truth-conditions. This is so due to the difference between the cases in which they are true (*li-ftirāqihimā fī l-ṣidq*) given above, and their [common] truth in every matter for whose individuals it is impossible that there exist anything other than what exists externally. (*ḤQ* 255.14–256.8)

§47[141] Whereas neither a-proposition under one of the two readings implies the other—which is to say, neither is stronger (*akhaṣṣ*) than the other—in both e- and i-propositions, one proposition is stronger than the other. So, if the externalist i-proposition is true, the essentialist i-proposition with the same terms must be true, but not the other way round (see Figure 22); and if the essentialist e-proposition is true, the externalist e-proposition with the same terms must be true, but not the other way round (see Figure 23). Finally, al-Ḥillī claims that if the o-proposition is true in either reading, it will be true in the other.

**Text 47.1** The essentialist i-proposition is weaker than its a-proposition, and than the externalist a- and i-propositions. The essentialist e-proposition is stronger than[142] the externalist e-proposition (because whenever the essentialist e-proposition is true, so is the externalist e-proposition, the members (*afrād*) of its subject being some of the members of the essentialist). The converse is not the case, due to the truth of the externalist e-proposition in the example we have given (limiting figures to squares); for it may be true that "no figure is a triangle" as an externalist, but not as an essentialist e-proposition, because some of that which, were it to exist, would be a figure, would be, insofar as it were to exist, a triangle. The o-propositions [in the two readings] imply each other (*wa-l-sālibatān al-juz'iyyatān mutalāzimatān*). (*ḤQ* 256.9–15)

I worry there is an error in the text recording the last claim, and I have left it out of Figure 23. Consider "some figures are not triangles" in a world in which the only figures are triangles; the proposition is true as an essentialist, but false as an externalist. I agree with al-Taftāzānī on this (and his treatment incidentally shows how insights from §§26 and 27 can be put to use).

**Text 47.2** The essentialist i-proposition is weaker than the externalist i-proposition (*aʿamm min al-khārijiyyah muṭlaqan*), because the judgment on some externally existent individuals is a judgment on the individuals hypothesized to exist [for the essentialist reading], but not the reverse (because it is possible that there is no externally existent individual, so the predicate will not be affirmed of it [as an externalist proposition]). The externalist e-proposition is weaker [than the essentialist e-proposition] because the contradictory of the stronger is weaker. There is partial disjunction between the two o-propositions[143] (as is the status of the contradictories of overlapping terms) (*ḥukm naqīḍ al-ʿumūm min wajh*).[144] (*TŠ* 224.9–pu)

**The third discussion, on the indefinite and the determinate**

The next three lemmata discuss the distinction between propositions with at least one term negated by a nominal negation (as against propositional negation introduced in §41), and propositions with both terms positive and determinate (*wujūdī muḥaṣṣal*). It parallels Avicenna's discussion in *Pointers* 3.7 (*AI* 27.9–29.2), though al-Kātibī does not even mention the question of the relation between expressions like "not-seeing" and "blind" and the range of subjects of which they are legitimately predicated.[145] The discussion in §50 underlines one aspect of the truth-conditions of affirmative and negative propositions (that the subject of a true affirmative proposition exists, already touched on in the discussion of externalist propositions), an aspect that plays a role in the discussion of conversion, contraposition, and the fourth figure.

§48[146] The criterion that distinguishes a proposition as metathetic (*maʿdūlah*) is whether one or both of its extremes is indefinite. Al-Kātibī gives two examples, the first of a proposition with an indefinite subject ("the not-living is inanimate"),[147] the second of a proposition with a retracted predicate ("the inanimate is not-knowing"). Al-Taḥtānī defends al-Kātibī's decision not to give a third example with both terms indefinite because the examples given show how each term is made indefinite (*TT* 264.3–5). Al-Taḥtānī explains the use of the term *maʿdūlah*.

> **Text 48.1** It is only called "modified" (*maʿdūlah*) because the particles of negation, such as *laysa* and *ghayr* and *lā*, were imposed originally on negation and removal (*li-l-salb wa-l-rafʿ*); if they are set down with another [expression] as a single thing of which it is affirmed that something belongs to it, or that it belongs to something else, or of which something is negated, or that it does not belong to something else, then [the expression] has been modified by [the

negative particle] (*ʿudila bi-hi*) from its original imposition to something else. (*TT* 263.pu–264.2)

Propositions that have both terms positive and determinate (*wujūdī muḥaṣṣal*) are determinate (*muḥaṣṣalah*) if affirmative, and—for al-Kātibī at least—simple (*basīṭah*) if negative; his name for the negative may derive from the simplicity of its terms (*TT* 264.9–12). Al-Kātibī gives no examples for it because all the examples of negative propositions up to now (which is to say, the examples in §§41 and 42) are simple.

§49[148] Al-Kātibī recurs to the test for a negative proposition (given in §41) to ensure that the presence of nominal negation—that is, the negation in an indefinite term—does not mislead his readers.

Text 49.1 You have already come to know that affirmation is projecting a relation [between subject and predicate] (*īqāʿ al-nisbah*) and negation is removing it (*rafʿuhā*), so the important consideration in whether a proposition is affirmative or negative is in the projection or removal of the relation, and not in [the proposition's] two extremes. (*TT* 265.5–6)

§50[149] It is with this lemma that the discussion moves beyond definitional matters. Al-Kātibī only deals with metathetic propositions that have an indefinite predicate and a positive and determinate subject; in fact, he only deals with the implicational relations between the metathetic affirmative proposition and the simple negative. The commentators begin by explaining why he limits himself in this way.

Text 50.1 The reason for focusing on the second [that is, the difference between the metathetic affirmative and the simple negative] is that taking indefiniteness

> and determination into account in the predicate leads to a four-fold division . . . determinate affirmative, like "Zayd is a writer"; determinate negative, like "Zayd is not a writer"; metathetic affirmative, like "Zayd is a not-writer"; and metathetic negative, like "Zayd is not a not-writer." (*TT* 267.5–12)

Al-Taḥtānī argues that, of the six possible ways these propositions can be paired, confusion can only arise between the determinate (or simple) negative and the metathetic affirmative; this is the only pair in which both propositions have exactly the same number of particles of negation.

The two propositions can be confused not just because of matters to do with expression (*lafẓī*), but also because of those that are semantic (*maʿnawī*).

> **Text 50.2** The semantic [difference between the two] is that the simple negative is implicationally weaker (*aʿamm*) than the affirmative with an indefinite predicate, which is to say, when the affirmative with an indefinite predicate is true, so is the simple negative, but not [necessarily] the reverse. (*TT* 268.8–10)

This is because—and this may be the first time this aspect of the semantics of affirmative propositions has come up in the *Risālah* itself—neither the a- nor i-proposition is true unless the subject exists, whereas the e- and o-propositions are true if the subject does not exist, or if the subject exists and all (or some, in the case of the o-proposition) of the items that come under it are such that the predicate is not true of them. So "every Martian is not-green" is true only if there are Martians and they are not green, whereas "no Martian is green" is true if there are no Martians, or if they are not green.

Al-Kātibī immediately goes on to clarify that this implicational relation holds for both readings of the proposition that have just been set out in §§45–47; that is, the externalist and the essentialist.

**Text 50.3** [Al-Kātibī's text here] is as though it is an answer to a question that has been posed—namely, if you mean by the phrase "affirmation invokes the existence of the subject" that affirmation invokes the existence of the subject in external reality (*fī l-khārij*), then the essentialist affirmative is fundamentally never true, because the judgment in it is not limited to subjects that exist in external reality. (*TT* 270.11–14)

I conclude with the summary al-Ḥillī offers on implication and indefinite terms.

**Text 50.4** The result of this (*al-ḥāṣil*) is that if the two propositions differ in quality and agree in indefiniteness and determination, they contradict; and if [the situation] is the reverse, they cannot be true together as affirmatives or false together as negatives; and if they differ in these two considerations, then the affirmative is stronger than the negative. (*ḤQ* 258.14–16)

Which is to make the following claims: (1) "A is not-B" is the contradictory of "A is not not-B"; (2a) "A is B" and "A is not-B" cannot be true together but they can be false together; (2b) "A is not B" and "A is not not-B" cannot be false together but they can be true together; and (3) "A is B" implies "A is not not-B," but not the reverse.

The distinction in expression between these propositions is sensitive to whether the proposition used is three-part or two-part (see the distinction in §40). If three-part, what matters is where the negative particle comes with respect to the copula; if two-part, what matters is whether the negative particle is one specifically set aside for nominal or propositional negation.

## The fourth discussion, on modal propositions

**§51**[150] In the fourth discussion, al-Kātibī develops further the fundamental aspects of modal logic. With this lemma, al-Kātibī deals with issues that Avicenna deals with in *Pointers* 4.1 (*AI* 32.1–10). Al-Kātibī does not use the term, but he analyzes the proposition here as four-part (*rubāʿiyyah*), completing the analysis into two-part (*thunāʾiyyah*) and three-part (*thulāthiyyah*) he began in §40. A four-part proposition will make the copula explicit in the way it is expressed, and also the modality by which the predicate belongs to the subject.

> **Text 51.1** We have already explained that the proposition comprises three parts: that on which judgment is passed, the judgment made on it, and the relation between the two. Know now that the relation, whether affirmative or negative, inevitably has a quality (*kayfiyyah*) in the fact of the matter (*fī nafs al-amr*), which is necessity or perpetuity, nonnecessity or non-perpetuity, or others that arise; in the fact of the matter, a proposition cannot be without this quality. This quality is called the matter of the proposition. What is understood (*al-maʿqūl*) or expressed (*al-malfūẓ*) of this quality is called the mode of the proposition. For example, the relation of ANIMAL to MAN in the fact of the matter is necessary (*al-wujūb*). Suppose we were not aware of this quality, the relation in what we understand would be the relation of general possibility; then the mode of the proposition would differ from the matter on one kind of consideration. (*ḤQ* 259.apu–260.7)

Al-Kātibī is not limiting matter and its corresponding modes to the four he lists in the lemma (*TŠ* 232.2); they are given by way of example. Every proposition, even if expressed as a two-part proposition, has in itself both a copula and a mode. Although contingent matter is expressed as *māddat al-imkān*, and remote or impossible matter is expressed as *māddat al-imtināʿ*, note that natural or necessary matter is expressed as *māddat al-wujūb*, which is to say, it is signified by a term different from the term signifying the mode.

Al-Ḥillī in Text 51.1 may not be setting out al-Kātibī's position on the topic in exact terms; he claims that "what is understood or expressed . . . is called the mode," whereas al-Kātibī stipulates that "the expression signifying" the matter of the proposition is the mode. On the face of it, al-Kātibī takes a mode to be an expression signifying the matter of the proposition, not an expression signifying what the speaker takes to be the matter.

> Text 51.2 According to the technical usage of the ancients, matter is the quality of the affirmative relation in terms of necessity, possibility, and impossibility, and mode is the expression signifying what someone considers to be the quality of that relation, whether it is the matter itself, or more general or more particular than it, or distinct from it. So the mode on this understanding can also differ from the matter in the true proposition, as "man is an animal by one-sided possibility" so the matter is necessary (*al-wujūb*) and the mode is something more general than [necessity]. Since the technical usage of the ancients is not adequate to providing a detailed account of propositions, the later scholars modified it (*ʿadala ʿanhu*). (*TŠ* 233.12–234.1)

Finally, let me draw attention to two other uses of *māddah* in the *Risālah*. The first came earlier, in commentary on §45, where al-Taḥtānī says that al-Kātibī uses dummy letters rather than concrete terms to avoid the misconception that the logical point is specific to a certain matter; al-Taḥtānī is using "matter" simply to refer to the concrete terms of a proposition. Here in §51, in dealing with propositional matter, the relation between the meanings of the subject term and the predicate term is assessed as a function of the necessity, possibility, and impossibility of the semantic relation between the two (irrespective of the person asserting the relation). Later, from §116 on, the notion of syllogistic matter (*mawādd al-aqyisah*) is introduced. There, the relation between the meanings of the subject and the predicate is assessed in terms of epistemic considerations, dealing with how we came to bring the meanings into relation with each other, and how certain we can be that we were right to do so.

§52[151] After al-Rāzī, it became common to speak of "the thirteen propositions into which it is usual to inquire"; that is, the thirteen modal propositions that are central to al-Kātibī's investigation. A few more over and above the thirteen come up in the discussion as their contradictories, or as conclusions to inferences, but do not make it onto the "official" list.[152] In Appendix 1, I offer a unified list of the propositions in the order al-Kātibī presents them, the way they are referred to by Rescher in his groundbreaking work (which I adopt for the translation of the *Risālah*, and of the commentators),[153] and the way Strobino refers to corresponding propositions in Avicenna's work.[154] In Appendix 2, I offer a fuller list, with these thirteen propositions set out in AEIO forms, along with other propositions assumed or referred to by al-Kātibī but not among the thirteen.

A few points should be made before the propositions are presented. The first has to do with how the modal propositions are generated. Taking four modalities and four temporality conditions as primitives allows the generation of fourteen simple propositions; these may then be made into compound propositions. The modalities are (1) necessity (**L**), (2) perpetuity (**A**), (3) actuality (**X**), and (4) possibility (**M**). (3) "C is at least once B" deserves special mention. The *muṭlaqah* proposition—*muṭlaqah* is used to translate the term for the assertoric proposition in Aristotle's *Prior Analytics*—has the elided temporal operator, "at least once."

Al-Kātibī never devotes a section of the *Risālah* to set out the temporality conditions, though they come up throughout the presentation of the modal propositions that begins at §52. Here is how al-Kātibī's colleague al-Ṭūsī introduces them in his commentary on Avicenna's *Pointers*, where they are gathered and formalized. A proposition may be under a condition (*mashrūṭah*):

> TEXT 52.1 Either [1] by the duration of the existence of the essence (*dhāt*) of the subject, or [2] by the duration of the existence of the description of the subject set down with the subject, or [3] by the duration of the predicate as predicate. These three are conditioned by what is included in the proposition. Or it can be [4] according to a definite time, or [5] according to an indefinite time; these two are conditioned by what is extrinsic to the proposition. It is as though [Avicenna] says that a condition is either intrinsic or extrinsic to the proposition. The intrinsic [condition] is either connected to the subject or connected to the predicate. What is connected to the subject is either [the subject] itself, or a description set down with it. [The condition] connected to the predicate is one thing, because [the predicate] is also a description and it has no essence distinct from that of the subject. The extrinsic is relative either to a definite time, or to an indefinite time. (*ṬḤ* 265.5–266.3)

The temporality conditions that matter for al-Kātibī are (1) as long as the substance underlying the subject term exists (no symbol, the referential reading), (2) as long as the substance underlying the subject term is described by the subject term (subscripted **D**), (4) at a specified time (subscripted **T**), and (5) at some unspecified time (subscripted **X**). Simple propositions can be conjoined with other simple propositions to form compound propositions, such as two-sided possibility, "every C is possibly B and possibly not B"; being two-sided is noted with a subscripted 2 (except for the nonnecessary existential, $\mathbf{X}_{\sim\mathbf{L}}$; $\mathbf{M}_2$ might be better as $\mathbf{M}_{\sim\mathbf{L}}$).

Obviously, with the four modalities, the four temporality conditions, and the possibility of forming compound propositions, many more than just thirteen propositions can be constructed. How did the thirteen propositions presented in the *Risālah* come to be the ones traditionally investigated? There is a story here (about interpretive preferences), but this is how al-Khūnajī puts it after setting out the conditions and modalities:

> **Text 52.2** If you know this much about the differentiation of propositions according to their modalities, you can take account of the modality however you like and construct propositions from them as much as you want. Those about which we shall speak, the propositions mentioned with respect to their conversions and contradictories and syllogistic reasoning (whether in simple or mixed [modal premise sets]) are thirteen; you will know from them the valuations of the remainder of those mentioned, and of others that can be constructed from them. (*Ḫ̮K* 104.7–11)

Al-Rāzī also mentions thirteen propositions; I think he may be the first to have come to this set. In any event, he speaks of these thirteen when he comes to deal with syllogisms with mixed modality premises in the *Mulakhkhaṣ*:

> **Text 52.3** You have come to know that the propositions make up fifteen species, but we will not devote attention to the strongest possible proposition or the future possible proposition, because anyone who knows the valuations of the one-sided and two-sided possible propositions in the four figures will find it easy to account for the valuations of the other two [possible propositions], except in some rare cases for which such consideration must be defined. We take account of the valuation of the remaining propositions. (*RM* 272.4–apu)

For my comments, but not for the translation, I have adopted a number of conventions from Paul Thom's *Medieval Modal Systems* and extended them to deal with the propositions customarily investigated in the Arabic logical tradition. In consequence, a proposition in which a property is said to belong necessarily to a subject is not referred to as a "necessary proposition" but a "necessity proposition," and one in which a property is said to belong possibly to a subject is not referred to as a "possible proposition" but a "possibility proposition." I extend this terminology to the temporal modalities of the Arabic logicians, and refer to a proposition asserting that a property always belongs to a subject as a "perpetuity proposition." Were "actuality proposition" not the obvious way to translate *fiʿliyyah*, that would be how I would refer to the *muṭlaqah*; in the event, I have continued with Rescher's "absolute."

For my comments (but, again, not for the translations), I tend to a convention Thom institutes that respects natural English usage, whereby he gives the modality in negative propositions as the dual of the modality in the affirmative propositions. So the necessity (**L**) a-proposition is "every C is necessarily B," but its e-proposition is "no C is possibly B"; similarly, its i-proposition is "some C is necessarily B," while its o-proposition is "some C is not possibly B." The possibility ($\mathbf{M_1}$) a-proposition is "every C is possibly B," its e-proposition is "no C is necessarily B," its i-proposition is "some C is possibly B," and its o-proposition is "some C is not necessarily B." This convention may be extended from the alethic ("necessarily," "possibly") to the temporal modalities ("always," "at least once"). Thus, the perpetuity (**A**) a-proposition is "every C is always B," its e-proposition is "no C is ever B," its i-proposition is "some C is always B," and its o-proposition is "some C is not ever B." So too, the absolute ($\mathbf{X_1}$) a-proposition is "every C is at least once B," its e-proposition is "no C is always B," its i-proposition is "some C is at least once B," and its o-proposition is "some C is not always B."

The compound propositions (or two-sided, or "special": *al-khāṣṣah*) are simple propositions conjoined with a rider agreeing in quantity and disagreeing in quality. If it is a two-sided possibility proposition ($\mathbf{M_2}$) or a nonnecessary absolute proposition ($\mathbf{X_{\sim L}}$), the rider is a possibility proposition; in every other case (for al-Kātibī) it is an absolute proposition. If the compound proposition is an i- or o-proposition, the second conjunct must be understood to refer to the individuals under the subject of the first conjunct; for example: "some Cs are at least once B while C, and those same Cs are not always B" (see §71). The compound is expressed in the shorthand: "some Cs are at least once B while C, not always." I often expand this shorthand in my comments.

I follow al-Kātibī's order of exposition from §52 on, going on at the end of §52 and §59 to mention simple and compound propositions beyond the thirteen that come up later. For the relative strength of the propositions, see Figures 24 and 25.[155] In introducing each proposition, I give Strobino's symbolic name for the proposition (or a lightly modified alternative), followed by Rescher's translation of the Arabic term, the Arabic term, and Strobino's alternative term. I then give the examples of the a- and e-propositions from my translation of the *Risālah*, followed by a second English version I take to be more idiomatic, and then the original Arabic. In the second appendix, I set out a summary of all four quantified propositions in each modality.

1. **L**: absolute necessary proposition (*ḍarūriyyah muṭlaqah*); referential necessity.

Necessarily, every man is an animal (every man is necessarily an animal; *bi-l-ḍarūrah kull insān ḥayawān*); necessarily, no man is a stone (no man is possibly a stone; *bi-l-ḍarūrah lā shay' min al-insān bi-ḥajar*).

2. **A**: absolute perpetual proposition (*dā'imah muṭlaqah*); referential perpetuity.

Always, every man is an animal (every man is always an animal; *dā'iman kull insān ḥayawān*); always, no man is a stone (no man is ever a stone; *dā'iman lā shay' min al-insān bi-ḥajar*).

3. **L**$_{D1}$: general conditional (*mashrūṭah ʿāmmah*); descriptional unrestricted necessity.

Necessarily, every writer moves his fingers as long as he is writing (everyone writing necessarily moves his fingers as long as he is writing; *bi-l-ḍarūrah kull kātib mutaḥarrik al-aṣābiʿ mā dāma kātiban*); necessarily, no writer has his fingers still as long as he is writing (no one writing possibly has his fingers still as long as he is writing; *bi-l-ḍarūrah lā shayʾ min al-kātib bi-sākin al-aṣābiʿ mā dāma kātiban*).

4. **A**$_{D1}$: general conventional (*ʿurfiyyah ʿāmmah*); descriptional unrestricted perpetuity.

Always, every writer moves his fingers as long as he is writing (everyone writing always moves his fingers as long as he is writing; *dāʾiman kull kātibin mutaḥarrik al-aṣābiʿ mā dāma kātiban*); always, no writer has his fingers still as long as he is writing (no one writing ever has his fingers still as long as he is writing; *dāʾiman lā shayʾ min al-kātib bi-sākin al-aṣābiʿ mā dāma kātiban*). Note that *dāʾiman* is normally left out (for example, *ḤQ* 296.4), being understood from the *mā dāma*.

Al-Kātibī's examples of descriptional necessity and perpetuity propositions have denominative subjects and predicates. The descriptional is able to display predicates that necessarily or always belong to a subject under a given description, but perhaps do not belong necessarily or always to the underlying substance of which the subject term is the title (*ʿunwān*; see Text 45.2 above). But the descriptional is still true with univocal subject and predicate (it is implied by, but does not imply, the referential, so it is weaker (*aʿamm*) than the referential): "every man is necessarily an animal as long as he is described as a man." It does not come up in the *Risālah*, but the default proposition in Avicennian demonstration theory is **A**$_{D1}$, the descriptional perpetuity proposition (for example, Avicenna, *Najāt* [*AN* §§123, 133]).[156]

5. $\mathbf{X}_1$: general absolute (*muṭlaqah ʿāmmah*); referential one-sided absoluteness.

By general absoluteness, every man is breathing (every man is at least once breathing; *bi-l-iṭlāq al-ʿāmm kull insān mutanaffis*); by general absoluteness, no man is breathing (no man is always breathing; *bi-l-iṭlāq al-ʿāmm lā shayʾ min al-insān bi-mutanaffis*). Variants: §55: *kull insān ḍāḥik bi-l-fiʿl* (every man actually laughs).

6. $\mathbf{M}_1$: general possible (*mumkinah ʿāmmah*); referential one-sided possibility.

By general possibility, every fire is hot (every fire is possibly hot; *bi-l-imkān al-ʿāmm kull nār ḥārrah*); by general possibility, no fire is cold (no fire is necessarily cold; *bi-l-imkān al-ʿāmm lā shayʾ min al-nār bi-bārid*).

Al-Kātibī explicitly or implicitly calls on eight further simple propositions (numbered as given in the second appendix).

14. $\mathbf{L}_{T1}$: absolute temporal (*al-waqtiyyah al-muṭlaqah*); assumed in working out the contradictories for $\mathbf{L}_{T2}$ as one of its component propositions, and also the conclusion to some first-figure syllogistic mixes.

Necessarily, every C is B at time T (every C is necessarily B at time T; *kull jīm bāʾ bi-l-ḍarūrah fī waqt muʿayyan*); necessarily, no C is B at time T (no C is possibly B at time T; *lā shayʾ min jīm bāʾ bi-l-ḍarūrah fī waqt muʿayyan*).

15. $\mathbf{L}_{X1}$: absolute spread (*al-muntashirah al-muṭlaqah*); assumed in working out the contradictories for $\mathbf{L}_{X2}$ as one of its component propositions, and also the conclusion to some first-figure syllogistic mixes.

Necessarily, every C is B at some time (every C is necessarily B at some time; *kull jīm bāʾ bi-l-ḍarūrah fī waqt mā*); necessarily, no C is B at time T (no C is possibly B at time T; *lā shayʾ min jīm bāʾ bi-l-ḍarūrah fī waqt mā*).

16. $\mathbf{X}_{T1}$: temporal absolute (*al-muṭlaqah al-waqtiyyah*); conclusion in some first- and second-figure mixes.

By general absoluteness, every C is B at time T (every C is actually B at time T; *kull jīm bāʾ bi-l-fiʿl fī waqt muʿayyan*); by general absoluteness, no C is B at time T (no C is actually B at time T; *lā shayʾ min jīm bāʾ bi-l-fiʿl fī waqt muʿayyan*).

17. $\mathbf{X}_{X1}$: spread absolute (*al-muṭlaqah al-muntashirah*); a conclusion in some first- and second-figure mixes.

By general absoluteness, every C is B at some time (every C is actually B at some time; *kull jīm bāʾ bi-l-fiʿl fī waqt mā*); by general absoluteness, no C is B at some time (no C is actually B at some time; *lā shayʾ min jīm bāʾ bi-l-fiʿl fī waqt mā*).

18. $\mathbf{M}_{T1}$: temporal possible (*al-mumkinah al-waqtiyyah*); given as contradictory of $\mathbf{L}_{T1}$, a component of $\mathbf{L}_{T2}$. The Arabic is given for the o-proposition in *ḤQ* 296.12–14, though with *fī dhālika l-waqt* for *fī waqt muʿayyan*.

Possibly, every C is B at time T (every C is possibly B at time T; *kull jīm bāʾ bi-l-imkān fī waqt muʿayyan*); possibly, no C is B at time T (no C is necessarily B at time T; *lā shayʾ min jīm bāʾ bi-l-imkān fī waqt muʿayyan*).

19. $\mathbf{M}_{A}$: perpetual possible (*al-mumkinah al-dāʾimah*); given as contradictory of $\mathbf{L}_{X1}$, a component of $\mathbf{L}_{X2}$. The Arabic is given

for the o-proposition in *ḤQ* 296.15–16, where, however, it is given as the possible perpetual (*al-dāʾimah al-mumkinah*); I have followed the name for it given in *ḪK* 126.11, and Rescher and vander Nat, "Theory of Modal Syllogistic," 25.

Always, every C is possibly B (*kull jīm bāʾ bi-l-imkān dāʾiman*); always, no C is necessarily B (*lā shayʾ min jīm bāʾ bi-l-imkān dāʾiman*).

20. $\mathbf{X_{D1}}$: absolute continuing (*al-ḥīniyyah al-muṭlaqah*); given as the contradictory of $\mathbf{A_{D1}}$, and as the conclusion to a number of third- and fourth-figure syllogistic mixes. The *ḥīna*-clause is given in some examples as *fī baʿḍ awqāt kawnihi jīm*, as for example in §69.3: "Everyone afflicted with pleurisy may cough at times while afflicted" (*kull man bi-hi dhāt al-janb yumkinu an yasʿala fī baʿḍ awqāt kawnihi majnūban*). *Bi-l-iṭlāq al-ʿāmm* could be put at the beginning or end of the proposition.

Every C is [at least once] B while it is C (every C is at least once B while C; *kull jīm bāʾ ḥīna huwa jīm*); no C is [always] B while it is C (no C is always B while C; *lā shayʾ min jīm bāʾ ḥīna huwa jīm*).

21. $\mathbf{M_{D1}}$: possible continuing (*al-ḥīniyyah al-mumkinah*); given as the contradictory of $\mathbf{L_{D1}}$. As with $\mathbf{X_{D1}}$, the *ḥīna*-clause can be replaced with *fī baʿḍ awqāt kawnihi jīm; bi-l-imkān al-ʿāmm* can be replaced as in the example given for 19; alternatively, below it would be replaced by the modalized copula, *yumkinu an yakūna.*

Every C is possibly B while C (*bi-l-imkān al-ʿāmm kull jīm bāʾ ḥīna huwa jīm*); no C is necessarily B while C (*bi-l-imkān al-ʿāmm lā shayʾ min jīm bāʾ ḥīna huwa jīm*).

Both $\mathbf{X_{D1}}$ and $\mathbf{M_{D1}}$ are stronger than their corresponding referential propositions (that is, $\mathbf{X_1}$ and $\mathbf{M_2}$), because they stipulate not only that the predicate holds of what underlies the subject in a given way, but also that it holds of what underlies the subject in a given way at some time that the subject is true of it.

§53[157] The compound propositions are made up of one of the simple modals conjoined with a second proposition that is, first, taken to be anaphorically linked to the same items under the subject of the first proposition (see §71). Second, it is a one-sided possibility proposition (**M**$_1$) when the compound proposition as a whole is said to be nonnecessary—that is, for the general possibility (**M**$_2$) and the nonnecessary existential (**X**$_{\sim L}$)—and otherwise a one-sided absolute (**X**$_1$). Finally, it is the same quantity but the opposite quality of the proposition it restricts (§59.2).

7. **L**$_{D2}$: special conditional (*mashrūṭah khāṣṣah*); descriptional restricted necessity.

Necessarily, every writer moves his fingers as long as he is writing, not always (everyone writing necessarily moves his fingers as long as he is writing, and no writer is always moving his fingers; *bi-l-ḍarūrah kull kātib mutaḥarrik al-aṣābiʿ mā dāma kātiban lā dāʾiman*); necessarily, no writer has his fingers still as long as he is writing, not always (no one writing possibly has his fingers still as long as he is writing, and every writer at least once has his fingers still; *bi-l-ḍarūrah lā shayʾ min al-kātib bi-sākin al-aṣābiʿ mā dāma kātiban lā dāʾiman*).

§54[158]

8. **A**$_{D2}$: special conventional (*ʿurfiyyah khāṣṣah*); descriptional restricted perpetuity.

Always, every writer moves his fingers as long as he is writing, not always (everyone writing always moves his fingers as long as he is writing, and no writer is always moving his fingers; *dāʾiman kull kātib mutaḥarrik al-aṣābiʿ mā dāma kātiban lā dāʾiman*); always, no writer has his fingers still as long as he is writing, not always (no one writing ever has his fingers still as long as he is writing, and every writer at least once has his fingers still; *dāʾiman lā shayʾ min al-kātib bi-sākin al-aṣābiʿ mā dāma kātiban lā dāʾiman*).

§55[159]

9. $\mathbf{X}_{\sim L}$: nonnecessary existential (*wujūdiyyah lā-ḍarūriyyah*); referential nonnecessary absoluteness.

Every man is actually laughing, not necessarily (every man is at least once laughing, and no man is necessarily laughing; *kull insān ḍāḥik bi-l-fiʿl lā bi-l-ḍarūrah*); no man is actually laughing, not necessarily (no man is always laughing, and every man is possibly laughing; *lā shayʾ min al-insān ḍāḥik bi-l-fiʿl lā bi-l-ḍarūrah*).

§56[160]

10. $\mathbf{X}_2$: non-perpetual existential (*wujūdiyyah lā-dāʾimah*); referential two-sided absoluteness.

Every man is actually laughing, not always (every man is at least once laughing, and no man is always laughing; *kullu insān ḍāḥik bi-l-fiʿl lā dāʾiman*); no man is actually laughing, not necessarily (no man is always laughing, and every man is at least once laughing; *lā shayʾ min al-insān ḍāḥik bi-l-fiʿl lā dāʾiman*). As with the two-sided possibility proposition, a- and e-propositions are made up of the same components but in reverse order. (Al-Kātibī gives no examples here; those I offer are modified from the preceding proposition.)

§57[161]

11. $\mathbf{L}_{T2}$: temporal (*waqtiyyah*); referential temporal determinate.

Necessarily, every moon is eclipsed at the time of the earth's coming between it and the sun, not always (every moon is necessarily eclipsed at the time of the earth's coming between it and the sun, and no moon is always eclipsed; *bi-l-ḍarūrah kull qamar munkhasif waqt ḥaylūlat al-arḍ baynahu wa-bayna l-shams lā dā'iman*); necessarily, no moon is eclipsed at the time of quadrature, not always (no moon is possibly eclipsed at the time of quadrature, and every moon is at least once eclipsed; *bi-l-ḍarūrah lā shay' min al-qamar bi-munkhasif waqt al-tarbīʿ lā dā'iman*).

Al-Kātibī names the first component of each of these compounds the absolute temporal (*waqtiyyah muṭlaqah*), noted above at the end of commentary on the simple propositions.

§58[162]

12. **$L_{X2}$**: spread (*muntashirah*); referential temporal indeterminate.

Necessarily, every man breathes at a given time, not always (every man necessarily inhales at some time, and no man is always inhaling; *bi-l-ḍarūrah kull insān mutanaffis fī waqt mā lā dā'iman*); necessarily, no man breathes at some time, not always (no man possibly inhales at some time, and every man is at least once inhaling; *bi-l-ḍarūrah lā shay' min al-insān bi-mutanaffis fī waqt mā lā dā'iman*).

As before, al-Kātibī names the first component of each of these compounds the absolute spread (*muntashirah muṭlaqah*), noted above at the end of the comments on the simple propositions.

§59[163]

13. **$M_2$**: special possible (*mumkinah khāṣṣah*); referential two-sided possibility.[164]

This is the last of the thirteen propositions, the special possible (*al-mumkinah al-khāṣṣah*), the two-sided possible. By special possibility, every man is writing (every man is possibly writing, and no man is necessarily writing; *bi-l-imkān al-khāṣṣ kull insān kātib*); by special possibility, no man is writing (no man is necessarily writing, and every man is possibly writing; *bi-l-imkān al-khāṣṣ lā shay' min al-insān bi-kātib*). As in the case of the non-perpetual existential, the a- and e-propositions are made up of the same components set out in a different order.

In the treatment of conversion, the propositions appear with the adverbial phrase—"by necessity," or "by general absoluteness," or whatever—at the end of the proposition, thus: *ba'ḍ bā' jīm bi-l-iṭlāq al-'āmm, ba'ḍ bā' laysa bā' bi-l-ḍarūrah, ba'ḍ bā' laysa bā' dā'iman* (§75). The modality is unstated in the absolute continuing (§76.1), and, as mentioned, the use of *ḥīna* rather than *mā dāma* indicates that the modality is either general absoluteness or possibility (and, obviously, the use of *mā dāma* signals either necessity or perpetuity; §78). As mentioned in presenting the general absolute, it can be formulated as *kull jīm bā' bi-l-fi'l* (in §76.2). A number of differently modalized propositions are occasionally referred to with phrases like *kull jīm bā' bi-iḥdā l-jihāt al-arba' al-madhkūrah* (§78.1, §78.4).

Al-Kātibī mentions six more compound propositions as conclusions to inferences; again, I number them as they appear in the second appendix.

22. **L₂**: non-perpetual necessary (impossible proposition) (*al-ḍarūriyyah al-lā-dā'imah*), given as conclusion to a first-figure mix.

Every C is necessarily B, not always (every C is necessarily B, and no C is always B; *bi-l-ḍarūrah kull jīm bā' lā dā'iman*); necessarily, no C is B, not always (no C is possibly B, and every C is at least once B; *bi-l-ḍarūrah lā shay' min jīm bā' lā dā'iman*).

23. **A₂**: non-perpetual perpetual (impossible proposition) (*al-dā'imah al-lā-dā'imah*), given as conclusion to some first-figure mixes.

Always, every C is B, not always (every C is always B, and no C is always B; *dā'iman kull jīm bā' lā dā'iman*); always, no C is B, not always (no C is ever B, and every C is at least once B; *dā'iman lā shay' min jīm bā' lā dā'iman*).

24. **$A_{D(2)}$**: non-perpetual-for-some conventional (*al-ʿurfiyyah lā dā'imah fī l-baʿḍ*), given as converse of certain propositions, and as conclusion for some fourth-figure mixes.

Always, every C is B as long as it is C, not always for some (every C is always B as long as it is C, and some C is not always B; *dā'iman kull jīm bā' mā dāma jīm lā dā'iman fī l-baʿḍ*); always, no C is B as long as it is C, not always for some (no C is ever B as long as it is C, and some C is at least once B; *dā'iman lā shay' min jīm bā' mā dāma jīm lā dā'iman fī l-baʿḍ*).

25. **$X_{T2}$**: non-perpetual temporal absolute (*al-muṭlaqah al-waqtiyyah al-lā-dā'imah*); given as conclusion for a first-figure mix.

Every C is B at time T, not always (every C is B at time T, and no C is always B; *kull jīm bā' fī waqt muʿayyan lā dā'iman*); no C is B at time T, not always (no C is B at time T, and every C is at least once B; *lā shay' min jīm bā' fī waqt muʿayyan lā dā'iman*).

26. **$X_{X2}$**: non-perpetual spread absolute (*al-muṭlaqah al-muntashirah al-lā-dā'imah*); given as a conclusion for a first-figure mix.

Every C is B at some time, not always (every C is B at some time, and no C is always B; *kull jīm bā' fī waqt mā lā dā'iman*); no C is B at some time, not always (no C is B at some time, and every C is at least once B; *lā shay' min jīm bā' fī waqt mā lā dā'iman*).

27. **$X_{D2}$**: non-perpetual absolute continuing (*al-ḥīniyyah al-muṭlaqah al-lā-dā'imah*).

Every C is [at least once] B while it is C, not always (every C is at least once B while C, and no C is always B; *kull jīm bāʾ ḥīna huwa jīm lā dāʾiman*); no C is [always] B while it is C, not always (no C is always B while C, and every C is at least once B; *lā shayʾ min jīm bāʾ ḥīna huwa jīm lā dāʾiman*).

*The second section, on the divisions of the hypothetical proposition*

As noted in commentary on §39 above, the material presented in §§60–66 goes much more deeply into matters first touched on in §39. These seven lemmata begin with §60, which introduces the technical terms for the parts of the propositions. It goes on to divide the following (*luzūm*) in conditionals into what is now commonly translated as implicative (*luzūmiyyah*) and coincidental (*ittifāqiyyah*), and concludes by setting out the three kinds of disjunction (exclusive, inclusive, and what I call alternative denial).[165] Lemma 61 sets out the incompatibility in disjunctives as either oppositional (*ʿinādiyyah*) or coincidental, with examples of coincidental incompatibility in the three kinds of disjunction. Lemma 62 deals with how to negate hypothetical propositions. Lemma 63 sets out the possible combination of true and false component propositions, which, over and above the strong following stipulated in §60, determine the truth-conditions for the implicative conditional; §64 sets out the parallel combinations for disjunctives. One of Avicenna's notable innovations in dealing with the hypothetical propositions was to quantify conditionals and disjunctives, and §65 stipulates what it is for a hypothetical proposition to be universal or particular, and then lists the expressions used to indicate quantification. Lemma 66 closes this section of al-Kātibī's treatment of the hypotheticals by gesturing toward the more complex hypothetical propositions that can be built up out of the simple ones already introduced.

§60[166] Lemma 60.1 presents the terms of art for the parts of hypothetical propositions, whether conditional or disjunctive; the first component is the antecedent, the second the consequent. For the disjunctive, as al-Kātibī notes later, the distinction between the components is merely a question of placement of the disjuncts. Lemma 60.2 turns to issues of real substance, and I quote al-Ḥillī. Note the examples offered for the implicative (which exhibit a strong relation between antecedent and consequent like causality and correlation) and coincidental conditionals (for which truth of the components is enough). Note also that al-Kātibī and Avicenna have different definitions for the coincidental.

> TEXT 60.1 The conditional divides into the implicative and the coincidental, and that which covers both is the associative (*al-istiṣḥāb*).[167] Implication is the relation of necessity, coincidence the relation of [two-sided] possibility, while association is the relation of general possibility.
>
> The implicative is that in which the truth of the consequent is [dependent] on the assumption (*taqdīr*) of the truth of the antecedent due to a connection (*ʿalāqah*) between the two that requires the association of one with the other in truth, like causality and correlation (*al-ʿilliyyah wa-l-taḍāyuf*). So, when a cause exists, so does its effect, as in "if the sun is up, then it is day"; for the sun's being up is cause for it being day. Similarly, if one of two correlatives is true the other is true, as in "if father exists, then child exists."
>
> The coincidental has two interpretations. The first—the one the author uses—is that in which the consequent is true with the antecedent (*mujāmiʿan li-l-muqaddam fī l-ṣidq*) without any connection between the two, as in "if man is rational, then donkey brays." The second interpretation is that the consequent in [the conditional] is true in fact (*fī nafs al-amr*), whether the antecedent is true or false. This is the interpretation Avicenna used in the *Cure*, and it is weaker than the first.[168] (*ḤQ* 276.6–277.2)

Lemma 60.3 turns to the three kinds of disjunctive proposition, implicitly dealing with the strength of disjunction by giving examples that—so we are told in §61—exhibit the stronger oppositional relation between the disjuncts (examples for the weaker coincidental relation are given in §61). I translate *māniʿat al-jamʿ* as alternative denial ("this thing is either a stone or a tree"): it could be one or the other, or neither, but it cannot be both. The exclusive has contradictories or opposites as disjuncts ("this number is either even or odd"): it can only be one or the other. And the inclusive disjunction ("either Zayd is in the water or else he will not drown"): it can be one or the other, or both; it cannot be neither. The fact that these relations are modalized comes out strongly in al-Ḥillī's commentary on the lemma. First, alternative denial (*māniʿat al-jamʿ*):

> **Text 60.2** It has two interpretations. The first—used by the author—is that in which it is judged that the two parts are incompatible in truth though not in falsity, as in "either this is a stone or a tree"; for the judgment here is only of the impossibility of conjunction in truth (*imtināʿ al-ijtimāʿ ʿalā l-ṣidq*) not in falsity, due to the possibility of their being false together (*li-jawāz kidhbihimā maʿan*). And it comes about (*taḥdath*) from the proposition and what is more particular (*akhaṣṣ*) than its contradictory (for tree is more particular than not-stone).
>
> The second interpretation is that in which it is judged that it is impossible to conjoin its two parts in truth. This sense is weaker than the first, and covers both the first and the real disjunction. (*ḤQ* 277.apu–278.6)

Al-Kātibī's preferred usage is that the alternative denial "either P or Q" means "not-possible (P and Q), and possible (not-P and not-Q)"; the weaker usage is "not-possible (P and Q)." As for inclusive disjunction (*māniʿat al-khulūw*):

**Text 60.3** It also has two interpretations. The first is that it is that in which it is judged only to be impossible to conjoin its two parts in falsity, as in "either Zayd is in the water or he is not drowned"; for the judgment here is that it is impossible to conjoin them in falsity, for it is impossible that he not be in the water and drowned. It comes about from the proposition and what is more general (*aʿamm*) than its contradictory, for "he does not drown" is more general than his not being in the water.

The second interpretation holds that in [this disjunction] it is judged that it is impossible to conjoin the two parts in falsity. This sense is weaker than the first, and covers both the first and the exclusive (*al-ḥaqīqiyyah*). (*ḤQ* 278.10–u)

In Texts 60.2 and 60.3, the first interpretations (the stronger) are stronger by virtue of the "only," which is effectively a conjunct, "yet it is possible." So, for the stronger inclusive disjunction we have "not-possible (not-P and not-Q), and possible (P and Q)," and for the weaker, "not-possible (not-P and not-Q)." As al-Ḥillī notes, the weaker senses of both alternative denial and inclusive disjunction are true of the exclusive disjunction.

A note in closing this section of the commentary. One aspect of the treatment of conditionals that finds its way into al-Ḥillī's commentary is the insistence that the distinction between necessity and possibility in categorical propositions parallels the distinction between implicative (*luzūmiyyah*) and coincidental (*ittifāqiyyah*) conditionals, and that, moreover, the coincidental corresponds to two-sided possibility. This prompts al-Ḥillī to note the *istiṣḥābiyyah* conditional (implied by either an implicative or a coincidental conditional) is like one-sided possibility (mentioned at the beginning of Text 60.1, but I think the statement in the *Asrār* is clearer):

**Text 60.4** Implication resembles necessity, coincidence resembles two-sided possibility, and association (*al-istiṣḥāb*) resembles one-sided possibility. (*ḤA* 79.12)

I believe that the opposition between the oppositional (*ʿinādiyyah*) and the coincidental disjunctives also parallels the opposition between the implicative and the coincidental conditional.

**§61**[169] It is in §61 that we are told that the examples of disjunctive propositions given so far in the *Risālah* are all oppositional (*ʿinādiyyah*); the lemma goes on to give us examples of coincidental disjunctive propositions on al-Kātibī's assumption of a state of affairs such that there is a black person who does not write. The truth-conditions that make each of these disjunctives true are congenial with those given in modern propositional logic for, respectively, exclusive disjunction, alternative denial, and inclusive disjunction (see §64).

**§62**[170] As for Avicenna, what matters in negating a hypothetical is the relation between its parts, and not the quality (or quantity) of those parts themselves.[171] This is what al-Kātibī is referring to when he talks about removing "what is judged to be in their affirmatives." As for the eight propositions:

**Text 62.1** He means by "these eight propositions" the implicative conditional, the coincidental, and the three disjunctives taken as oppositional and coincidental. (*ḤQ* 280.5–6)

Which is to say, the propositions to be negated are (1) the implicative conditional, (2) the coincidental conditional, (3) the oppositional exclusive disjunction, (4) the coincidental exclusive disjunction, (5) the oppositional inclusive disjunction, (6) the coincidental inclusive disjunction, (7) the oppositional alternative denial, and

(8) the coincidental alternative denial. Text 64.2 presents some of the relevant truth-conditions; see also §72.

§63[172] The truth-conditions of the affirmative conditional differ according to whether the conditional is implicative or coincidental,[173] and—for the coincidental—according to which interpretation of the coincidental is being used (al-Ḥillī has told us in commentary on §60—the interpretations are set out in Text 60.1—that Avicenna in the *Cure* uses the weaker of the two). For the implicative, there are two considerations. The first has to do with the relation between the antecedent and the consequent (are they inseparable?), the second with the truth or falsity of the component propositions. Section 60.2 has set out the first consideration—basically, that the two components are related to each other causally or as correlatives—and §63 sets out the second consideration (which is the only consideration for the truth of the coincidental).

This is what al-Ḥillī has to say about the truth of the affirmative implicative conditional:

> **Text 63.1** The truth and falsity of conditionals is not a function [simply] of the truth and falsity of the parts (*laysa li-ṣidq ajzā'ihā wa-kidhbihā*); for the affirmative conditional is true with two true propositions, as in "if man is an animal, it is a body"; with two false propositions, as in "if man is a donkey, then he brays"; with two unknown as to truth and falsity, as in "if Zayd has money, then he is rich"; and with a false antecedent and a true consequent, as in "if man is a donkey, then he is a body."
>
> The reverse is not the case—that is, that the antecedent be true and the consequent false—due to the impossibility of the true entailing the false. This is because the meaning of *luzūm* is the necessity of the truth of the consequent if the antecedent is true or the necessity of the falsity of the antecedent on the falsity of the consequent.

> Were the true to entail the false, the falsity of the true implicant would follow from the falsity of its implicate, and the truth of the false implicate would follow from the truth of its implicant; so two contradictories would be conjoined, and that is absurd. (*ḤQ* 281.1–10)

So the affirmative implicative conditional will be false with a true antecedent and a false consequent irrespective of the relation between the two parts; but it will also be false when the relation between the two parts falls short of the relation set out in §60.2, irrespective of the truth or falsity of the parts:

> TEXT 63.2 The false affirmative is composed of two false propositions, as in "if man is a horse, then he is a donkey"; and from a false antecedent and a true consequent, as in "if man is a donkey, then he is rational," and the reverse—that is, from a true antecedent and a false consequent—as in "if man is rational, then he is a donkey"; and from two true propositions, as in "if man is an animal, then he is rational." (*ḤQ* 282.2–6)

The coincidental conditional is true on al-Kātibī's account only when both the antecedent and the consequent are true. On Avicenna's weaker account, it is true when the consequent is true. Specifically on al-Kātibī's account:

> TEXT 63.3 If, however, [the conditional] is coincidental then its falsity from two true propositions is impossible, because the meaning of the coincidental is association (*muṣāḥabah*) in truth (this in the coincidental in the stronger sense). (*ḤQ* 282.7–8)

§64[174] Lemma 64 begins with a consideration of the truth-conditions for affirmative disjunctive propositions. It follows on with a brief indication of the truth-conditions for the various negative hypothetical propositions (set out in broad terms in §62).

Like the conditional, the disjunctives have different truth-conditions according to whether they are oppositional or coincidental. As for the implicative conditional, there are two considerations for the oppositional: the first the relation between the terms themselves (are they incompatible?); the second the truth of the component disjuncts. For the first consideration there are two views, set out in Texts 60.2 and 60.3 above; al-Kātibī prefers the strong sense. For the coincidental—set out in §61—the only consideration is the truth of the component disjuncts. So the truth-conditions in the first part of §64 apply to both oppositional and coincidental, but the oppositional have further requirements set out at the beginning of §61 (mutual exclusion due to the two parts themselves). Here is what al-Ḥillī has to say about the real, or exclusive, disjunction:

> Text 64.1 The affirmative real disjunction is true from a true and a false proposition, because it judges of them the impossibility of their joint truth and their joint falsity (as in "number is either even or odd"); so it is not true from two true propositions due to the impossibility of their joint truth, or from two false propositions due to the impossibility of their joint falsity. (*ḤQ* 282.9–10)

Al-Kātibī offers a single sentence for the truth-conditions of the negatives ("true of that of which the affirmative is false, and false of that of which the affirmative is true"); al-Ḥillī goes through aspects of the resulting truth-conditions.

> Text 64.2 The negative conditional may be true with two true propositions, as in "not, whenever man is animal, he is rational"; and with two false propositions, as in "not, whenever man is a donkey, he is a horse"; and from a true antecedent and a false consequent, as in: "not, whenever

man is rational, he is a horse"; or the reverse, as in "not, whenever man is a horse, he is rational." It may be false from two true propositions, as in "never, if man is a body, then he is an animal"; and from two false propositions, as in "never, if man is a donkey, then he brays"; and from a false antecedent and a true consequent, as in "never, if man is a donkey, then he is a body"; [the false conditional] is not composed of a true antecedent and a false consequent, otherwise the affirmative will be true [against the stipulation in Text 63.1].

The negative real disjunctive may be true from two false propositions, as in "not, either the man is a donkey or a horse"; from two true propositions, as in "not, either the man is an animal or rational"; and from a true and a false proposition if they are not contradictories (or with the force of contradictories), as in "not, either the man is an animal or a horse." And it may be false from a true and a false proposition that are contradictories (or that have the force of contradictories), as in "not, the number is either odd or even." (*Ḥ Q* 283.2–15)

§65[175] One of Avicenna's innovations is to quantify hypothetical propositions.[176] Lemma 65.1 deals with what is meant by, respectively, a universal conditional, a particular, and a singular. Lemma 65.2 sets out the quantifiers used for the propositions in their various quantifications; although this part of the lemma is clear without commentary, it seems the obvious moment to introduce the forms of the quantified conditionals and disjunctives.

Hypothetical propositions are quantified over circumstances or situations. An a-proposition is true if it is true that the consequent follows/is opposed to the antecedent in all cases in which the antecedent can possibly occur; an i-proposition is true if it is true that the consequent follows/is opposed to the antecedent in some cases in which the antecedent can possibly occur; a singular proposition is true if it is true that the consequent follows/ is opposed to the antecedent in one case in which the antecedent can possibly occur.

> **Text 65.1** If we have "whenever A is B then C is D" or "always, either A is B or C is D," we do not mean that "C is D" is an implicate of or opposed to "A is B" in all contexts in which "A is B" occurs (*fī jamīʿ al-madār allatī yaqaʿu ʿalayhā alif bāʾ*), for the antecedent may be something unchanging (*amran thābitan*), as in "whenever God is knowing he is living." Rather, we mean by it that "C is D" is an implicate of or opposed to "A is B" in all situations (*fī jamīʿ al-awḍāʿ*) we may suppose with which "A is B" is compatible; and the situations are those that occur by reason of connecting (*al-iqtirān*) [it] to matters with which the antecedent is compatible . . .
>
> In the particular, it is judged that the antecedent entails the consequent (or is opposed to it) under some situations that are supposed, as in "sometimes, if this is a body then it is an animal," for body entails animal only in the situation of its being connected to sense and not otherwise. Similarly for "sometimes, number is either abundant or deficient."
>
> The singular (*al-makhṣūṣah*) is that entailment or opposition is judged in it in a specified situation or time, as in "if you bring me Zayd I will honor you," or "if you come today I will honor you," or "at this moment, either Zayd is in the water, or he is not."[177] (*ḤQ* 284.6–285.6)

Al-Kātibī's account of the hypotheticals has few examples. A shorthand for the hypotheticals has been devised by Strobino, and the form of three of the propositions is illustrated by examples offered by al-Ḥillī (*ḤQ* 285.apu–286.14). I present shorthand first, then examples of the form in what follows (and again in summary in Appendix 3). Here are the conditionals (given in shorthand with a-propositions as the component propositions; this is arbitrary and does not reflect the examples—all with unquantified components—that al-Ḥillī actually offers):

A-conditional: (a-ℂ)aa. Whenever the sun is up then it is day (*kullamā kānat al-shams ṭāliʿah fa-l-nahār mawjūd*; alternatives to *kullamā*: *mahmā*, *matā*);
E-conditional: (e-ℂ)aa. Never, if the sun is up then it is night (*laysa l-battata idhā kānat al-shams ṭāliʿah fa-l-layl mawjūd*);
I-conditional: (i-ℂ)aa. Sometimes, if the sun is up then it is day (*qad yakūnu idhā kānat al-shams ṭāliʿah fa-l-nahār mawjūd*);
O-proposition: (o-ℂ)aa. Two forms (no examples given): (1) Sometimes not, if P then Q (*qad lā yakūnu*); (2) Not always, if P then Q (*laysa kullamā*, or *laysa mahmā*, or *laysa matā*).

And here are the disjunctives:

A-proposition: (a-𝔻)aa. Always, either the sun is up, or it is not (*dāʾiman immā an takūna l-shams ṭāliʿah aw lā takūna*);
E-proposition: (e-𝔻)aa. Never, either the sun is up, or it is day (*laysa l-battata immā an takūna l-shams ṭāliʿah wa-immā an yakūna l-nahār mawjūdan*);
I-proposition: (i-𝔻)aa. Sometimes, either the sun is up, or it is night (*qad yakūnu immā an takūna l-shams ṭāliʿah wa-immā an yakūna l-layl mawjūdan*);
O-proposition: (o-𝔻)aa. Two forms (no examples given): (1) Sometimes not, either P or Q (*qad lā yakūnu*); (2) Not always, either P or Q (*laysa dāʾiman*).

No equivalences between conditionals, or between disjunctives, are called on in the *Risālah*, but they are included in the square of opposition that I take from Strobino. Figure 30 assumes that Avicenna's account of equivalences is accepted by al-Kātibī (specifically, that (a-ℂ)aa is equivalent to (e-ℂ)ao, (o-ℂ)ao to (i-ℂ)aa, (o-ℂ) aa to (i-ℂ)ao, and (a-ℂ)ao to (e-ℂ)aa); it may not be the account al-Kātibī would offer outside an introductory text like the *Risālah*. See further discussion in commentary on §72 (on the square of opposition), on §86 (on contraposition), and on §87 (on the co-implication of hypothetical propositions).

§66[178] We are told at the end of §66 that we should work out the various ways in which hypothetical propositions can be composed (*murakkab*). The order followed by the commentators (categorical-categorical, conditional-conditional, disjunctive-disjunctive, categorical-conditional, categorical-disjunctive, conditional-disjunctive) is conventional, and is followed in the presentation of hypothetical arguments in §§105–9 (though they are like disjunctive propositions with respect to their component disjuncts, the arguments do not take account of the ordering of the premises, and so only have six rather than nine classifications). Al-Taftāzānī gives us the examples al-Kātibī has asked us to find as an exercise (*TŠ* 272–73). Here are the divisions of the conditionals; I note in square brackets after each what kind it represents on al-Kātibī's division.[179]

1. Whenever (something is man) then (it is an animal). [Categorical-categorical]
2. Whenever (whenever something is a man it is an animal) then (whenever it is not an animal it is not a man). [Conditional-conditional]
3. Whenever (always, a number is either even or odd) then (always, it is either divisible into two equal parts or not so divisible). [Disjunctive-disjunctive]
4. If (animal is more general than man) then (whenever something is man it is animal). [Categorical-conditional]
5. Whenever (whenever something is a man it is an animal) then (it is an implicant of animal). [Conditional-categorical]

6. If (this is a number) then (it is either even or odd). [Categorical-disjunctive]
7. If (this is either even or odd) then (it is a number). [Disjunctive-categorical]
8. If (whenever something is a man it is an animal) then (either it is a man or it is not an animal). [Conditional-disjunctive]
9. If (always, either the sun is up or it is night) then (whenever the sun is up, then it is not night). [Disjunctive-conditional]

And here is the division of the disjunctives:

1. A number is either even or odd. [Categorical-categorical]
2. Either (if the sun is up then it is day) or (if the sun is up then it is night). [Conditional-conditional]
3. Either (a number is either even or odd) or (it is even or indivisible into two equal parts). [Disjunctive-disjunctive]
4. Either (the sun is not an implicant for day) or (whenever the sun is up it is day). [Categorical-conditional]
5. Either (something is one) or (it is either even or odd). [Categorical-disjunctive]
6. Either (if number is odd it is even) or (number is either even or odd). [Conditional-disjunctive]

The study of hypothetical propositions carries on with the square of opposition in §72 (see Figure 30).

### *The third section, on the valuations of propositions*

Let me begin by explaining my choice of "valuation" as a translation here of *ḥukm,* a term rendered elsewhere in the translation as "judgment." This section treats four topics (contradiction, straight conversion, contraposition, and the implicates of hypotheticals), the last three of which evaluate what proposition of a certain form the first proposition can imply. Contradiction is an important preliminary for these evaluations. Many of the proofs for these implications—which is to say, of these one-premise arguments (to introduce a phrase that al-Kātibī did not use)—depend on putting forward the contradictory of the putative conclusion and deriving an impossible conclusion from it and the first proposition.

> TEXT 67.A He begins with contradiction because some of the proofs for conversion and co-implication depend upon it. (*TŠ* 274.9)

Furthermore, the contradictories are themselves a function of the truth-conditions stipulated for the various propositions; specifying a proposition's contradictory specifies precisely what the assertion of the proposition denies.

**The first discussion, on contradiction**

Lemmata 67–72 lay out the contradictories of the six simple and seven compound categorical propositions, and of the hypothetical propositions, that have so far been introduced (see Appendix 1 and Figures 26–30). Other simple categorical propositions—introduced in commentary on §§52–59—play a role in the further discussion of those propositions "customarily investigated" by Arabic logicians. For example, the perpetuity proposition (**A**) has the general absolute ($\mathbf{X_1}$) as its contradictory, and both of these are presented among the thirteen, whereas the conventional ($\mathbf{A_{D1}}$: "every C is always B as long as it is C") has as its contradictory the absolute continuing (*ḥīniyyah muṭlaqah*, $\mathbf{X_{D1}}$: "some C is not always B while C"). These further propositions are listed in the second appendix.

§67[180] The definition of contradiction given in §67 ("a difference between two propositions in affirmation and negation such that it requires of itself that one is true and the other false") incites the commentators to identify the genus and the differentiae deployed to narrow it.

**Text 67.1** "Difference" (*al-ikhtilāf*) is like a genus, for what occurs between propositions also occurs between terms, and restricting "difference" with "between two propositions" excludes the difference between terms. Next, the difference between two propositions may occur through affirmation and negation, as in "Zayd is knowing," "Zayd is not knowing," and it may occur through difference between subject and predicate, as in "Zayd is knowing" and "'Amr is ignorant." Moreover, the difference through affirmation and negation may require [that the two propositions divide] in truth and falsity, though it may not, as in "Zayd is knowing," "Zayd is not not-knowing."[181] This division [in truth and falsity] may be due to the difference [in affirmation and negation] itself, as in the case of two mutually contradictory propositions, and it may not, as in "this is a man" and "this is not rational." For the first is true and the second is false, but not due to the difference itself, but because being a man entails rationality. (*ḤQ* 289.9–290.2)

§68[182] The lemma proceeds by investigating ever more complex propositions and the factors that need to be taken into account to find a proposition's contradictory. The first stipulations apply even to the simplest propositions, the singular (*al-makhṣūṣah*):

**Text 68.1** If [the proposition] is singular, the widely held doctrine is that contradiction is only realized with eight conditions: unity of the subject, of the predicate, of relation (*al-iḍāfah*), of potentiality and actuality, of part and whole, of condition (*al-sharṭ*), of place, and of time (*al-zamān*). (*RM* 177.10–apu)

In short, these factors must all be the same so that two propositions can be each other's formal contradictory. The first two mean that the subject and the predicate are the same in the two propositions. Unity of relation is breached in "Zayd is 'Amr's father" and "Zayd is not Khālid's father"; unity of potentiality and actuality is breached in "the sword is cutting" (in that it is sharp and has the potential to cut) and "the sword is not cutting" (in that it is not actually being used to cut); unity of part and whole is breached in "the black person is black" (in respect of his complexion) and "the black person is not black" (in respect of his teeth); unity of condition is breached in "the black thing compresses the vision" (when it is black) and "the black thing does not compress the vision" (when it is not black); unity of place is breached in "Zayd is sitting" (in the house) and "Zayd is not sitting" (in the marketplace); unity of time is breached in "Zayd is here" (now) and "Zayd is not here" (at some other time) (all examples from *ṬḤ* 301.apu–304.3 on *Pointers* 5.1.3, *AI* 44.8–14). Al-Rāzī had tried to allocate different unities to either the subject or the predicate and thereby reduce their number (*RM* 177–179), but his attempt at reduction was resisted by al-Ṭūsī and al-Ḥillī:

> **Text 68.2** This is what the author mentions following Fakhr al-Dīn. The truth is that these things belong to [both] the subject and the predicate; specifying some as "of the predicate" and some as "of the subject" is simply arbitrary. (*ḤQ* 291.14–pu)

Al-Rāzī's reduction was, however, accepted by al-Kātibī, and §68 stipulates the conditions to be observed to ensure that the propositions differentiated by contradiction are unified with respect to their predicates and subjects.

Al-Kātibī sets out the further condition for finding the formal contradictory of a quantified proposition, which is that the two contradictories must also differ in quantity:

> **Text 68.3** The first is specific to quantified propositions, which is difference in quantity. For the two particulars may

> be true together, and the two universals false together; that is, in every matter in which the subject is more general than the predicate. So "some animal is human" and "some animal is not human" are both true, and "every animal is human" and "no animal is human" are false. But if we say "some animal is human" and "no animal is human," it is impossible to conjoin them so that both are true or both false. (*ḤQ* 292.6–12)

Al-Kātibī sets out a final condition, specific to modalized propositions.

> **Text 68.4** The second condition is difference in mode (and this extends to the quantified and the singular propositions). For the two possible propositions may be true in contingent matter with the falsity of the two necessary propositions: "possibly, every man is a writer" and "possibly, not every man is a writer"; they are both true, while "necessarily, every man is a writer" and "necessarily, not every man is a writer" are false. (*ḤQ* 292.13–pu)

§69[183] There are six simple propositions that are named in §52 (the possibility, the absolute, the necessity, the perpetuity, the conventional, and the conditional; respectively, $\mathbf{M_1}$, $\mathbf{X_1}$, **L**, **A**, $\mathbf{A_{D1}}$, and $\mathbf{L_{D1}}$), and four unnamed in the first list by al-Kātibī, which however crop up elsewhere in the treatise: the possible continuing (*ḥīniyyah mumkinah*), the absolute continuing (*ḥīniyyah muṭlaqah*), the absolute temporal, and the absolute spread; respectively, $\mathbf{M_{D1}}$, $\mathbf{X_{D1}}$, $\mathbf{L_{T1}}$, and $\mathbf{L_{X1}}$. Leaving the absolute temporal and absolute spread to one side for the moment, the remaining eight propositions can be set out as four opposed pairs (see for examples Figure 26 for the square generated by the propositions dealt with in 1 below, and Figure 27 for the square generated by the propositions dealt with in 4 below):

1. The absolute necessity proposition (**L**) has as its contradictory the general possibility proposition (**$M_1$**): "every A is necessarily B" contradicts "some A is not necessarily B" (or "some A is possibly not B").
2. The absolute perpetuity (**A**) has the general absolute (**$X_1$**): "every A is always B" contradicts "some A is not always B" (or "some A is sometimes not B").
3. The general conditional (**$L_{D1}$**) has the possible continuing (**$M_{D1}$**, *ḥīniyyah mumkinah*): "every A is necessarily B as long as it is A" contradicts "some A is possibly not B while A" (or "some A is not necessarily B while A").
4. The general conventional (**$A_{D1}$**) has the absolute continuing (**$X_{D1}$**, *ḥīniyyah muṭlaqah*): "every A is always B as long as it is A" contradicts "some A is sometimes not B while A" (or "some A is not always B while A").

To repeat: I use "as long as it is" to translate *ma dāma*, which means "at every moment it is," and "while" to translate *ḥīna*, which means "for at least one moment it is"; this is simply to reflect Arabic usage, which renders the same temporality condition differently according to whether the modality it is associated with is necessity or perpetuity (*mā dāma*), or possibility or actuality-at-a-time (*ḥīna*). The temporal modality can be left out; we assume perpetuity with *mā dāma*, at-least-once with *ḥīna*. Further, note that in holding the possible continuing (**$M_{D1}$**) to be the contradictory of the general conditional (**$L_{D1}$**), al-Kātibī talks about a proposition "in which it is judged to remove the opposing necessity with respect to the description"; so "someone cannot ever cough as long as he is afflicted" is opposed in quantity, quality, and modality to "everyone may cough at times while afflicted."

As noted, "absolute" (*muṭlaqah*) was used by the tenth-century translators of Aristotle to translate "assertoric,"[184] yet in 2 above its contradictory is not a general absolute (**$X_1$**) but a perpetuity proposition (**A**). This looks odd to an Aristotelian (and in Text 69.1

al-Ḥillī is using *al-qudamāʾ* to refer to Aristotle and his followers rather than to Avicenna), for whom an assertoric is contradicted by another assertoric of opposing quantity and quality:

> **Text 69.1** Most of the ancients (*jamāhīr al-qudamāʾ*) were negligent (*sahaw*) about the contradictory of the absolute; they reckoned that it was an absolute too, and were not struck by the truth of two contraries in non-perpetual matter. (*ḤQ* 294.6–7)

A common example for two such contraries is "every man is sleeping," which is true on the truth-conditions for the general absolute with "no man is sleeping" (put differently, "every man is at least once sleeping" can be true with "no man is always sleeping").

§70[185] The compound propositions are conjunctions of simpler propositions, so their contradictories are alternations of the contradictories of those simpler propositions. Al-Taḥtānī tells us (*TT* 337.2) that the disjunction in the disjunctive contradictories are inclusive (*māniʿat al-khulūw*). Here is the example in less compressed language: For the proposition, "every A is at least once B and at least once not B," we take the opposing propositional form (here, an o-form) and the dual of the modality (here, always) and produce "some A is never B"; the proposition "which agrees with the original" agrees in quality, is also a perpetuity proposition, and is limited to the items made subject in the first proposition (see §71), so the disjunct is "or those same As are always B."

Al-Ḥillī gives a complete list of the a-propositions and their o-proposition contradictories (*ḤQ* 295.7–296.u); I summarize it here and in Appendix 4, along with al-Ḥillī's Arabic for the propositions:

1. **L**$_{D2}$ a-proposition contradicts either **M**$_{D1}$ o-proposition or **A** i-proposition: the contradictory of "every C is necessarily B as

long as it is C, not always"—the "not always" is shorthand for "and no C is always B"—is "either some C is not necessarily B while C, or some C is always B" (*naqīḍ kull jīm bāʾ bi-l-ḍarūrah mā dāma jīm lā dāʾiman immā baʿḍ jīm laysa bāʾ bi-l-imkān ḥīna huwa jīm aw baʿḍ jīm bāʾ dāʾiman*).

2. $\mathbf{A}_{D2}$ a-proposition contradicts either $\mathbf{X}_{D1}$ o-proposition or **A** i-proposition: the contradictory of "every C is always B as long as it is C, not always" is "either some C is not always B while C, or some C is always B" (*naqīḍ kull jīm bāʾ mā dāma jīm lā dāʾiman immā baʿḍ jīm laysa bāʾ ḥīna huwa jīm aw baʿḍ jīm bāʾ dāʾiman*).
3. $\mathbf{X}_2$ a-proposition contradicts either **A** o-proposition or **A** i-proposition: the contradictory of "every C is B, not always" is "either some C is never B, or some C is always B" (*naqīḍ kull jīm bāʾ lā dāʾiman immā baʿḍ jīm laysa bāʾ dāʾiman aw baʿḍ jīm bāʾ dāʾiman*).[186]
4. $\mathbf{X}_{\sim L}$ a-proposition contradicts either **A** o-proposition or **L** i-proposition: the contradictory of "every C is B, not necessarily" is "either some C is never B, or some C is necessarily B" (*naqīḍ kull jīm bāʾ lā bi-l-ḍarūrah immā baʿḍ jīm laysa bāʾ dāʾiman aw baʿḍ jīm bāʾ bi-l-ḍarūrah*).
5. $\mathbf{L}_{T2}$ contradicts $\mathbf{M}_T$ or **A**:[187] the temporal is a compound of an absolute temporal (*waqtiyyah muṭlaqah*) and a general absolute, so its contradictory is either a possibility temporal or a perpetuity; so the contradictory of "every C is B necessarily at a specified time, not always" is "either possibly at that time some C is not B, or some C is always B" (*naqīḍ kull jīm bāʾ bi-l-ḍarūrah fī waqt muʿayyan lā dāʾiman immā baʿḍ jīm laysa bāʾ bi-l-imkān fī dhālika l-waqt aw baʿḍ jīm bāʾ dāʾiman*).
6. $\mathbf{L}_{X2}$ contradicts $\mathbf{M}_A$ or **A**: the spread is a compound of an absolute spread (*muntashirah muṭlaqah*) and a general absolute, so its contradictory is either a possible perpetual or a perpetuity; so the contradictory of "every C is B necessarily at some time, not always" is "either some C is not necessarily B always, or

some C is always B" (*naqīḍ kull jīm bāʾ lā bi-l-ḍarūrah fī waqt mā lā dāʾiman immā baʿḍ jīm laysa bāʾ bi-l-imkān dāʾiman aw baʿḍ jīm bāʾ dāʾiman*).

7. **M2** contradicts either **L** o-proposition or **L** i-proposition: the contradictory of "some C is B by a special possibility" is "either some C is not possibly B or some C is necessarily B" (*naqīḍ kull jīm bāʾ bi-l-imkān al-khāṣṣ immā baʿḍ jīm laysa bāʾ bi-l-ḍarūrah aw baʿḍ jīm bāʾ bi-l-ḍarūrah*).

§71[188] This is the moment in the treatment of contradiction when al-Kātibī deals explicitly with particular (that is, i- and o-) compound propositions, and so it is here that he sets out precisely how the conjunction operates in a compound proposition and, by extension, how the disjunction operates in the contradictory of the original compound; all examples up to now should be read in this more precise manner. Take a compound i-proposition. The shorthand (1) "some body is an animal, not always" could either unpack to (1.1) "some body is at least once an animal, and some body is at least once not an animal," or—and this is the reading al-Kātibī insists on—to the stronger (1.2) "some body is at least once an animal and [that same body is] at least once not an animal." For (1.1), the contradictory would be (2.1) "no body is ever an animal or every body is always an animal," whereas for the preferred version (1.2) the contradictory would be (2.2) "every body is either never an animal or always an animal." In (2.1), the disjunction has two sentences as its disjuncts, each with its own subject, but in (2.2), the disjunction is restricted to having the terms in the predicate as disjuncts. Al-Ḥillī agrees with al-Kātibī, and expands on the meaning of the contradictory (2.2):

**Text 71.1** "Every body is either always an animal or always not an animal": this covers three meanings, first, that every body is always an animal; second, that no body

> is ever an animal; and third, that some bodies are animals always and some others are never animals. (*ḤQ* 297.10–15)

I take it that (1.1) is plainly true (I am at least once an animal, and my desk is at least once not an animal), and so (2.1) is plainly false. Since al-Kātibī states without argument that (1) is false, he must expect his readership to hear it as (1.2). In short, he seems to assume that we know that the conjunction in a compound proposition has predicates and not propositions as its conjuncts. I worry that I cannot hear the specific example as he expects his readers to hear it. "Some bodies are at least once animals, and those bodies are at least once not animals" does not seem to me to be obviously false without further stipulations about the continuity of animal bodies: my body is for the moment an animal, but surely on my death it will continue to be a body but cease to be an animal?

§72[189] This lemma resumes the treatment of hypothetical propositions from §66. It takes up from the introduction of the truth-conditions and formal aspects of the propositions—in particular their quantification—and sets out elements to sketch squares of opposition for them. Al-Kātibī's rule for finding the contradictories of hypothetical propositions states that the contradictory must be of the same "genus" (a conditional for a conditional, a disjunctive for a disjunctive) and the same "species" (an implicative for an implicative, a coincidental for a coincidental, see §60.2; and in the case of a disjunctive, an oppositional for an oppositional, a coincidental for a coincidental, see §61) (*TŠ* 289.pu–u). If species and genus are preserved, the contradictory is produced by changing the quantity and quality of the proposition (in other words, from A to O, from E to I, as in the categoricals). Al-Ḥillī writes:

> **Text 72.1** So the contradictory of the affirmative implicative conditional is the negative implicative conditional: I

> mean, the judgment in it is of the negation of implication, not the implication of negation; so it is a species of the implicative. So the contradictory of "whenever A is B, C is D" is "not always, if A is B, C is D," and vice versa. (*ḤQ* 298.3–5)

There are no grounds in §72 of the *Risālah* to attribute to al-Kātibī the whole of the square of opposition set out in Figure 30, at any rate, not (as already noted in comment on §65) the equivalences between (a-ℂ)aa and (e-ℂ)ao, (o-ℂ)ao and (i-ℂ)aa, (o-ℂ) aa and (i-ℂ)ao, and (a-ℂ)ao and (e-ℂ)aa (the central oppositions are certainly to be found in §72). Khaled El-Rouayheb has examined Avicenna's argument for the equivalence between (a-ℂ)aa and (e-ℂ)ao, and shown that it is effectively a formulation of a thesis attributed to Boethius, associated with connexive logic.[190] It is clear from what the commentators say about later lemmata of the *Risālah* (and specifically §86 and §87) that al-Kātibī himself rejected the thesis; al-Taḥtānī's attribution to al-Kātibī of the position set out in Text 86.4, and al-Ḥillī's similar attribution in Text 87.5, both entail rejection of the thesis. That said, al-Kātibī goes on in both §86 and §87 to set out positions he probably does not accept; a teacher has to make his or her students aware of the most commonly held views in the field. With the contradictories in hand, al-Kātibī is ready to go on to prove conversions for the conditional propositions when he returns to the topic of hypothetical propositions in §81.

**The second discussion, on straight conversion**

The following fifteen lemmata (which is to say, §§73–87) deal with immediate inferences (also called in modern treatments one-premise inferences).[191] In the *Risālah*, these include conversion, contraposition, and inferences among hypothetical propositions. I defer making observations on the inferences among hypothetical propositions to §81, where al-Kātibī picks up his intermittent treatment, which I have been tying together through cross-reference. The reader should bear in mind, however, that the definition of conversion is broadened by the post-Avicennian logicians specifically so it applies to hypothetical propositions as well as categorical (see comments to §73).

A couple of notes on the terms of art and how I translate them, given the juxtaposition of these two inferences in the exposition. The conversion of categorical propositions is called "straight conversion" (*al-ʿaks al-mustawī*; "regular conversion" would also reflect the technical phrase, and Sprenger quite reasonably rendered it "even conversion"), referring to conversion in which the terms in the original proposition (*al-aṣl*, here, the convertend) appear unchanged in the resulting converse (also *al-ʿaks*). Contrast this with contraposition (*ʿaks al-naqīḍ*), in which at least one of the extremes in the original proposition is transformed into its contradictory term in the contrapositive. Because al-Kātibī treats these two kinds of inference together, and yet mainly uses the same term (*ʿaks*) for both the inference and its result, some confusion may arise. In consequence, I have translated *ʿaks* as "conversion" or "converse" and its related verb as "convert" in the passage §§73–80, and as "contraposition" or "contrapositive" and the related verb as "contrapose" in §§82–85. Note, finally, that al-Kātibī does not use distinct terms for simple and per accidens conversion, unlike Western treatments (between, that is to say, a conversion that results in a converse of the same quantity as its convertend, and one that results in a particular converse for a universal convertend).

The proofs that are given for these valuations are of three kinds: reductio, ecthetic, and by way of the converse. An example of the reductio proof is first given by Alexander of Aphrodisias:[192] if "no C is B" does not convert to "no B is C," then "some B is C,"[193] but this with the first proposition gives us by Ferio (see §91.5) "some B is not B," which is impossible; therefore the first converse proposed is correct. Al-Kātibī's first use of this form of proof—his favorite—is in §75. (It is worth reiterating that as a general absolute (**X**$_1$), "some B is not B" is not self-contradictory on its Avicennian truth-conditions; it simply means that something that is at some stage B is at least once not B; see Text 69.1.) An example of the ecthetic proof is first given in Aristotle: if "some C is B" is true, then there must be some C—call it D—which is both C and B, which means there is a B which is C, which allows us to infer "some B is C." Al-Kātibī's first use of ecthesis is in §77.1.[194] The third method, by way of the converse, converts the contradictory of the converse to obtain something incompatible with the original proposition. So "no C is B" must convert to "no B is C"; otherwise, "some B is C," from which i-conversion allows us to infer "some C is B"; but "no C is B"; therefore, the original conversion proposed must be correct. Obviously, the third method is cumulative, drawing on conversions that have been proved in the account before the proof in question. Al-Kātibī first uses this method in §76.2 (for the affirmative component of a compound e-proposition), and makes special mention of it in §79, reserving its use for affirmative propositions because—so it seems to me—it calls on conversions of negative propositions that come first in this exposition.

Proofs to reject invalid conversions are by counterexample. One counterexample serves to reject the conversion of a given proposition and, by extension, to reject the convertibility of all weaker propositions. We find examples of rejections in §74 and §77. The proofs depend for their economy on the relative implicational strength of the propositions, developed (in a somewhat desultory fashion) in the course of laying out the propositions (see Figure 24 for simple propositions, Figure 25 for a frequently referred to set of five compound and two simple propositions, and Figures 28 and 29 for squares of opposition with implicational relations). I refer to one of two propositions as stronger (*akhaṣṣ*) if it implies the second proposition but is not implied by it, and the second proposition as weaker (*aʿamm*). Anything that follows from the weaker follows from the stronger, which is stated by the Arabic logicians as "the implicate of the weaker is the implicate of the stronger" (*lāzim al-aʿamm lāzim al-akhaṣṣ*); the contrapositive of this maxim is "what does not follow from the stronger does not follow from the weaker" (*mā lā yalzamu min al-akhaṣṣ lā yalzamu min al-aʿamm*). So if there really is a counterexample to show that the stronger cannot convert (which is to say, that it cannot have its converse as one of its implicates), then none of the propositions weaker than that proposition can convert; if they could, then—since they themselves are implicates of the stronger—that converse would be the stronger's converse (*lāzim al-lāzim lāzim al-malzūm*).

The exposition begins (§§74–76) with e-propositions (of the form, "no C is B"), moves on to o-propositions (§77), and finishes with affirmatives, all of which result in i-propositions (§78); see Conversions in Table 1. Al-Ḥillī offers the slightly misleading note:

> **Text 73.a** The custom of the ancients (*ʿādat al-awāʾil*) was first to mention the status of the negative propositions in conversion, and so—in imitation of his forebears—the author begins with these propositions. (*ḤQ* 299.17–apu)

The earliest essay on conversion in this tradition that I have read is in Avicenna's *Najāt*. There, Avicenna deals with the conversion of absolute propositions, then necessity propositions, then possibility propositions (*AN* §§55–57, 45–51). He goes through negative then affirmative propositions in each modality. He does the same in Path Five of *Pointers* (*AI* 51–55). Al-Rāzī followed roughly the same layout in first discussing conversion in the *Mulakhkhaṣ* (*RM* 184–97), but when he came to summarize his own position on the conversions and the disputes surrounding them (*RM* 197–99), he offered the summary doctrine first as it relates to negative propositions irrespective of their modality, then as it relates to affirmative. He did not touch on o-propositions because no one had yet worked out that $\mathbf{L}_{D2}$ and $\mathbf{A}_{D2}$ o-propositions convert (see §77.1 below). It is the structure of al-Rāzī's concluding statement that determines the structure for the treatment of conversion offered by al-Kātibī: he not only begins with negative propositions in a given modality, he begins by covering the negatives of all the modalized propositions.

§73[195] Al-Kātibī's definition of straight conversion (*al-ʿaks al-mustawī*) refers to parts of a proposition rather than terms. The relative breadth of al-Kātibī's definition is clear when contrasted with Avicenna's from *Pointers* 5.3.1:

> **Text 73.1** Conversion is putting the predicate of the proposition as subject, and the subject as predicate, while preserving the quality and keeping truth and falsity as it was [in the original]. (*AI* 51.1–3)

Note that Avicenna only has categorical propositions in mind, whereas the definition we find in the *Risālah* stretches to include—arguably—all hypothetical propositions (for more on which, see Texts 73.3 and 81.1). Note also the phrase "keeping truth and falsity as it was" in Avicenna's definition, which—after challenge from the Rāzians—is modified by al-Kātibī so that only truth is preserved in the converse. Here is al-Ḥillī on these points:

> **Text 73.2** The expression "the first part" is general for the subject and the antecedent, so the conversion of both categoricals and conditionals enter under [the definition]. Preservation of truth is necessary for the converse, otherwise it would not be an implicate of the first proposition. We do not mean that it must be true, just that it follows the first proposition in truth, so if the first proposition is actually true, so too is the converse; if it is [true] by supposition, so too the converse. We do not stipulate preservation of falsehood due to the possibility that the implicate is true while the implicant is false; so "every animal is a man" is false while its converse is true, "some man is an animal."

Preservation of quality is part of what conversion is stipulated to be (*amr iṣṭilāḥī*). (*ḤQ* 299.1–9)

The question that troubles two of the commentators I have read is whether the definition is too broad; as it stands, the definition includes disjunctive propositions, which certainly have parts, one stated before the other. I do not think the outcome of the debate is important, but the discussion illustrates the kind of considerations taken into account, and one aspect of the truth-conditions of the disjunctive. For al-Ḥillī, the question does not arise, simply because he understands "the first part" to cover the subject of a categorical and the antecedent of a conditional and—seemingly—nothing more (*ḤQ* 299.1–2). Al-Taḥtānī argues the disjunctive has a converse, but that it is of no value:

> **Text 73.3** It is not to be said: It follows on this [account] that the disjunctive has a converse, because its two parts are distinct in how they are stated and placed, even if they are not distinct in respect of nature (*bi-ḥasab al-ṭabʿ*). So if one of them is exchanged with the other, [the disjunctive] will have a converse because the definition holds of this [operation], but they have been explicit (*ṣarraḥū*) that [disjunctives] have no converse. Because we answer: We do not concede that the disjunctive has no converse, because the meaning (*al-mafhūm*) of "either the number is even or odd" is a judgment on the evenness of number being incompatible with oddness (*bi-muʿānadat al-fardiyyah*), and the meaning of "either the number is odd or even" is a judgment on the oddness of number being incompatible with evenness (*bi-muʿānadat al-zawjiyyah*). There is no doubt that "this is incompatible with that" is different in meaning from "that is incompatible with this." So the disjunctive also has a converse different from it in meaning. It is simply that since there is no benefit in [this conversion], no one

considered it; it is as though this is all that is meant by the claim that disjunctives have no converse. (*TT* 344.11–u)

Al-Taftāzānī is unimpressed by this line of argument:

> **Text 73.4** "Either the number is odd or even" is not a converse for "either the number is even or odd," since there is no difference (*taghāyur*) in meaning [between them]. This is because the judgment in it is only of conflict between "this is even" and "this is odd," as is borne out by the interpretation of the disjunctive (*tafsīr al-munfaṣilah*) and understanding its meaning (*taʿaqqul mafhūmihā*). (*TŠ* 290.9–12)

§74[196] The four lemmata from §74 to §77 consider all negative propositions (e- and o-propositions) in all thirteen modalities "customarily investigated." Seven of the thirteen are proved not to convert by counterexample. As mentioned in the introduction to the commentary on the section, this is done neatly. Al-Kātibī assumes his readers will have in mind the relative implicational strength of the seven propositions—$\mathbf{L}_{T2}$, $\mathbf{L}_{X2}$, $\mathbf{X}_2$, $\mathbf{X}_{\sim L}$, $\mathbf{X}_1$, $\mathbf{M}_2$, and $\mathbf{M}_1$ (see Figure 25). He takes the strongest, $\mathbf{L}_{T2}$, and sets out a proposition which is true in that modality (assume that the eclipse in question is a lunar eclipse): "no moon is possibly eclipsed at the time of quadrature, and every moon is at least once eclipsed." This proposition is true, mutatis mutandis, in all the weaker modalities. But its converse (first part second, second part first, truth and quality as in the original proposition) in the weakest negative proposition—the $\mathbf{M}_1$ o-proposition—is false: "some of what is eclipsed is not necessarily a moon" (or "some of what is eclipsed is possibly not a moon"); so none of the seven propositions converts. Al-Ḥillī writes:

> **Text 74.1** Seven of the e-propositions do not convert—the ones the author mentions. This is because the temporal

is the strongest of these seven, and—as we said earlier—it does not convert; and if the strongest does not convert, nor does the weaker. The proof (*bayān*) that [the temporal] does not convert is that "necessarily, no moon is eclipsed at the time of quadrature, not always" may be true, but its converse (namely, "some of what is eclipsed is not a moon," by the weakest of the modalities, general possibility [$\mathbf{M_I}$]) is false, because every eclipsed is necessarily a moon. The proof that the remaining e-propositions fail to convert is because they are weaker than the temporal; were they to convert, so would the temporal, because the implicate of the weaker is the implicate of the stronger (*li-anna lāzim al-ʿāmm lāzim al-khāṣṣ*). (*ḤQ* 299.pu–300.8)

Al-Ḥillī goes on straight after this to deal with al-Khūnajī's argument that these seven propositions—if taken with his interpretation of the essentialist subject (see §45 for al-Kātibī's conflicting interpretation, and Text 45.7)—all convert as **A** o-propositions (so the example would convert as "some eclipsed is never a moon"). As al-Ḥillī says: "This proof only goes through if it is granted that the subject of the essentialist proposition be taken in such a way that the impossible enters into it" (*ḤQ* 300.apu–pu); here, that impossible would be eclipsed-which-is-not-a-moon. I merely note this in passing.[197] I think al-Kātibī in the *Risālah* is exploring propositional implication when taken under the externalist reading of the subject. In any event, he has blocked al-Khūnajī's interpretation of the essentialist subject by his phrase in §45, by limiting the subject to "every possible . . . C" (*kull . . . jīm min al-afrād al-mumkinah*).

§75[198] Having proved seven propositions do not convert, al-Kātibī has six propositions still to consider (see e-conversion in Table 1). He takes them in two passes, dealing first with propositions read as referential necessity and perpetuity (**L** and **A**), and then those read as descriptional necessity and perpetuity ($\mathbf{L_{D1}}$, $\mathbf{A_{D1}}$, $\mathbf{L_{D2}}$, and

$\mathbf{A}_{D2}$). This is the first of the reductio proofs I mentioned in the introduction to this section. Al-Kātibī's exposition is clear, but I set out one proof—for the conversion of the necessity e-proposition—in numbered steps, both for the purposes of illustration and because it is the first point where a difference becomes apparent between al-Kātibī and Avicenna in their respective accounts of the modal syllogistic. Al-Kātibī's proof runs like this:

1. no C is possibly B
   (**L** e-proposition, premise)
2. no B is ever C
   (**A** e-proposition, to prove)
3. some B is at least once C
   ($\mathbf{X}_1$ contradictory of 2; assumed)
4. some B is not possibly B
   (3, 1 by Ferio LXL; absurd)

By contrast, Avicenna's followers prove a stronger converse; not just an **A** converse as al-Kātibī has proved, but an **L** converse:

1. no C is possibly B
   (**L** e-proposition, premise)
2. no B is possibly C
   (**L** e-proposition, to prove)
3. some B is possibly C
   ($\mathbf{M}_1$ contradictory of 2, assumed)
4. some B is not possibly B
   (3, 1 by Ferio LML; absurd)

Al-Kātibī rejects **L** e-conversion, because he does not accept Ferio LML—that is, stating minor first—"some C is possibly B, no B is possibly A, therefore some C is not possibly A." This is not a valid argument according to al-Kātibī. I say more about this claim in my commentary on the next lemma, and on §98, but for the meantime, note that it ramifies through the account of conversion, and that al-Ḥillī disagrees with al-Kātibī and defends the validity of Ferio LML.

§76[199] Al-Kātibī comes to the remaining four e-propositions, the descriptionals (**$L_{D1}$**, **$A_{D1}$**, **$L_{D2}$**, and **$A_{D2}$**). Here is a step-by-step version of the proof both al-Kātibī and his purist Avicennian detractors agree on, for **$A_{D1}$** e-conversion.

1. no C is ever B as long as it is C
   (**$A_{D1}$** e-proposition, premise)
2. no B is ever C as long as it is B
   (**$A_{D1}$** e-proposition, to prove)
3. some B is at least once C while B
   (**$X_{D1}$** contradictory of 2; assumed)
4. some B is not always B while B
   (3, 1 by Ferio $A_DX_DX_D$, absurd)

The validity—indeed, the self-evidence—of the syllogism is accepted in §99(1). But again, if the minor premise—here an absolute continuing (**$X_{D1}$**, *ḥīniyyah muṭlaqah*) in step 3—is instead a possible continuing (**$M_{D1}$**, *ḥīniyyah mumkinah*), al-Kātibī holds that there can be no productive syllogism. But, as with the proof in the preceding lemma for referential **L** e-conversion, followers of Avicenna such as al-Ḥillī claim that there is a proof for descriptional **$L_{D1}$** e-conversion:

1. no C is possibly B as long as it is C
   (**$L_{D1}$** e-proposition, premise)
2. no B is possibly C as long as it is B
   (**$L_{D1}$** e-proposition, to prove)
3. some B is possibly C while B
   (**$M_{D1}$** contradictory of 2, assumed)
4. some B is not necessarily B while B
   (3, 1 by Ferio $L_DM_DM_D$; absurd)

But the possible continuing ($\mathbf{M}_{\mathrm{D1}}$, *ḥīniyyah mumkinah*) is for al-Kātibī simply another possibility proposition, not an actuality proposition (*fiʿliyyah*; see §98), and therefore not able to serve as minor premise in a productive syllogism.

Al-Ḥillī takes himself to address the rejection of both **L** e-conversion and $\mathbf{L}_{\mathrm{D1}}$ e-conversion in the following passage, though he only makes one comment directly on the descriptional. I consider first his recapitulation of the argument in favor of the conversion, then aspects of his opponents' view, and finally how al-Ḥillī parses the descriptional.

> TEXT 76.1 Know that the writer differs from the earlier scholars with respect to the conversions of the necessary and conditional [categorical] propositions; they held that both convert as themselves. With respect to the necessary proposition, this is because if "necessarily, no C is B" is true, then "necessarily, no B is C" is true, otherwise "some B is possibly C," which is impossible for a number of reasons. The first of these is that, were it true in actuality (*law ṣadaqa bi-l-fiʿl*), it would form with the original proposition ["necessarily, no C is B"] a syllogism producing "necessarily, some B is not B," which is impossible, so the truth [of the putative conclusion] in actuality is impossible. (*ḤQ* 303.1–7)

A few points on this passage: Both al-Kātibī and al-Ḥillī accept Ferio LXL (here stated minor first: "some C is at least once B, no B is possibly A, therefore some C is not possibly A") as perfect. It is the strength of the minor premise required for productivity that matters for how strong a converse can be proved. Because Ferio LXL ("some B is at least once C, no C is possibly B, therefore some B is not possibly B") and Ferio AXA ("some B is at least once C, no C is ever B, therefore some B is never B") both lead to an impossibility when used in the reductio proofs above, they can be used to prove that the contradictory of "some B is at least once C" is true, which is to say, the **A** e-proposition "no B is ever C." To prove the stronger **L** e-proposition ("no B is possibly C"), it would be necessary to have the reductio syllogism go through with a possibility proposition as its minor ("some B is possibly C, no C is possibly B, therefore some B is not possibly B"). But this is ruled out by al-Kātibī in §98. Al-Ḥillī, by contrast, accepts the syllogism as valid, arguing in the last sentence of Text 76.1 that if one supposes the possibility proposition that is the minor to be true in actuality, it leads to an impossibility whose truth in actuality is impossible. Here is al-Ḥillī's response to al-Kātibī's claim in §98:

> TEXT 76.2 The ancients (*al-qudamā'*) claimed to produce a necessary conclusion from a possible minor with a necessary major. On the hypothesis that the possible occurs (*'alā taqdīr wuqū' al-mumkin*), the conclusion would be necessary, and thus it is necessary in the way things in fact are (*fī nafs al-amr*); otherwise, the possible entails the impossible (namely, what is not necessary being necessary on the assumption of the possible). (*ḤQ* 356.5–8)

The dispute involves both how we interpret a modal proposition, and how we interpret the modalities themselves. I simply note two comments by al-Kātibī's admired predecessor, the first quoted by al-Ḥillī himself (these expand the notes given before comments on §45).

> TEXT 76.3 A certain later scholar [al-Khūnajī] said: "We do not concede that the original [proposition] remains true on the hypothesis that the possible occurs (*'alā taqdīr wuqū' al-mumkin*), such that an impossibility follows." To which we answer: One of two matters follows—namely, either the original proposition is false on the hypothesis that the possible occurs, or it entails the impossible. Yet each one of these alternatives is impossible, so the occurrence of the

possible is impossible—so it is not possible, which is what is sought. (*ḤQ* 303.8–12)

In his *Kashf al-asrār*, al-Khūnajī enlarged on his concerns, and argued by counterexample against "no C is possibly B" converting as "no B is possibly C" (**L** e-conversion) because

> **Text 76.4** there is no impossibility in an attribute possibly belonging to two distinct species, but belonging actually only to one and not the other. So "necessarily, none of those things of which this attribute is actually affirmed in external reality is this second species" may be true, as a necessary consequence of the fact that all the things described actually by this attribute in external reality are without exception individual members of the first species; and [as a necessary consequence of the fact] that the second species is necessarily negated of the individual members of the first species. Yet the converse of the original proposition, "necessarily, none of those things under the second species in external reality has this attribute" may not be true, as a necessary consequence of the fact that it is possible to describe the second species with this attribute. In exactly the same way, "necessarily, nothing inside a certain house at a certain moment is a man" may be true if we assume that whatever is inside the house at that time is limited to not-men, while "necessarily, no man is inside that house at that time" may not be true as a converse. There are many analogous cases here. (*ḪK* 135.4–apu)

In this line of argument against al-Kātibī, al-Ḥillī offers an insight into how he reads the descriptional propositions ($\mathbf{L}_{\mathrm{D1}}$), with "no C is possibly B as long as it is C" in mind; in this, I think he differs from al-Kātibī, but I do not propose to pursue exactly how.

**Text 76.5** The meaning of the general conditional proposition [$\mathbf{L}_{D1}$] is that it is impossible to conjoin the descriptions C and B in a single essence—this entails the truth of the converse mentioned. [This can also be proved] by the proof given for the necessary proposition. (*ḤQ* 303.apu–u)

The second part of §76 deals with the two-sided descriptional propositions, the special conditional ($\mathbf{L}_{D2}$) and the special conventional ($\mathbf{A}_{D2}$). Bear in mind how these propositions unpack from—to take the special conditional as the example—"no C is possibly B as long as it is C, not always," which is short for "no C is possibly B as long as it is C, and every C is at least once B." The conversion will be by two steps. The general conditional component ($\mathbf{L}_{D1}$) converts as "no B is ever C as long as it is B," whereas the general absolute component ($\mathbf{X}_1$) converts as "some Bs are at least once C" (proved by way of the converse referred to in §79). The resulting "no B is ever C as long as it is B and some Bs are at least once C" is called the non-perpetual-for-some (*lā dā'imah fī l-baʿḍ*).[200]

§77[201] There are only two o-propositions that convert—that is, the special conditional ($\mathbf{L}_{D2}$) and the special conventional ($\mathbf{A}_{D2}$; see Table 1, o-conversion). The proof in §77 is the first ecthetic proof in the *Risālah*. This kind of ecthetic proof takes an i-proposition—in both cases, the $\mathbf{X}_1$ i-proposition "some C is at least once B"—and, taking one of the Cs that is B and calling it D, produces two propositions: "D is at least once C" and "D is at least once B." The proof is clear, so long as it is remembered that the rider "not always" hides a second proposition (in this case, "some C is at least once B"), from which we infer both that some C exists and that some B exists.[202] Here is a slightly reordered line-by-line version, with the proposition to be converted given already simplified into its two components:

1. some C is not possibly B as long as it is C (first conjunct of $\mathbf{L}_{D2}$ o-proposition, premise)
2. those same Cs are at least once B (second conjunct of $\mathbf{L}_{D2}$ o-proposition, premise)
3. D is at least once C (2, ecthesis)
4. D is at least once B (2, ecthesis)
5. D is not possibly C as long as it is B (1 and 3)
6. some B is not possibly C as long as it is B (4 and 5)
7. some B is at least once C (3 and 4)
8. some B is not possibly C as long as it is B, not always (6 and 7)

Al-Kātibī pauses to prove step 5:

5. D is not possibly C as long as it is B (to prove)
5a. D is possibly C while B (contradictory of 5; assumed)
5b. D is possibly B while C (5a)
5c. some C is possibly B while C (1, 3, 5b; absurd)

Al-Ḥillī seems to imply that the proof for o-conversion is al-Kātibī's discovery, though the best evidence suggests that it was in fact al-Khūnajī who first gave the proof.[203]

> **Text 77.1** The ancients were convinced that there is absolutely no conversion for the o-proposition. But the author has proved the conversion of the o-proposition (if it is one of the two specials) by ecthesis. (*ḤQ* 306.2–4)

The conversion of other o-propositions is rejected by counterexamples for the strongest simple proposition (the necessity, **L**) and the strongest remaining compound (the temporal, $\mathbf{L}_{T2}$); each of the rejected converses is a one-sided possibility ($\mathbf{M}_1$), which is the weakest of the modalities (see Figures 24 and 25). Here are the counterexamples with the rejected converses made explicit:

the **L** o-proposition, "some animals are not possibly human," is true, while the $\mathbf{M_1}$ o-proposition, "some humans are not necessarily animals," is false; the $\mathbf{L_{T2}}$ o-proposition, "some moon is not possibly eclipsed at quadrature, not always," is true, while the $\mathbf{M_1}$ o-proposition, "some eclipsed is not necessarily a moon," is false.

§78[204] This lemma considers and proves the conversions of all affirmative convertible (*mun'akisah*) propositions. All converses are i-propositions; al-Kātibī invites us to consider "every animal is a man" as a counterexample against a stronger converse. He moves on to prove that **L**, $\mathbf{L_{D1}}$, **A**, and $\mathbf{A_{D1}}$ all convert as $\mathbf{X_{D1}}$. Consider **L**:

| | | |
|---|---|---|
| 1. | every C is necessarily B | (**L** a-proposition, premise) |
| 2. | some B is at least once C while B | ($\mathbf{X_{D1}}$ i-proposition, to prove) |
| 3. | no B is ever C as long as it is B | ($\mathbf{A_D}$ contradictory of 2, assumed) |
| 4. | no C is ever C | (1, 3 by Celarent $A_D$LA; absurd) |

The proofs take Celarent $A_D$LA, $A_D$AA, $A_DL_DA_D$, and $A_DA_DA_D$ to be self-evident (see §99).

In §78.2, al-Kātibī directs the proof for the conversion of special conditional ($\mathbf{L_{D2}}$) and special conventional ($\mathbf{A_{D2}}$) a-propositions to proving that the converse has a non-perpetuity rider; in short—and here I take the special conventional ($\mathbf{A_{D2}}$) as an example—that "every C is always B as long as it is C, not always" converts to $\mathbf{X_{D2}}$, "some B is at least once C while B, not always." The first part ("some B is at least once C while B") has just been proved in §78.1; the second part, the rider, is proved by assuming it (that is, "some B is at least once not C") to be false, whereupon "every B is always C" would be true. This is then added to the first and second parts of the original proposition. Consider it joined to the first part:

1. every C is always B as long as it is C (first conjunct of $\mathbf{A}_{D2}$ a-proposition)
2. every B is always C (contradictory of **X** o-proposition)
3. every B is always B (1, 2 by Barbara $A_{D1}AA$)

Now consider it in tandem with the second part:

4. no C is always B (second conjunct of $\mathbf{A}_{D2}$ a-proposition)
2. every B is always C (contradictory of **X** o-proposition)
5. no B is always B (4, 2 by Celarent XXX)

But 3 and 5 are contraries, so to conjoin them would be absurd; so 2 is false and “some B is at least once not C” is true.

In §78.3, it is clear that the proofs in §78.2 do not work for the i-propositions of the special conditional and special conventional, because we do not have a universal proposition as a major premise for the syllogisms that lead to an impossibility (consider the role of 1 in the first part of the proof just offered).

> **Text 78.1** He only turned to ecthesis for the two particulars because the proof mentioned for the universals does not work here, because a particular cannot be the major in the first [figure of the syllogism]. (*ḤQ* 311.6–7)

This means that the proofs presented for the special conditional ($\mathbf{L}_{D2}$) and special conventional ($\mathbf{A}_{D2}$) i-propositions involve an ecthetic component to show that the rider of the convertend passes on to the converse. Consider the $\mathbf{A}_{D2}$ i-proposition: “Some C is always B as long as it is C, and those Cs are not always B”; al-Ḥillī expands al-Kātibī’s telegraphic version of the proof:

> **Text 78.2** If the two specials are particular, like “some C is B as long as it is C, not always,” they convert as a non-perpetual [absolute] continuing. The proof is by ecthesis, which is that

we suppose the C which is B to be D, so D is not C actually [at least once]; otherwise, it would be C always and so be B always, since the perpetuity of B is a function of the perpetuity of the description of C [which is to say, because of the first component of the proposition to be converted]; but we have already stated "not always," so [its being C always] would be absurd. And D is B actually; this is clear. So "some B is not C" is true, along with "some B is C while B," due to what was said about the general [conditional and conventional] propositions before. So it follows that "some B is C while B, not always," and that is what is sought. (*ḤQ* 310.apu–311.5)

In §78.4, the five remaining affirmative propositions that convert ($\mathbf{L}_{T2}$, $\mathbf{L}_{X2}$, $\mathbf{X}_{2}$, $\mathbf{X}_{\sim L}$, $\mathbf{X}_{1}$) are shown to convert to $\mathbf{X}_{1}$ by reductio. Take for example $\mathbf{L}_{T2}$: "every moon is eclipsed at the earth's alignment, not always," which will convert to "some eclipsed is at least once a moon." Were this not the case, "no eclipsed is ever a moon" would be true, which would produce with the original proposition "no moon is ever a moon" by Celarent (in this case, $AL_{T2}A$; see §99).

§79[205] To provide an example for al-Kātibī's alternative method set out in this lemma, al-Ḥillī gives the proof that the **L** a-proposition converts as an $\mathbf{M}_{D1}$ i-proposition (that is, that "every C is necessarily B" converts as "some B is possibly C while B").

**Text 79.1** This is an allusion to a general proof for the conversions of affirmatives, like when you say: The affirmative necessary proposition converts as a possible continuing (*al-ḥīniyyah*); otherwise, its contradictory is true, which is "no B is [possibly] C as long as it is B," which converts as itself—that is, "no C is [possibly] B as long as it is C"; but this is implicationally stronger (*akhaṣṣ*) than [and therefore implies] the contradictory of the necessary proposition and

> is therefore false, because were it true, then the contradictory of the necessary proposition assumed to be true [as the premise] would be true, so two contradictories would be true. (*ḤQ* 312.1–6)

This method also works to prove the convertibility of negative convertible propositions. Take "no C is ever B," the converse of which is "no B is ever C"; were this not the case, "some B is at least once C" would be true, which converts as "some C is at least once B." But this is the contradictory of "no C is ever B." But al-Kātibī limits the method to affirmative propositions, presumably because their proofs call on the negative conversions already proved.

§80[206] The issues touched on in this lemma are those first raised in §§75 and 76. As mentioned in my commentary on those lemmata, the issues involve how a proposition regimented for use in logic should be read, and the modal notions it displays. This is the issue in modal logic that most divides the post-Avicennian revisionist logicians like al-Khūnajī and al-Kātibī from Avicenna. I have no intention of grappling with the second issue, important though it is. I do, however, offer al-Ḥillī's sketch of the interrelation among the readings of the necessity and possibility propositions for the modal conversions.

> **Text 80.1** Our predecessors held that the two possible propositions [$\mathbf{M_1}$ and $\mathbf{M_2}$] convert as a general possible proposition [$\mathbf{M_1}$], and they sought to prove this conversion with two arguments.
>
> First, were the converse false, its contradictory (the necessary e-proposition) would be true, which converts as itself, whereupon it follows that two contradictories are true, which is absurd. For example, if every, or some, C is B by one of the two possibilities, then "some B is possibly C" is true; otherwise, "necessarily, no B is C,"

which converts to "necessarily, no C is B," which contradicts the original i-proposition and is contrary to (*yuḍādd*) the a-proposition.

Second, were the contradictory of the converse true (that is, "necessarily, no B is C"), we make it the major and the original proposition ("every" or "some C is B" by either one-sided or two-sided possibility) the minor, which produces in the first figure "necessarily, some C is not C" or "necessarily, no C is C"—this is absurd.

Since the author has proved the necessary proposition does not convert as itself, he has—in his opinion—refuted the first argument. And since—in his opinion—the possible minor is not to be used in the first figure (as will be explained presently),[207] he has refuted the second argument. And since no proof for the conversion of the possible proposition other than these two has become apparent to him, he has undoubtedly to suspend judgment (*tawaqqafa*) as to its convertibility or otherwise. (*ḤQ* 312.pu–313.15)

§81[208] This lemma returns to the treatment of hypothetical propositions begun in §38, and uses the contradictories covered in §72 above (the last lemma in which the hypotheticals were treated) to prove the converses of convertible conditional propositions. (Al-Kātibī, following the tradition, takes it to be meaningless to say that a disjunctive proposition converts, given that the order of the two disjuncts is arbitrary; see the discussion in Texts 73.3 and 73.4.) Al-Kātibī offers guidelines to prove that conditional a- and i-propositions both convert to a conditional i-proposition, and that the conditional e-proposition converts to a conditional e-proposition; he also offers a counterexample against the convertibility of the conditional o-proposition.

The proof for the conversion of the a-proposition in the conditional is of the common type, and should work for both implicative and coincidental conditionals:[209] "always, if A is B then C is D" converts as "sometimes, if C is D then A is B"; if not, then "never, if C is D then A is B," which with the original produces by Celarent the absurd conclusion, "never, if A is B then A is B." The proof for the conversion of the e-proposition is that if it is true "never, if A is B then C is D," then it is true "never, if C is D then A is B"; if not, then the contradictory is true, "sometimes, if C is D then A is B"; as minor with the first proposition it produces by Ferio "sometimes not, if C is D then C is D," which is absurd. (Both proofs depend on syllogisms mentioned by al-Kātibī in broad terms in §105.)

The counterexample for o-conversion (with the putative converse, "sometimes not, if this is a man then this is an animal") is self-explanatory. For al-Kātibī, there is no meaningful way to talk about conversion of disjunctives; here is al-Ḥillī prefiguring al-Taftāzānī's argument in Text 73.4.

> **Text 81.1** We have explained already that there is no differentiation in nature between its parts, but only in placement. If one of the two parts is opposed to its counterpart, then the second is opposed to the first; whichever is supposed as antecedent or consequent, the disjunctive does not alter. (*ḤQ* 315.1–3)

**The third discussion, on contraposition**

§82[210] This is the second of the three discussions devoted to immediate inferences (see Table 1). Again, as in the case of conversion, the Avicennian definition is abandoned. This time, however, the definition is not abandoned in search of generality (which for conversion extended the definition to include hypothetical propositions), but validity. The replacement definition offered in §82 defines an inference that is not typically called contraposition in English, but conversion by negation.[211] Here, however, I continue to call it contraposition because it was offered by the post-Avicennian logicians as a replacement for Avicennian contraposition.

Avicenna claimed to be able to prove that from a categorical a-proposition a contrapositive follows that is, arguably, stronger than what can in fact be proved to follow on his doctrine.[212] Later scholars came to accept a modified, weaker contrapositive. The original Avicennian definition that is implicitly rejected in the *Risālah* runs:

> **Text 82.1** [Contraposition] involves taking what contradicts the predicate and making it subject, and what contradicts the subject and making it predicate.[213] (*Ḫ K* 147.2–3)

For "every C is B," this would give us the contrapositive "every not-B is not-C." Al-Khūnajī says that Avicenna's account fails even on Avicenna's own doctrine, the important elements of which are set out faithfully in the *Risālah* in §§48–50.

> **Text 82.2** Because [Avicenna] said of the contrapositive of the a-proposition, if we have "every C is B," then "every not-B is not-C" follows. But if the predicate in this [second] proposition is the negative of C (*salb jīm*), [the proposition] is an affirmative with two indefinite terms (*mūjibatan maʿdūlat al-ṭarafayn*), and so its contradictory is a negative that also has two indefinite terms [which is to say, "some not-B is not not-C"]. The affirmative with a determinate predicate (namely, "some not-B is C") does not, however, follow [this contradictory], because such an affirmative is stronger than the negative with an indefinite predicate; the affirmative with determinate predicate cannot follow the contradictory of the affirmative with indefinite predicate, otherwise it would be possible that both [putative] contradictories [namely, "every not-B is not-C" and "some not-B is C"] be false together, due to the possibility that both are false when the subject does not exist. (*Ḫ K* 147.6–12)

Take "every C is B." Let us say that its contrapositive is "every not-B is not-C," otherwise "some not-B is not not-C"; we cannot claim that this with the original proposition gives us "some not-B is B" (which would be absurd and prove the assumed contrapositive to be a valid inference), because we cannot take "some not-B is not not-C" to imply "some not-B is C" to derive the absurdity. Here and in al-Khūnajī's argument, we are not entitled to assert the existence of the subject term of the o-proposition that is joined to the original proposition (see §50.1), but we must assert it to exist in the conclusion, which is an i-proposition.

Al-Kātibī's definition (differing from al-Khūnajī's [*ḪK* 148.3–4] by including hypotheticals, and by making it explicit that the truth of the contrapositive must agree with that in the original proposition) gives a weaker contrapositive than Avicenna's, so that for "every C is B" the contrapositive is "no not-B is C"; it also gives—as has become obvious in the discussion to this point—the i-proposition "some C is B" the contrapositive "some not-B is not C." Here is al-Ḥillī's summary of al-Kātibī's position:

> **Text 82.3** If we have "every C is B," its contrapositive is "no not-B is C." So not-B is the contradictory of the predicate, which we have made the subject, and C is the subject, which we have made the predicate; the quality [of the contrapositive] differs from [the quality of the original]: this is according to the opinion of the writer. But he has differed in this from the opinion of the ancients, because they made it consist of making the first part the contradictory of the second, and the second part the contradictory of the first, keeping quality the same. So they took the contrapositive of "every C is B" to be "every not-B is not-C," whereas the author took an implicate of this contrapositive and made [the implicate] the contrapositive. (*ḤQ* 315.9–apu)

Let me note before descending to the details of the specific propositions for which al-Kātibī proves al-Khūnajī's modified contraposition that al-Sharīf al-Jurjānī claims that Avicenna's original account works for the sciences.

> **Text 82.4** The contraposition used in the sciences is the contraposition in this sense [Avicenna put forward]; the sense set out by the later scholars is not used in [the sciences]. (*TT* 364n1)

I imagine that this is because every term in a science refers to something, and no term exhausts the subject matter of the science.

Contradictory terms as considered in §§26 and 27 in the *Risālah* model some of these relations; the contrapositive of an a-proposition is represented by Figures 15 and 16. Note that in both these figures, however, Avicenna's claims for the contrapositive of "every B is A" as "every not-A is not-B" are justified;[214] so too, the inference of "some not-B is A" from "some not-B is not not-A" seems to be justified by Figures 16, 17, 18, and 19 (see Text 83.3).

§83[215] The claims given in this lemma may be taken in four distinct sections, all to do with affirmative universal propositions (a-propositions). Let me preface these sections with a general comment offered by al-Ḥillī.

> **Text 83.1** Affirmatives in contraposition are interchangeable (*yatabādalāni*) with negatives in straight conversion, according to the ancients; that is, the negatives there are like the affirmatives here, and so too [the affirmatives are like the negatives]. The author disputes the second [of these claims]. (*ḤQ* 316.2–5)

So al-Kātibī by and large agrees with the claims Avicenna makes about the contrapositives of negative propositions (in other words, if a negative proposition of a given modality converts by way of straight conversion, an affirmative proposition of the same modality has one of al-Kātibī's weaker contrapositives), but not of affirmative propositions (see Table 1); reasons for differing from Avicenna have been rehearsed in commentary on §82.

I say "by and large"; one of the reasons al-Kātibī comes to different conclusions from those who follow Avicenna is that he rejects syllogisms with possibility minors for the reductio proofs. These have been mentioned in the course of commenting on straight conversions (§§73–80); al-Kātibī uses Darii LXL and Darii AXA but rejects Darii LML and Darii AMA. That this matters becomes apparent in (for example) Text 83.3.

For §83.1, the first of the two guidelines offered in Text 83.1 means that if a negative proposition does not convert by straight conversion, the affirmative proposition of the same modality has no contrapositive. The counterexamples given to show which e-propositions do not convert may be modified to identify the a-propositions with no contrapositive; this means that the discussion in §74 applies mutatis mutandis to the affirmatives. "Every moon is necessarily not-eclipsed at the time of quadrature, not always" is true as a temporal ($\mathbf{L}_{T2}$), the strongest of the seven propositions set out in Figure 25. The weakest of its putative contrapositives, a general possibility ($\mathbf{M}_1$) o-proposition, "some eclipsed is not necessarily a moon" (the weakest of the propositions set out in Figure 25), which is however false, because every eclipsed is necessarily a moon. The counterexample shows that there is no valid contrapositive for the universal affirmative of the seven propositions set out in Figure 25, nor for the particular affirmative of those propositions, because the o-proposition that has just been mentioned is the only candidate contrapositive, and it is false. Al-Ḥillī confirms that first of the two guidelines offered in Text 83.1 works for the doctrine of the ancients:

> **Text 83.2** Nor does this contrapose according to the ancients, because "necessarily, every moon is not-eclipsed at the time of quadrature, not always" is true, along with the falsity of "every eclipsed is a not-moon" by a general possibility. (*ḤQ* 316.14–apu)

Lemma 83.2 turns to the contrapositives of necessity (**L**) and perpetuity (**A**) a-propositions. As in the treatment of the conversion of the corresponding e-propositions (in §75), the ancients contraposed the necessity e-proposition as a necessity e-proposition ("as itself," *ka-nafsihi*), whereas al-Kātibī has them both as a perpetuity e-proposition.

> **Text 83.3** The ancients contraposed the necessary [a-proposition] as itself, because if it is true "every C is B necessarily," then it is true "every not-B is not-C necessarily," otherwise "some not-B is not not-C"[216] as a general possibility, from which "some not-B is possibly C" follows, which added to the original proposition produces "some not-B is B necessarily." The same is the case for the perpetual proposition.
>
> The later scholars said that the negative with two indefinite extremes does not entail the affirmative with an indefinite subject, because [the affirmative] is stronger than [the negative], and the weaker does not entail the stronger. The truth is that this [criticism by the later scholars] of the ancients is misdirected (*ghayr wārid*), because [the ancients] suppose all of what is not-B to exist and on that basis judge it to be not-C; on this hypothesis the negative and the affirmative imply each other. Further, the author has already judged this contraposition to be clear when he said that the contradictory of the more general is more particular than the

> contradictory of the more particular [as set out in §27]. (*ḤQ* 317.14–318.9)

Al-Ḥillī's last comment is a reference back to §27, where al-Kātibī has proved what amounts to the claims of the ancients to do with contraposition (see for this specific point Figure 16). The proofs that are given by al-Kātibī in §83.2 assume Darii LXL and AXA; the contrapositive of the necessity proposition cannot be the stronger "no not-B is possibly C" (let alone the ancients' "every not-B is necessarily not-C") because of al-Kātibī's rejection of Darii LML (see §98 below).

Similarly, §83.3 proves that general conditional and conventional a-propositions convert as conventional e-propositions with indefinite subjects. Again, the proofs are clear, and they assume that Darii with descriptional a-major and descriptional i-minor produces a descriptional i-conclusion. Once again, the ancients differ in two respects: first, that the contrapositive is an a-proposition with two indefinite terms, and second, that from the conditional categorical proposition ($\mathbf{L}_{D1}$) we infer a conditional proposition ($\mathbf{L}_{D1}$), and not merely the weaker conventional ($\mathbf{A}_{D1}$).

> **Text 83.4** According to the doctrine of the ancients, the conditional [categorical, that is, $\mathbf{L}_{D1}$] contraposes as a conditional, because if "every C is necessarily B as long as it is C," then "necessarily every not-B is not-C as long as it is not-B," otherwise "some not-B is possibly C while not-B." This is absurd, because were it true actually with the original proposition, it would produce "some not-B is B while not-B," which is absurd. The [contrapositive] conversion of the conventional as a conventional is the same style of proof. (*ḤQ* 319.3–9)

The fourth section of the lemma, which I have marked off in the translation as §83.4, deals with the remaining a-propositions in the privileged set—namely, the special conditional and conventional propositions (that is, **L**$_{D2}$ and **A**$_{D2}$). Their general form is: "every C is always B as long as it is C, and every C is at least once not B" (consider "writer" and "pen-holding"). Because they are compound propositions, and as in the case of straight conversion, the contraposition of these propositions is given by adopting the proof for the first part from (in this case) the preceding discussion in §83.3, and joining that contrapositive to the contrapositive of the second component proposition. I think al-Kātibī's statement of the second part of the proof is clear, but here it is line by line:

| | | |
|---|---|---|
| 1. | every C is at least once not B | (**X** e-proposition, second conjunct of premise) |
| 2. | some not-B is at least once C | (**X** i-proposition, to prove) |
| 3. | no not-B is ever C | (**A** contradictory of 2, assumed) |
| 4. | no C is ever not-B | (3 by **A** e-conversion; absurd) |

The "non-perpetual-for-some" rider goes through "due to the existence of the subject": al-Kātibī means that we know the not Bs exist because of the second component of the original proposition. Al-Ḥillī offers an alternative contrapositive:

> **Text 83.5** According to the canon of the ancients, "every C is B as long as it is C, not always" converts to "every not-B is not-C as long as it is not-B, not always for-some." The first part is due to its being an implicate of the two generals; the second is due to what went before. (*ḤQ* 320.12–15)

§84[217] Al-Kātibī completes his treatment of the contraposition of affirmative propositions by dealing with i-propositions. This lemma is made up of two parts. The first part gives a proof for the contraposition of the two special descriptional i-propositions (**L**$_{D2}$ and **A**$_{D2}$), a proof that—in parallel with the case of straight o-conversion of the specials (§77.1)—depends on the fact that the second part of the compound proposition guarantees the existence of not-B. The second part of the lemma presents counterexamples showing that there are no contrapositives for the remaining eleven propositions. Again, al-Kātibī broadly follows the first of the general guidelines in Text 83.1.

We need to keep the unpacked proposition in mind to follow al-Kātibī's proof: "some C is always B as long as it is C, and those same Cs are at least once not B." As noted, the proof has strong affinities with the proof for the o-conversion of the specials given in §77, and also uses ecthesis.

1. some C is always B as long as it is C (first conjunct of $\mathbf{A}_{\mathbf{D}2}$ i-proposition)
2. those same Cs are at least once not B (second conjunct of $\mathbf{A}_{\mathbf{D}2}$ i-proposition)
3. D is one of the Cs (ecthesis)
4. D is at least once not-B (3, 2)
5. D is never C as long as it is not-B (3, 1)
6. some not-B is never C as long as it is not-B, not always (4, 5, 3)

The justification for 5 (D is never C as long as it is not-B) is this:

5. D is never C as long as it is not-B (to prove)
5a. D is at least once C while not-B (contradictory of 5, assumed)
5b. D is at least once not-B while C (5a)
5c. one of the Cs in 1 is at least once not-B while C (5b, 1; absurd)

For the other eleven modalities of i-propositions, al-Kātibī takes the strongest simple and compound propositions (respectively, **L** and $\mathbf{L}_{\mathbf{T}2}$), and their putative contrapositives as the weakest simple proposition ($\mathbf{M}_1$). (See Figures 24 and 25 for the relative strengths of the propositions.) So "some animal is necessarily not-man" is a true **L** i-proposition, while "some man is not necessarily animal" is a false $\mathbf{M_1}$ o-proposition. And "some moon is necessarily not-eclipsed at the time of quadrature, not always" is a true $\mathbf{L_{T2}}$ i-proposition, while "some eclipsed is not necessarily a moon" is a false $\mathbf{M_1}$ o-proposition. As al-Ḥillī notes (*ḤQ* 322.8), the counterexamples were used to show that o-propositions fail in straight conversion (see §77.2, where al-Kātibī offers somewhat more explanation as to why it is enough only to show that conversion fails for these two propositions).

§85[218] The last two lemmata of the third discussion deal with contraposition of negative propositions, which mirror some but not all aspects of the straight conversion of affirmative propositions (see Text 83.1). Al-Kātibī begins by gesturing toward a general argument that the contrapositive of an e-proposition cannot be an a-proposition; al-Ḥillī expands, referring back to §78.1:

> **Text 85.1** Whether universal or particular, none of the negatives contrapose (*tan'akisu*) as a universal (as with the affirmatives in straight conversion), because the contradictory of the predicate might be more general than the original subject (*'ayn al-mawḍū'*), whereupon it would not be true to affirm the subject of all the individuals under the contradictory of the predicate. This is like "no man is a stone"; "every not-stone is a man" is not true, because not-stone is more general than man, and it is not correct to affirm [man] of all the individuals [under not-stone] (*'alā jamī' afrādihi*). (*ḤQ* 322.u–323.4)

Only two-sided propositions contrapose. Al-Kātibī claims that $\mathbf{L_{D2}}$, $\mathbf{A_{D2}}$, $\mathbf{L_{T2}}$, $\mathbf{L_{X2}}$, $\mathbf{X_2}$, and $\mathbf{X_{\sim L}}$ contrapose. His proof for $\mathbf{A_{D2}}$ runs:

1. no C is ever B as long as it is C (first conjunct of $\mathbf{A}_{D2}$ e-proposition)
2. every C is at least once B (second conjunct of $\mathbf{A}_{D2}$ e-proposition)
3. D is one of the Cs (ecthesis)
4. D is at least once not-B (3, 1)
5. D is at least once C while not-B (1; see Text 85.2)
6. some of what is not-B is at least once C while not-B (4, 5)

The justification for 5 is that because of 1, D is not-B at all times that it is C; here is al-Ḥillī on the matter:

> **Text 85.2** Because we expose (*nafriḍu*) the subject as a specific thing—let it be D—two premises are true. First, and clearly, D is not-B by absoluteness (*bi-l-iṭlāq*);[219] second, D is C at some times that it is not-B, because it is not-B at all times that it is C. [This is] due to the truth of the first proposition (*al-aṣl*): if it is true that it is not-B at all times it is C, then it is true that it is C at some times it is not-B. (*ḤQ* 323.13–pu)

Al-Kātibī's proof for $\mathbf{X}_2$, the weakest but one of the remaining four ($\mathbf{L}_{T2}$, $\mathbf{L}_{X2}$, $\mathbf{X}_2$, and $\mathbf{X}_{\sim L}$) runs:

1. no C is always B (first conjunct of $\mathbf{X}_2$ e-proposition)
2. every C is at least once B (second conjunct of $\mathbf{X}_2$ e-proposition)
3. D is one of the Cs (ecthesis)
4. D is at least once not-B (3, 1)
5. some not-B is at least once C (4, 3)

**§86**[220] This lemma deals with two final aspects of the discussion of contraposition. Dealing with the first aspect—to do with the contrapositives of the seven remaining negative propositions (that is, **L**, **A**, $\mathbf{L}_{D1}$, $\mathbf{A}_{D1}$, $\mathbf{X}_1$, $\mathbf{M}_1$, and $\mathbf{M}_2$)—al-Kātibī regrets that there has been no success in finding the requisite proofs. It is here that he differs from the second guideline in Text 83.1. The second part of the lemma has to do with hypothetical propositions, and so forms part of the piecemeal treatment begun in §38, and carried on with some interruptions through truth-conditions, quantification, contradiction, and conversion. Particularly on the first aspect, to do with al-Kātibī on modalized categorical propositions, al-Ḥillī is a hostile commentator; he believes that Avicenna has a perfectly good proof for the conversion of a possibility proposition. He is strangely less hostile to the second part, in which al-Kātibī is also rejecting Avicenna's position.

Al-Ḥillī begins his consideration of al-Kātibī's claims about the remaining propositions with the necessity proposition: does "no C is possibly B" (**L**) contrapose to "some not-B is possibly C" ($\mathbf{M}_1$, its weakest possible contrapositive)?

> **Text 86.1** The e-necessary proposition is the strongest of the simple negatives, and—according to [al-Kātibī's] doctrine—it does not contrapose, due to the lack of success in finding a proof. This is because the demonstration is either by reductio [or ecthesis], and it is not possible to come forward with such a proof here, because—given "necessarily, no C is B," if "some not-B is C" by a one-sided possibility is not true, then its contradictory is, "necessarily, no not-B is C," which converts to "necessarily, no C is not-B," which is absurd—[the putative proof] does not go through because it is possible to have [these] two negatives when the subject is empty (*kidhb al-mawḍūʿ*). Nor will ecthetic proofs work here, because—in [al-Kātibī's] view—ecthesis is only for affirmative [components of compound negatives], and not for simple negatives. And if the necessary proposition does not contrapose, nor do any of the other simple propositions, because [the **L** e-proposition] is the strongest. (*ḤQ* 325.4–13)

This would eliminate **L**, **A**, $\mathbf{L_{D1}}$, $\mathbf{A_{D1}}$, $\mathbf{X_1}$, and $\mathbf{M_1}$. The two-sided possibility ($\mathbf{M_2}$) cannot provide an adequately strong subject term for contraposition.

> **Text 86.2** The two-sided possibility among the compound propositions is also unknown as to contraposition, because a reductio proof will not go through. [This is] because, if we make the claim: if "no C is B" is true by a two-sided possibility, "some not-B is C" is true by a one-sided possibility, otherwise its contradictory is true, which is "necessarily, no not-B is C," which converts to "necessarily, no C is not-B," which is absurd, [the claim] does not go through, due to the possibility of the truth of the two negatives when the subject is empty. (In this there is occasion for reflection, because the subject of the possible proposition must be existent actually, as we explained in the verification of the quantified propositions.) An ecthetic proof does not work here either, because were we to say: suppose from C a D, so it is true of [D] that it is possibly not-B and it is C, and hence it is true that "some not-B is possibly C"; this does not go through, because the subject being taken must be insofar as it is in actuality, not in possibility, according to what we have explained. (*ḤQ* 325.14–326.8)

The second part of §86 moves on to the hypothetical propositions, and concerns the contraposition of conditionals (to be clear, the hypothetical *muttaṣilah*, not the categorical *mashrūṭah*). As one would expect, someone—the ancients—defended the contraposition of conditional hypothetical propositions (*ḤQ* 326.9). Al-Taḥtānī gives the clearest account of why al-Kātibī thinks the proofs fail. Here are the proofs he rejects:

> **Text 86.3** [The proof for] the contraposition of the affirmative conditional is because if (1) "whenever A is B then

> C is D" is true, then (2) "never, if C is not D then A is B," otherwise (3) "sometimes, if C is not D then A is B," which with the original proposition produces (4) "sometimes, if C is not D then C is D," which is absurd. Or (3) converts by straight conversion to (5) "sometimes, if A is B then C is not D." But then "A is B" implies two contradictories [that is, in (1) and (5)].
>
> [The proof for] the contraposition of the negative conditional is because if (6) "never, if A is B then C is D," then (7) "sometimes, if C is not D then A is B," otherwise (8) "never, if C is not D then A is B," so (9) "sometimes not, if A is B then C is not D," from which it follows (10) "sometimes, if A is B then C is D," which contradicts the original proposition [that is, (6)].
>
> Since these proofs did not go through according to the author, and he was not successful by way of another proof, he suspended judgment on whether or not they contrapose (*tawaqqafa fī l-inʿikās wa-ʿadamihi*). (*TT* 375.7–u)

Why reject these proofs? Al-Taḥtānī rejects the assumption that there is a problem with "A is B," implying two contradictories:

> **Text 86.4** Nor do we concede that having "A is B" entail two contradictories is impossible; because "A is B" may be impossible, and the impossible may entail the impossible. (*TT* 377.5–6)

We will see in Texts 87.2 and 87.5 that al-Ḥillī claims—and al-Taftāzānī backs him up in Text 86.5—that al-Kātibī in his *Jāmiʿ al-daqāʾiq* agrees with Text 86.4.[221]

Al-Taftāzānī goes on to say that negative coincidental conditionals contrapose, though affirmative coincidentals do not, and nor do disjunctives (*TŠ* 310.3, 310.7, 310.10); I note but do not propose to explore these claims. I conclude by drawing attention to the fact that the claims defended in the *Risālah* may not wholly reflect al-Kātibī's considered position. At the end of the argument against the contraposition of disjunctives, al-Taftāzānī says:

> **Text 86.5** This is what the author said in the *Jāmiʿ* [*al-daqāʾiq*], and by this he made it clear that what he intended by "hypotheticals" here was not the coincidentals, and that his own doctrine was not suspension [of judgment] (*al-tawaqquf*) with respect to contraposition and its failure; rather, what he meant was that [the status of] contraposition was unknowable, although in some [of the propositions] failure of contraposition was known. (*TŠ* 310.14–16)

### The fourth discussion, on the co-implication of hypothetical propositions

§87[222] This lemma follows directly on the treatment of the contraposition of conditional hypothetical propositions, and makes up part of the nineteen lemmata al-Kātibī devotes to the hypothetical propositions and their role in inference. Like the treatment of conversion in §81 and of contraposition in the preceding lemma, this is a treatment of immediate or single-premise inference; unlike conversion and contraposition, the proposition inferred is not the same species (see §72) as the premise from which it is inferred. The discussion is confined to three broad issues: what disjunctive propositions are entailed by, and entail, conditional propositions; what conditional propositions are entailed by, and entail, exclusive disjunctive propositions; and what conditional propositions are entailed by, and entail, inclusive disjunction and alternative denial (see Figures 31–33). According to al-Taftāzānī, it is so limited a treatment because this part of the syllogistic is of little value (*li-qillat jadwāhu*) (*TŠ* 310.pu).

Al-Kātibī claims to base all his proofs in this lemma on the fundamental meaning of implication and disjunction:

> **Text 87.1** Al-Kātibī alludes to the demonstration of all [these claims] with the words: "otherwise implication and disjunction mean nothing," which is to say, if there is a universal implication between two matters, then were it not impossible to conjoin (*manʿ jamʿ*) the implicant and the contradictory of the implicate, it would be possible to conjoin them so that the implicant would be affirmed without the implicate (*maʿa ʿadam al-lāzim*) such that the implicate would not be an implicate. And were it not impossible to exclude (*manʿ khulūw*) the contradictory of the implicant and the implicate, it would be possible to remove them both, so the implicant would be affirmed without the implicate, so the implicate would not be an implicate. If it is impossible to conjoin universally, were each [disjunct] not to entail the contradictory of the other, it would be possible to assert (*thubūt*) one with the other, and there would not be a disjunction—alternative denial—between them. If there is inclusive disjunction between them, then were the contradictory of each of them not to entail the other disjunct, it would be possible to affirm the contradictory of one while supposing the contradictory of the other; so then there would be no inclusive disjunction between them. (*TŠ* 311.8–16)

Al-Kātibī lists a number of implicates of the hypothetical propositions, without proofs. Al-Ḥillī assesses the claims in three passes, considering the proofs for the co-implication among a conditional, an inclusive disjunctive with the conditional's antecedent negated, and an alternative denial with the conditional's consequent negated (see Figure 31). He denies that al-Kātibī is entitled to rely on them, which is to say that al-Kātibī has an incoherent account of the conditionals:[223]

TEXT 87.2 If "whenever A is B then C is D" is true, then so is "always, either A is B or C is not D" (as an alternative denial), otherwise it would be possible to conjoin "A is B" and "C is not D" such that "A is B" is established but with "C is not D," whereupon the universal conditional ("whenever A is B then C is D") would not be true.

But on the rule [al-Kātibī] mentioned in his other books—such that it is problematic by reason of [the rule] to have contraposition for conditionals, I mean [the rule] that something entails its contradictory—this will not go through.

"Always, either A is not B or C is D" (as an inclusive disjunction) would also be true, because were both disjuncts false (*law khalā l-amr ʿanhumā*), "A is B" would be established but "C is D" would be false, and that is absurd, due to what we established at the outset; this is the sense of [al-Kātibī's] claim "otherwise the implication would be void."

But this also would not go through on his rule. (*ḤQ* 327.9–14)

Proofs are given for the claims in §87.2 by al-Taftāzānī (see Figure 32):

TEXT 87.3 Since both alternative denial and inclusive disjunction entail two conditional connections (*li-ttiṣālayn*), and the real disjunctive covers both blocking conjunction of both disjuncts and blocking exclusion of both disjuncts, it in consequence entails four conditionals, two with one of the two disjuncts as antecedent and the contradictory of the other disjunct as consequent, and two with reversed components; since were one of the disjuncts not to entail the contradictory of the other there would be no relation between them blocking conjunction of both disjuncts (*lam yakun baynahumā manʿ jamʿ*), and were the contradictory of one of the disjuncts not to entail the other disjunct, there would be no relation between them blocking exclusion of both disjuncts. For example, "this number is either even or odd" entails "always, if it is even then it is not odd" and "always, if it is odd then it is not even," and "always, if it is not even then it is odd," and "always, if it is not odd, then it is even." (*TŠ* 311.17–312.2)

And for the co-implication between alternative denial and inclusive disjunction (see Figure 33):

**Text 87.4** Further, alternative denial and inclusive disjunction each entail the other with the contradictories of both parts [of the original proposition], which is to say, blocking conjunction of both disjuncts entails blocking exclusion of their contradictories, since were the exclusion of both contradictories possible, the original parts (*al-ʿaynayn*) could conjoin, which vitiates blocking conjunction. So too, blocking exclusion of the two matters requires blocking conjunction of their contradictories, since were it possible to conjoin the two contradictories it would be possible to remove the two original parts (*irtifāʿ al-ʿaynayn*), which vitiates blocking exclusion. For example, if "either the thing is a man or horse" is true as an alternative denial, "either it is not-man or not-horse" is true as an inclusive disjunctive, and vice versa. (*TŠ* 312.2–u)

Al-Ḥillī, assessing the proofs for al-Kātibī's claims, comes at the end to say:

Text 87.5 According to his rule which has been mentioned (and that is [the possibility of] something entailing two contradictories, and the possibility of something entailing something as a universal and its absence as a particular), none of these implications goes through. (*ḤQ* 329.11–13)

In making this claim, al-Ḥillī is reinforcing the ascription of a position to al-Kātibī already ascribed to him by al-Taḥtānī in Text 86.4.

## The Third Treatise, on Syllogisms

### *The first section, on the definition and division of syllogism*

The lemmata on syllogism are presented by all commentators on the *Risālah* as treating the most important element of the logic, because it is the most important means for establishing new assertions. The first ten lemmata (§§88–97) define the syllogism and the technical terms for its components, then sketch the moods of what in Latin logic is referred to as the categorical syllogistic (what Avicenna and the later Arabic tradition affiliated with his work called connective syllogisms with categorical premises). The lemmata touch on but do not develop some of the most important notions of logic—in particular, that of the relation the conclusion has to the premises of the syllogism. The commentators develop some of these notions—and I offer here a few of their comments—but their primary concern, given that the *Risālah* is a book for beginners, is to make sure that readers are able to follow the proofs al-Kātibī sets out for the productive moods, and to be aware of the rules—and the reasons for them—to which he alludes in rejecting sterile moods.

Before I descend to the details covered in §§88–97, I should say something about how the proofs for the moods relate, on the one hand, to the passage that introduces the propositions deployed in the syllogisms (§§51–59), and, on the other, to the passage that examines how those propositions used as premises determine the modality of the proposition produced as conclusion to a syllogism (§§98–104). As I see it, the only claim al-Kātibī is making for the moods set out in this passage is that there is at least one kind of proposition covered in §§51–59, which, when used for the premises, makes the mood productive. He is presenting the syllogism taken without restriction (*al-qiyās al-muṭlaq*) as to what kind of alethically or temporally modalized propositions serve as premises. He is not, in other words, offering an assertoric syllogistic. He is simply claiming that if there are propositions that make the mood productive, this is the way a proof can be constructed to prove that productivity. The clearest indication that this is what he is doing is in the three moods presented in the lemmata I have numbered as §§95.7–97 (the last three of the eight moods he presents for the fourth figure). There, al-Kātibī says that these moods are valid when the negative proposition is one of the two "specials" (that is, $\mathbf{L}_{D2}$ and $\mathbf{A}_{D2}$, described in §§53 and 54, whose o-propositions are proved to convert in §77); it is enough that he has at least one proposition that works for the mood to include it in the presentation.

In terms of procedure, what al-Kātibī tries to show in the following treatment is that some combinations of premises must be rejected because they never produce a conclusion, and that those that are left should be accepted in the account because proofs can be constructed for their productivity.

In rejecting a number of moods as sterile, al-Kātibī refers to conditions of productivity for the figures. These conditions are given for the first figure (§91.1: that the minor premise be affirmative, and the major premise universal) with reasons for why they are necessary, for the second figure (§92: that the two premises differ in quality, and that the major be universal), for the third (§94: that the minor be affirmative, and that one of the premises be universal), and for the fourth (§95: either that both premises be affirmative and the minor universal, or that they differ in quality with one a universal). Reasons are offered why some of these conditions should be observed, and at three points (while considering the second, third, and fourth figures) al-Kātibī alludes to countermodels that produce (as I translate the phrase, first used in §92) "discrepant conclusions revealing lack of productivity" (*al-ikhtilāf al-mūjib li-ʿadam al-intāj*), "which is a syllogism with true premises leading in some cases to an affirmative conclusion, and in others to a negative conclusion." The commentators provide us with some appropriate countermodels in dealing with §§92, 94, and 95,[224] and I follow in their footsteps (though less and less doggedly as the account goes on).

The presentation of the proofs that the remaining moods are indeed productive calls on conversion (discussed above in §§67–80, though all that matters for the current discussion is that e-, a-, and i-conversion go through for some propositions, and o-conversion goes through for $\mathbf{L}_{D2}$ and $\mathbf{A}_{D2}$), reductio (*qiyās al-khalf*), or ecthesis (*al-iftirāḍ*). These last two techniques have been deployed in the treatment of conversion (reductio is used often from its first appearance in §75, and ecthesis somewhat less frequently from its first appearance in §77). Al-Kātibī reflects on the structure of a reductio proof in §113. He does not discuss ecthesis, so I offer comments distinguishing its use in §93 from the ecthesis in §75.

§88[225] The delineation of the syllogism al-Kātibī offers ("syllogism is a discourse composed of propositions from which alone, if admitted, another discourse follows necessarily") is very much like the last one Avicenna formulated, in *ʿUyūn al-ḥikmah*;[226] this is the most common definition (using "definition" for now in the loose sense of *taʿrīf*) given by post-Avicennian logicians, and differs from Avicenna's earlier definitions, and from Aristotle's and al-Fārābī's.

The commentators on the *Risālah* clarify the definition's coverage, and the force of the various elements that make it up. To begin: "Discourse composed of propositions" must include the syllogism held in the mind (*al-qiyās al-maʿqūl*) and, secondarily, the syllogism actually uttered (*al-qiyās al-malfūẓ*). Both the following (*luzūm*) of the conclusion and the syllogicity of the syllogism belong primarily to the syllogism held in the mind: "expressing the propositions entails the intellection of their meanings by one familiar with imposition, and intellecting their meanings on the hypothesis they are conceded (*ʿalā taqdīr al-taslīm*) entails the conclusion" (*TŠ* 312.9–11); it is the conclusion as understood in the mind that is primarily referred to in the definition as the "other discourse" (*TŠ* 312.11–12). The point is made by al-Rāzī with reference to the definition from *ʿUyūn al-ḥikmah*:

> TEXT 88.1 What is intended by "that which follows necessarily from admitting the premises is admitting the conclusion" is not oral discourse (*al-qawl al-lisānī*); for uttering the conclusion does not follow necessarily from uttering the premises, but rather the psychological thoughts [follow one from another].[227] (*RM* 244.u–245.2)

Al-Khūnajī directs his comments in the *Kashf al-asrār* to the delineation in the *Cure* (*AQ* 54.6–7),[228] which runs (*ḪK* 231.2–3): "a discourse in which, if more than one thing is posited, from the things posited alone, and not accidentally, another discourse different from them follows necessarily" (*qawl idhā wuḍiʿat fīhi ashyāʾ akthar min wāḥid lazima ʿan tilka l-ashyāʾ al-mawḍūʿah li-dhātihā lā bi-l-ʿaraḍ qawl mā ākhar ghayruhā bi-l-iḍṭirār*).[229] Like al-Rāzī, al-Khūnajī offers some comments on the relation between syllogism as concepts understood and as propositions uttered (more or less relaying Avicenna's comments [*AQ* 54.9–u]):

> TEXT 88.2 Know that there are intelligible syllogisms, and they are thoughts that are composed in the soul in such a way as to lead to the assertion in the soul of something else; and there are audible syllogisms, and they are uttered discourse that are composed of propositions with the restrictions which have been mentioned. [The latter] are not syllogisms insofar as they are audible—since uttering the syllogism does not require uttering what is sought, nor

> does [what is sought] follow from it—but rather insofar as they signify meanings that are understood, which are syllogisms in the first sense. (*ḪK* 239.11–pu)

The genus in the definition of syllogism is "discourse" (*qawl*). "Propositions" (*qaḍāyā*) is used in the plural to exclude single-premise inferences that, when involving a compound proposition (like for example the conversion or the contraposition of $\mathbf{L}_{D2}$), trouble the limits of the definition (the problem is solved by claiming that the elements of a compound proposition are not taken themselves as propositions). "Propositions" is used rather than "premises" because a premise is a proposition that is part of a syllogism, so using "premises" would make the definition circular (*ḤQ* 331.u–332.1). "If admitted" points to the fact that the premises need not be actually conceded or accepted; all that matters is what follows from the premises were they to be conceded. This means the definition includes syllogisms with false premises as well as those with true premises. "Follows" (*lazima*) defines a strong enough relation between premises and conclusion to exclude induction and example. (Note that *lazima* is a compression of the Arabic Aristotle's original *lazima . . . min al-iḍṭirār*; this has led me often to translate the word in the *Risālah* as "follows necessarily.") In first-figure syllogisms, the following is self-evident (see §22). "From which" (*ʿanhā*, in some formulations *minhā*) excludes a conclusion that follows from the matter of the premises (*bi-ḥasab khuṣūṣ al-māddah*) rather than from the premises by virtue of their form; for example, "no man is a stone, every stone is inanimate, no man is inanimate" is excluded. Al-Taḥtānī emphasizes the necessity implicit in "follows from them" (*lazima ʿanhā*); he agrees that the effect of the whole phrase is to exclude induction and example, "due to the possibility of a counterexample to what they prove" (*TT* 384.8–9). "Alone" (*bi-* or *li-dhātihā*) is to exclude inferences that entail a conclusion by means of a proposition not in the premise-set, whether that proposition is foreign (not entailed by the premise-set) or not (entailed by the premise-set; the example given involves a contrapositive of one of the premises). "Another discourse" points to the fact that the conclusion must differ from each one of the premises; without this restriction, any two premises would be a syllogism from which either of the two premises could be concluded (though this might also breach the "from them" condition).[230]

§89[231] The distinction between connective (*iqtirānī*) and repetitive (*istithnāʾī*) syllogisms is one Avicenna explicitly claimed as his own (*Pointers* 7.2.1 [*AI* 65.u–66.10]); it is a distinction made by all who belong to the broader logical tradition he initiated. The distinction turns on whether the conclusion is in the premises actually (*bi-l-fiʿl*) or only potentially (*bi-l-quwwah*). Whereas the connective syllogism is so-called because it establishes a connection between extremes, the repetitive is so-called "because it includes a repetitive particle; namely, 'but' (*li-shtimālihi ʿalā ḥarf al-istithnāʾ aʿnī lākin*)" (*TT* 386.9).

It was recognized by the post-Avicennian tradition that the new distinction was an important point of divergence from the Aristotelian tradition, because it made space for an extraordinary extension to the syllogistic system, an extension that was to become even larger in the works of some post-Avicennian logicians (see §§105–9 for an overview of the simpler syllogisms in this extension; these are effectively being placed alongside the categorical syllogism set out in §§91–97). This is one of the occasions on which al-Ḥillī uses the term "ancients" (in this case, actually "ancient logicians") to refer to the logicians who came before Avicenna rather than to Avicenna himself.

> **Text 89.1** The ancient logicians divided the syllogism into that composed of categoricals and that composed of hypotheticals, and they considered the first to be the connective and the second to be the repetitive. The cause of their error here was their failure to apprehend the

connective hypotheticals. When Avicenna had extracted these [syllogisms] from potentiality to actuality, he introduced a primary division of the syllogism into connective and repetitive, exactly as the author has done here. (*ḤQ* 334.6–10)

Al-Ḥillī mildly rebukes al-Kātibī's formulation of the delineation. Al-Ḥillī says that the components of a hypothetical are not taken as propositions insofar as they are parts of a hypothetical proposition (see commentary on §§60 to 66 above), which is to say, they are neither true nor false insofar as they are components of the hypothetical.

Text 89.2 We say "of the genus of the conclusion," not, as the author does, "the conclusion itself"; because the conclusion is a discourse that bears truth and falsehood, yet when it is a part of the hypothetical it does not; so the part mentioned in the syllogism is not itself the conclusion. (*ḤQ* 334.pu–335.1)

But the most crucial element of the delineation is the distinction between a conclusion that is actually in the premises, and one that is only potentially in the premises. On this, al-Taḥtānī says:

Text 89.3 Al-Kātibī restricted the mention of the conclusion and its contradictory in the definition with "actually" simply because, were it not restricted like this, the connective syllogisms would come under the definition of the repetitive syllogism; since the conclusion is a compound of matter (its two extremes) and of form (its compositional structure), and a thing's matter is that through which potentiality comes about, so the conclusion is mentioned in [the connective syllogisms] potentially. (*TT* 386.13–apu)

Further doubts are raised about the delineation, among them whether—given that the definition of syllogism in §88 insists that the conclusion be other than either of the premises—the fact that the repetitive syllogism is defined as actually mentioning the conclusion or its contradictory breaches that part of the definition of syllogism. It does not:

> **Text 89.4** We do not concede that if the conclusion is actually mentioned in the syllogism it will not be distinct (*mughāyirah*) from each of the premises. It would only be like that were the conclusion not part of the premise, which is rejected, because the premise in the repetitive syllogism is not "the sun is up" but rather its entailing the presence of day (*bal istilzāmuhu li-wujūd al-nahār*). (*TT* 387.6–9)

So too the fact that the part of a hypothetical does not have a truth-value insofar as it is a part of a hypothetical—and therefore is not a proposition, unlike the conclusion—does not prevent it being an actual mention of the conclusion; all that is required for actual mention is both extremes in the order given in the conclusion.

§90[232] Al-Kātibī's exposition of the terms of art specific to the syllogism requires no commentary. He includes fourth-figure syllogisms, though the fourth figure is only distinguishable when the syllogism (which in the Arabic tradition is the major and minor premises, excluding the conclusion) is considered relative to the conclusion. Considered in itself, the syllogism can only have three figures.[233] Note that al-Kātibī, in line with the later Arabic tradition, puts minor premise before major, and subject before predicate (so *Prior Analytics* 25b38 *anna alif in kānat maqūlah ʿalā kull bāʾ wa-kānat bāʾ tuqālu ʿalā kull jīm* is for al-Kātibī *kull jīm bāʾ wa-kull bāʾ alif*); I follow al-Kātibī in my translations, but when I use the Latin mnemonics, Barbara Celarent, or a, e, i, o for premises (as in "the premise-pair a-e"), reference is to the major first.

Al-Kātibī begins with the categorical syllogisms:

> **Text 90.1** The connective syllogism is either categorical (if it is made up of two categorical propositions) or hypothetical (if it is not so constructed). Since the categorical is simpler, let us begin with it. (*TT* 388.13–14)

Al-Taḥtānī lays out the two sets of conditions that need to be covered:

> **Text 90.2** Know that for the productivity of the four figures there are conditions that have to do with the quantity and quality of the premises, and conditions that have to do with the modality of the premises. (*TT* 391.apu–pu)

Al-Kātibī deals with the first set of conditions from §§91 to 97, and moves on to the second set in Section 2 (§§98–104).

**§91**[234] The two conditions for productivity in the first figure are that the minor premise be affirmative (because if it is not affirmative, the minor term will not come under the middle [*TT* 392.4–9]), and that the major premise be universal (because if it is not universal, the minor term may not come under the major term predicated of the middle [*TT* 392.10–14]). The first condition rules out eight premise-pairs (stating major premise first), a-e, a-o, e-e, e-o, i-e, i-o, o-e, and o-o, and the second condition rules out (I repeat those already eliminated by the first condition; that is, the last four I have just listed) i-a, i-e, i-i, i-o, o-a, o-e, o-i, and o-o; together the two conditions rule out twelve premise-pairs of the possible sixteen. Unlike Aristotle, neither al-Kātibī nor his commentators go any further into the rejection of these twelve or the moods they can make up.[235] The remaining four are taken to make up moods that are said to be self-evident (*bayyinah bi-nafsihā*); they are (given major first):[236]

| | | |
|---|---|---|
| §91.2 | Barbara: | BaA, CaB ⊢ CaA |
| §91.3 | Celarent: | BeA, CaB ⊢ CeA |
| §91.4 | Darii: | BaA, CiB ⊢ CiA |
| §91.5 | Ferio: | BeA, CiB ⊢ CoA |

§92[237] Al-Kātibī sets out the two conditions for productivity in the second figure: that the premises differ in quality, and that the major premise be universal; "otherwise we get discrepant conclusions revealing lack of productivity (*wa-illā la-ḥaṣala l-ikhtilāf al-mūjib li-ʿadam al-intāj*)." Al-Taḥtānī provides relevant examples leading to such conclusions; these show us that breaching either of the two conditions leaves us with a premise combination for which we can find true premises and a true affirmative putative conclusion, and for which we can also find true premises and a true negative putative conclusion.

> **Text 92.1** And the fact is that such discrepancy requires the sterility of the syllogism, because, when it is true with the affirmative it does not produce the negative, and when it is true with the negative it does not produce the affirmative. This is because what is meant by "production" is that the syllogism entails one of the two specifically (*istilzām al-qiyās li-aḥadihimā ʿalā al-taʿyīn*). (*TT* 396.10–12)

Here are two compressed passages in which al-Taḥtānī presents triplets of terms. The first is designed to show that the first condition—that the premises differ in quality—must be observed. If the condition is breached, the premises will agree in quality:

> **Text 92.2** Consider the case that the two premises are affirmative. [It leads to discrepant conclusions] because it is true "every man is an animal" and "every rational is an animal," and the true [conclusion, "every man is rational,"] would be affirmative; but were we to change the major

> premise [from "every rational is an animal"] to "every horse is an animal," the true [conclusion, "no man is a horse,"] would be negative.
>
> Now consider the case that the two [premises] are negative. [It leads to discrepant conclusions] due to the truth of "no man is a stone" and "no horse is a stone," and the true [conclusion, "no man is a horse,"] would be negative; but were we to have "no rational is a stone" [in place of the major premise "no horse is a stone,"] the true [conclusion, "every man is rational,"] would be affirmative. (*TT* 395.14–u)

The second passage assumes that the second condition—that the major be universal—is breached, so the major is either an i-proposition or an o-proposition.

> **Text 92.3** Consider the case that it is an i-proposition. [It leads to discrepant conclusions] because "no man is a horse" and "some animal is a horse" are true, and the true [conclusion, "some man is an animal,"] is affirmative; but were we to change the major ["some animal is a horse"] to "some thing-that-neighs is a horse," the true [conclusion, "some man is not a thing-that-neighs,"] is negative.
>
> Then consider the case that it is an o-proposition. [It leads to discrepant conclusions] because "every man is an animal" and "some body is not an animal" are true, and the true [conclusion, "some man is a body,"] is affirmative; but with "some stone is not an animal" the true [conclusion, "some man is not a stone,"] is negative. (*TT* 396.4–9)

With these four pairs of triplets, al-Taḥtānī takes himself to have established the two conditions of productivity for the second figure. He does not consider and reject every invalid mood. He would be entitled to assume that premises weaker than those he considers must also be rejected;[238] this would be another application of the rule (see §74) that what follows from the weaker follows from the stronger (*lāzim al-aʿamm lāzim al-akhaṣṣ*) and—more specifically—its contrapositive, what does not follow from the stronger does not follow from the weaker. Stronger conclusions must also be rejected.[239] But this is not the path al-Taḥtānī follows.

§93[240] The conditions defended in §92 leave four productive moods, named by Peter of Spain as Cesare, Camestres, Festino, and Baroco, and treated by both Peter and al-Kātibī in that order. In Strobino's shorthand:

| | | |
|---|---|---|
| §93.2 | Cesare: | AeB, CaB ⊢ CeA |
| §93.3 | Camestres: | AaB, CeB ⊢ CeA |
| §93.4 | Festino: | AeB, CiB ⊢ CoA |
| §93.5 | Baroco: | AaB, CoB ⊢ CoA |

As noted above, al-Kātibī proves that these syllogisms are productive by calling on the four self-evident first-figure moods, the conversions proved in §§73–80, reductio, and syllogistic ecthesis. Al-Kātibī begins with Cesare (§93.2). I expand al-Kātibī's shorthand proofs for Camestres (§93.3), Festino (§93.4), and Baroco (§93.5) to show the methods he has in mind; I give the proof for Camestres by conversion, for Festino by ecthesis, and for Baroco by reductio.

Camestres by conversion; note that the minor will have to be a convertible proposition (*munʿakisah*):

| | | |
|---|---|---|
| 1. | every A is B | (major) |
| 2. | no C is B | (minor) |
| 3. | no B is C | (2, e-conversion) |
| 4. | no A is C | (1, 3 by Celarent) |
| 5. | no C is A | (4, e-conversion) |

Festino by ecthesis; in 3, al-Kātibī exposes that part of C which is B and calls it D; note that the ecthesis here and in commentary on the fourth figure is syllogistic ecthesis, to be distinguished from the perceptual ecthesis (*al-iftirāḍ bi-l-ḥiss*) used in proving i-conversion (see comments before the treatment of §73 above):

| | | |
|---|---|---|
| 1. | no A is B | (major) |
| 2. | some C is B | (minor) |
| 3. | every D is B, some C is D | (2, i-ecthesis) |
| 4. | no D is A | (1, first proposition in 3 by Cesare) |
| 5. | some C is not A | (4, second proposition in 3 by Ferio) |

Baroco is by reductio (see §113), where in 3 the contradictory of the conclusion is assumed:

| | | |
|---|---|---|
| 1. | every A is B | (major) |
| 2. | some C is not B | (minor) |
| 3. | every C is A | (contradictory of conclusion, assumed) |
| 4. | every C is B | (3, 1 by Barbara; absurd) |
| 5. | not (every C is A) | (contradictory of 3) |

Some had sought to prove Baroco by ecthesis:

> **Text 93.1** The ancients proved it also by ecthesis, by supposing that some [of "some C is not B"] as D, so it is not B; so it is true "no D is B," and "every A is B," so "no D is A." Then we say "some C is D," and "no D is A," which produces "some C is not A," which is what is sought. The author does not mention this [method] because according to him ecthesis invokes the existence of the subject, and the subject of the negative can be nonexistent;[241] but there is no doubt their argument is flawed.[242] (*ḤQ* 343.5–11)

§94[243] The exposition of the third figure follows the model established in the treatment of the second; I sketch rapidly the rejections and proofs to which al-Kātibī alludes. There are again two conditions for productivity in the third: first, that the minor is affirmative, and second, that one of the premises is universal. Take the first condition: If the minor were to be negative, it would form a premise-set with either an affirmative or a negative proposition. Consider it with an affirmative major (so "no C is B" and "every A is B") with "horse" as minor, "man" as middle, and "animal" and "rational" as major terms. So we have:

1.1 no man is a horse, every man is an animal; every horse is an animal
1.2 no man is a horse, every man is rational; no horse is rational

With a negative major, consider examples with "that-which-neighs" and "horse" as major terms.

2.1 no man is a horse, no man is that-which-neighs; every horse is that-which-neighs
2.2 no man is a horse, no man is a donkey; no horse is a donkey

Al-Taḥtānī goes on to explain why we cannot breach the second condition.

> **Text 94.1** One of the premises must be universal because, were they both particular, it would be possible that the part of the middle that is judged to come under the major is not the part of the middle that is judged to come under the minor, and so the judgment may not pass from the middle to the minor. This is like "some animals are human" with "some animals are horses." The judgment on some animals as being horses does not pass to the part judged to be humans. (*TT* 401.12–16)

Observing both conditions leaves six productive moods, referred to by the Latin tradition as Darapti, Felapton, Disamis, Datisi, Bocardo, and Ferison; al-Kātibī presents them in the following order: Darapti (§94.3), Felapton (§94.4), Datisi (§94.5), Ferison (§94.6), Disamis (§94.7), and Bocardo (§94.8). Aside from when he gives the ecthetic proof for Datisi, al-Kātibī merely names the methods by which the moods may be proved productive. Here are the syllogisms in Strobino's shorthand:

| | | |
|---|---|---|
| §94.3 | Darapti: | BaA, BaC ⊢ CiA |
| §94.4 | Felapton: | BeA, BaC ⊢ CoA |
| §94.5 | Datisi: | BaA, BiC ⊢ CiA |
| §94.6 | Ferison: | BeA, BiC ⊢ CoA |
| §94.7 | Disamis: | BiA, BaC ⊢ CiA |
| §94.8 | Bocardo: | BoA, BaC ⊢ CoA |

§95[244] The conditions for productive fourth-figure moods are the most complex of those offered, being set out as disjuncts: either that both premises be affirmative and the minor be a universal, or that the two premises differ in quality and one of them be universal. As al-Taḥtānī says:

> **Text 95.1** That is because, were one of the two [conditions] not met, one of three outcomes would follow: both premises would be negative, or both would be affirmative and the minor particular, or they would differ in quality and both would be particular. In these cases, we have discrepant conclusions, which reveal nonproductivity. (*TT* 405.15–17)

Al-Taḥtānī once again offers pairs of triplets to reject sterile moods. For the first case where the conditions are not met (e-e-4):

1.1 no man is a horse, no donkey is a man; no horse is a donkey

1.2 no man is a horse, no thing-that-neighs is a man; every horse is a thing-that-neighs

For the second case (a-i-4):

2.1 some animal is a man, every rational is an animal; some man is rational
2.2 some animal is a man, every horse is an animal; some man is not a horse

For the first possibility under the third case (o-i-4):

3.1 some rational is man, some animal is not rational; some man is an animal
3.2 some rational is man, some horse is not rational; some man is not a horse

And for the second possibility under the third case (i-o-4):

4.1 some man is not a horse, some animal is man; some horse is an animal
4.2 some man is not a horse, some rational is man; some horse is not rational

If al-Taḥtānī has shown that the conditions must be observed, al-Kātibī is left with eight productive fourth-figure moods, rather than the five normally given, which are the first five in the *Risālah*: Bramantip, Dimaris, Camenes, Fesapo, Fresison.[245] The proofs for their productivity are easily recovered from al-Kātibī's directions (which are all for reduction through conversion and inversion of premise order). Al-Kātibī goes on to give another three moods (§§95.8–95.10), and comes back to meditate on their relatively recent acceptance as valid in §97. Here are the moods in Strobino's shorthand:

| | | |
|---|---|---|
| §95.3 | Bramantip: | AaB, BaC ⊢ CiA |
| §95.4 | Dimaris: | AaB, BiC ⊢ CiA |
| §95.5 | Camenes: | AaB, BeC ⊢ CeA |
| §95.6 | Fesapo: | AeB, BaC ⊢ CoA |
| §95.7 | Fresison: | AeB, BiC ⊢ CoA |
| §95.8 | A-O-O: | AaB, BoC ⊢ CoA |
| §95.9 | O-A-O: | AoB, BaC ⊢ CoA |
| §95.10 | I-E-O: | AiB, BeC ⊢ CoA |

§96[246] Al-Kātibī notes that all moods in the fourth can be proved by reductio (first used in the *Risālah* in §75), but goes on to point out that Dimaris and Fresison can also be proved by ecthesis. His further comments relate to Dimaris, but what follows is at least one way they can be made to apply to Fresison (though i-conversion on 1 and e-conversion on 2, followed by Ferio would surely be easier):

| | | |
|---|---|---|
| 1. | some B is C | (minor) |
| 2. | no A is B | (major) |
| 3. | every D is B, some D is C | (1, i-ecthesis) |
| 4. | no B is A | (2, e-conversion) |
| 5. | no D is A | (first proposition in 3, 4 by Celarent) |
| 6. | some C is D | (second proposition in 3, i-conversion) |
| 7. | some C is not A | (5, 6 by Ferio). |

§97[247] I give al-Taḥtānī's comments here in full, because they record not only the countermodels the ancients gave against the productivity of the last three moods noted in §95, but also the reason these moods were subsequently accepted. As is so often the case with innovations in the later logic, the eminent scholar who showed how to prove productivity for these moods with the appropriate proposition (which is to say, $\mathbf{L}_{\mathrm{D2}}$ or $\mathbf{A}_{\mathrm{D2}}$) may be—once again—Afḍal al-Dīn al-Khūnajī (although al-Ṭūsī credits al-Abharī with discovering the proof).[248] That said, al-Khūnajī and al-Rāzī are named by al-Ḥillī as opposing the validity of syllogisms beyond the first five (*ḤQ* 354.6) (wrongly, as al-Ḥillī says, because the arguments rehearsed and then rejected in Text 97.1 do not take $\mathbf{L}_{D2}$ or $\mathbf{A}_{D2}$ o-conversion into account [*ḤQ* 355.11–13]).

> **Text 97.1** The ancients used to limit the productive moods of this figure to the first five; according to them, the last three moods were sterile due to discrepant conclusions arising in them.
>
> Consider the sixth mood [A-O-O], it is true that "some animal is not human," and "every horse is an animal," and the truth is the negative [conclusion; "some human is not a horse"]; or [with a different major] "every rational is animal," and the truth is the affirmative [conclusion: "some human is rational"].
>
> Consider the seventh [O-A-O], it is [sterile] because it is true that "every man is rational," and "some horse is not man," and the truth is the negative [conclusion; "some horse is not rational"]; or [with a different major] "some animal is not man," and the truth is the affirmative [conclusion; "some rational is animal"].
>
> Consider the eighth [I-E-O], it is like "no man is a horse," and "some rational is a man" [which terms are true as a negative conclusion, "some horse is not rational"], or [with a different major] "some animal is man" [which terms are true as an affirmative conclusion, "some rational is animal"].
>
> The writer alludes to his answer by the fact that the proof for discrepant conclusions in these moods only goes through if the syllogism is made up of simple premises; but if we stipulate for its productivity that the negative that is used must be one of the two specials [$\mathbf{L}_{D2}$ or $\mathbf{A}_{D2}$], these objections have no traction. Know that their productivity is based on the conversion of the special o-proposition as itself; because the sixth

> and the seventh simply reduce through its conversion to the second [figure] and the third [figure], and the eighth only produces were it such that if its premises were reversed, there would result in the first figure a negative special that would convert to the conclusion sought. The conversion of the [special] was not apparent to the ancients, but a certain eminent later scholar (*baʿḍ al-afāḍil min al-mutaʾakhkhirīn*) hit upon it and proved it. (*TT* 412.1–413.u)

*The second section, on mixes of modalized propositions*

In setting out al-Kātibī's take on the modal mixes (that is, syllogisms with mixes of modalized premises, taken with reference to the strongest modal conclusion they produce), I have been guided above all by the pioneering work of Nicholas Rescher. His exposition was aided enormously by a series of tables of the mixes (each of the modals given as minor along the vertical axis, and each given as major along the horizontal axis), and I have presented these tables too. As far as I can tell, the first commentator to present al-Kātibī's claims in this way was al-Taḥtānī (though I present versions from Ibn Mubarakshāh; see opening comments to the Tables). Here, I mainly present a paraphrase of what al-Taftāzānī has to say in support of al-Kātibī's account in reaction to al-Ḥillī's hostile comments.

I have noted already in treating the propositions, their contradictories, and their conversions, that although there are thirteen propositions "that are customarily investigated," there are in fact more propositions called on to serve as contradictories. Even more propositions come into play in treating the modal mixes, above all because of the way the rules of production operate on the temporal ($\mathbf{L}_{T2}$) and spread ($\mathbf{L}_{X2}$) propositions.

Since this is an important part of al-Kātibī's logic, and is often at odds with Avicenna's, I make reference to Avicenna's alternative account in *Pointers*. There, Avicenna had—for the first time in his treatments of the modals, so far as I am aware—decided to treat modal mixes one figure at a time, rather than by taking one mix of modal propositions and following that premise-pair through all figures (as he does in the *Najāt*). The way Avicenna presents his account is as a modified version of the broadly Aristotelian rule of the major, which has it that the modality of the conclusion follows the modality of the major premise (*al-natījah tābiʿah li-l-kubrā*); since al-Kātibī adopts most of Avicenna's modifications to the rule, I deal with them below.

§98[249] The Rāzian logicians differ from Avicenna in that they take all first-figure syllogisms with a possibility proposition (whether $\mathbf{M_1}$, $\mathbf{M_2}$, $\mathbf{M_{D1}}$, or $\mathbf{M_{D2}}$) as minor premise to be sterile (see Text 45.a and preceding notes). Avicenna accepted first-figure syllogisms with a possibility proposition as minor premise: Barbara MMM ("every C is possibly B, every B is possibly A, therefore every C is possibly A"; M-BaA, M-CaB $\vdash$ M-CaA), Barbara XMM: ("every C is possibly B, every B is A, therefore every C is possibly A"; X-BaA, M-CaB $\vdash$ M-CaA), and Barbara LML ("every C is possibly B, every B is necessarily A, therefore every C is necessarily A"; L-BaA, M-CaB $\vdash$ L-CaA).[250] The thrust of §98 is to exclude these mixes. Al-Ḥillī fought against al-Kātibī here more than on any other point of logic; the second paragraph of Text 98.1 gives his defense of "assuming the occurrence of the possible," his name for a proof by upgrading, a move al-Ṭūsī refers to as supposing the possible actual (*farḍ dhālika l-mumkin mawjūdan*):[251]

> **Text 98.1** The ancients claimed to produce a necessary conclusion from a possible minor with a necessary major. Assuming the possible to be the case (*ʿalā taqdīr wuqūʿ al-mumkin*), the conclusion would be necessary, and thus it is necessary in the way things are in themselves (*fī nafs al-amr*); otherwise the possible entails the impossible (namely, what is not necessary being necessary on the assumption of the possible).

[And the ancients also claimed] that from a possible minor and a possible major a one-sided possible [is produced]. [This is because,] assuming the possible to be the case, the possible [conclusion] is true; so it is that the possible [conclusion] is true in the way things are in themselves. Otherwise, what is not possible in the way things are in themselves could be possible on assuming the possible to be the case, and this is absurd.

So too if the major is existential and the minor a possible. If it is a two-sided possible, then, with one of its two parts, the minor forms a syllogism that produces a one-sided possible, and with its other part, a syllogism produces a one-sided possible conclusion differing [in quality] from the first—so the conclusion will be two-sided.

The later scholars rejected the truth of the major on the assumption of the occurrence of the minor. This is an error [which they should reject], otherwise they are mired in what they seek to flee. For were the necessary or possible majors false on the occurrence of the possible [predicate in the possible minor], then the possible would entail the impossible, because the falsity (*kidhb*) of the necessary or the possible is impossible in itself. [This falsity] may, however, be the case for the existential, due to the possibility (*iḥtimāl*) that the judgment follow not the essence of the middle but its description, which is unknown as to whether it applies to the essence of the minor term; so here one may rebut the truth as to actuality. But the possible [must follow], for the possible follows in any case.

According to the doctrine of the ancients, the productive connections in this figure are 169 moods, coming about from 13 squared. According to the doctrine of the author, 26 of these are dropped, the result of 13 times 2 possible propositions. (*ḤQ* 356.5–357.4)

As mentioned, all of the syllogisms with possibility minors (the three listed at the beginning of this section of the commentary) are rejected by the Rāzian logicians, at least, unless a special reading of the subject term (*bi-ḥasab al-ḥaqīqah*) is adopted. The problem as they see it is that the middle term ("B" in all the examples above) may not actually come to belong to the minor term ("C"), whereupon the judgment made of B will not pass to C (*fa-yajūzu an lā yakhruja ilā l-fiʿl fa-lā yataʿaddā l-ḥukm ilayhi*). Al-Taftāzānī reflects specifically on the last syllogism (Barbara LML), offers a countermodel, and distinguishes Avicenna's view from his own. To consider Barbara LML, he imagines a situation in which Zayd only rides horses.

> **Text 98.2** For this reason it is true on the supposition that has been mentioned, "every donkey is possibly a mount for Zayd," and "every mount for Zayd is necessarily a horse," along with the falsity of the conclusion [that is, "every donkey is necessarily a horse"]. This is clear if what is taken into account with respect to the subject term is describing the essence with a qualification that is actually the case (*bi-l-fiʿl fī nafs al-amr*); but if what is taken into account is describing it with what is actual in mental existence (*bi-l-fiʿl bi-l-dhihn*), which is Avicenna's position, then the possible proposition as minor premise (*al-ṣughrā l-mumkinah*) produces just as if simple possibility were taken into account (as is the case on al-Fārābī's view, since there is no difference between the two views in real but only in notional terms). [On Avicenna's position,] the counterexample would have no traction because the major would be false. As you learned in the section on propositions, there is matter here for reflection. (*TŠ* 335.8–14)

Which is to say, the major premise in the counterexample on al-Taftāzānī's reading ("Every actual mount for Zayd is necessarily a horse") is unproblematically true; whereas when it is read on Avicenna's understanding ("Every possible mount for Zayd is necessarily a horse"), it is false, and Avicenna need not worry about the counterexample. But for the purposes of the *Risālah*, the subject term is read throughout all the inferences presented in the way al-Taftāzānī reads it here.

This is one part of a long discussion reviewing some of the considerations at play in deciding that the possibility proposition could not serve as minor premise in a modal syllogism. Note that al-Taftāzānī has not brought up issues of how modalities are defined—other writers did that—but only how the subject term of a proposition was to be understood.

§99[252] The *Risālah* has set down the minimum requirements for the modalities of the premises for a first-figure mood to produce a conclusion (that the minor premise not be a possibility proposition). In §99, al-Kātibī considers the strength of the conclusion; this is where he directly accosts the second set of problems dealt with by Avicenna's interpretation of the Rule of the Major. It is worthwhile stating Avicenna's rule before considering the variations al-Kātibī introduces (and has already introduced by virtue of §98). Here is how al-Ṭūsī states it:

> **Text 99.1** So from this discussion it emerges that the necessary major, with all actual and non-actual minors (*al-ṣughrayāt al-fiʿliyyah wa-ghayr al-fiʿliyyah*), produces a necessary conclusion. If a nonnecessary major and the minor are two actuals, an actual is produced. If one of [the premises], or both, are possible, a possible is produced. A major that may be either produces something that may be actual or non-actual. So some conclusions happen to follow the major, like what results from an actual minor with whatever major, so long as it is not descriptional. Some of them happen to follow the minor, like what results from a

possible and an absolute, whether both are one-sided or two-sided (*ʿāmmatayn aw khāṣṣatayn*). And some happen to differ from both [major and minor], like what results from a possible and an absolute, one of which is one-sided, the other two-sided. Then the conclusion is like the minor in possibility, and the major in whether it is one-sided or two-sided. (*ṬḤ* 394.10–395.5)

The first rule pressed upon us by al-Kātibī (§98) is that the minor premise must be one of the actuals (*al-fiʿliyyāt*), which is to say, one of the eleven left from the customary thirteen after the one- and two-sided possibility propositions ($\mathbf{M_1}$ and $\mathbf{M_2}$) are taken out. As al-Ḥillī has told us in Text 98.1, the modal mixes we have left to consider are not thirteen squared, but thirteen times eleven.

Once we have set the mixes with possibility propositions as minor premises to one side, does al-Kātibī now—like Avicenna—by and large follow the major? Yes, unless (and in this he also imitates Avicenna) the major is a descriptional. This step in the process of working out modal mixes calls on the deeply Avicennian distinction between referential (*dhātī*) and descriptional (*waṣfī*) readings (see commentary on §52 above), a distinction that is crucially important for Avicenna's own account of the modal mixes in Text 99.1 (see Text 52.1). We must treat the nine non-descriptionals as one group (group 1), and the four descriptionals (*al-waṣfiyyāt*, which is to say $\mathbf{L_{D1}}$, $\mathbf{A_{D1}}$, $\mathbf{L_{D2}}$, and $\mathbf{A_{D2}}$) as another (group 2). When a proposition from group 1 is major premise, the conclusion has the modality of the major, which is to say that for these propositions, the Avicennian rule stands without modification. When, however, a proposition from group 2 is major premise, the conclusion by and large follows the modality of the minor, with a few exceptions.

Al-Taftāzānī sets out five matters to explain why the rules apply (*TŠ* 337.1–338.5). (1) Group 1 conclusions follow the major due to the clear subsumption of the minor under the middle (*li-l-indirāj al-bayyin*); the major premise makes clear that everything of which the middle is established is judged by the major term, and by the same modality. (2) Group 2, by contrast, has a conclusion that follows the minor premise, because the major premise signifies that the major term belongs (to the middle, and by the middle to the minor) exactly as long as the middle exists; so the major term will belong to the minor term as long as the middle belongs to the minor. In short, if the minor premise signifies that the middle belongs to the minor perpetually as a referential predication (that is, as the predicate in a *dhātī* proposition), the major term in the major premise will also belong as a referential predication, even if the major premise is descriptional. (3) We drop the second element of compound propositions when they serve as minors (this applies to both referential and descriptional propositions); there is no reason that the conclusion will be limited by the second element given that the minor has come under the middle. Anyway, it will be the affirmative element of the compound that meets the condition for first-figure productivity, not the negative element. (4) The only non-Avicennian rule in this part of the *Risālah*, however, is that the specific necessity (*al-ḍarūrah al-makhṣūṣah*) is dropped; this is to say, if one of the premises is nonnecessary and necessity is specific only to the other premise, the necessity is stripped out, appearing in the conclusion as perpetuity or even something weaker. Finally, (5) the rider on the major will remain as an element of the conclusion.

There is, however, a combination (*ta'līf*) from which no syllogism with true premises can be constructed. In his presentation of the first figure in *Pointers* 7.3.13, Avicenna closes with the words (and "pure" here has the sense of two-sided):

> **Text 99.2** Know that if the minor is necessary and the major pure existential (*wujūdiyyah ṣirfah*) among those in the sense of "while the subject is described in a certain way," there is no syllogism with true premises that can be constructed (*lam tantaẓim minhu qiyās ṣādiq al-muqaddamāt*). (*AI* 70.5–7)

Al-Ṭūsī illustrates the point with the following example (*ṬḤ* 399.12–13):

| | | |
|---|---|---|
| minor: | every sphere is necessarily moving | (**L** a-proposition) |
| major: | every moving thing necessarily changes, not always | ($\mathbf{L}_{D2}$ a-proposition) |

Remember that the "not always" rider is short for (using the concrete terms of this example) "and no moving thing is always changing"; this amounts to the claim that no moving thing is always moving. But the minor is making the claim that celestial spheres are necessarily—and therefore always—moving; to assert both at once would be absurd. Al-Taftāzānī sets out the problem in his treatment of the next lemma from another angle:

> **Text 99.3** It will be obvious to you that no syllogism with true premises is constructed from the necessary proposition with either the special conditional or special conventional; this because the conclusion that is implied—I mean the non-perpetual necessary, or the non-perpetual perpetual—is absurd, and the absurd cannot be implied by the true (*wa-l-muḥāl lā yakūnu lāziman li-l-ṣādiq*). (*TŠ* 338.6–8)

Rescher was able to set out a clear statement of the rules for the first figure, which I modify slightly to fit with the conventions I have been following:[253]

1. The minor premise must be one of the actuality propositions (that is, the eleven propositions left over after taking out $\mathbf{M}_1$ and $\mathbf{M}_2$).
2. If the major is not one of Group 2 (that is, if it is not one of $\mathbf{L}_{D1}$, $\mathbf{A}_{D1}$, $\mathbf{L}_{D2}$, or $\mathbf{A}_{D2}$), then the mode of the conclusion is the mode of the major.

3. If the major is from Group 2, then the mode of the conclusion is that of the minor except that (a) the conclusion is under whatever rider the major was under, and (b) the conclusion is **L** if and only if both the minor and the major are (see Table 2, first-figure mixes).

§100[254] Once again, the first consideration for mixes in the second figure is the minimum conditions for productivity; strength of conclusion is deferred to the next lemma. Here is a paraphrase of the first condition according to al-Taftāzānī (*TŠ* 338.14–15):

First condition: (1a) minor one of the two perpetuals (**L** or **A**), or (1b) major one of six convertible e-propositions (**L**, **A**, $\mathbf{L}_{\mathbf{D1}}$, $\mathbf{L}_{\mathbf{D2}}$, $\mathbf{A}_{\mathbf{D1}}$, $\mathbf{A}_{\mathbf{D2}}$).

If both conditions are breached, then the minor would be one of the eleven that are not **L** or **A** (the strongest of which are $\mathbf{A}_{\mathbf{D2}}$ and $\mathbf{L}_{\mathbf{T2}}$), and the major would be one of the seven e-propositions that do not convert, the strongest of which is $\mathbf{L}_{\mathbf{T2}}$. Al-Taftāzānī finds pairs of triplets with discrepant conclusions for Cesare and Camestres (which are the strongest of the moods). He begins with Camestres (*TŠ* 339.3–6). Read each minor with major 1 and the first actual state of affairs, then with the major 2 and the second actual state of affairs; these actual states of affairs are putative conclusions that are discrepant in form.

| | | |
|---|---|---|
| minor: | no eclipsed shines as long as it is eclipsed, not always | ($\mathbf{A}_{\mathbf{D2}}$) |
| minor: | no eclipsed shines at the time of quadrature, not always | ($\mathbf{L}_{\mathbf{T2}}$)[255] |
| major 1: | every moon shines necessarily at a certain time, not always | ($\mathbf{L}_{\mathbf{T2}}$) |
| major 2: | every sun shines at a certain time, not always | ($\mathbf{L}_{\mathbf{T2}}$) |
| in fact 1: | every eclipsed is always or necessarily a moon | (**A** or **L**) |
| in fact 2: | no eclipsed is ever or possibly a sun | (**A** or **L**) |

Al-Taftāzānī goes on to Cesare (*TŠ* 339.7–11):

| | | |
|---|---|---|
| minor: | every eclipsed is not-luminous necessarily as long as it is eclipsed, not always | ($\mathbf{A}_{D2}$) |
| minor: | every eclipsed is not-luminous at a given time, not always | ($\mathbf{L}_{T2}$) |
| major 1: | no moon is not-luminous at a given time, not always | ($\mathbf{L}_{T2}$) |
| major 2: | no sun is not-luminous at a given time, not always | ($\mathbf{L}_{T2}$) |
| in fact 1: | every eclipsed is necessarily a moon | (**L**) |
| in fact 2: | no eclipsed is possibly a sun | (**L**) |

We can generalize from these two sets of triplets to cover Festino (by Cesare) and Baroco (by Camestres):

> **Text 100.1** When these two mixes do not produce in these two moods, the rest of the mixes do not produce in the rest of the moods, because the sterility in production of the stronger requires the absence of productivity in the weaker (*wa-matā lam yuntij hādhāni l-ikhtilāṭān fī hādhayni l-ḍarbayn lam yuntij sā'ir al-ikhtilāṭāt fī sā'ir al-ḍurūb li-anna ʿadam intāj al-akhaṣṣ yūjibu ʿadam intāj al-aʿamm*). (*TŠ* 339.9–11)

This brings us to the second condition for productivity in the second figure:

Second condition: The possible ($\mathbf{M}_1$ and $\mathbf{M}_2$) can only be used with **L**, $\mathbf{L}_{D1}$, and $\mathbf{L}_{D2}$.

The reasoning is that (a) it is known from the first condition that—because neither **M** entails **L** or **A**—it could only produce with **L**, **A**, $\mathbf{L}_{D1}$, $\mathbf{A}_{D1}$, $\mathbf{L}_{D2}$, or $\mathbf{A}_{D2}$; but, (b) we can provide triplets of terms with discrepant conclusions against **A**, $\mathbf{A}_{D1}$, and $\mathbf{A}_{D2}$. Here is a pair of triplets with **M** as minor:

| | | |
|---|---|---|
| minor: | every Greek is possibly black | (**M**) |
| major 1: | no Greek is ever black | (**A**) |
| major 2: | no Turk is ever black | (**A**) |
| in fact 1: | every Greek is necessarily Greek | (**L**) |
| in fact 2: | no Turk is possibly Greek | (**L**) |

So we know that possibility minors only produce with necessity majors. Al-Taftāzānī goes on to show that, similarly, possibility majors only produce with necessity minors:

> **Text 100.2** This is the case if it is the minor; but if it is the major, it could only be used with the absolute necessary proposition (because it is known from the first condition that the possible major only produces with the two perpetuals [**L** and **A**] due to otherwise breaching the two conditions—namely, the perpetuity of the minor and the major being one of the six convertibles). Its producing with the perpetual is, however, impossible due to the following counterexample: "every Greek is always white, and possibly, no Greek is white" (with the truth of the affirmative ["every Greek is necessarily Greek"]) and [the formally identical syllogism producing a different quality conclusion:] "possibly, no Indian is white" (with the truth of the negative [when considered with "every Greek is always white"; namely, "no Greek is possibly Indian"]). (*TŠ* 340.6–11)

§101[256] A few notes are in order to set al-Kātibī and al-Taftāzānī's discussion of the second figure in context. They are both Avicennian logicians, however much they protest against some of Avicenna's claims about the modal syllogistic; they both accept Avicenna's reading of the absolute proposition as having an elided "at least once." On this understanding of the absolute—which is unlike Aristotle's assertoric proposition (even though they share the same name in the translation of, for example, *Prior Analytics* 25a1: *kull muqaddamah immā an takūna muṭlaqah wa-immā ḍṭirāriyyah wa-immā mumkinah*)—the second-figure syllogisms with two absolute premises are unproductive (they fail against the first condition for second-figure productivity given in commentary on §100). The exclusion was controversial in Avicenna's day, and he begins by saying that there can be no second-figure mixes from two absolute propositions (nor—as Aristotle also had it—from two possibles or from a mix of an absolute and a possible). This is a moment where Avicenna follows truth rather than Aristotle; as he says in the *Najāt*, if the absolute e-proposition does not convert "according to true doctrine, there is no conclusion from two absolutes in the second" (*AN* §63, 58.apu–pu). A century before al-Kātibī, Abū l-Barakāt al-Baghdādī still fumed about how perverse Avicenna's reading was (al-Baghdādī, *al-Kitāb al-muʿtabar fī l-ḥikmah*, 120.18–21), but everyone in the eastern realms of Islam had accepted it by the time al-Kātibī took up his pen. Avicenna spends the first four lemmata of *Pointers* 7.6 on the conditions of productivity for the second figure (*AI* 70.15–71.apu), and they are much like al-Kātibī's account. Avicenna's claims about first-figure mixes that are rejected by al-Kātibī will, however, ramify through the imperfect figures. Al-Kātibī's changes are explained by al-Taftāzānī and questioned by al-Ḥillī. I return to them after I have set out the conditions governing the strength of the conclusion in a second-figure syllogism; the remarks of the commentators are important for the light they throw on how the various participants in the debate stipulated different truth-conditions for the propositions.

Seventy-seven moods are dropped from the possible 169 by the first condition (leaving 92), and 8 by the second, (leaving 84) (*TŠ* 340.14–u). After the first condition, al-Taftāzānī pauses in his exposition of the conditions for the second-figure mixes by disputing a central feature of Avicenna's account of the modal syllogistic; I omit it from the following text, and return to it as Text 101.3. I also omit the reasons al-Taftāzānī gives for each of the rules.[257]

> **Text 101.1** The rule for the mode of the conclusion [of these remaining 84 moods] is that if one of the two premises is necessary or perpetual, the conclusion is perpetual; otherwise the conclusion is like the minor (though on condition that the existence rider (*qayd al-wujūd*) is dropped—I mean the "not necessarily" or "not always"—and that the temporal or descriptional reading of necessity is dropped). (*TŠ* 341.1–3)

Al-Taftāzānī then dwells on a number of mixes, and especially $\mathbf{L}_{\mathbf{D1}}$ with $\mathbf{L}_{\mathbf{T2}}$, and $\mathbf{L}_{\mathbf{D1}}$ with $\mathbf{L}_{\mathbf{D1}}$. He disagrees with al-Khūnajī and defends the account recorded in Rescher (see Table 3, second-figure mixes)[258] by stating that these premises do not produce necessity propositions of some kind (*TŠ* 342.5). Al-Taftāzānī works from what is sought in a proposition; namely, the relation between an underlying essence and a description. The reason al-Khūnajī claims a stronger conclusion from each premise pair is that he understands the proposition in a different way (*TŠ* 342.4–343.3). I note this merely to indicate that there are differences among post-Avicennian logicians.

In concluding these comments, however, I want to draw attention to how the post-Avicennian logicians differ from Avicenna himself. The following discussion is revealing. Consider Camestres LML: no C is necessarily B (**M** minor), every A is necessarily B (**L** major), therefore no C is possibly A (**L** conclusion). This is a mix that follows from claims Avicenna made about the first-figure mixes, and in *Pointers* 7.6.11 he invites us to the following reflection:

> **Text 101.2** You know that if C is such that B is true of it in its totality affirmatively without necessity (so B is

> nonnecessary for everything which is C, or nonnecessary for what is the exposited part of C), while A differs from this (since of everything that is A, B is necessary for it), then the nature of C (*fa-inna ṭabīʿat jīm*) or the exposited part of it is disjoined from the nature of A (*mubāyanah li-ṭabīʿat alif*), neither of them entering under the other, not even possibly . . . You likewise know that the conclusion is always necessary negative. (*AI* 74.4–11)

Al-Taftāzānī again rejects the argument on the grounds of the two relata at issue; as noted in commentary on §45 (especially Texts 45.3 and 45.5), al-Taḥtānī takes the subject insofar as it is a title for the essence of the subject, and the predicate as a description.

> **Text 101.3** It should not be said: If the middle is necessarily affirmed of one of the two extremes, and necessarily negated of the other, there is a necessary separation (*mubāyanah ḍarūriyyah*) between the two, so the conclusion from two necessaries is a necessary. Because we answer: The only thing that follows from this is the incompatibility between the essences of the two extremes, and what is sought is the incompatibility between the essence of the minor term and the description of the major term, so what is sought does not follow necessarily, and what follows is not what is sought. For this reason it is true on the celebrated assumption, "no donkey is possibly a horse" [**L** minor], and "every mount for Zayd is necessarily a horse" [**L** major], along with the falsity of "some donkey is not possibly a mount for Zayd" [which would be the L conclusion to Avicenna's Camestres LLL]. (*TŠ* 341.6–11)

§102[259] Al-Taftāzānī sets out the first condition for the third figure, which is that the minor premise be one of the actuality propositions (*al-fiʿliyyāt*), and defends it by presenting counterexamples.

**Text 102.1** [The minor must be actual] because the strongest of the mixes with possible minor premise (I mean the mix of the special possible minor premise with the necessary or conditional major) in the strongest moods (I mean the first two) are sterile due to discrepant conclusions (*li-l-ikhtilāf*).[260] Suppose that Zayd rides a horse and not a donkey, and ʿAmr rides a donkey and not a horse, then "every mount for Zayd is possibly a mount for ʿAmr" and "every mount for Zayd is necessarily a horse" are true, along with the impossibility of an affirmative [conclusion, because the truth is no mount for ʿAmr is a horse]. But change the major to "necessarily, no mount for Zayd is a donkey," then we have Felapton (*al-ḍarb al-thānī*), yet with the impossibility of a negative [conclusion, because the truth is that every mount for ʿAmr is a donkey]. (*TŠ* 343.5–11)

Al-Taftāzānī calculates the mixes excluded by this condition as 26 (2 possibility propositions times 13 customarily investigated propositions), leaving 134 productive mixes. Avicenna need not feel bound by this condition, as al-Ḥillī explains:

**Text 102.2** The later scholars stipulated for the third figure the actuality of its minor just as for the first; because if the minor is possible for the middle and the major is affirmed (*thābitan*) for it, the affirmation of the major of the minor does not follow, due to what went before in the first figure to do with the fact that the judgment of the major is only on that which is the middle actually, not what is possibly [the middle]. But Avicenna produced a possible from two possible propositions, and from [a possible] and an absolute a possible also; and from a possible and a necessary a possible if the major is a possible, otherwise a necessary. (*ḤQ* 363.pu–364.4)

Al-Taftāzānī states the condition for the modality of the conclusion (see Table 4):[261]

> **Text 102.3** The rule for the modality of the conclusion is that, if the major[262] is not one of the four descriptionals, the conclusion is like the major; and if it is one of the four descriptionals, then the conclusion is—by the proofs mentioned for the unmodalized propositions—like the converse of the minor, but on condition that (1) if there is a non-perpetuity rider, it is dropped from the converse (because it will be negative, and the negative has no role as the minor of this mood), and (2) that we add to the converse the non-perpetuity of the major if there is such a rider, as in the case of the two specials. [This second condition is] because, with the minor, it produces non-perpetuity of the conclusion, as in "every B is always C," and "every B is A as long as it is B, not always," which produces "some C is A while C, not always." The main component of the proposition ["some C is A while C"] is due to what went before in the [exposition to do with the] absolute propositions; the non-perpetuity rider is because we add the minor to the non-perpetuity rider of the major thus: "every B is always C," and "no B is always A (*lā shay' min bā' alif bi-l-iṭlāq*)," which produces "some C is not always A (*laysa baʿḍ jīm alif bi-l-iṭlāq*)." And this is what is meant by "the non-perpetuity of the conclusion." (*TŠ* 344.4–u)

§103[263] There are five conditions to take into account for productivity in the fourth figure. Only the first two conditions (that both premises be actual, and that negative premises must be convertible) apply without exception to all moods (though the second does not really apply to Bramantip or Dimaris, because neither has a negative premise); the other three conditions are each specific to one mood alone. For this reason, it is important to bear in mind throughout the commentary on this lemma and the next the moods and the order in which al-Kātibī gives them. Further, for those seeking to shed light on my account by comparison with Rescher and vander Nat's "Theory of Modal Syllogistic," note that he follows someone he refers to as al-Shirwānī,[264] who departs from al-Kātibī's ordering of the moods. So—for reference—al-Kātibī has (1) Bramantip, (2) Dimaris, (3) Camenes, (4) Fesapo, (5) Fresison, (6) AOO, (7) OAO, and (8) IEO. As noted, al-Kātibī says that the last three moods are only productive by virtue of the convertibility of the special conditional and conventional o-propositions.

Here, as before, the commentators take each condition one by one, work out what propositions are excluded by it, take the strongest of the excluded propositions, and find a pair of term-triplets that lead to discrepant conclusions, or a counterexample against the conclusion proposed for the syllogism; syllogisms with these and all weaker premises are thus rejected. In this case, I provide al-Ḥillī's argument on behalf of al-Kātibī for the first two conditions, and then simply summarize the remaining three conditions. So, for the condition that the syllogism must have actuality propositions as its premise:

> **Text 103.1** We cannot use the possible in this figure, whether as minor or major, because it will be either affirmative or negative, and in both cases it will fail.
>
> The negative case is due to what we will explain, that the negative used in this figure must be convertible. The affirmative case is because—if it is the minor—it does not determine decisive production due to the possibility that a property may belong to one species [actually] and yet be possible for another, just as when we suppose that man is picked out specifically by being in a house at a certain time, yet [being in the house] is possible for a horse; it is true "every horse is possibly in the house" and "every neighing thing is a horse necessarily," along with the impossibility of "some in the house is a neighing

> thing." Were we to have as major "necessarily, no man is a horse," the negative (namely, "some in the house is not a man") is false.
>
> If [a possible premise] is the major, it is similarly [unproductive], due to the truth of "everyone in the house is necessarily a man" and "every horse is possibly in the house," along with the falsity of the affirmation [that every man is possibly a horse]. Were we to have as the minor "necessarily, nothing in the house is a neighing thing," the negative [that is, that no horse is possibly a neighing thing] is false. (*ḤQ* 365.7–u)

The second condition is that the negative premise must be convertible; this affects Camenes, Fesapo, Fresison, AOO, OAO, and IEO. Al-Ḥillī takes the temporal (**L**$_{T2}$, the strongest of the inconvertible negatives, §74), and provides a counterexample against it producing as minor premise with the strongest of the simple propositions (**L**) as major. So, if the minor is **L**$_{T2}$ (as in the true premises "no man is possibly a writer, not always, but at the time of his being still," and "every rational is necessarily a man") along with the falsity of a negative conclusion ("no writer is rational," no matter how weak the modality), all seven inconvertibles as minor fail to produce. Since **L** does not produce with the inconvertibles, nor will the weaker simple propositions. And since the productive component of the strongest of the compounds (**L**$_{D2}$) is **L**$_{D1}$, and **L** implies **L**$_{D1}$, nor will any compound produce.

> **Text 103.2** The second [—that it fails as major—] is due to the sterility of the necessary with the temporal major, due to the truth of "necessarily, every writer is a man" and "no man is a writer" as necessary temporal, with the impossibility of negating man of himself.
>
> [And it fails as a major due to] the sterility of the special conditional with [the temporal] also, because it is

> true “everyone laughing is astonished necessarily as long as he is laughing, not always” and “no man is laughing” as a necessary temporal, along with the impossibility of negating man of being astonished.
>
> So, since it has been proved that the temporal is not productive with the strongest of the simple propositions and of the compound propositions, it has also been proved that it does not produce with the rest. And it is proved that the other propositions aside from the temporal that have inconvertible negatives do not produce. (*ḤQ* 366.pu–367.7)

Here are the remaining conditions, presented without supporting argument. The third condition is that for Camenes, either “perpetuity must be true of the minor” (it must be either a necessity or a perpetuity proposition) or “the general conventional must be true of the major” (it must be one of the six with convertible negatives; that is, **L**, **A**, $\mathbf{L}_{\mathrm{D1}}$, $\mathbf{A}_{\mathrm{D1}}$, $\mathbf{L}_{\mathrm{D2}}$, or $\mathbf{A}_{\mathrm{D2}}$). The fourth condition relates only to the sixth mood (AOO): the major must be of a modality the negative propositions of which convert (the six mentioned in the third condition). On the face of it, this is strange (the major is an a-proposition), but the o-minor converts in the first stage of the proof to reduce the mood to Baroco, so it must be one of the two specials (conditional or conventional) to convert; “whereupon the major must be one of the six, as you learned in [rules for] the second figure: if perpetuity is not true of the minor then the major must be one of the six with convertible negatives” (*TŠ* 349.apu–u). The fifth condition relates only to the eighth mood (IEO), that—once again—the minor must be one of the two specials, so the major must be one of the six just mentioned. This is the same condition, but the reasons are different: the proof is made cogent by metathesis (which in this context means swapping the two premises, *ʿaks al-tartīb*), which in the first stage of the proof reduces the fourth figure to the first figure, and then, in the final stage of the proof, converts the conclusion.

> Text 103.3 So it is unavoidable for the two premises of the eighth mood that they be such that if they are presented in reverse order (*in buddilatā*), they produce a special negative in the first figure. But the first figure only produces the special negative if the major is one of the two specials, and the minor is one of the six [with convertible negatives]. Inevitably, then, here the minor must be one of the two specials because it is the major in the first-figure reduct, and the major must be one of the six [with convertible negatives] because it is the minor in the first-figure reduct. (*TŠ* 350.5–9)

§104[265] The conclusions to the fourth-figure moods are taken in four passes, corresponding to the four tables presented in Rescher (though numbered differently because al-Kātibī orders his treatment differently). So Bramantip and Dimaris have 121 productive mixes each (eleven times eleven, the number of the customarily investigated propositions left once the two possibility propositions are taken out) (*TŠ* 351.2–4). The mood of the conclusion is that of the converse of the minor if it is either **L** or **A**, or the syllogism is from the six with convertible negatives; otherwise the conclusion is an absolute; see Table 5 for these two moods (*TŠ* 351.apu–u).[266] In Camenes, there are 46 productive mixes (from two perpetual minors times the eleven actuals, plus the four descriptional minors times the six propositions with convertible negatives) (*TŠ* 351.5–7). The mood of the conclusion is a perpetuity proposition if perpetuity is true of one of the premises, otherwise the mood of the converse of the minor; see Table 6 (*TŠ* 351.u–352.1).[267] In Fesapo and Fresison, there are 66 productive mixes (from the eleven actuality minors times the six propositions with convertible negatives) (*TŠ*

351.8–10). The conclusion is a perpetuity proposition if the major is **L** or **A**, otherwise it is the mood of the converse of the minor dropping the non-perpetual rider; see Table 7 (*TŠ* 352.1–2).[268] For all the moods to now:

> TEXT 104.1 The proof for everything is by the proofs mentioned for the unmodalized propositions, and the proof that the conclusions are no stronger is by counterexample (*bayān ʿadam luzūm al-zāʾid bi-l-naqḍ*). (*TŠ* 352.3)

Finally, we come to the three moods made valid by the convertibility of the special conditional or conventional o-proposition. In the sixth mood (AOO) and the eighth (IEO) there are 12 productive mixes (from two specials as minor times six propositions with convertible negatives), while in the seventh (OAO) there are 22 productive mixes (from the two specials as major times the eleven actuality propositions) (*TŠ* 352.9–12). Their conclusions are governed by the following considerations:

> TEXT 104.2 The conclusion in the sixth is like that in its second-figure [reduct, Baroco,] after reducing [the sixth to it] through converting the minor;[269] in the seventh, as it is in the third figure after converting the major (to reduce it by that means to [the third]); and in the eighth, like the converse of the conclusion resulting from the first figure, which comes about through metathesis of the premises (*min ʿaks al-tartīb*).[270] (*TŠ* 352.4–7)

*The third section, on connective syllogisms with hypothetical premises*

The hypothetical syllogistic is made up of those connective syllogisms (see §89) in which there is at least one hypothetical premise (*TŠ* 352.11–12). Avicenna developed the hypothetical syllogistic for a number of applications. It underpins his analysis of the reductio proof (see §113), it provides a method to prove conclusions of a certain form that are integral to sciences like geometry, and it remedies a textual gap that, on one reading, Aristotle had left in his exposition of logic. Avicenna was proud of his extraction (*istikhrāj*) of the hypothetical syllogistic, though al-Kātibī's immediate predecessor al-Khūnajī presented himself as consciously correcting and expanding work in which Avicenna had expressed too much pride. Most of these points are rehearsed by al-Taftāzānī at the beginning of his treatment of the section.

> **Text 105.a** This chapter is one that must be included in logic, because there are assertions sought (*al-maṭālib al-taṣdīqiyyah*) that are hypothetical propositions, especially in geometry, set out in Euclid's *Elements*. Because Aristotle did not deal with the matter in the *Organon*, some have claimed that there is no need for it, because the knowledge of categorical syllogisms can do without mentioning [the hypothetical syllogistic]. But this claim fails due to the manifest difference between the valuations [of the hypothetical and the categorical syllogistic]. Avicenna said: "Perhaps Aristotle worked on it but it was not translated into Arabic"; he claimed to have singlehandedly invented [this part of logic] and put it in a book; he said: "We wrote a book on this subject nearly eighteen years ago, and after extracting it, I came across a book attributed to al-Fārābī; but it must be wrongly ascribed, because it was so unclear and full of errors and weak proofs." In spite of this, Avicenna got much of [the hypothetical syllogistic] wrong; he claimed much that is productive to be sterile, and made certain matters conditions that have no effect on productivity. Indeed, al-Khūnajī and those who follow him treated [this kind of syllogism] extensively;[271] of this, al-Kātibī has limited himself in the *Risālah* to a small portion appropriate to a summary, and left most of it to one side due to its lesser value or its distance from nature. (*TŠ* 352.13–353.9)

The hypothetical syllogisms may be divided according to the composition of their premises: two conditional premises, two disjunctive premises, a categorical and a conditional, a categorical and a disjunctive, or a conditional and a disjunctive. This is not Avicenna's ordering of treatment of the divisions, and may have been first used by al-Rāzī.[272]

§105[273] Hypothetical syllogisms made up of two conditional premises further divide into three subdivisions. This is where commentators first mention the "incomplete part" (*juz' ghayr tāmm*), which became culturally synonymous with whatever is abstruse and impenetrable. The examples al-Taftāzānī gives clarify his understanding of "incomplete part" as he delivers the division of syllogisms with two conditional premises; note that the part may be a term or a proposition, because its parthood is defined relative to the premise's dominant operator. The syllogisms may be divided:

> **Text 105.1** [Either] the sharing between the two conditionals is in a complete part of both—I mean, the whole antecedent (*tamām al-muqaddam*) or the whole consequent—as in "whenever A is B then C is D" and "whenever C is D then H is Z"; or in an incomplete part of both—I mean one of the two extremes of the antecedent or the consequent—as in "whenever A is B then C is D" and "whenever D is H then W is Z"; or in a complete part of one of [the two premises] and an incomplete part of the other, as in "whenever C is D then whenever A is B then H is Ṭ" and "whenever H is Ṭ then W is Z." (*TŠ* 353.12–354.2)

The normal form (*al-maṭbū'*)—that is, the naturally available form of this kind of hypothetical syllogism—is the first, with two conditional premises that share in a complete part (*ḤQ* 372.10–16). It generates a syllogistic that almost perfectly parallels the categorical syllogistic, one of the reasons that critics of the hypothetical syllogistic like Abū l-Barakāt al-Baghdādī complained that there was nothing new or valuable in Avicenna's extension.[274] Al-Taftāzānī notes that al-Kātibī's account relates only to syllogisms in which both premises are either implicative (*luzūmī*) or coincidental (*ittifāqī*)—assuming that a syllogism with coincidental premises is productive—but does not touch on the much more complicated question of production from an implicative premise with a coincidental (*TŠ* 354.3–6).

It is at this point that an important distinction relating to implicative conditionals is introduced by al-Taftāzānī to deal with an objection to using two implicative conditionals to construct a syllogism.

> **Text 105.2** It is raised against two implicative premises (*al-luzūmiyyatayn*) that "whenever two is odd it is a number" and "whenever [two] is a number it is even" are both true, while the conclusion is false, I mean "whenever two is odd it is even." I answer that if the implicative is taken as true in the fact of the matter (*in uʿtubira fī l-luzūmiyyah al-ṣidq bi-ḥasab nafs al-amr*), we do not concede that the minor ["whenever two is odd it is a number"] is true; and if it is taken counterfactually (*bi-ḥasab al-ilzām*), we do not concede the falsity of the conclusion, for whoever takes two as odd inevitably takes it to be even. (*TŠ* 354.7–11)

§106[275] As before, hypothetical syllogisms made up of two disjunctive premises further divide into three subdivisions.

> **Text 106.1** The syllogism composed of disjunctives also forms a set of three divisions. The first is when what is shared between the two premises is a complete part of both; the second is when what is shared between them is a complete part of one and an incomplete part of the other, and the third is when what is shared between them is an incomplete part in both. Since the first two are remote from

> nature and the last is proximate, the author mentioned it and left the first two to one side. (*ḤQ* 374.9–375.1)

Al-Taftāzānī's examples for these (reordered to fit with al-Ḥillī) run as follows. First, a syllogism in which the premises share in a complete part is like "always, either A is B or C is D" and "always, either C is D or H is Z"; second, a syllogism in which premises share a part that is a complete part in one and incomplete in the other is like "always, either whenever A is B then C is D, or whenever A is B then H is Z" and "always, either every H is Z or every Ḥ is Ṭ"; and third, a syllogism in which premises share an incomplete part is—and this is the normal form (*al-maṭbūʿ*) al-Kātibī decides to exemplify in the *Risālah*—like "always, either every A is B or every A is C" and "always, either every C is D or every H is Z" (*TŠ* 354.pu–355.4).

The conditions for production in what is the third form on my presentation are, first, that both premises are affirmative; second, that one of them is universal; and third, that the disjunctives are inclusive (*ṣidq manʿ al-khulūw ʿalayhā*). Here is an example of the first figure in this form:

| | |
|---|---|
| minor: | always, either every A is B or every C is D |
| major: | either every D is H or every W is Z |
| conclusion: | always, either every A is B or every C is H or every W is Z |

Al-Taftāzānī claims that this is a valid argument

> **Text 106.2** because inevitably in each of the two disjunctives one of the disjuncts must occur (as a necessary consequence of their being inclusive disjunctions); so what occurs in the first disjunctive is that the first part (I mean "every A is B") is the first of the parts of the conclusion; and if it is the second part (I mean "every C is D"), what occurs from it is with the second disjunctive; and the first part [of

> the second disjunctive] (I mean "every D is H") forms a syllogism thus: "every C is D, and every D is H," which produces "every C is H"; this becomes the second of the parts of the conclusion. The second part [of the second disjunctive] (I mean "every W is Z") is [also] one of the parts of the conclusion. On every hypothesis, one of the three parts of the stated disjunctive is inevitably true. (*TŠ* 355.8–apu)

The categorical syllogism at the heart of the second disjunct of the conclusion ("every C is D, and every D is H, therefore every C is H") is in the first figure; the whole syllogism is categorized according to this syllogism, and obviously can come about in any of the four figures (examples of second-, third-, and fourth-figure syllogisms are given in al-Taftāzānī [*TŠ* 356.1–7]).

§107[276] This form of syllogism is composed of a categorical and a conditional, and it too divides into a number of subdivisions.

> **Text 107.1** This division divides into four subdivisions, because the categorical occurs either as major or as minor. On both assumptions, it shares with the conditional in either [the conditional's] consequent or antecedent. The last three are remote from nature, so the author turns from them and mentions the first division, which is the categorical as major and the sharing with the consequent of the conditional. (*ḤQ* 376.11–14)

Al-Taftāzānī gives examples, reordered here to match al-Ḥillī's division (that is, categorical major sharing consequent, categorical major sharing antecedent, conditional major sharing consequent, conditional major sharing antecedent). So an example of the natural (*al-maṭbūʿ*) syllogism with the categorical as major, sharing with the conditional's consequent, is:

minor: whenever A is B then C is D
major: every D is H
conclusion: whenever A is B then C is H

This is valid "because whenever the antecedent is true the consequent is necessarily true" (*TŠ* 356.15–16). This is the form al-Kātibī expects his students to learn. The categorical must be true in the fact of the matter (*fī nafs al-amr*). The composition of the antecedent and the categorical determine the figure the syllogism is counted under; here, the form of the consequent "C is D" and the major "every D is H" make the whole syllogism count as first figure. What follows are the less natural forms inappropriate to a summary of logic. The first example is of a categorical major sharing with the antecedent:

minor: whenever A is B then C is D
major: every B is H
conclusion: whenever A is H then C is D (not given in al-Taftāzānī)

A categorical minor sharing with the consequent (in the second figure; note the presence of the quantifier in the consequent):

minor: every A is B
major: whenever C is D then every H is B
conclusion: whenever C is D then some A is H
(not given in al-Taftāzānī)

A categorical minor sharing with the antecedent:

minor: every A is B
major: whenever B is C then D is H
conclusion: whenever A is C then D is H (not given in al-Taftāzānī)

§108[277] Al-Kātibī gives three natural forms under two broad types for the fourth kind of hypothetical syllogism, composed from a number of categorical propositions and a disjunctive. These are divided into those in which the categoricals are the same number as the disjuncts of the disjunctive, and the second kind al-Kātibī illustrates, in which the categoricals are fewer in number than the disjuncts of the disjunctive. The first kind further subdivides into those in which the categoricals all have the same predicate and thus lead to a categorical conclusion with a single predicate (this is the first example in §108.1, and is called divided syllogism; it is taken to serve as an analysis of complete induction), and those in which the categoricals have different predicates and thus lead to a categorical conclusion with a disjunctive predicate. Al-Taftāzānī takes al-Kātibī's exposition to be clear in itself, though he makes four points over and above what we find in the *Risālah*. The first three points he makes are to confirm that all three of these natural forms of syllogism with categorical and disjunctive premises have moods in all four figures (*TŠ* 357.13, 358.2, 358.11). Finally, al-Taftāzānī does not here follow his normal practice of setting out the forms al-Kātibī is excluding, but concludes his commentary on this lemma thus:

> TEXT 108.1 Al-Kātibī ignores [two cases], when the categoricals are more numerous than the disjuncts of the disjunction, or when they are the same number, but are such that not every one of the categoricals shares in one of the disjuncts of the disjunction; he does so because they are remote from nature. (*TŠ* 358.apu–u)

§109[278] The fifth form of syllogism with at least one hypothetical premise is composed of a conditional and a disjunctive. Again, al-Kātibī is highly selective about the forms he includes in the *Risālah*.

**Text 109.1** This division subdivides into a number of divisions. The first is that the sharing is in a complete part of the two premises, and the conditional is the minor. The second is that the sharing is in a complete part of them both and the conditional is the major. The third is that the sharing is in an incomplete part of the two premises and the conditional is the minor. The fourth is that the sharing is in an incomplete part of them both and the conditional is the major. The fifth is that the sharing is in a complete part of one of them and not the other; here there are two divisions, and if you add to this the conditional being minor or major it comes to be four more. The author mentions the natural inferences (*al-maṭbūʿ*) among these; namely, the first and the third. (*ḤQ* 380.3–13)

Aside from ignoring subdivisions with the conditional as major, an example of the form al-Kātibī completely ignores in the *Risālah* (number five in al-Ḥillī's list in Text 109.1) is: "always, either whenever A is B then C is D, or whenever H is W then Z is Ḥ" and "whenever Z is Ḥ then Ṭ is Y" (*TŠ* 359.5–8).

Al-Taftāzānī examines the inferences al-Kātibī does include; his analysis goes no deeper than to restate the rule al-Kātibī gives in the *Risālah* (roughly, if p is incompatible with q, then p is incompatible with the implicant of q). His remarks in Text 109.2 have the following syllogism in mind:

| | |
|---|---|
| minor: | whenever A is B then C is D |
| major: | always (or sometimes), either C is D or H is Z (alternative denial) |
| conclusion: | always (or sometimes), either A is B or H is Z |

**Text 109.2** This is because "C is D" is an implicate of "A is B," and "H is Z" is incompatible (*yamtaniʿ ijtimāʿuhu*) with

"C is D" both as a universal and as a particular; so "H is Z" is also incompatible with "A is B," because incompatibility with the implicate—whether always or generally—entails a similar incompatibility with the implicant. This is the case if the disjunctive is alternative denial. (*TŠ* 359.11–14)

Al-Taftāzānī turns to consider the same example with an inclusive disjunction in the major, and here his analysis adds a great deal to what we find in the *Risālah.*

| | |
|---|---|
| minor: | whenever A is B then C is D |
| major: | always (or sometimes), either C is D or H is Z (inclusive disjunction) |
| conclusion: | sometimes, if A is not B then H is Z |

Text 109.3 This is because the contradictory of the middle (I mean the contradictory of "C is D") entails the two extremes of the conclusion (I mean the contradictory of "A is B" and the proposition "H is Z"). It entails the first because the contradictory of the implicate entails the contradictory of the implicant; it entails the second because of the inclusive disjunction between "C is D" and "H is Z"—for every two cases related in this way, the contradictory of either entails the other. So if the contradictory of the middle entails the two extremes, [the syllogism] produces that the first extreme (I mean the contradictory of "A is B") may entail "H is Z" by a third-figure syllogism in the following way: "whenever the contradictory of the middle is realized, the first extreme is realized" (I mean "A is not B"), and "whenever the contradictory of the middle is realized, the other extreme is realized" (I mean "H is Z"), which produces "sometimes, if A is not B then H is Z," which is what is sought. (*TŠ* 359.15–360.2)

Going beyond al-Kātibī, al-Taftāzānī concludes from the analysis of the two preceding texts that if the disjunction in the major is exclusive (*ḥaqīqiyyah*) then the syllogism produces both conclusions at once.

Al-Taftāzānī takes the example of the second kind of inference al-Kātibī considers here and offers a proof for it. The syllogism is:

minor: whenever A is B then C is D
major: always, either every D is H or W is Z
(inclusive disjunction)
conclusion: whenever A is B then either every C is H or W is Z

> **Text 109.4** This is because "every C is D" is affirmed on the supposition (*taqdīr*) of "A is B," whereupon what comes about in the disjunctive given the first part (I mean "every D is H") is "every C is D" and "every D is H," which produce "every C is H"; so "every C is H" is affirmed on the supposition of "A is B." Whereas, given the second part [of the disjunctive] (I mean "W is Z"), what comes about on the supposition of "A is B" is "W is Z." So, on the supposition of "A is B," one of two cases follow: either "every D is H," or "W is Z." This is what the conclusion amounts to. (*TŠ* 360.7–11)

*The fourth section, on the repetitive syllogism*

§110[279] The repetitive syllogism is one of the two kinds of syllogism distinguished by Avicenna's novel analysis.[280] It first comes up in the *Risālah* in §89, where the commentators deal with how the repetitive fits in under the broad definition of syllogism (given in §88), particularly in relation to the condition that the premises lead to another discourse (that is, it leads to a new proposition not given in the premise-set in the sense set out by al-Ḥillī in Text 89.2). A further question arises in relation to the definition specifically of the repetitive syllogism in §89, and what it means for the conclusion to be mentioned in actuality (*bi-l-fiʿl*) as opposed to in potentiality (*bi-l-quwwah*); briefly, it means that the conclusion must be given though not asserted, in the same structure and with the same terms, though not necessarily in the same quality, as one of the components of the major premise.

Al-Kātibī comes back in this lemma to lay out the conditions for a valid repetitive syllogism. He presents five conditions (the last two being alternative conditions): one premise must be a hypothetical (*sharṭiyyah*); the other premise must affirm or deny one of the two parts of the first premise; the hypothetical must be affirmative and—if conditional—implicative and universal; or—if the hypothetical premise is not universal—the other premise must be universal or must hold at precisely the same time the first premise holds.

A few remarks from the commentators throw more light on these conditions. Clearly, it must be one of the components of the hypothetical premise that is produced as conclusion; otherwise a premise would be repeated as conclusion, breaching the condition in the general definition of syllogism that it lead to another discourse. Since, however, hypothetical propositions can be composed from categorical or from hypothetical propositions, it is not a condition that the other premise be a categorical—because it may be a component hypothetical proposition of the first proposition—nor that the conclusion be categorical, for exactly the same reason (*TŠ* 360.u).

Some points should be made about hypothetical propositions that bear on issues not explored in the *Risālah* itself. The conditional must be affirmative because a negated conditional denies the implication between the antecedent and the consequent (see above §62); so too a negated disjunctive denies the opposition between the disjuncts. Yet "if there is no implication or opposition between two matters, the presence or absence of one will not imply the presence or absence of the other" (*TŠ* 361.6–7). Further, the reason that the hypothetical must be either implicative (*luzūmī*) or oppositional (*ʿinādī*) (see §§60 and 61) is that if the hypothetical were merely coincidental (*ittifāqī*), then "because knowing the truth or falsity of the coincidental depends on knowing the truth or falsity of one of its parts, then were we to acquire knowledge of the truth or falsity of one of the parts from the coincidental, that would be circular" (*TŠ* 361.8–10).

Either the hypothetical premise must be necessary and universal (whether conditional or disjunctive, which must be, respectively, an implicative a-proposition or an oppositional a-proposition), or the other premise must be universal or true at the time the major premise holds. The second part of the disjunctive condition for a valid repetitive means that even if the hypothetical is not universal, there will be a valid argument if there is perpetual positing of the antecedent of a particular conditional, or of a disjunct of an appropriate particular disjunctive; or the perpetual denying of the consequent of a particular conditional, or of a disjunct of an appropriate particular disjunctive. As it happens, al-Taḥtānī disagrees on this point, and thereby tells us more about how to interpret the universal hypothetical.

> **Text 110.1** It is said in some books that the perpetuity of positing [the antecedent of the conditional, or of one of the disjuncts] or of removing [the consequent of the conditional, or of one of the disjuncts] is productive; but this is only correct if we interpret the universal hypothetical as that in which the implication or opposition is realized (*mutaḥaqqiqan*) with actually realized situations (*al-awḍāʿ al-mutaḥaqqiqah fī nafs al-amr*), so that from the perpetuity of positing or removing, the realization [of the implication or opposition] follows with all the situations taken into account.
>
> But this is not [how we interpret the universal hypothetical]; rather, it is interpreted as the realization of implication or opposition in situations that are not incompatible with the antecedent, so it is possible that the implication in the particular has a condition that never exists in spite of the perpetual presence of the

> implicant; whereupon the existence of the implicate does not follow due to the fact that a situation of the implicant is not realized with the implicate and its condition (due to their always being negated together). This is like the truth of the proposition, "it may be if the Necessary exists then atom exists"—in the third figure[281]—and [of the proposition] "the Necessary always exists." It does not follow from this that atom exists tout court, because the implication here is just for the situation the Necessary and the atom exist together, even though [this situation] does not come about at all. (*TT* 448.9–u)

§111[282] Al-Kātibī lists the productive moods of repetitive syllogisms that meet the conditions set out in §110. With a conditional major, there are two moods, what in the Latin West would be called modus ponens and modus tollens. Al-Kātibī sketches a proof that these moods must be valid if the major is indeed an implication, and sketches why other moods must be rejected. He goes on to list valid moods with a disjunctive major. With an exclusive disjunction, we have modus ponendo tollens and modus tollendo ponens; with alternative denial, only modus ponendo tollens; and with inclusive disjunction, only modus tollendo ponens.

Al-Taḥtānī adds little to what we find in the *Risālah* itself here, though what he and al-Kātibī say expands on the notions of implication and opposition as they relate to inferences (first set out in §§60 and 61). So "the repetition of the conditional's antecedent produces the consequent, otherwise it would follow that the implicate is separable from the implicant, so the implication would be void (*illā lazima nfikāk al-lāzim ʿan al-malzūm fa-yabṭulu l-luzūm*)" (*TT* 449.14–15). So too, the denial of the consequent entails the denial of the antecedent, "otherwise [we would have] the presence of the implicant without the implicate, so the implication would be void (*illā lazima wujūd al-malzūm bi-dūn al-lāzim fa-yabṭulu l-luzūm*)" (*TT* 449.16). The further comments on oppositional disjunctives define them relative to the impossibility of affirming both disjuncts (*imtināʿ al-jamʿ*) and the impossibility of denying both disjuncts (*imtināʿ al-khulūw*).

*The fifth section, on matters appended to the syllogism*

The following four lemmata deal with four topics that are only loosely related to each other. So the first lemma deals with aspects of how related syllogisms can be regarded as forming a unity of some kind, the second lemma deals with the reductio (which lies at the heart of the formal syllogistic), and the last two lemmata deal with inferences that are not deductions but that figure in the broader applications of logic in science and law. That said, the first topic deals with the pragmatic matter of referring to the collection of premises and inferences that relate a theorem in a science back to first principles, the second with reflections on how to analyze indirect reasoning, the third with the main inductive method used in some sciences, and the fourth with a style of forensic reasoning developed outside the philosophical sciences.

§112[283] The compound syllogism is not defined by al-Kātibī to have special relevance to science, but al-Taḥtānī's comments seem to envisage a role for it in organizing principles and interim conclusions relative to a scientific question.

> **Text 112.1** The compound syllogism is a syllogism made up of a number of premises, two of which produce a conclusion that, taken with another premise [from the initial set], produces another conclusion, and so on until reaching what is sought (*al-maṭlūb*). And that is just if the premises (or one of them) of the syllogism that produces what is sought need likewise to be acquired through another syllogism; [this goes on] until the acquisition ends in principles that are primitive (*al-mabādiʾ al-badīhiyyah*). So there will

be [a number of] syllogisms ordered and determined to what is sought, and for this reason it is called a compound syllogism. (*TT* 451.13–u)

The collection of premises can either be presented so that the interim conclusions that serve as premises in later syllogisms on the way to what is sought are made explicit (*mawṣūl al-natā'ij*), or so that these interim conclusions are elided (*mafṣūl al-natā'ij*). Presumably, the approach of eliding interim conclusions is the more common way to set out a science, and the lemma effectively prescribes a study method for students of such sciences.

§113[284] The analysis of the reductio is as a compound syllogism, though not in the narrow and precise sense of §112. Al-Taftāzānī notes that it is called *qiyās al-khalf*—syllogism through the impossible—because it leads to the impossible by supposing that what is sought is not true (I ignore the dispute about the vowel in *kh-l-f*, and alternative etymologies).

TEXT 113.1 Since the syllogism is limited to the connective and the repetitive (along with their divisions, which have been mentioned), the syllogism must be reduced and analyzed to that. Yet great difference of opinion has occurred here; Avicenna's settled view is that the reductio is a compound of two syllogisms, one connective and the other repetitive.[285] (*TŠ* 364.3–7)

I doubt I can do much better than to fill out al-Kātibī's analysis. He takes it that we want to prove Baroco (see §93.5):

minor: some C is not A
major: every B is A
conclusion: some C is not B

Take the conclusion posited above, and suppose it to be untrue (if "some C is not B" is not true, then "every C is B"). Can we show that this leads to an impossibility? Take the other premise ("every B is A"), which as a premise is assumed to be true (*musallamah*; see §88, and Text 118.1 below); by Barbara we know that "every C is B" and "every B is A" produce "every C is A." Up to here, we have assembled the components of the first connective syllogism of the reductio (of the form set out in §107):

1. if *some C is not B* is false, then *every C is B*
(statement of contradictory)
2. but *every B is A* (major premise of Baroco restated)
3. if *some C is not B* is false, then *every C is A*
(by schema cited in §107)

But we have assumed (as the minor premise of the original syllogism) "some C is not A." So we can take the conclusion of the connective and, with the minor premise, assemble a repetitive syllogism (modus tollens):

3. if *some C is not B* is false, then *every C is A*
4. but *some C is not A* (minor premise of Baroco restated)
5. therefore *some C is not B* is not false
(by second repetitive syllogism in §111)

Al-Taftāzānī's analysis is as follows ("question" is the conclusion sought):

**Text 113.2** The connective is a compound of two conditionals, one of which is the implication (*al-mulāzamah*) between the posited question (*al-maṭlūb al-mawḍūʿ*) on the assumption that it is not true, and the contradictory of the question; this implication is self-evident. The other is between the contradictory of the question, on the assumption it is true, and an impossible matter; this implication may need explanation. So this connective produces a conditional that is a compound of the conditional (on the assumption that [the question] is not true) and the impossible matter. The repetitive is a compound of an implicative conditional that is the conclusion of the connective and of the repetition of the contradictory of the consequent to produce the contradictory of the antecedent; so the verification (*taḥaqquq*) of the question follows. (*TŠ* 364.8–apu)

His overall account of what is going on is this:

> **Text 113.3** In summary, were the question not to be verified, its contradictory would be; but if its contradictory were to be verified, an impossibility would come about; an impossibility cannot come about, so the contradictory of the question cannot come about, so the question is verified. (*TŠ* 364.pu–u)

§114[286] Induction is a defeasible inference, and therefore differs from the inferences considered in the *Risālah* up to now. It is described by al-Kātibī as arriving at a universal judgment on the basis of most of its particulars. One line of thinking among al-Kātibī's contemporaries was that it ceases to be induction when all particulars have been taken into account, whereupon it becomes a divided syllogism (*qiyās muqassam*) (*TŠ* 365.6), under the kind sketched in §108.[287] As al-Taftāzānī rightly says, however, once every particular has been taken into account, so too have most of them. In light of this, some say that induction divides into complete (*tāmm*)—and this is the divided syllogism, a kind of syllogism set out in the first example in §108.1—and incomplete (*nāqiṣ*), which is the kind of induction commonly understood from the term, a kind of induction that leads only to supposition but not knowledge. (If this is true, then one would think induction should be used in rhetoric, but not in dialectic; whereas al-Ḥillī claims that complete induction is used in sciences, but incomplete in dialectic [*ḤQ* 388.12–16].)

But in fact, it is not the process of induction itself that matters, but the universal assertion to which it leads; it seems as if some intend the affirmation of what is sought by induction to be the affirmation of a universal judgment because it exists in most particulars. But—as the imam made clear (I assume this is al-Ṭūsī, because the mention is followed by *ḥujjat al-Islām raḍiya llāh ʿanhu*)—it consists of examining one by one (*taṣaffuḥ*) particular matters under a judgment to judge them against a single matter that takes in all those particulars (*TŠ* 365.12–13). If I understand al-Taftāzānī rightly, the goal is not to abstract a judgment from particulars, but to test a judgment's fit against particulars. Whatever al-Taftāzānī has in mind, he claims that it agrees with what al-Fārābī had to say:

> TEXT 114.1 Induction is the examination of particulars under a given universal matter, one after the other, to show the correctness (*taṣḥīḥ*) of a given judgment judged affirmatively or negatively of that matter; so our examining the particulars under that universal to seek the judgment in each one is induction. Affirming or negating the judgment of that universal matter is the conclusion of the induction. Induction is so called because the inductive reasoner (*al-mustaqriʾ*) investigates successively one particular after another to determine the conclusion. (*TŠ* 365.apu–366.2)

§115[288] Following earlier logicians (for example, Avicenna in *Pointers* 7.1.3 [*AI* 64.apu–65.4]), al-Kātibī is concerned to set out and criticize the method of those who defend the use of example in his own milieu, and his commentators refer to those culturally specific argument techniques by name.[289] Al-Taftāzānī notes that the description al-Kātibī gives ("taking a judgment belonging to one particular and affirming it of another particular because of a meaning common to both") is loose, as was the description of induction. More correctly:

> **Text 115.1** It involves drawing attention to a similarity one particular has to another by virtue of a meaning common to both, in order to affirm of the first, [the derivative case,] the judgment affirmed of the second, [the principal case,] a judgment caused by that [common] meaning . . . The theologians call example inference from the seen to the unseen (*al-istidlāl bi-l-shāhid ʿalā l-ghāʾib*) . . . the lawyers call it analogy (*qiyās*). (*TŠ* 366.7–apu)

Induction and example are commonly reduced to syllogisms. Al-Taftāzānī takes the argument by example given by al-Kātibī (the heavens are created in time because they are like a house in terms of its being a composite, which is the real cause (*ʿillah*) a house is known to be created in time) and turns it into a syllogism (*TŠ* 367.8–9):

minor: the heavens are composite
major: everything composite is created in time
conclusion: the heavens are created in time

Whereas the flaw (*khalal*) in induction lies in the minor premise of its syllogistic form (has every subject claimed to have the property predicated of its kind in the conclusion really been examined?), the weakness in example lies in the major premise (in the example just presented, in "everything composite is created in time"). Clearly, everything turns on the defense of the major, for which the proponents of example as a valid argument have two methods, concomitance (*dawarān*) and division (*taqsīm*), which are attacked by al-Kātibī one after the other after his dismissive "But this kind of argument is weak."

The first attack is on concomitance—specifically, special concomitance (*al-dawarān al-khāṣṣ*), which is the causal subordination (*tarattub*) of the judgment to something that has an appropriately causal link to that judgment both in being present and in being absent (*al-shay' alladhī la-hu ṣulūḥ ʿilliyyat dhālika l-ḥukm wujūdan wa-ʿadaman*).[290] The judgment (*al-ḥukm*) is the presumed concomitant effect (*al-dā'ir*) of the thing that has such an appropriate causal link; that is, the presumed concomitant cause (*al-madār*). But how can we come to know about this link? If we know about it by complete induction, we have some grounds to assert it, but we are no longer using example as our method (*TŠ* 367.2–12). In short, as al-Kātibī asks, how could we know that two permanently linked concomitants are actually causally related?

The second attack is on the division that supports the connection of the principal analogue with the judgment; in this form of argument, the division is not produced by dichotomous division. Both al-Taftāzānī and al-Kātibī worry about the lack of system in generating disjuncts, the seemingly arbitrary collection of disjuncts that might result, and the risk of producing a division that is not exhaustive (*TŠ* 367.13–u).

> **Text 115.2** Be aware that no one contests the fact that induction and example only produce supposition and not certainty. (*TŠ* 368.7)

## The Conclusion

Up to this point, virtually the entire focus of the *Risālah* has been on issues to do with form (*ṣūrah*). In the concluding section, al-Kātibī enlarges on issues to do with matter (*māddah*). According to al-Taftāzānī, it is this order of treatment that allows al-Kātibī to move smoothly from the formal division of the syllogism (into connective and repetitive, and under the connective into categorical and hypothetical, and under the categorical into the four figures) to a division under the criterion of matter (*bi-ʿtibār al-māddah*) into the five arts of logic, "I mean, demonstration, dialectic, rhetoric, fallacy theory, and poetry, because each conveys either an assertion or something else with [affective] impact, like what provokes the imagination" (*TŠ* 368.10–12). How are these five arts distinguished from each other?

> **Text 116.a** Assertion is either declarative (*jāzim*) or not, and the declarative is either considered with respect to its truth (*ḥaqīqatuhu*) or not. What is considered [in this way] is either actually true or not; what conveys declarative true assertion is demonstration, and what conveys declarative untrue assertion is sophistry (*al-safsaṭah*). The assertion that is not considered with respect to its being true or untrue, but rather with respect to its being generally acknowledged, is dialectic (if [the assertion] really is generally acknowledged, otherwise it is eristic, which, along with sophistry, comes under fallacy theory). That which conveys non-declarative assertion is rhetoric, and that which conveys what elicits images (*al-mufīd li-l-takhyīl*) rather than assertion is poetry. (*TŠ* 368.13–u)

What al-Kātibī is referring to as the matter of syllogisms (*māddat al-aqyisah*) is a function of the truth of an assertion, its epistemic justification and its presentation in terms of that truth and justification. This use of matter is a further development of the notion of propositional matter (*māddat al-qaḍiyyah*) set out in §51, and of terms as a proposition's matter first set out at the beginning of the comment on §45.

In short, the different propositional matters are used to distinguish among different disciplinary uses of syllogistic. From the time of Avicenna, particularly in his exposition of logic in *Pointers and Reminders*, it had become common merely to mention the five arts, and concentrate on demonstration (which leads to truth) and sophistry (which looks like demonstration, and deceives the student on the path to learning demonstrative truth). It was a topos to lament this change in coverage (see al-Taftāzānī in Text 0.1; his comments are echoed by Ibn Khaldūn), though rare—as far as I am aware—not to accept it. The fact remains that we are looking at the remnants of a grand theory of discourse, an attempt to offer a unified theory of the persuasive power of language as used across the disciplines.[291]

In what follows, al-Kātibī deals in turn with the six propositions of certainty used for demonstration (§116) and the demonstrations that can be constructed using them (§117), then goes on to consider various epistemically weaker premises and the kinds of arguments that are constructed from each of them (§118). He pauses to deal with propositions used in the pathological discourse of sophistry (§119) before concluding with an account of how a science is constructed, touching on aspects of its internal structure, its structure in the broader system of sciences, and the nature of the theorems it is directed to demonstrating (§120). A prominent part of what follows involves the classification of propositions in terms of their respective epistemic force, and it is worth bearing in mind that they are distinguished as types (*aṣnāf*) and not species (*anwāʿ*); this is not an essential division, and no claim is implied that they or the further distinctions that depend on them are natural or unchanging.

### *The first discussion, on syllogistic matters*

Propositions taken in terms of their syllogistic matter are taken in terms of their epistemic justification. The first six syllogistic matters are propositions taken to be certain (*al-yaqīniyyāt*; sometimes the necessary propositions, *al-ḍarūriyyāt*); these are the propositions that provide data for demonstrative science. Al-Ḥillī sets out three necessary conditions for a proposition to be certain (*yaqīnī*): it must be declarative (*jāzim*), correspondent with reality (*muṭābiq*), and stable through justification by some rational consideration (*thābit*). The antonyms for each of these are, respectively, that it be merely supposition (*ẓann*), that it be compound ignorance (*jahl murakkab*),[292] and that it be a belief accepted on authority (*iʿtiqād al-muqallid*) [*ḤQ* 394.9–apu]. So an assertion that is certain must be presented as justified, it must be the case, and it must be justified by a consideration which guarantees that it is the case. The separate ways each of the sources of data for demonstrative science are justified by some consideration distinguish them as different syllogistic matters. As just mentioned, these distinctions are not ultimately dictated by the way things are in themselves; they are, to use once again the terms al-Ṭūsī uses, types (*aṣnāf*) and not species (*anwāʿ*).

There is a further restriction on the way "certain" is being used to qualify assertion. The conclusion of a demonstration inherits certainty if all conditions of a demonstration are met, and there are more than six grounds for this kind of demonstratively secured certainty. The use of "certain" in this section of the *Risālah*, however, is limited: "What is meant is that the primary certain matters (*al-mawādd al-uwal al-yaqīniyyah*) are limited to six, whereas acquired [certain assertions] are not primary but rather secondary or even more remote [from primary certain propositions]" (*TŠ* 369.6–8); see Text 117.1 below.

§116[293] Primary premises (*awwaliyyāt*) are defined as those for which the intellect needs nothing more than conceiving the two extremes (*taṣawwur al-ṭarafayn*) to assert that the premises are certain. This was the criterion for primitive assertion (*taṣdīq badīhī*) set out in Text 2.1 (indeed, al-Ḥillī refers to *awwaliyyāt* as primitive premises, *badīhiyyāt* [*ḤA* 197.9]), so in this lemma we see the way the foundational elements of propositional knowledge introduced at the beginning of the treatise ground the development of demonstrative science.

> **Text 116.1** The primaries are propositions on which the intellect judges simply by virtue of conceiving its extremes, like "the whole is greater than the part," "every assertion must be denied or affirmed," and "the same body is not in two places at a single moment." If the extremes are clearly

> conceived and related (*jaliyyat al-taṣawwur wa-l-irtibāṭ*), then the judgment is absolutely clear; otherwise it is clear to one for whom the conception and relation is clear, and unclear for others. Sometimes the intellect hesitates in a primary judgment after conceiving the extremes, either due to deficiency of natural disposition (*al-gharīzah*) as in the young or the dull-witted, or due to the natural operation of the intelligence (*al-fiṭrah*) being tarnished by beliefs that are at odds with the primaries, as in the case of some vulgar or ignorant people. (*TŠ* 370.1–7)

The remaining five propositions of certainty require something over and above the conception of the extremes to aid the intellect in coming to assert them (*TŠ* 369.10–11). Observational propositions (*al-mushāhadāt*)—based on sense-perception—issue in a judgment (*ḥukm*), whether to do with the observed world (*ẓāhirah*) such as "the sun is hot," or with internal (*bāṭinah*) states such as "I am afraid"; the second kind makes a judgment to do with our affective (*wijdāniyyah*) states (*ḤQ* 395.5).

> **Text 116.2** All the judgments based on sense-perception are, however, particular, for the senses only convey that this fire is hot; the judgment that every fire is hot is an intellectual judgment that the intellect acquires from perceiving particulars of that judgment and coming to understand its causes. From this, it appears that what makes a judgment on observed data is a compound of the senses and the intellect, and not the senses alone. (*TŠ* 370.10–13)

Premises based on experience (*al-mujarrabāt*) involve, over and above observation, repeated experience, such that one matter occurs on the occurrence of another, or is absent on the absence of another (al-Kātibī's example is the occurrence of purgation after taking scammony). Al-Ḥillī explains the underlying structure. It is a syllogism that allows the soul to move from repeated experience to the universal proposition (here, "scammony is purgative"). The syllogism is repetitive (see §110 and following): were the occurrence of purgation coincidental (*ittifāqī*), it would not always be the case after taking scammony; but it is always the case; therefore it is not coincidental. It is this syllogism that distinguishes premises based on experience from data acquired by induction discussed in §114 (*ḤQ* 395.11).

We find out more about premises based on experience by considering the next kind of certain proposition. Premises provided by intuiting the middle term of a syllogism (*al-ḥadsiyyāt*, *ḤQ* 396.5) are like those based on experience, except that in a judgment provided by intuiting the middle term, the judgment is given as to both the fact that a given thing is the case, and as to what that thing is; that is, judgment is given as to the causality and quiddity (*sababiyyah*, *māhiyyah*) of the thing. By contrast, in premises based on experience, the judgment is given only as to the causality (*sababiyyah*), the fact that something is the case. For example, from "moonlight is light reflected from the sun," we know not simply that the sun causes moonlight, we know what moonlight is (reflected sunlight); whereas from "scammony is purgative" we know only that scammony causes purgation, but not what it is.

> **Text 116.3** Intuited premises are propositions on which judgment is made by a strong intuition from the soul conveying knowledge, like the judgment that the light of the moon is acquired from the sun due to the formations of its light in accordance with its different states relative to the sun. So it is like premises based on experience in terms of repeated observations and the addition of a hidden syllogism; it differs in that the cause in premises based on experience is known only in terms of its being a cause, not in terms of what it is,

> whereas in intuited propositions it is known in both respects. [This type of premise] depends only on intuition and not on thinking, otherwise it would be an acquired knowledge claim (*min al-ʿulūm al-kasbiyyah*). (*TŠ* 370.pu–371.4)

For premises based on sequential testimony (*al-mutawātirāt, ḤQ* 397.1), al-Kātibī sets down two conditions. First, the claim cannot be impossible, and second, trust must be generated by widespread agreement on the matter (there is no arbitrary number of witnesses that can guarantee that agreement on a matter; the requisite number is a function of producing the requisite trust). Al-Ḥillī sets down a third condition, which is that the data must ultimately be such that it can be derived from the sense-perception (*al-istinād ilā l-ḥiss*). By this condition, sequential testimony as to—for example—the existence of God is excluded.

> Text 116.4 Premises based on sequential testimony are propositions on which judgment is made due to manifold witness after the possibility of what is judged and trust in there being no agreement to lie among the witness-bearers. This is like the judgment that Mecca exists, and Baghdad, and the stipulation [that the data] are traced back to the senses—since this kind of report is only considered for what is traced back to observation (*al-mushāhadah*). The criterion (*al-ḍābiṭ*) for the minimum number [of witnesses] for sequential testimony is that certainty in the judgment result, and the possibility [that it is false] cease. There is no proof for what those hold who stipulate five or twelve or twenty or forty or seventy, for we decide (*qāṭiʿūn*) that we have knowledge through data from sequential testimony without knowledge of a specified number; [that number] would differ according to differences among events and informants and auditors. (*TŠ* 372.4–10)

Al-Kātibī excludes from a debate data from experience, intuition, and sequential testimony; at least, such premises cannot be used to compel an opponent to accept an argument. Al-Ḥillī explains that this is because the data are derived from sense-perception (*li-stinādihi ilā l-ḥiss*), and are therefore particular; and because—I take this to be a separate argument—people have differing levels of ability to intuit middle terms. I have to say I find confusing the claim that these data are particular. Surely the whole point of the syllogistic condition in (4) and (5) is that it makes the claim universal. Further, data given by (5) are from an expert; the whole notion of a functioning scientific community is based on recognizing expertise in specific sciences and agreeing to defer to the appropriate experts. In any event, al-Kātibī and al-Ḥillī caution that these premises cannot guarantee success in a debate. At the same time, they both accept that such data can be used in demonstrations. At the least, this means that some demonstrations cannot be used in debate. It may mean further that some demonstrations are for the demonstrator alone.

Lastly, (6) implicitly syllogistic premises (*al-qaḍāyā llatī qiyāsātuhā maʿahā*, *ḤQ* 398.2) depend on a middle always present to the mind ("its divisibility into two equal parts," which is always present to the mind and determines the certainty of "four is even"). What is always present to the mind is not obtained by reflection but, according to al-Ḥillī, by the natural operation of the intellect (*fiṭrah*) and what is inherent to it as it operates.

> Text 116.5 Implicitly syllogistic premises, also called propositions with inherently available syllogisms (*al-qaḍāyā al-fiṭriyyat al-qiyās*), are propositions on which judgment is made by mediation of a syllogistic middle always available to the mind on the occurrence of the two extremes of the proposition, as in "four is even because it is divisible into two equal parts." (*TŠ* 372.13–15)

§117[294] A necessary condition for a syllogism to be a demonstration is that its premises be taken from among the premises of certainty (*al-yaqīniyyāt*) set out above. It is not, however, a sufficient condition for a syllogism to be a demonstration, as might seem to be implied by the way al-Kātibī opens this lemma. Further necessary conditions involve the causal relations discussed in this lemma, as well as appropriate subject term and predicate, discussed in §120. In this lemma, in fact, two issues are dealt with. The first is how the conditions considered in §116 relate to, and are to be distinguished from, considerations that were introduced in dealing with the modal propositions. The second is the kind of causal relations between middle and major terms that determine whether a demonstration can be produced, and what kind can be produced.

*Yaqīniyyāt*—what I have translated as "premises of certainty"—was interpreted by early scholars to entail that the premises are necessary in the sense discussed in §§51 to 59.[295] Due to demonstrations given in physics, however, it became clear that weaker modal grades such as for-the-most-part premises had to be accepted as adequate for demonstration. Avicenna insisted that even lower modal grades such as merely contingent propositions could be used, so long as it was recognized that the conclusion would be of correspondingly lower modal grade (for example, in *Pointers* 9.2, *AI* 81.10–82.10). Presumably, he meant to dissociate *yaqīniyyāt* from any particular modal grade; to say that such a proposition is necessary should be taken to refer to its epistemic status (specifically, to the nature of the justification for holding the proposition to be true).

> **Text 117.1** The premises of demonstration need not be taken from the six necessary propositions (*al-ḍarūriyyāt*), but rather may include the derived propositions that culminate in [those six] (*al-kasbiyyāt al-muntahiyāt ilayhā*); so what is intended by al-Kātibī is that the syllogism whose ultimate material (*mawādduhu l-uwal*) is from the six necessary propositions—whether its premises are two

necessary propositions, or two acquired propositions, or a mix—is called a demonstration.

When it is said that demonstration is only composed of necessary propositions, we mean that it can only be composed of propositions it is necessary to assert (*qaḍāyā yakūnu l-taṣdīq bi-hā ḍarūriyyan*), whether in themselves they are necessary, possible, or existential propositions, and whether they are primitive or acquired. (*TŠ* 372.pu–373.5)

Al-Kātibī distinguishes between a demonstration of the fact and a demonstration of the reasoned fact. He states the classic condition for a demonstration of the reasoned fact (rephrased slightly by al-Ḥillī [*ḤQ* 399.5])—namely, that the middle term must be the cause for the occurrence of the major term to the minor term both in the mind and in existence—and of the demonstration of the fact (again, in al-Ḥillī's terms) that the middle term is the cause for the occurrence of the major term to the minor term in the mind but not in existence. *Burhān annī* is the preferable reading of the Arabic for demonstration of the fact, *burhān limmī* for demonstration of the reasoned fact; but note that for al-Ḥillī—and for everyone else in this tradition—the proofs are, respectively, *burhān in* and *burhān lim*.[296]

Text 117.2 So it is a syllogism made up of propositions of certainty to convey another proposition of certainty. The middle term must inevitably be a real cause (*ʿillah*) for the occurrence of the assertion of the judgment sought, otherwise the demonstration would not be a demonstration of [the judgment sought]. At this point, it must be that either it is moreover a cause for the existence of that judgment extramentally as well, and is called a demonstration of the reasoned fact (*burhānan limmiyyan*) because it conveys the reason why [the predicate exists] (*al-limmiyyah*), I mean, the causality of the judgment (*ʿilliyyat al-ḥukm*) absolutely; or it is

> not [a cause for the extramental existence of the judgment], and is called a demonstration of the fact (*burhānan anniyyan*) because it conveys the fact that [the predicate obtains], I mean, the affirmation in the intellect without the causality for its existence (*dūn al-ʿilliyyah fī l-wujūd*). (*TŠ* 373.6–11)

Al-Kātibī does not go on in the *Risālah* to identify a further, more specific way that the causality of the terms may be related, but most of his commentators do.

> **Text 117.3** If the middle in a demonstration of the fact is an effect of the existence of the judgment extramentally, it is called a proof (*dalīl*), as in "Zayd is fevered, and every fevered suffers putrid humors"; otherwise [the argument-form] is not given a special name, as in "this fever is tertian, every tertian fever has acute periods," because being tertian is not an effect of acute periods of fever; rather, both [having tertian fever and having acute bouts] are effects of putrid bile exuding from the veins. (*TŠ* 374.1–4)

§118[297] The syllogistic matters given to this point can serve for premises in a demonstration. The epistemically less secure premises that follow are acknowledged as justified in ways weaker than those above, and they are used in levels of discourse less scientifically beneficial than demonstration, though perhaps more broadly beneficial to society. The different contexts in which these premises occur are, in descending order of epistemic robustness, dialectic, rhetoric, and poetry. The theory that systematically distributes differing syllogistic matters to differing discursive contexts is, as mentioned above, called by some modern scholars the context theory. Al-Kātibī adopts the version of the theory that Avicenna had settled on in his final writings.

The criterion for a premise being (1) endoxic is that it is widely recognized as true (*ʿumūm al-iʿtirāf*). Of course, primary premises may be as widely recognized as those that are endoxic, and when used along with other dialectical premises, it is their widespread acceptance that matters. The causes of widespread acceptance of an opinion (*shuhrah*) are various, and al-Ḥillī enumerates four: truth; general social utility; passions resulting from humoral disposition; and the effects of rules, laws, and manners on dispositions. The test to distinguish the endoxic from the primary is a thought experiment: were a man "to suppose his soul empty of all matters other than his intellect (*law faraḍa nafsahu khāliyatan min jamīʿ al-umūr al-mughāyirah li-ʿaqlihi*)," he would judge a primary premise to be true, but not the endoxic. The test for making the distinction, according to al-Taftāzānī, comes down to "the pure mind, which only looks at the content of the extremes (*al-ʿaql al-ṣarīḥ alladhī lā yanẓuru ilā ghayr buṭūn al-ṭarafayn*)." Every nation accepts its own endoxic data; so too the practitioners of every art accept endoxic premises relative to their art (*bi-ḥasab ṣināʿatihim*). Endoxic premises are used in dialectical arguments, along with conceded premises.

On one usage, premises that are conceded (*musallamāt*) may include those that are certain and those that are not, but al-Kātibī uses the term in §118 as a counterpart (*qasīmah*) of the certain. The test for (2) whether a premise is conceded is obvious, but the way such premises are used calls for explanation. A premise is conceded by an opponent in a dialectic exchange; once conceded, the questioner tries to build on the conceded premises an argument that refutes the larger claim of the opponent (*fa-idhā tasallamahā minhu banā ʿalayhā mā yubṭilu bi-hi kalāmahu*). A classic example of such an exchange is that which takes place in legal methodology as to whether consensus is probative. The utility of dialectic is in convincing someone unable to grasp the demonstration of a truth by means of a less difficult kind of argument, and in compelling someone to accept what he does not believe.

> **Text 118.1** What is intended is that its propositions are taken insofar as they are endoxic or conceded, even if

actually they are certain or even primary. The truth is that it is more general than demonstration in respect of form too, because what is considered in it is production insofar as [the premises are] conceded, being so whether as syllogism or induction or example, unlike demonstration; so it is just syllogism.

The goal of dialectic is to persuade someone who falls short of apprehending demonstration, and compelling an opponent. The dialectician may be the respondent protecting a view—his goal being to avoid being compelled [to relinquish it]—or he may be the questioner objecting to, and trying to destroy, a given posit—his goal being to compel his opponent [to relinquish the view]. (*TŠ* 375.4–10)

Rhetorical discourse is socially useful. It uses premises that are approved on authority, or that are merely suppositional. (3) A received proposition (*maqbūlah*) is taken from someone whose credibility derives from some religious matter (at least in all of al-Kātibī's examples, though al-Ḥillī extends the source of credibility to include proverbial wisdom [*ḤQ* 402.13]). (4) A premise that is merely supposed (*maẓnūn*) as true may include what is not declarative (*jāzim*) in the sense introduced above (Text 116.a), or what is not certain (*yaqīn*), whereupon it covers compound ignorance, pure supposition, and the belief of those bound by authority (*ḤQ* 403.1).

**Text 118.2** What is intended by supposition is the judgment on the proposition preponderantly one way while acknowledging the possibility that it be the other way (even if those who use [these propositions] in rhetorical discourse declare them certain without entertaining the possibility that things are otherwise). These propositions include for-the-most-part premises based on experience

> (*al-tajrībiyyāt*), sequential testimony, and intuited propositions that are not certain. (*TŠ* 375.apu–u)

There is nothing much to add to al-Kātibī's treatment of what elicits images in poetical discourse. Its impact is a physical affection; whether conceded or not, whether true or not, it imparts strength to its auditor through its expression or its meaning. Poetic syllogism exercises an effect on the soul, which is passive in receiving this effect; we are more inclined toward, and pliable (*aṭwaʿ*) before, this discourse. Other things like meter and a pleasing voice lend it even more force. It is worth noting that earlier logicians did not consider meter in their analysis of poetry, whereas later logicians (and in this case, al-Ḥillī presumably means Avicenna) do consider it, and even rhyme (*ḤQ* 403.apu).

> **Text 118.3** What is meant by meter is a form that follows the system of organization of the vowels and silences and their interrelation in number and extent such that the soul finds a special delight—which is called taste—in apprehending [this form]. (*TŠ* 376.14–15)

The last premise al-Kātibī considers in this lemma, (5) the estimative (*wahmiyyah*), leads him to consider sophistical refutations in the following lemma.

> **Text 118.4** Estimative propositions are false propositions in which judgment is made by the human estimative faculty with respect to imperceptible matters. It is qualified by the phrase ["with respect to imperceptible matters"] just because the intellect [rightly] believes the judgments of the estimative faculty about matters perceived by the senses (*al-maḥsūsāt*). And due to the concord through extreme clarity between the intellect and the estimative faculty in whatever is like geometry, dispute rarely occurs about

> [these judgments]. In pure intelligibles, however, [the judgments of the estimative faculty] are false; this is proved by the fact that the estimative faculty helps the intellect in [acquiring] premises of certainty that produce a conclusion which is certain, yet disputes [with the intellect] about the conclusion, as in "the dead are inanimate, and every inanimate is such that it is not to be feared."
>
> The judgments of the estimative faculty are endoxic for the most part (*fī l-akthar*), because it is closer to sensible things, and has more impact on people (*awqaʿ fī l-ḍamāʾir*).
>
> The syllogism composed of [these propositions] is sophistry, the goal of which is to silence and overcome the opponent. The strongest benefit in knowing [sophistry] is to [be able to] avoid it. (*TŠ* 377.1–10)

So powerful is the hold that estimative propositions have over certain people that such propositions are only overcome by intellectual arguments and provisions in religious law.

§119[298] Al-Kātibī's treatment of fallacy theory comes before rather than after his treatment of demonstration theory; he follows the same order in *Jāmiʿ al-daqāʾiq*. In this, he departs from Avicenna's ordering of material in *Pointers*, where we find fallacy theory as the final chapter of the logic volume. It is hard to say what led al-Kātibī to this decision. He had predecessors in ordering the subjects like this (not least al-Fārābī), but I suspect it is mainly because he treats all material considerations in logic together, rather than—as Avicenna did—first as they have to do with propositions (*Pointers* Path 6) and then as they have to do with arguments (*Pointers* Paths 9 and 10). By contrast, §118 deals with premises for arguments that fail to meet the criteria for demonstration, and §119 develops the topic by moving straight on to the fallacious arguments in which some of those premises find a place. Unlike Avicenna, however, al-Kātibī makes no mention of specious premises (*al-mushabbihāt*), which is where in Path 6 of *Pointers* Avicenna deals with fallacious propositions. Indeed, al-Kātibī presents estimative premises (*al-wahmiyyāt*) in terms closely modeled on Avicenna, but goes straight on to say that it is these which are the premises used in fallacious syllogisms.[299]

The treatment in the *Risālah* is short and highly selective. I do not think that this is due to influence from al-Rāzī, who omitted fallacy theory from the *Mulakhkhaṣ*, saying that "the discussion of the details of fallacies is also rather like an extra we can do without . . . So it is better to set them out in the extended treatments [of logic]" (*RM* 354.9–u). Al-Kātibī sets out a substantial treatment of fallacies in his *Jāmiʿ al-daqāʾiq*, and adds such a treatment to his commentary on the *Mulakhkhaṣ*. And there is clear evidence—presented at the end of this section—that he thinks proper analysis of fallacies is essential even in short treatises like the *Risālah*, especially for theology students.

We can say, however, that the treatment of fallacies was in flux through the period in which the *Risālah* was written. Al-Kātibī's commentator al-Ḥillī epitomizes a different approach to dealing with fallacy theory, which reflects deeper differences to do with the continuing direct relevance of Aristotle for logic. Al-Kātibī sets out five fallacies in the *Risālah*, and names them only in broad terms (a fallacy may be one "whose matter is corrupt," or it "may be false but seem true with respect to expression," or its falsity "may be with respect to meaning"), whereas al-Ḥillī in his commentary gives each fallacy its name under the Aristotelian division. Furthermore, in the *Asrār*, al-Ḥillī gives the list of fallacies first treated by Aristotle, set out in substantially the same way as they were in *Sophistical Refutations* (*ḤA* 218.1–222.3). Nonetheless, I will stick to the fallacies treated by al-Kātibī.

Al-Ḥillī disagrees with al-Kātibī's analysis of begging the question (the first syllogism in the lemma, the example that concludes "every man is risible"); al-Kātibī, following al-Rāzī, claims that the problem derives from corrupt matter. Against al-Rāzī, al-Ṭūsī claims rather that the fallacy derives from a formal problem (*ṬḤ* 498.7–10). But according to al-Ḥillī:

> **Text 119.1** The truth is that the defect in this is due neither to matter nor to form, because the matter is correct and true, so too the form of the syllogism. The defect here is only with respect to the fact that it begs the question because the discourse implied does not differ from the discourse in the premises.[300] (*ḤQ* 408.9–12)

Al-Ḥillī agrees with al-Kātibī's analysis of the painted-horse problem as equivocation:

> **Text 119.2** The error in this only arises due to confusion (*ishtibāh*) of the expression "horse" between the engraved image and the specific animal; it is one of the kinds of error to do with expression. (*ḤQ* 409.1–2)

He also agrees with the analysis of the fallacy arising from "man-and-horse" as a fallacy of meaning, though he names precisely what kind of fallacy it is:

> **Text 119.3** This is an error to do with meaning, which is due to a confusion of the true with the false; it involves a judgment being made in the affirmative on a subject not specified to exist. The truth is that the error in this comes under the category of secundum quid (*min bāb sūʾ iʿtibār al-ḥaml*). (*ḤQ* 409.6–8)

The fourth example (taking the natural proposition—see §43—as a universal) is worth special mention, because according to al-Taftāzānī, al-Kātibī analyzed it differently before changing his mind.

> **Text 119.4** If it is said: Putting the natural proposition in place of the universal, as in "man is an animal, animal is a genus," is not a corruption of matter (*fasād al-māddah*), but a corruption of form due to leaving out the universal quantifier of the major (*kulliyyat al-kubrā*). I answer: The principle of the major here is true as a natural proposition (whereupon the form [of the syllogism] is corrupt), and it is false as a universal (whereupon the matter is corrupt); so al-Kātibī took the corruption of the syllogism here to arise from the matter, having regard to [the proposition] not being true when expressed as a universal. In the *Jāmiʿ*, al-Kātibī took [the fallacy] as arising from the form, having regard to the universal quantifier of the major being left out when expressed as a natural proposition.[301] (*TŠ* 379.1–6)

Finally, al-Ḥillī agrees that the fifth example in §119 (taking mental matters as real) is a fallacy of meaning (more precisely, another example of secundum quid, though—pace al-Ḥillī—in Text 119.6 it looks to me like it's a part of a false cause) (*ḤQ* 410.5). Al-Taftāzānī offers an example of what is under discussion:

> **Text 119.5** An example of al-Kātibī's "taking what is merely mental to be real" is: Were the partner of the Creator impossible in external reality, then [the cocreator's] impossibility would obtain in external reality, so that which is described by impossibility (*al-mawṣūf bi-l-imtināʿ*) would be realized in external reality (because the realization of the description (*taḥaqquq al-ṣifah*) in external reality necessarily requires the realization of what is described by it). The

error here is that the impossibility is in mental matters that fundamentally have no realization. (*TŠ* 379.14–u)

And it is here that we can see how much fallacy theory matters for al-Kātibī, because we find out in the *Jāmiʿ* just who it is whose work is riddled with this fallacy.[302]

**Text 119.6** Also under [the second broad division of fallacies] is what occurs because of taking mental considerations as external, as when it is said, were the partner of God impossible in extramental existence, its impossibility would occur in extramental reality. And what is described with impossibility occurring in extramental reality in fact occurs in extramental reality; so that which is impossible in extramental reality would occur in extramental reality, which is absurd. The error here is that the impossibility is a mental consideration that is not realized in extramental reality . . . This fallacious reasoning occurs frequently in scientific books, especially the books connected to the imam [Fakhr al-Dīn]; so you have to pay attention to it. By this, many obscurities will be solved for you. (*Jāmiʿ al-daqāʾiq*, 78a.1–14, Chester Beatty 3577)

*The second discussion, on the parts of the sciences*

**§120**[303] This is the last lemma of the *Risālah*, appropriately given to what al-Kātibī and his contemporaries took to be the culmination and highest goal of logic, demonstration theory. It carries on with discussions opened up in the Conclusion, specifically in §116 on the kinds of propositions that can be used in a demonstration, and in §117, on further conditions (to do with the middle term, modality and causality) for a successful demonstration. But in fact, nearly every point al-Kātibī has developed in the *Risālah* so far can be brought to bear on demonstration, and it is natural that he refers back to §5 in opening this lemma, and specifically to the definition of a scientific subject given there: "that whose essential accidents are investigated in the science, accidents that attach to the subject due to what it is (that is, due to its essence), or due to what is coextensive with it, or a part of it." The range of scientific subjects is explored by al-Kātibī and by al-Taftāzānī in Text 120.2. Essential accidents (*aʿrāḍ dhātiyyah*), mentioned before and crucial for this lemma, are defined before Text 120.2 below. "Subject" is used in the plural ("subjects," *mawḍūʿāt*) to include all subjects of propositions used in the science. As noted in Text 5.1, a given science is distinct from another by virtue of the distinction between the subjects each studies.

> **Text 120.1** Know that a single science may have a single subject, either absolutely like number for arithmetic or insofar as a property occurs to it (whether an essential property, like natural body insofar as it is subject to change for physics, or a foreign property,[304] like moving sphere for its science [astronomy]). And the science may have a number of subjects on condition that they are interrelated (*mutanāsibah*). The sense of interrelation [of subjects] is their sharing in an essential property like line and plane and body if they are made subjects for geometry (they share extended magnitude), or in an accidental property (*ʿaraḍī*) like the body of man and its parts and states and medicine and nutrition and whatever shares with these things when they are all taken as subjects of the science of medicine (for they share in being related to health, which is the goal of that science). (*TŠ* 381.1–8)

What al-Kātibī does not consider in the *Risālah* is the way subjects of different sciences relate to each other.[305] The goal of scientific research is to produce a system of interrelated knowledge claims where higher sciences establish claims more abstract and fundamental than those established in the lower sciences; the theorems proved in the higher science are taken up as principles in the lower science. (The reverse can also happen if the principles of the lower science used in establishing the claim to be borrowed do not depend on the higher science that borrows the claim.) Al-Taftāzānī in particular among the commentators writes on the matter, but the clearest contribution is from al-Ḥillī in his *Asrār* (*ḤA* 208.9–209.2); I mention it but follow al-Kātibī in leaving it to one side.

The subject (and the subjects under it) are defined according to the rules set out in §§35–37;[306] the resulting definitions are considered to be among the principles of the science. As such—and al-Kātibī stresses this again as he closes his treatise—they cannot be proved in the science, because they constitute the subjects that must be assumed for the propositions of the science (they are, to put it another way, preconditions for the investigation). What must be proved to belong to the subjects are the essential accidents (*al-aʿrāḍ al-dhātiyyah*)—never defined in the *Risālah*—a technical term, which in this context refers to an attribute in whose definition the subject is taken (*yu'khadh al-mawḍūʿ fī ḥaddihi*), like "snub" in "snub nose," which is defined as "a nose possessing a bend" (*anf dhū taqʿīr*) (*ḤA* 203.6–7); these are—again, most commonly—accidents that belong only to the subjects of the science. A much-cited example of a theorem (*mas'alah*) to be proved in geometry is "triangle has internal angles that sum to two right angles" (*Elements* 1.32). The essential accident ("internal angles that sum to two right angles") belongs only to the subject "triangle," and it is proved by using postulates (in this case, derivatively on 1.31, which uses postulate 1 "to draw a straight line from any point to any point"), by using common notions (in this case, first, common notion 2, "if equals are added to equals, then the wholes are equals"), and by using other conclusions already proved.[307] These essential accidents belong to their subjects as extrinsic to the meaning (they are not constitutive of the subject), but they hold as implicates of the subject. Since every conclusion in a science relates a subject to an essential accident, and essential accidents cannot be constituents of a quiddity, there must ultimately be essential accidents of quiddity that are immediate (see §22).[308]

In §120.2, al-Kātibī focuses more closely on how the subjects of the theorems may relate to the subject of the science (he takes these examples from Avicenna [*AN* §§126, 135–36]); these examples serve to show how the theory of demonstration is applied to a science (in this case, geometry).[309] Al-Taftāzānī expands on al-Kātibī's examples and adds one more:

> **Text 120.2** The questions are the propositions for which the science seeks to demonstrate a relation between their predicates and their subjects. These propositions can only be acquired, and this is something no one disputes (to claim they could be available without acquisition would be bizarre). The subjects of the questions can be the subject of the science if [that subject] is taken without qualification (*mujarradan*), as in geometry. So "every magnitude is either commensurable or incommensurable"; here, magnitude is the subject of geometry, and the meaning of two magnitudes being commensurable is that both have a common measure, and being incommensurable is the opposite.[310] Or [the subject of the theorem could be the subject of the science] with a per se attribute, like "every [magnitude which is a] mean proportional is a side contained by the two other extremes"; here "magnitude" is the subject, though it has been taken with one of its per se accidents (namely, its being a mean proportional—that is, its being between two magnitudes, its relation to one being the same as the other to it, like four cubits between two and eight, which is half eight, and two is half of it). The meaning of it being a side contained by the two other extremes is that the result of squaring it is the result of multiplying one extreme by the other; so the result of multiplying four

by four is sixteen, which is the result of multiplying two by eight. And [the subject of the theorem] may be a species of the subject of the science, either unqualified (*mujarrad*), as "every line may be bisected," line being a species of magnitude; or [it may be a species of a subject of the science] with a per se attribute, as in "every line set upon another line produces angles that are either right angles or that sum to right angles"; here line is taken with its being set upon another line (which is one of its per se accidents). And [the subject of the theorem] may be a per se accident of the subject, as in "every triangle has angles that sum to two right angles"; triangle is a per se attribute of magnitude. And [the subject of the theorem] may be a species of per se attribute, as in "every isosceles triangle has base angles that are equal to each other"; the triangle that is described is a species of triangle. (*TŠ* 386.8–387.10)

In §120.3, al-Kātibī stresses once again in closing that a demonstration must be of an extrinsic property belonging to a subject. Were it of something intrinsic to the subject, the demonstration would amount to demonstrating that a constitutive belongs to the subject. But we had to conceive the subject before beginning the demonstration, and we can only conceive the subject with all its constituents. So we cannot demonstrate a constituent (or, as it is more commonly expressed, it is impossible to demonstrate a definition).[311]

# Notes

1 Asaph: The son of Berechiah the Gershonite (2 Chronicles 20:14); psalmist charged by King David to worship God in song and praise (1 Chronicles 15:16–17).

2 Q Fuṣṣilat 41:42.

3 "The rope of God," an allusion to Q Āl ʿImrān 3:103.

4 Among other meanings, the Arabic *ʿayn* is equivocal between "eye" and "spring."

5 Al-Kātibī is referring back to the division set out in §16 above.

6 A reference to §15 above.

7 A reference to §16 above.

8 An allusion to a phrase in Q ʿAṣr 103:2.

9 The Arabic for "inanimate" is a positive term (see §49).

10 Because I adopt Rescher's translations of the names of propositions, "conditional" is used both for the categorical necessity proposition under a descriptional reading and for the hypothetical proposition first set out in §39 above.

11 This is what Euclid would call a postulate (his first and third postulates are given as examples).

12 This is one of Euclid's common notions (his first is the example).

13 *TT* 21 (no comment); *TŠ* 88. *ḤQ* omits the exordium.

14 I adopt the convention of using "intellect" for sublunary intellect and "intelligence" for superlunary; see Davidson, *Alfarabi, Avicenna, and Averroes on Intellect: Their Cosmologies, Theories of the Active Intellect, and Theories of Human Intellect*, 4.

15 Perhaps because it presents logic detached from metaphysics and physics; scholars were more negative to the logic section in al-Bayḍāwī's *Ṭawāliʿ al-anwār min maṭāliʿ al-anẓār* (translated in al-Bayḍāwī et al., *Nature, Man and God in Medieval Islam*), on the face of it no more logically objectionable than *al-Risālah al-Shamsiyyah*; El-Rouayheb, "Sunni Muslim Scholars on the Status of Logic, 1500–1800," 227.

16 See §36; a delineation (or description) makes something known using nonessential elements.

17 *TT* 30; *TŠ* 97; *ḤQ* 182.

18 For reflections on the difficulties in reaching a definitive translation for *taṣdīq*, see Sabra, "Avicenna on the Subject Matter of Logic," 758; for an argument that *taṣdīq* should be translated as "belief," see Lameer, *Conception and Belief in Ṣadr al-Dīn al-Shīrāzī: Introduction, Translation and Commentary*. I follow Strobino's preference for "assertion"; see "Ibn Sina's Logic." A common alternative for *taṣawwur* is "conceptualization" (e.g., Ahmed in *AN*) to reflect the process of coming to a conception; I believe that throughout the *Risālah* al-Kātibī uses the term to refer to the conception attained.

19 One common definition of knowledge is—as for conception—"the occurrence of the form of something in the intellect" (*TŠ* 98.2).

20 A disjunction—*mānīʿat al-khulūw*—presented in §60.3, second section of the second treatise.

21 *ḤQ* 184; *TT* 44; *TŠ* 104.

22 I take al-Ḥillī's use of *badīhiyyāt* for *awwaliyyāt* in *ḤA* 197.9 to be a relevant consideration. I avoid "innate" due to the examples "hot" and "cold" in Text 2.1.

23 Al-Khūnajī sets out the distinction, with implicational relations between the two; *ḪK* 115.4–apu.

24 See Strobino, *Avicenna's Theory of Science: Logic, Metaphysics, Epistemology*, Chapter 1, especially page 28, Text 1.7 (Avicenna, *Al-Shifāʾ: al-Manṭiq: Burhān* 77.1–5); from page 24, Strobino examines how Avicenna's discussion relates to the learner's paradox from Plato's

*Meno*, the impact of the paradox on the *Posterior Analytics*, and Avicenna's foundationalism.

25 Al-Rāzī is, however, strongly associated with the position set out in the *Muḥaṣṣal*; see, e.g., *ṬḤ* 124.20, and al-Rāzī's late *Mafātīḥ al-ghayb al-mushtahar bi-l-Tafsīr al-kabīr*, 2.143.15 and following (I am grateful to Tareq Moqbel for the reference). See also Benevich, "Scepticism and Semantics in Twelfth-Century Arabic Philosophy," Section 1.

26 *ḤQ* 185 (not from start of lemma); *TT* 52; *TŠ* 106.

27 For Avicenna's delineations of logic, see Gutas, *Avicenna and the Aristotelian Tradition: Introduction to Reading Avicenna's Philosophical Works*, 316–18.

28 See especially Sabra, "Avicenna on the Subject Matter of Logic," 752.

29 *ḤQ* 187; *TT* 64; *TŠ* 112.

30 *ḤQ* 188; *TT* 68; *TŠ* 114.

31 "Subject" can mean the subject matter of a science; in the plural, it means the subjects of the propositions used or proved in the science; see commentary to §120 below.

32 Meaning what is called a per se 2 attribute; see Strobino "Per Se, Inseparability, Containment and Implication: Bridging the Gap between Avicenna's Theory of Demonstration and Logic of the Predicables," 187–208, at 190. I mention the definition in commentary on §120. See further *AN* §§7, 11, and §§121, 131.

33 The opening sentence draws on Avicenna's wording in *al-Taʿlīqāt* 167 (quoted in *SQ* 109n7).

34 As I understand it, this is the reading put forward by El-Rouayheb, "Post-Avicennan Logicians on the Subject Matter of Logic: Some Thirteenth- and Fourteenth-Century Discussions," 74. For the origin of the revision, see *Ḫ̌K* 8.13–9.2.

35 As does al-Ḥillī. He agrees, however, with Avicenna, *ḤA* 10.14, as does al-Samarqandī, *SQ* 108–112.6.

36 *ḤQ* 190; *TT* 74; *TŠ* 116.

37 Avicenna, *Pointers* 1.12.1 (*AI* 8.pu–9.1), records the convention that "implication" (*luzūm*) is reserved for the relation of one meaning to

another that is extrinsic to the first, even though in ordinary usage it also refers to the relation between one meaning and another contained in the first. The passage is translated in Strobino, "Per Se," 245–46, see comments in Kalbarczyk *Sprachphilosophie in der Islamischen Rechtstheorie*, 85–86nn54, 55.

38 *ḤQ* 194; *TT* 82; *TŠ* 119.

39 Since the distinction between expression and meaning is important throughout this first section of the first treatise, in Text 7.1 and the following discussion I use small capitals for MEANING and quotation marks for "expression."

40 Recounted in Section 2 of Street, "The Reception of *Pointers* 1.6 in Thirteenth-Century Logic: On the Expression's Signification of Meaning."

41 *ḤQ* 196; *TT* 89; *TŠ* 123.

42 That is, implicates that cannot be removed in the imagination (*fī l-wahm*); see Strobino, "Per Se," 237–43, the second kind. Al-Khūnajī and al-Kātibī are using a distinction finer than those in Avicenna.

43 I summarize here aspects of *Ḫ K* 11.u–13.u and *RM* 20.u–21.pu; see Section 5 of Street, "Reception of *Pointers*."

44 *ḤQ* 197; *TT* 91; *TŠ* 123.

45 *ḤQ* 199; *TT* 96; *TŠ* 128.

46 The same alternative is given and rejected in *Ḫ K* 14.11–14, though he reverses the usage for the second two terms in the proposed new terminology: "the composite comes under the simple on Avicenna's definition."

47 See Zimmermann, *Al-Fārābī's Commentary and Short Treatise on Aristotle's "De Interpretatione"*, 17 and 17n3, and *AM* 50–53 with Di Vincenzo's comments 285–87. I think Aristotle is dealing with issues that may cloud the distinction between simple and compound, and (as Di Vincenzo says) Avicenna is making the same point. Perhaps the doctrine reported in Text 10.1 is an attempt to provide a term for borderline cases.

48 *ḤQ* 200; *TT* 102; *TŠ* 132.

49 The full story is more complex: The grammarians' *fiʿl* is not the logicians' *kalimah*, which does not conjugate fully; Avicenna, *ʿIbārah* (*AʿI* 18.12). Notably, al-Rāzī adopts the grammarians' term of art, *fiʿl*.

50 *AʿI* 7.4–5, 17.4–5; cf. *ḪK* 14.15–15.11, whence I take some of my observations.

51 That is, it is syncategorematic; see Copenhaver et al., *Peter of Spain: Summaries*, 105.

52 *ḤQ* 201; *TT* 108; *TŠ* 134.

53 Philoponus, *On Aristotle Categories 1–5*, 52.

54 See Schöck, "Name (*ism*), Derived Name (*mushtaqq*), and Description (*waṣf*) in Arabic Grammar, Muslim Dialectical Theology and Arabic Logic."

55 For further distinction into three kinds of *tashkīk*, see *TT* 112.5–15.

56 *ḤQ* 204; *TT* 115; *TŠ* 136.

57 *ḤQ* 205; *TT* 117; *TŠ* 137.

58 *ḤQ* 207; *TT* 124; *TŠ* 139.

59 Note that al-Taftāzānī reads what I give as "conception of its meaning" (*taṣawwur maʿnāhu*) as "its conception" (*taṣawwuruhu*), on the grounds that "meaning" is redundant, since only a meaning can be conceived (*TŠ* 139.apu). I think the evidence of the manuscripts is against al-Taftāzānī on this point.

60 I draw what I have to say here from the opening section of Thom, "Avicenna's Mereology."

61 There is no systematic presentation in the *Risālah* of scientific questions, the interrogatives (*maṭlab*, pl. *maṭālib*) deployed in the process of a scientific investigation, and the protocols involved in answering them. This lemma, §19, and Text 33.1 present some relevant points, but see Strobino, "What If That (Is) Why? Avicenna's Taxonomy of Scientific Inquiries" for a full account; see also *AN* §§115–18, 128–30.

62 *ḤQ* 208; *TT* 129; *TŠ* 134.

63 See Figures 6 and 7 for alternative divisions presented by al-Ṭūsī in commentary on *Pointers* 2.5 (*ṬḤ* 201.7–24); mentioned again in commentary on §23.

64 I assume al-Kātibī is basing his division on notions gathered by Avicenna in *Pointers* 1.17.2 (*AI* 11.16–12.9).

65 Al-Taḥtānī condemns al-Kātibī's decision as stepping beyond the bounds of logic, first, by limiting his interest to species with actual instantiations (*al-nawʿ al-khārijī*), and, second, by confusing species (when it is taken with respect to pure specificity) with definition (*TT* 135.pu–136.2). I translate *maqūl* as "that may be said" to reflect the point al-Ḥillī is making.

66 *ḤQ* 210; *TT* 136; *TŠ* 143.

67 To repeat: al-Kātibī only uses the first of these terms in this section of his treatise (but not until §34), and the second, in the sense of essential accident, at the close of his whole treatise (in §120). Avicenna distinguishes the two senses of *dhātī* (e.g., *AI* 10.1–4); see generally Strobino, "Per Se," and Text 7 on page 201.

68 Al-Taḥtānī offered this definition for "the whole of the part shared," and defended it against an alternative definition, the sum of parts shared between the quiddity and the other species (*TT* 137.7); consider the simple (ultimate) genera, like SUBSTANCE, which have no parts.

69 *ḤQ* 211; *TT* 139; *TŠ* 145.

70 *ḤQ* 213; *TT* 142; *TŠ* 147.

71 See remarks in comment on §12. I follow Thom, "Avicenna's Mereology," but note that *mushtaqq* is more general than Buridan's denominative.

72 I am guided by the rubrication of *SQ* 154.4, *wujūh fī nḥiṣār juzʾ al-māhiyyah fī l-jins wa-l-faṣl.*

73 See Porphyry in Barnes, *Porphyry*, 10.

74 *ḤQ* 215; *TT* 148; *TŠ* 150.

75 That is, what causes the species to be the portion of the generic meaning that it is.

76 *AM* 166.pu–u.

77 *Pointers* 2.6 [*AI* 16.15–16].

78 I think al-Kātibī is holding back from endorsing al-Rāzī's position, at least for the *Risālah*; see al-Rāzī, *Sharḥ al-ishārāt*, 98.3–11.

79 *ḤQ* 216; *TT* 150; *TŠ* 152.

80 *ḤQ* 217; *TT* 153; *TŠ* 154.

81 My account derives from Strobino, "Per Se," insofar as it relates to Avicenna's theories; the article gives a full account of how the *Eisagoge* material relates to the *Posterior Analytics* material.

82 Strobino, "Per Se," Section 2.1, 237–43. Al-Kātibī uses the phrase "impossible to separate" without further explanation; drawing directly on Strobino, I simply note the basic notions Avicenna uses in delivering the original distinctions on which al-Kātibī draws. Al-Kātibī implicitly assumes that the implicate is posterior to what is called its substrate, or—in some versions of the lemma—its underlying quiddity. Cf. *SQ* 148–50.

83 *ḤQ* 219; *TT* 160; *TŠ* 160.

84 As when defining differentia, Avicenna has two definitions for proprium, and al-Kātibī is closer to the one in *Pointers* (*AI* 15.apu).

85 *ḤQ* 221; *TT* 165; *TŠ* 163.

86 *ḤQ* 221; *TT* 167; *TŠ* 164.

87 See Marmura, "Avicenna's Chapter on Universals in the *Isagoge* of his *Shifāʾ*"; the three universals developed here (especially the first) are alluded to in *Pointers* 1.11 (*AI* 7.pu–8.apu, especially 8.15–16), and laid out in more detail by al-Ṭūsī.

88 As is, in fact, the existence of the natural universal; for a counterargument, see *SQ* 140.8–141.5.

89 *ḤQ* 223; *TT* 171; *TŠ* 171.

90 From Keynes, *Studies and Exercises*, 172.

91 Joseph, *An Introduction to Logic*, 41.

92 *ḤQ* 226; *TT* 175; *TŠ* 173.

93 See at the outset Fallahi, "Fārābī and Avicenna on Contraposition"; *SQ* 133 and, especially, from 134 (where, at 134.10–11, al-Kātibī provides a counterexample against the first and second claims set out in this lemma).

94 *ḤQ* 227; *TT* 186; *TŠ* 179.

95 *ḤQ* 228; *TT* 191; *TŠ* 182.

96 Take for example al-Ṭūsī's comment in *Pointers* on 6.4: "Know that these divisions are not essential . . . for this reason, Avicenna called

them 'types' not 'species'" (*ṬḤ* 392.18–19). The distinction between *ṣinf* and *nawʿ* is said by al-Kātibī's commentators to matter in reading the *Risālah*; see, e.g., Text 38.4.

97 *ḤQ* 229; *TT* 194; *TŠ* 183.

98 Not, I think, Avicenna, though the discussion is perhaps a development of his consideration of "universal at the top under which no other universal is subsumed," like "point" (in the geometrical sense) according to some philosophers; *AM* 118.17–18. I am grateful to Silvia di Vincenzo for important references on this and the following lemmata.

99 As noted in comment on §0 above, I adopt Davidson's convention of referring to the superlunary intelligences as such, and their sublunary congeners as intellects.

100 *ḤQ* 230; *TT* 197; *TŠ* 183.

101 *ḤQ* 232; *TT* 200; *TŠ* 185.

102 "Ancients" as a group term generally includes Avicenna, but not this time; see *Pointers* 2.1.3 (*AI* 14.8–10).

103 *ḤQ* 233; *TT* 202; *TŠ* 186.

104 *ḤQ* 234; *TT* 205; *TŠ* 188.

105 His major contribution is in the *Burhān*; see Strobino, *Avicenna's Theory of Science*, Part 5.

106 I draw from Strobino, "Per Se," 188, where a more formal account is presented.

107 *ḤQ* 236; *TT* 208; *TŠ* 191.

108 I have earlier translated *musāwin* as coextensive; perhaps "equal" is better in this context, because the definition must not only be true of what the definiendum is true of, but also mean the same.

109 *ḤQ* 238; *TT* 212; *TŠ* 195.

110 Cf. Avicenna, *Burhān* 52.3–20; Strobino, *Avicenna's Theory of Science*, Text 12.1.

111 *ḤQ* 239; *TT* 216; *TŠ* 197.

112 *ḤQ* 242; *TT* 220; *TŠ* 201.

113 A different argument for the same conclusion is given by al-Ḥillī, *ḤQ* 243.4–7.

114 Cf. al-Ṭūsī (*ṬḤ* 392.18–19) quoted in comment on §29 making much the same point.

115 *ḤQ* 244; *TT* 226; *TŠ* 203.

116 *RM* 313–319; *ḪK* Section 7, 195–229, Section 10, 317–423, remarks critical of Avicenna, 317.11–u.

117 Strobino, "Ibn Sina's Logic," 3.2.1. Cf. *AN* §§24–26, 19–20; §§78–84, 79–93.

118 *ḤQ* 246; *TT* 231; *TŠ* 204.

119 See *AM* 57.pu–58.2 for Avicenna's presentation of the distinction, and *SQ* 131–133.1; further comments given at §§12 and 13 above.

120 Al-Fārābī, *Kitāb al-Ḥurūf* §§85 and 86 (not a direct quotation).

121 I cut my remarks short; for more, see Klinger, "Language and Logic in the Graeco-Arabic Tradition: A History of Propositional Analysis from the Hellenic Commentators on Aristotle to Theories of the Proposition in Arabic Philosophy, 900–1350," Section 3. Cf. *SQ* 227.9–228.7.

122 Translated in El-Rouayheb, "Does a Proposition Have Three Parts or Four? A Debate in Later Arabic Logic," 306–7; the paper traces the origins, long history, and demise of the four-part doctrine.

123 *ḤQ* 248; *TT* 235; *TŠ* 210.

124 See Klima, *John Buridan, Summulae*, 269.

125 *ḤQ* 248; *TT* 236; *TŠ* 211.

126 *ḤQ* 251; *TT* 241; *TŠ* 214.

127 *AʿI* 45.8–pu (not a direct quote).

128 There is no unified theory of reference presented in the *Risālah*, but in a proposition of the type "man is a species," "man" refers not to some or all individual men (as it does in quantified propositions), but to the meaning of the quiddity; see also the opening sentence of Text 45.1.

129 *ḤQ* 252; *TT* 244; *TŠ* 215.

130 Translated from a manuscript of Ibn Wāṣil's *Sharḥ al-Jumal* in El-Rouayheb's "Introduction" to his edition of Khūnajī (2010) (*ḪK*), xliii.

131 *ḤQ* 252; *TT* 245; *TŠ* 216.

132 For present purposes, "matter" refers to the two terms that fill the subject and predicate positions. *Māddah* is opposed to *ṣūrah*, form; see Text 51.2.

133 Strobino, "Ibn Sina's Logic," 3.1.1.

134 See al-Taftāzānī in Text 98.2 below on the difference between the positions of al-Fārābī and Avicenna.

135 So Qarāmalikī in commentary on al-Rāzī's *Mulakhkhaṣ* (*RM*), in notes to text at 400.

136 I am leaving to one side the complications of an alternative reading (preferred by the editor at *ḤQ* 252.u), *law wujida wa-kāna jīm*. I agree with the dominant interpretation: I restrict the protasis to *law wujida*, and read *law wujida kāna jīm*; see *TT* 257.10–15. Al-Ḥillī himself rejects the alternative (*ḤQ* 254.13–15).

137 The essence under C for which C is the title.

138 The proposition with an impossible subject is called the mental proposition (*qaḍiyyah dhihniyyah*) by al-Ḥillī; *ḤQ* 254.9.

139 Actuality propositions (*al-fiʿliyyāt*) are all propositions aside from $\mathbf{M}_1$ and $\mathbf{M}_2$. See Appendix 1.

140 *ḤQ* 255; *TT* 260; *TŠ* 224.

141 *ḤQ* 255; *TT* 261; *TŠ* 225.

142 Reading *akhaṣṣ min* for *akhaṣṣ*.

143 Including *al-sālibatayn* from the apparatus.

144 So, if a-propositions are represented by Figure 13, o-propositions are represented by Figure 17.

145 See *SQ* 259–68, and comments on §27 above, and Thom, "Al-Fārābī on Indefinite and Privative Names," on al-Fārābī's corresponding treatment in commentary on *De Interpretatione*. I translate *maʿdūlah* of the term as "indefinite," of the proposition, "metathetic."

146 *ḤQ* 256; *TT* 263; *TŠ* 226.

147 Note that what I translate here as "inanimate" (*jāmid*) is not an indefinite predicate in Arabic.

148 *ḤQ* 257; *TT* 264; *TŠ* 226.

149 *ḤQ* 257; *TT* 265; *TŠ* 227.

150 *ḤQ* 259; *TT* 273; *TŠ* 231.

151 *ḤQ* 260; *TT* 275; *TŠ* 234.

152 Al-Khūnajī lists thirty-two modal propositions (the central thirteen, and nineteen others), *ḪK* 107.8–109.4.

153 Rescher and vander Nat, "Theory of Modal Syllogistic."

154 Strobino, "Ibn Sina's Logic."

155 See Rescher and vander Nat, "Theory of Modal Syllogistic," 34–35, for a fuller sketch; this should be checked against, e.g., *ḪK* 104.12–107.2.

156 See Strobino, "Time and Necessity in Avicenna's Theory of Demonstration," 341–54.

157 *ḤQ* 266; *TT* 285; *TŠ* 240.

158 *ḤQ* 267; *TT* 288; *TŠ* 241.

159 *ḤQ* 268; *TT* 289; *TŠ* 241.

160 *ḤQ* 269; *TT* 290; *TŠ* 242.

161 *ḤQ* 271; *TT* 291; *TŠ* 243.

162 *ḤQ* 272; *TT* 294; *TŠ* 244.

163 *ḤQ* 273; *TT* 296; *TŠ* 245.

164 $\mathbf{M}_{\sim L}$ would be more consistent with my convention for $\mathbf{X}_{\sim L}$, but $\mathbf{M}_2$ is widely used.

165 I rarely depart from Strobino's terminology, but here I think his "exclusive non-exhaustive" for *māniʿat al-jamʿ*, though now common, is inelegant, and forces us into the equally inelegant "exclusive and exhaustive" for what modern logicians call the exclusive (in al-Kātibī's Arabic, *munfaṣilah ḥaqīqiyyah*). Were we to follow the Arabic, it would be real (*ḥaqīqiyyah*), inclusive (*māniʿat al-khulūw*), and exclusive (*māniʿat al-jamʿ*).

166 *ḤQ* 275–76; *TT* 299; *TŠ* 250–52.

167 Al-Kātibī never mentions the associative in the *Risālah*, whereas al-Ṭūsī in comment on *Pointers* does (*ṬḤ* 433.7 on *Pointers* 8.1 [*AI* 79.13]). I would have expected al-Ḥillī to use, like al-Ṭūsī, *al-istiṣḥābī*. See Text 60.4.

168 Avicenna's position is reported in Strobino, "Ibn Sina's Logic," 3.2.4; see *AQ* 279.2–283.9. For more on the differing truth-conditions, see

Text 63.2 and following. Avicenna may have shifted in his view; see *Ḫ̮K* 323.3–u, and editor's reference there to *AQ* 299–300 (thanks to Behnam Zolghadr for bringing this to my attention).

169 *ḤQ* 279; *TT* 305; *TŠ* 254.

170 *ḤQ* 280; *TT* 306; *TŠ* 260.

171 Strobino, "Ibn Sina's Logic," 4.2.

172 *ḤQ* 280; *TT* 308; *TŠ* 260.

173 Strobino, "Ibn Sina's Logic," 3.2.2.

174 *ḤQ* 281; *TT* 311; *TŠ* 264.

175 *ḤQ* 284; *TT* 313; *TŠ* 265.

176 Rescher, "Avicenna on the Logic of 'Conditional Propositions'"; Strobino, "Ibn Sina's Logic," 3.2, 4.2; Avicenna, *Pointers* 3.5 (*AI* 26.10–u).

177 Further light is shed on the truth-conditions of the conditional in al-Taḥtānī on §110 in Text 110.1, specifically, on the situations quantified over.

178 *ḤQ* 286; *TT* 319; *TŠ* 270.

179 See *Pointers* 3.8 (*AI* 29.3–30.8) for Avicenna's account of complex hypotheticals; see al-Ṭūsī's notes (*ṬḤ* 246–254), and Strobino "Ibn Sina's Logic," 3.2.1.

180 *ḤQ* 289; *TT* 323; *TŠ* 274.

181 I read *laysa lā ʿālim* with R, against Tabrīziyān's choice of *lā ʿālim*. Al-Kātibī has yet to introduce the unities between a proposition and its contradictory (he does so in the next lemma)—which this example obviously breaches—and I think the point here is that the two propositions are both true or both false, even though one is affirmative and the other negative.

182 *ḤQ* 290; *TT* 325; *TŠ* 276.

183 *ḤQ* 292; *TT* 332; *TŠ* 281.

184 See, e.g., the opening of *Prior Analytics* A.2: *wa-kull muqaddamah immā muṭlaqah wa-immā iḍṭirāriyyah wa-immā mumkinah*.

185 *ḤQ* 295; *TT* 336; *TŠ* 283.

186 The text actually has *immā baʿḍ jīm bāʾ dāʾiman aw baʿḍ jīm laysa bāʾ dāʾiman*; I emend this since it breaches the rule as stated in §70, and

departs from the format of the other contradictories. The passage is fiddly, and there are other equally trivial errors corrected without note.

187 The propositions that make up $\mathbf{L}_{T2}$ and $\mathbf{L}_{X2}$ are set out as component propositions, at §§57 and 58. I omitted mention there of the simple temporal components of their contradictories. $\mathbf{M}_T$: every C is possibly B at time T; $\mathbf{M}_A$: every C is possibly B always. See *H̱K* 108.10.

188 *ḤQ* 297; *TT* 338; *TŠ* 286.

189 *ḤQ* 297; *TT* 341; *TŠ* 289.

190 El-Rouayheb, "Impossible Antecedents and Their Consequences: Some Thirteenth-Century Arabic Discussions," 209–10; the relation between rejection of the thesis and analysis of the reductio is given further down page 210. See further comments on §113. I am grateful to Behnam Zolghadr for guidance on this matter.

191 Thom, *Syllogism*, 45–47.

192 See Łukasiewicz, *Aristotle's Syllogistic from the Standpoint of Modern Formal Logic*, 10.

193 Let us assume for the sake of argument that we are proving conversion for an **A** e-proposition (see §69.2); its square will be that in Figure 26 with "always" in place of "necessarily," and "at least once" in place of "possibly." The resulting syllogism leading to an impossibility assumes Ferio AXA, a self-evident syllogism (for which, see §91.5 and §99).

194 Al-Kātibī in the *Risālah* does not distinguish *iftirāḍ bi-l-ḥiss* (perceptual ecthesis) from *iftirāḍ qiyāsī*, but his colleague al-Ṭūsī does (*ṬḤ* 324.7–9). See Smith, *Aristotle: Prior Analytics*, xxiii–xxv, and Thom, *Syllogism*, 164–76. Syllogistic ecthesis, and al-Kātibī's preferred move, i-ecthesis, is used, for example, in §93. See Text 93.1 for al-Kātibī's dim view of Avicenna's favorite ecthetic move, o-ecthesis.

195 *ḤQ* 298; *TT* 342; *TŠ* 290.

196 *ḤQ* 299; *TT* 345; *TŠ* 291.

197 For relevant translated material, see Street, "Afḍal al-Dīn al-Khūnajī (d. 1248) on the Conversion of Modal Propositions" and "al-ʿAllāma al-Ḥillī."

198 *ḤQ* 301; *TT* 347; *TŠ* 292.

199 *ḤQ* 302; *TT* 349; *TŠ* 294.

200 Rescher and vander Nat, "Theory of Modal Syllogistic," 30; on the occasions it comes up, I symbolize it as $\mathbf{L}_{D(2)}$ or $\mathbf{A}_{D(2)}$.

201 *ḤQ* 305; *TT* 351; *TŠ* 296.

202 Recall the discussion in §§48–50 on the existence of the subject term of an affirmative proposition.

203 I do not think the ascription is certain. Al-Ṭūsī in comment on *Pointers* 5.4.9 (*AI* 53.2–5) seems to assume it is Athīr al-Dīn al-Abharī's proof (*ṬḤ* 333.10–u); cf. El-Rouayheb, "Introduction" to *Ḫ̮K*, xxiv–xxv.

204 *ḤQ* 307; *TT* 353; *TŠ* 297.

205 *ḤQ* 311; *TT* 356; *TŠ* 299.

206 *ḤQ* 312; *TT* 359; *TŠ* 301.

207 In §98. There is a variant in the received text here, seemingly preferred by al-Taḥtānī (and by the Sprenger and Cairo printings), such that the possibility minor is not used in the first or the third figures. This is certainly al-Kātibī's position, but it is irrelevant to the point at issue here.

208 *ḤQ* 313; *TT* 361; *TŠ* 302.

209 This and the following material comes from *ḤQ* 313.apu–314.u.

210 *ḤQ* 315; *TT* 364; *TŠ* 304.

211 Joseph, *Introduction*, 238–39.

212 The arguments against Avicenna here do not take account of counterarguments in *SQ* 321–38; see Fallahi, "Fārābī," and the references therein to a series of studies.

213 Quoting *AQ* 93.11–13.

214 So too in the more systematic exposition in Keynes, *Studies and Exercises*, 170–74; Keynes does, however, explicitly stipulate that the terms and their contradictories represent existing classes. Note that in Text 83.3 al-Ḥillī seems to agree with Keynes.

215 *ḤQ* 315; *TT* 368; *TŠ* 305.

216 Reading *laysa laysa jīm* for *laysa jīm* at *ḤQ* 317.pu.

217 *ḤQ* 320; *TT* 370; *TŠ* 305.

218 *ḤQ* 322; *TT* 372; *TŠ* 307.

219 Which is to say, D is at least once not B.

220 *ḤQ* 325; *TT* 374; *TŠ* 308.

221 To al-Kātibī is also attributed the rule that something can entail its own contradictory (Text 87.2), so (4) in the proof of Text 86.3 is unproblematic. See El-Rouayheb, "Impossible Antecedents," 210.

222 *ḤQ* 327; *TT* 378; *TŠ* 310.

223 One that al-Ḥillī himself came to share in his *al-Jawhar al-naḍīd fī sharḥ Kitāb al-Tajrīd* (*The Faceted Jewel in Commentary on the Book of Abstraction*); see Street, "al-ʿAllāma al-Ḥillī," 272.

224 Using triplets of terms, some taken from Aristotle, *Prior Analytics* 26a36–38 and 27a18–21; see Thom, *The Syllogism*, §§15 and 16, for an account of what Aristotle is doing, though note that al-Kātibī—as interpreted by his commentators—is only worried about what happens if his conditions are breached, and not in providing a full account of rejections.

225 *ḤQ* 331; *TT* 382; *TŠ* 313.

226 For a careful consideration of the evolving definition of syllogism, from Aristotle's (rendered into Arabic as *qawl matā wuḍiʿat fīhi ashyāʾ akthar min wāḥid lazima shayʾ ākhar min al-iḍṭirār li-wujūd tilka l-ashyāʾ al-mawḍūʿah bi-dhātihā*, El-Rouayheb, *Relational Syllogisms and the History of Arabic Logic, 900–1900*, 17) through Avicenna's ever briefer formulations, see ibid., Chapter 1.2. It should be noted that the Arabic from *ʿUyūn al-ḥikmah* in El-Rouayheb's transcription (on page 21) differs only in having *li-dhātihi* instead of al-Kātibī's *li-dhātihā*. Further, the definition given in *ʿUyūn* actually runs: *al-qiyās muʾallaf min aqwāl idhā sullimat lazima ʿanhā li-dhātihā qawl ākhar* (see Avicenna, *Fontes Sapientiae*, 5.17).

227 The entire discussion (with doubts and replies) takes up *RM* 241–48.

228 *ḪK* 231–43.

229 Thus al-Khūnajī. The *Qiyās* edition has: *qawl idhā wuḍiʿat fīhi ashyāʾ akthar min wāḥid lazima min tilka l-ashyāʾ al-mawḍūʿah bi-dhātihā lā bi-l-ʿaraḍ qawl ākhar ghayruhā min al-iḍṭirār*.

230 Notes mostly from *TŠ* 313–15.

231 *ḤQ* 333; *TT* 385; *TŠ* 316.

232 *ḤQ* 335; *TT* 388; *TŠ* 317.

233 Thom, *Syllogism*, §3.

234 *ḤQ* 337; *TT* 391; *TŠ* 319.

235 For an account of Aristotle's "highly elegant" procedure (called by Ross "proof by contrasted instances"), see Thom, *Syllogism* §15; none of al-Kātibī's commentators is so thorough or rigorous.

236 For an overview of the mnemonics, see Smith, *Aristotle: Prior Analytics*, 229–30; Thom, *Syllogism*, 54.

237 *ḤQ* 339; *TT* 395; *TŠ* 322.

238 Cf. Smith, *Aristotle: Prior Analytics*, 116 (in comment on 27b20–23): Aristotle "invokes the principle that if a set of premises yields no conclusion, then the set that results from it when one of the premises is replaced by a weaker premise also yields no conclusion."

239 Thom, *Syllogism*, 60.

240 *ḤQ* 340; *TT* 396; *TŠ* 322.

241 See §50.

242 Avicenna represents the ancients here; cf. *Pointers* 7.6.6 (*AI* 72.14–17). See Street, "An Outline of Avicenna's Syllogistic," 1.3.2. Al-Ḥillī agrees with Avicenna, *ḤA* 123.8–10.

243 *ḤQ* 343; *TT* 400; *TŠ* 325.

244 *ḤQ* 347; *TT* 404; *TŠ* 328.

245 I am taking the Latin names for these moods from Thom, *Syllogism*, 54.

246 *ḤQ* 352; *TT* 408; *TŠ* 330.

247 *ḤQ* 354; *TT* 411; *TŠ* 334.

248 See note in comment on §77 above.

249 *ḤQ* 355; *TT* 414; *TŠ* 335.

250 See Strobino, "Ibn Sina's Logic," Appendix C.

251 See Thom, "Logic and Metaphysics in Avicenna's Modal Syllogistic"; cf. El-Rouayheb, "Introduction" to *Ḫ̮K*, xl–xlv.

252 *ḤQ* 357; *TT* 415; *TŠ* 335.

253 Rescher and vander Nat, "Theory of Modal Syllogistic," 36.

254 *ḤQ* 360; *TT* 419; *TŠ* 337.

255 So the text; I would emend to "no eclipsed shines at the time of conjunction, not always."

256 *ḤQ* 362; *TT* 422; *TŠ* 340.

257 Rescher and vander Nat, "Theory of Modal Syllogistic," 39–41.

258 Rescher and vander Nat, "Theory of Modal Syllogistic," 40.

259 *ḤQ* 363; *TT* 425; *TŠ* 343.

260 That is, Darapti L-$M_2$, $L_{D1}$-$M_2$ and Felapton L-$M_2$, $L_{D1}$-$M_2$.

261 Rescher and vander Nat, "Theory of Modal Syllogistic," 41.

262 Reading *al-kubrā* for *al-ṣughrā* at *TŠ* 344.4.

263 *ḤQ* 365; *TT* 427; *TŠ* 345.

264 See El-Rouayheb, "*Takmīl al-Manṭiq*: A Sixteenth-Century Arabic Manual on Logic," 210, where the author is identified as Ḥasan ibn Muḥammad ibn Ḥusayn al-Amlashī l-ʿAjamī, active in the Ottoman Empire in the 1530s and 1540s (ca. 935–45).

265 *ḤQ* 369; *TT* 431; *TŠ* 351.

266 Results given in Rescher and vander Nat, "Theory of Modal Syllogistic," 43, as Table XI. Note that Rescher, following the so-called al-Shirwānī, has extended the number of propositions to include all assumed in the investigation, and not just those explicitly listed for investigation. This ramifies through his whole account for the fourth.

267 Rescher and vander Nat, "Theory of Modal Syllogistic," 44, Table XIC at 47.

268 Rescher "Theory," 44, Table XIA at 45.

269 This is how I would translate *baʿda ʿaks al-ṣughrā li-rujūʿihi ilayhi bi-ʿaks al-ṣughrā*. Perhaps the text needs emendation.

270 Rescher and vander Nat, "Theory of Modal Syllogistic," 44, deals with the sixth and the seventh, see also Table XID on 48; Rescher and vander Nat deal with the eighth on 49; see also Table XIE on 48.

271 Al-Taftāzānī is referring to Avicenna's comments in *AQ* 356.7–11, and al-Khūnajī's in *ḪK* 317.11–u.

272 Strobino, "Ibn Sina's Logic," 5.1.2; cf. *RM* 313–18.

273 *ḤQ* 371; *TT* 437; *TŠ* 352.

274 See Qaramālikī's comments on Abū l-Barakāt's possible influence, *RM* 441–42.

275 *ḤQ* 374; *TT* 439; *TŠ* 354.

276 *ḤQ* 376; *TT* 440; *TŠ* 356.

277 *ḤQ* 377; *TT* 441; *TŠ* 357.

278 *ḤQ* 379; *TT* 443; *TŠ* 359.

279 *ḤQ* 382; *TT* 446; *TŠ* 360.

280 See *Pointers* 7.2 (*AI* 65.u–66.u); the point raised here corresponds with *Pointers* 8.3 (*AI* 78.10–79.12). See Strobino, "Ibn Sina's Logic," 5.2.

281 I assume that al-Taḥtānī has this proposition in mind as conclusion to a third-figure syllogism like "possibly (sometimes), if substance is contingent then atom exists," and "necessarily (always), if substance is contingent then the necessary existent exists"; this would give al-Taḥtānī the hypothetical syllogism Disamis MLM, and the conclusion "possibly (sometimes), if the necessary existent exists then atom exists."

282 *ḤQ* 384; *TT* 449; *TŠ* 362.

283 *ḤQ* 386; *TT* 451; *TŠ* 363.

284 *ḤQ* 387; *TT* 452; *TŠ* 364.

285 E.g., *Pointers* 8.4 (*AI* 79.13–80.6). See El-Rouayheb, "Impossible Antecedents," 210, for a contemporary account of reductio; for a view opposed to Avicenna, see *ṬḤ* 455.19–456.1 referring to al-Kāshī, *al-Minhāj al-mubīn* (relevant part of text in Cambridge UL ms Browne D.19(10) ff. 71v–72v).

286 *ḤQ* 388; *TT* 454; *TŠ* 365.

287 See Strobino, "Ibn Sina's Logic," 5.1.2 type 5. See also Avicenna, *Pointers* 7.1.2 (*AI* 64.10–apu).

288 *ḤQ* 389; *TT* 454; *TŠ* 366.

289 For terminology, see Walter Young, "Concomitance to Causation: Arguing *Dawarān* in the Proto-Ādāb al-Baḥth," a study of inference taken from a treatise nearly contemporary with al-Kātibī, on juristic dialectic (*jadal*), the *Fuṣūl* of Burhān al-Dīn al-Nasafī (d. 687/1288) (the *Fuṣūl* was a curricular text taught to students more or less alongside the *Risālah*).

290 *TŠ* 367.2–3; I adopt an emendation of the text proposed by Young in "Concomitance to Causation," 265n192, and his translation of the passage.

291 See especially Black, *Logic and Aristotle's Rhetoric and Poetics in Medieval Arabic Philosophy*, 247–58. This theory is often called the

context theory (a theory of the way discourse is used according to its disciplinary context); see Lameer, "Aristotelian Rhetoric and Poetics as Logical Arts in Medieval Islamic Philosophy" for what may be a historically more precise account.

292 Simple ignorance is not knowing that P is Q; compound ignorance is, for example, believing wrongly that P is not Q.

293 *ḤQ* 394; *TT* 457; *TŠ* 368. See Black, *Aristotle's Rhetoric*, Gutas, "The Empiricism of Avicenna," and especially Strobino, *Avicenna's Theory of Science*, Chapter 2.

294 *ḤQ* 398; *TT* 460; *TŠ* 372.

295 **A**$_{\mathbf{D1}}$ is named by Avicenna as the default proposition for demonstration; *AN* §123 (iii), 101.

296 The double *mīm* clouds the etymology of *limmī*, which becomes clear in light of the earlier preference, *burhān al-limā* (or *burhān limā*); note also *burhān al-anna* (or *burhān anna*). In fact, al-Kātibī's choices are already options for Avicenna. See Strobino, *Avicenna's Theory of Science*, 217.

297 *ḤQ* 400; *TT* 461; *TŠ* 374.

298 *ḤQ* 405; *TT* 465; *TŠ* 377.

299 In this, I would speculate that al-Kātibī is influenced by an approach developed by al-Rāzī (*RM* 347–54).

300 In fact, al-Ḥillī disagrees with the taxonomy of Avicenna (and al-Ṭūsī) in *Pointers* Path 10, as well as with al-Kātibī's taxonomy (which seems to me to assign fallacies to more than one division; I present Figure 34 as a highly provisional reading).

301 I should note that Buridan (for example) relies on supposition theory in one of his analyses of this fallacy; see Klima, *John Buridan, Summulae*, 522. I am not aware of a unified treatment of a theory of reference in the Arabic texts, but the two analyses considered by al-Taftāzānī turn on what to take as the reference of "animal."

302 To sum up al-Kātibī's analysis of the fallacies: begging the question is named as such in Figure 34, equivocation ("the painted horse") comes under premises specious by expression; secundum quid (the man-and-horse fallacy, and taking the mental as real) comes under

premises specious by meaning; and the fallacy generated by the natural proposition is either a material fallacy under premises specious by meaning, or a formal fallacy under argument in a sterile figure (see Text 119.4).

303 *ḤQ* 410; *TT* 468; *TŠ* 380.

304 "Foreign" (*gharīb*) in the sense that moving need not apply to sphere in the way that change must apply to physical body.

305 See Strobino, *Avicenna's Theory of Science*, Chapter 5. Al-Taftāzānī does consider the matter (*TŠ* 381–82), but there are clearly problems in the edition at this point.

306 Though nothing is said about how they are acquired; see Avicenna, *Najāt* (*AN* §§140–43, 149–59).

307 I am using the more common geometrical terms here. Al-Kātibī gives Euclid's first and third postulates as examples, but speaks of them in the Aristotelian manner as "premises that are not self-evident but accepted by way of being posited" (*al-muqaddamāt ghayr al-bayyinah fī nafsihā al-ma'khūdhah ʿalā sabīl al-waḍʿ*), and he gives Euclid's first common notion as an example, but speaks of it as among "self-evident premises" (*al-muqaddamāt al-bayyinah fī nafsihā*).

308 Established in *Pointers* 1.12 (*AI* 8.pu–9.17).

309 See Strobino "Per Se," 215; the references al-Kātibī makes to Euclid and Avicenna's *Geometry* are given in footnote 64.

310 Reading the original *an yakūna la-humā miqdār wāḥid bi-qadri-himā jamīʿan wa-l-mubāyanah bi-khilāfihimā* (following Euclid) for the editor's preferred variant *an yaʿuddahā ʿadad ghayr al-wāḥid ka-l-arbaʿah wa-l-sittah wa-l-mubāyanah bi-khilāfihimā ka-l-arbaʿah wa-l-khamsah.*

311 Strobino, "Avicenna on the Indemonstrability of Definition."

# Tables

## Key to Symbols for Propositions

Both versions of al-Taḥtānī's *Taḥrīr* I use have some problems in the tables they present for the conclusions to syllogisms with mixed modal premises, and I have instead adopted the tables in Ibn Mubārakshāh's commentary on the *Risālah*. I am grateful to Khaled El-Rouayheb for alerting me to the value of this work and offering me a manuscript of it; and to Dustin Klinger for overcoming my reluctance to consult yet another commentator: Ibn Mubārakshāh, *Sharḥ al-Shamsiyyah* (El-Rouayheb, "Two Fourteenth-Century Islamic Philosophers: Ibn Mubārakshāh al-Bukhārī and Mullāzāde al-Kharziyānī," 4n10). The tables appear, in the order I give them below, on folios 96a, 98b, 99b, 102a, 102b, and 103a. I list again most of the propositional types given in Appendix 2; unlike the list in Appendix 2, however, I here follow the order Ibn Mubārakshāh adopts in setting out the major and minor premises in the tables.

| | |
|---|---|
| **L** | necessary (*al-ḍarūriyyah*) |
| **A** | perpetual (*al-dā'imah*) |
| $\mathbf{L_{D1}}$ | general conditional (*al-mashrūṭah al-ʿāmmah*) |
| $\mathbf{A_{D1}}$ | general conventional (*al-ʿurfiyyah al-ʿāmmah*) |
| $\mathbf{L_{D2}}$ | special conditional (*al-mashrūṭah al-khāṣṣah*) |
| $\mathbf{A_{D2}}$ | special conventional (*al-ʿurfiyyah al-khāṣṣah*) |
| $\mathbf{X_1}$ | general absolute (*al-muṭlaqah al-ʿāmmah*) |
| $\mathbf{L_{T2}}$ | temporal (*al-waqtiyyah*) |
| $\mathbf{L_{X2}}$ | spread (*al-muntashirah*) |

$\mathbf{X}_2$ non-perpetual existential (*al-wujūdiyyah al-lā-dā'imah*)

$\mathbf{X}_{\sim L}$ nonnecessary existential (*al-wujūdiyyah al-lā-ḍarūriyyah*)

$\mathbf{M}_1$ general possible (*al-mumkinah al-ʿāmmah*)

Simple propositions not customarily investigated that come up:

$\mathbf{L}_{T1}$ absolute temporal (*al-waqtiyyah al-muṭlaqah*)

$\mathbf{L}_{X1}$ absolute spread (*al-muntashirah al-muṭlaqah*)

$\mathbf{X}_{T1}$ temporal absolute (*al-muṭlaqah al-waqtiyyah*)

## Table 1: Conversion and Contraposition

| **E conversion** | **A contraposition (a → e)** |
|---|---|
| **L** → **A** (§75) | **L** → **A** (§83.2) |
| **A** → **A** (§75) | **A** → **A** (§83.2) |
| $\mathbf{L_{D1}}$ → $\mathbf{A_{D1}}$ (§76.1) | $\mathbf{L_{D1}}$ → $\mathbf{A_{D1}}$ (§83.3) |
| $\mathbf{A_{D1}}$ → $\mathbf{A_{D1}}$ (§76.1) | $\mathbf{A_{D1}}$ → $\mathbf{A_{D1}}$ (§83.3) |
| $\mathbf{L_{D2}}$ → $\mathbf{A_{D(2)}}$ (§76.2) | $\mathbf{L_{D2}}$ → $\mathbf{A_{D(2)}}$ (§83.4) |
| $\mathbf{A_{D2}}$ → $\mathbf{A_{D(2)}}$ (§76.2) | $\mathbf{A_{D2}}$ → $\mathbf{A_{D(2)}}$ (§83.4) |

| **O conversion** | **I contraposition (i → o)** |
|---|---|
| $\mathbf{L_{D2}}$ → $\mathbf{A_{D2}}$ (§77) | $\mathbf{L_{D2}}$ → $\mathbf{A_{D2}}$ (§84.1) |
| $\mathbf{A_{D2}}$ → $\mathbf{A_{D2}}$ (§77) | $\mathbf{A_{D2}}$ → $\mathbf{A_{D2}}$ (§84.1) |

| **A/I conversion** | **E/O contraposition (e → i)** |
|---|---|
| **L** → $\mathbf{X_{D1}}$ (§78.1) | **L** fails (§86) |
| **A** → $\mathbf{X_{D1}}$ (§78.1) | **A** fails (§86) |
| $\mathbf{L_{D1}}$ → $\mathbf{X_{D1}}$ (§78.1) | $\mathbf{L_{D1}}$ fails (§86) |
| $\mathbf{A_{D1}}$ → $\mathbf{X_{D1}}$ (§78.1) | $\mathbf{A_{D1}}$ fails (§86) |
| $\mathbf{L_{D2}}$ → $\mathbf{X_{D2}}$ (§78.2 for a, §78.3 for i) | $\mathbf{L_{D2}}$ → $\mathbf{X_{D1}}$ (§85.1) |
| $\mathbf{A_{D2}}$ → $\mathbf{X_{D2}}$ (§78.2 for a, §78.3 for i) | $\mathbf{A_{D2}}$ → $\mathbf{X_{D1}}$ (§85.1) |
| $\mathbf{X_1}$ → $\mathbf{X_1}$ (§78.4) | $\mathbf{X_1}$ fails (§86) |
| $\mathbf{L_{T2}}$ → $\mathbf{X_1}$ (§78.4) | $\mathbf{L_{T2}}$ → $\mathbf{X_1}$ (§85.2) |
| $\mathbf{L_{X2}}$ → $\mathbf{X_1}$ (§78.4) | $\mathbf{L_{X2}}$ → $\mathbf{X_1}$ (§85.2) |
| $\mathbf{X_2}$ → $\mathbf{X_1}$ (§78.4) | $\mathbf{X_2}$ → $\mathbf{X_1}$ (§85.2) |
| $\mathbf{X_{\sim L}}$ → $\mathbf{X_1}$ (§78.4) | $\mathbf{X_{\sim L}}$ → $\mathbf{X_1}$ (§85.2) |
| $\mathbf{M_1}$ fails (§80) | $\mathbf{M_1}$ fails (§86) |
| $\mathbf{M_2}$ fails (§80) | $\mathbf{M_2}$ fails (§86) |

## Table 2: Figure 1 Mixes

Major ⟶ (columns); ⟵ Minor (rows)

| | $L_{D1}$ | $A_{D1}$ | $L_{D2}$ | $A_{D2}$ |
|---|---|---|---|---|
| L | L | A | $L_2$ * | $A_2$ * |
| A | A | A | $A_2$ * | $A_2$ * |
| $L_{D1}$ | $L_{D1}$ | $A_{D1}$ | $L_{D2}$ | $A_{D2}$ |
| $A_{D1}$ | $A_{D1}$ | $A_{D1}$ | $A_{D2}$ | $A_{D2}$ |
| $L_{D2}$ | $L_{D1}$ | $A_{D1}$ | $L_{D2}$ | $A_{D2}$ |
| $A_{D2}$ | $A_{D1}$ | $A_{D1}$ | $A_{D2}$ | $A_{D2}$ |
| $X_1$ | $X_1$ | $X_1$ | $X_2$ | $X_2$ |
| $L_{T2}$ | $L_{T1}$ | $X_{T1}$ | $L_{T2}$ | $X_{T2}$ |
| $L_{X2}$ | $L_{X1}$ | $X_{X1}$ | $L_{X2}$ | $X_{X2}$ |
| $X_2$ | $X_1$ | $X_1$ | $X_2$ | $X_2$ |
| $X_{\sim L}$ | $X_1$ | $X_1$ | $X_2$ | $X_2$ |

* = impossible.

## Table 3: Figure 2 Mixes

Major ⟶ (columns); ⟵ Minor (rows)

| | L | $L_{D1}$ | $L_{D2}$ | A | $A_{D1}$ | $A_{D2}$ | $X_1$ | $L_{T2}$ | $L_{X2}$ | $X_2$ | $X_{\sim L}$ | $M_1$ | $M_2$ |
|---|---|---|---|---|---|---|---|---|---|---|---|---|---|
| L | A | A | A | A | A | A | A | A | A | A | A | A | A |
| A | A | A | A | A | A | A | A | A | A | A | A | | |
| $L_{D1}$ | A | $A_{D1}$ | $A_{D1}$ | A | $A_{D1}$ | $A_{D1}$ | | | | | | | |
| $A_{D1}$ | A | $A_{D1}$ | $A_{D1}$ | A | $A_{D1}$ | $A_{D1}$ | | | | | | | |
| $L_{D2}$ | A | $A_{D1}$ | $A_{D1}$ | A | $A_{D1}$ | $A_{D1}$ | | | | | | | |
| $A_{D2}$ | A | $A_{D1}$ | $A_{D1}$ | A | $A_{D1}$ | $A_{D1}$ | | | | | | | |
| $X_1$ | A | $X_1$ | $X_1$ | A | $X_1$ | $X_1$ | | | | | | | |
| $L_{T2}$ | A | $X_{T1}$ | $X_{T1}$ | A | $X_{T1}$ | $X_{T1}$ | | | | | | | |
| $L_{X2}$ | A | $X_{X1}$ | $X_{X1}$ | A | $X_{X1}$ | $X_{X1}$ | | | | | | | |
| $X_2$ | A | $X_1$ | $X_1$ | A | $X_1$ | $X_1$ | | | | | | | |
| $X_{\sim L}$ | A | $X_1$ | $X_1$ | A | $X_1$ | $X_1$ | | | | | | | |
| $M_1$ | A | $M_1$ | $M_1$ | | | | | | | | | | |

## Table 4: Figure 3 Mixes

| ← Minor / Major → | $L_{D1}$ | $A_{D1}$ | $L_{D2}$ | $A_{D2}$ |
|---|---|---|---|---|
| L | $X_{D1}$ | $X_{D1}$ | $X_{D2}$ | $X_{D2}$ |
| A | $X_{D1}$ | $X_{D1}$ | $X_{D2}$ | $X_{D2}$ |
| $L_{D1}$ | $X_{D1}$ | $X_{D1}$ | $X_{D2}$ | $X_{D2}$ |
| $A_{D1}$ | $X_{D1}$ | $X_{D1}$ | $X_{D2}$ | $X_{D2}$ |
| $L_{D2}$ | $X_{D1}$ | $X_{D1}$ | $X_{D2}$ | $X_{D2}$ |
| $A_{D2}$ | $X_{D1}$ | $X_{D1}$ | $X_{D2}$ | $X_{D2}$ |
| $X_1$ | $X_1$ | $X_1$ | $X_2$ | $X_2$ |
| $L_{T2}$ | $X_1$ | $X_1$ | $X_2$ | $X_2$ |
| $L_{X2}$ | $X_1$ | $X_1$ | $X_2$ | $X_2$ |
| $X_2$ | $X_1$ | $X_1$ | $X_2$ | $X_2$ |
| $X_{\sim L}$ | $X_1$ | $X_1$ | $X_2$ | $X_2$ |

## Table 5: Figure 4, Bramantip and Dimaris

| ← Minor / Major → | L | A | $L_{D1}$ | $A_{D1}$ | $L_{D2}$ | $A_{D2}$ | $X_1$ | $L_{T2}$ | $L_{X2}$ | $X_2$ | $X_{\sim L}$ |
|---|---|---|---|---|---|---|---|---|---|---|---|
| L | $X_{D1}$ | $X_{D1}$ | $X_{D1}$ | $X_{D1}$ | $X_{D1}$ | $X_{D1}$ | $X_{D1}$ | $X_{D1}$ | $X_{D1}$ | $X_{D1}$ | $X_{D1}$ |
| A | $X_{D1}$ | $X_{D1}$ | $X_{D1}$ | $X_{D1}$ | $X_{D1}$ | $X_{D1}$ | $X_{D1}$ | $X_{D1}$ | $X_{D1}$ | $X_{D1}$ | $X_{D1}$ |
| $L_{D1}$ | $X_{D1}$ | $X_{D1}$ | $X_{D1}$ | $X_{D1}$ | $X_{D1}$ | $X_{D1}$ | $X_1$ | $X_1$ | $X_1$ | $X_1$ | $X_1$ |
| $A_{D1}$ | $X_{D1}$ | $X_{D1}$ | $X_{D1}$ | $X_{D1}$ | $X_{D1}$ | $X_{D1}$ | $X_1$ | $X_1$ | $X_1$ | $X_1$ | $X_1$ |
| $L_{D2}$ | $X_{D2}$ | $X_{D2}$ | $X_{D2}$ | $X_{D2}$ | $X_{D2}$ | $X_{D2}$ | $X_1$ | $X_1$ | $X_1$ | $X_1$ | $X_1$ |
| $A_{D2}$ | $X_{D2}$ | $X_{D2}$ | $X_{D2}$ | $X_{D2}$ | $X_{D2}$ | $X_{D2}$ | $X_1$ | $X_1$ | $X_1$ | $X_1$ | $X_1$ |
| $X_1$ | $X_1$ | $X_1$ | $X_1$ | $X_1$ | $X_1$ | $X_1$ | $X_1$ | $X_1$ | $X_1$ | $X_1$ | $X_1$ |
| $L_{T2}$ | $X_1$ | $X_1$ | $X_1$ | $X_1$ | $X_1$ | $X_1$ | $X_1$ | $X_1$ | $X_1$ | $X_1$ | $X_1$ |
| $L_{X2}$ | $X_1$ | $X_1$ | $X_1$ | $X_1$ | $X_1$ | $X_1$ | $X_1$ | $X_1$ | $X_1$ | $X_1$ | $X_1$ |
| $X_2$ | $X_1$ | $X_1$ | $X_1$ | $X_1$ | $X_1$ | $X_1$ | $X_1$ | $X_1$ | $X_1$ | $X_1$ | $X_1$ |
| $X_{\sim L}$ | $X_1$ | $X_1$ | $X_1$ | $X_1$ | $X_1$ | $X_1$ | $X_1$ | $X_1$ | $X_1$ | $X_1$ | $X_1$ |

## Table 6: Figure 4, Camenes

Major ⟶

| ↓ Minor | L | A | $L_{D1}$ | $A_{D1}$ | $L_{D2}$ | $A_{D2}$ | $X_1$ | $L_{T2}$ | $L_{X2}$ | $X_2$ | $X_{\sim L}$ |
|---|---|---|---|---|---|---|---|---|---|---|---|
| **L** | **A** | **A** | **A** | **A** | **A** | **A** | **A** | **A** | **A** | **A** | **A** |
| **A** | **A** | **A** | **A** | **A** | **A** | **A** | **A** | **A** | **A** | **A** | **A** |
| **$L_{D1}$** | **A** | **A** | **$A_{D1}$** | **$A_{D1}$** | **$A_{D1}$** | **$A_{D1}$** | | | | | |
| **$A_{D1}$** | **A** | **A** | **$A_{D1}$** | **$A_{D1}$** | **$A_{D1}$** | **$A_{D1}$** | | | | | |
| **$L_{D2}$** | **A** | **A** | **$A_{D(2)}$** | **$A_{D(2)}$** | **$A_{D(2)}$** | **$A_{D(2)}$** | | | | | |
| **$A_{D2}$** | **A** | **A** | **$A_{D(2)}$** | **$A_{D(2)}$** | **$A_{D(2)}$** | **$A_{D(2)}$** | | | | | |

## Table 7: Figure 4, Fesapo and Fresison

Major ⟶

| ↓ Minor | L | A | $L_{D1}$ | $A_{D1}$ | $L_{D2}$ | $A_{D2}$ |
|---|---|---|---|---|---|---|
| **L** | **A** | **A** | **$X_{D1}$** | **$X_{D1}$** | **$X_{D1}$** | **$X_{D1}$** |
| **A** | **A** | **A** | **$X_{D1}$** | **$X_{D1}$** | **$X_{D1}$** | **$X_{D1}$** |
| **$L_{D1}$** | **A** | **A** | **$X_{D1}$** | **$X_{D1}$** | **$X_{D1}$** | **$X_{D1}$** |
| **$A_{D1}$** | **A** | **A** | **$X_{D1}$** | **$X_{D1}$** | **$X_{D1}$** | **$X_{D1}$** |
| **$L_{D2}$** | **A** | **A** | **$X_{D1}$** | **$X_{D1}$** | **$X_{D1}$** | **$X_{D1}$** |
| **$A_{D2}$** | **A** | **A** | **$X_{D1}$** | **$X_{D1}$** | **$X_{D1}$** | **$X_{D1}$** |
| **$X_1$** | **A** | **A** | **$X_1$** | **$X_1$** | **$X_1$** | **$X_1$** |
| **$L_{T2}$** | **A** | **A** | **$X_1$** | **$X_1$** | **$X_1$** | **$X_1$** |
| **$L_{X2}$** | **A** | **A** | **$X_1$** | **$X_1$** | **$X_1$** | **$X_1$** |
| **$X_2$** | **A** | **A** | **$X_1$** | **$X_1$** | **$X_1$** | **$X_1$** |
| **$X_{\sim L}$** | **A** | **A** | **$X_1$** | **$X_1$** | **$X_1$** | **$X_1$** |

# Figures

## Figure 1: The tripartite signification (for §7)

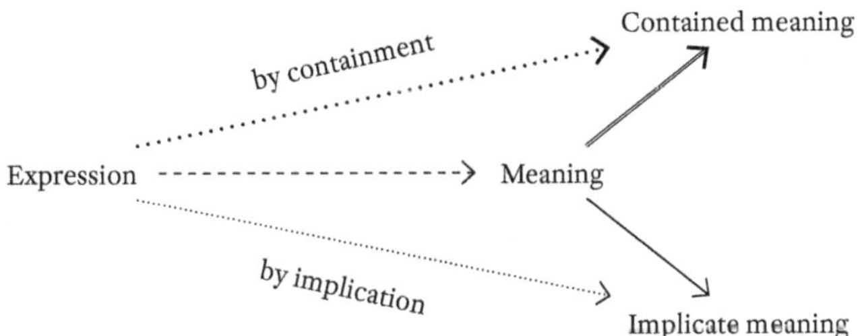


## Figure 2: The parts of speech (for §11)

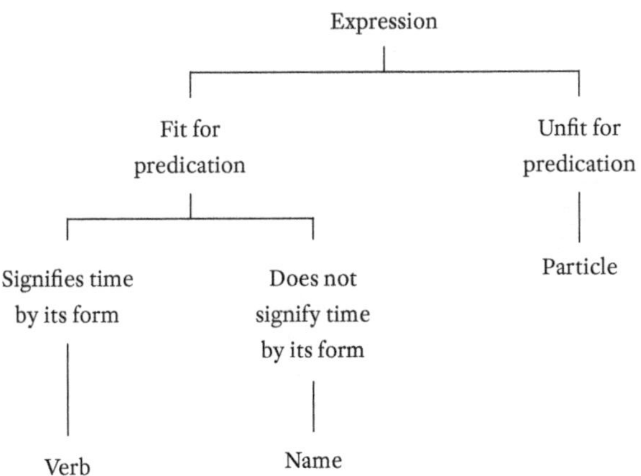

## Figure 3: Al-Ḥillī on the relation of expression to meaning (for §12)

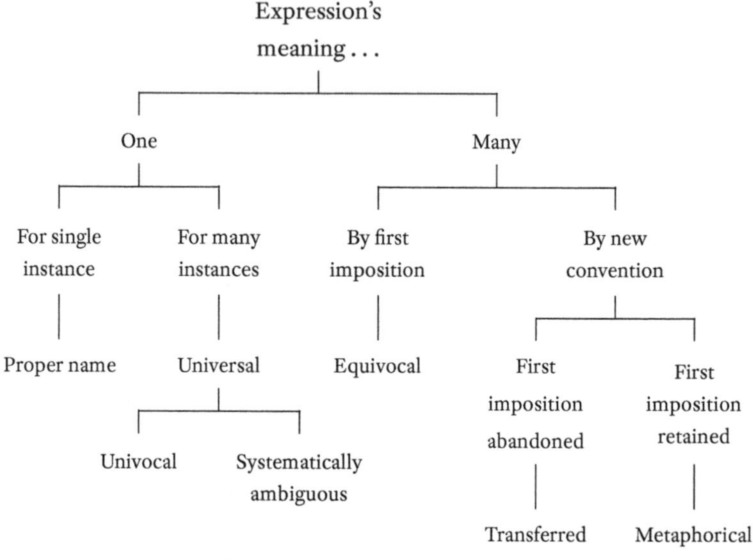

## FIGURE 4: AL-RĀZĪ ON THE RELATION OF EXPRESSION TO MEANING (FOR §§12 AND 13)

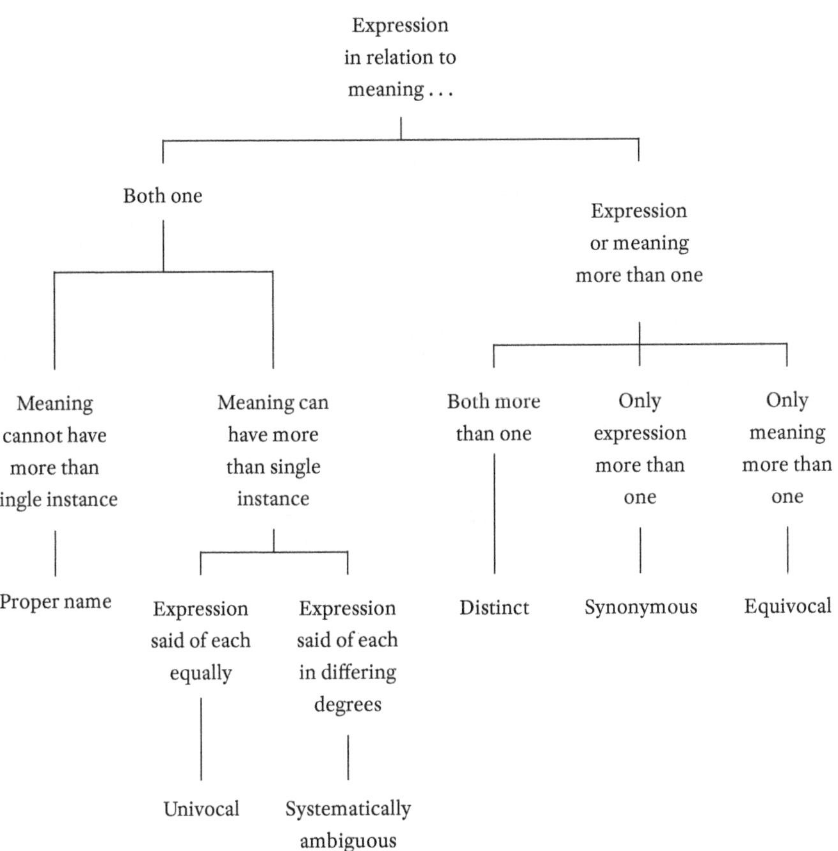

FIGURE 5: DIVISION OF THE PREDICABLES (FOR §16)

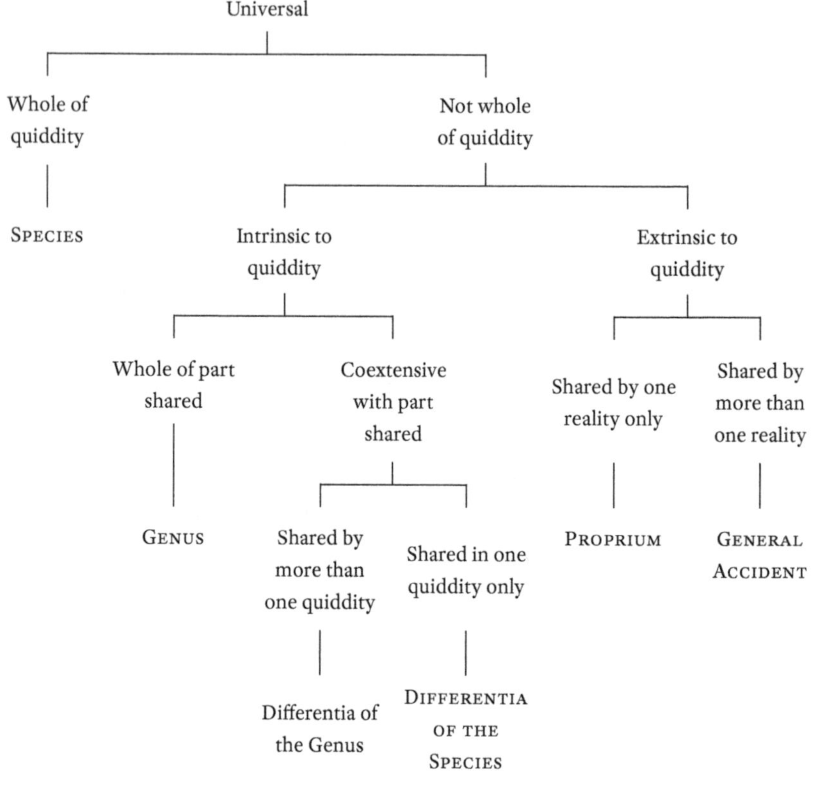

## Figure 6: *Ḥall mushkilāt al-ishārāt*, first division of the predicables (for §16)

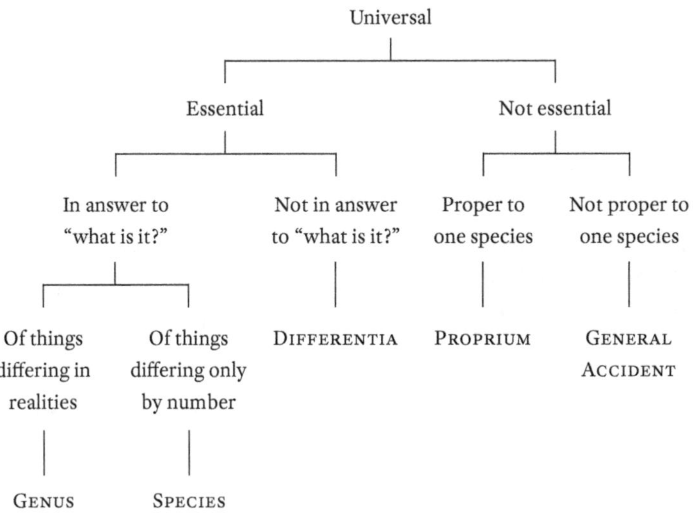

## Figure 7: *Ḥall mushkilāt al-ishārāt*, second division of the predicables (for §16)

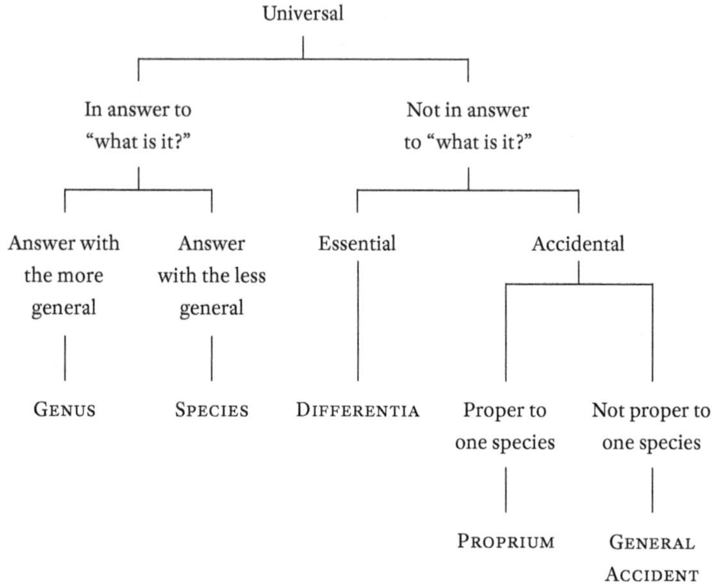

## Figure 8: Porphyrian tree (for §18)

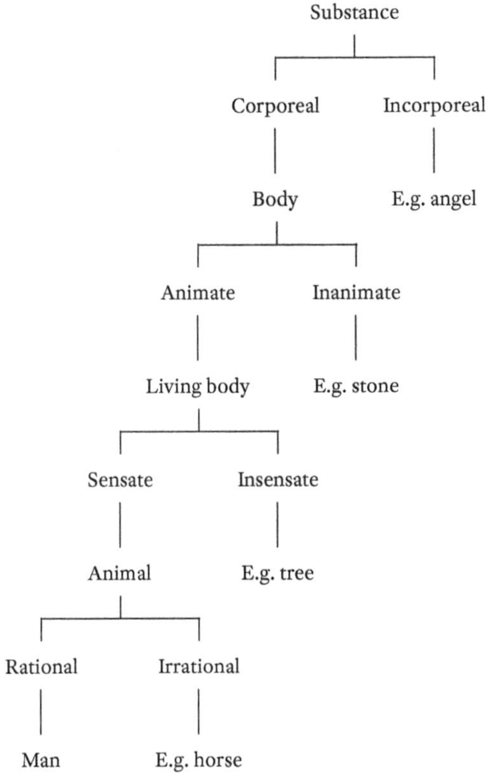

## Figure 9: Separable and inseparable (for §22)

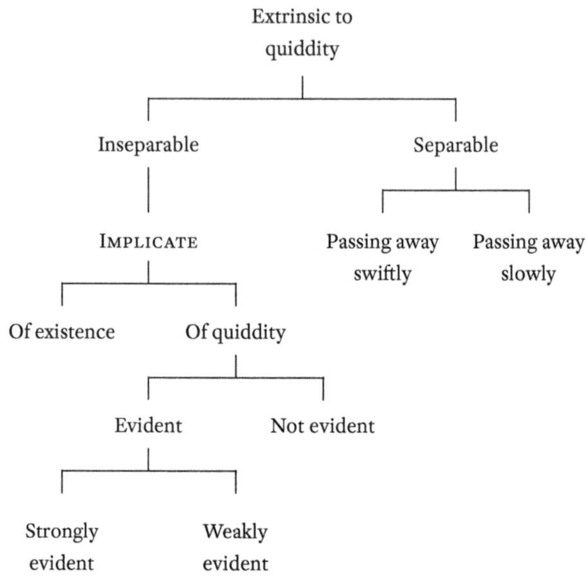

## Figure 10: Universals and existence (for §24)

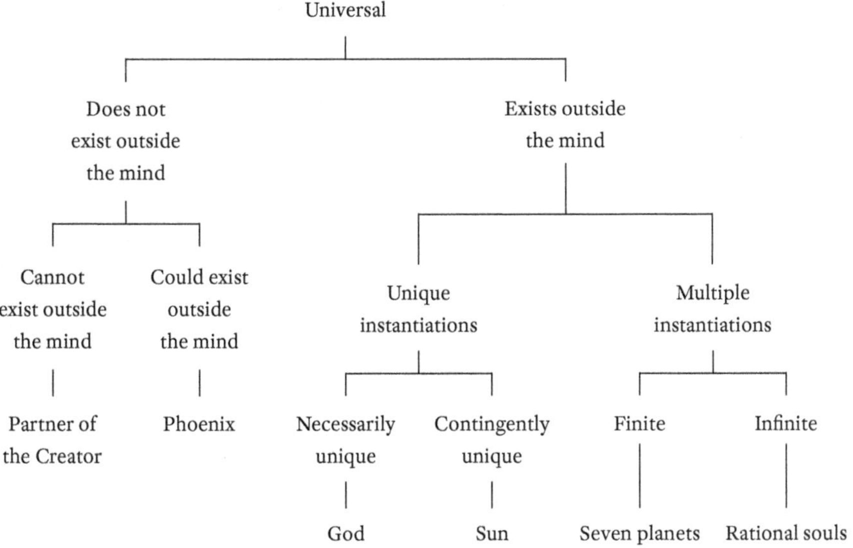

Figure 11: Coextensive terms (for §26)

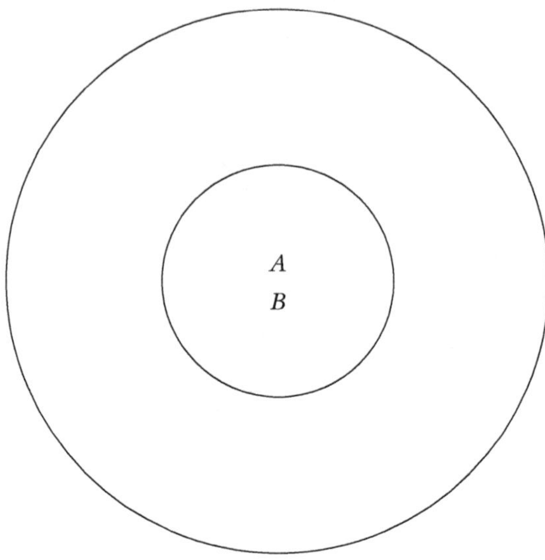


Figure 12: One term included in the other (for §26)

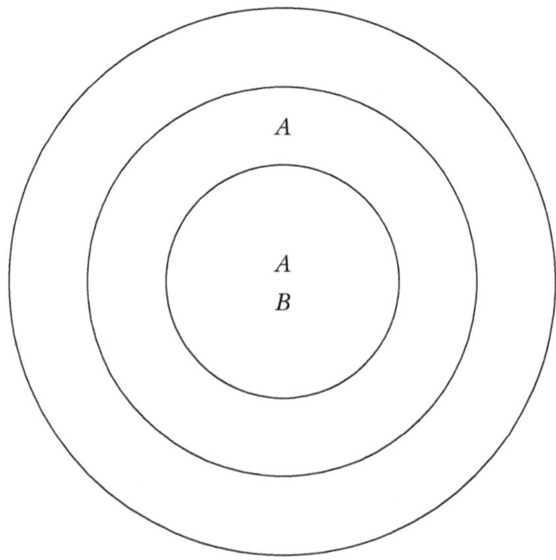

Figure 13: Overlapping terms (for §26)

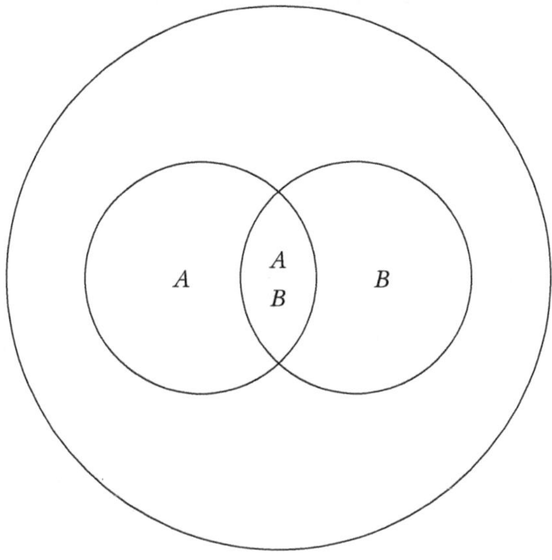


Figure 14: Disjoined terms (for §26)

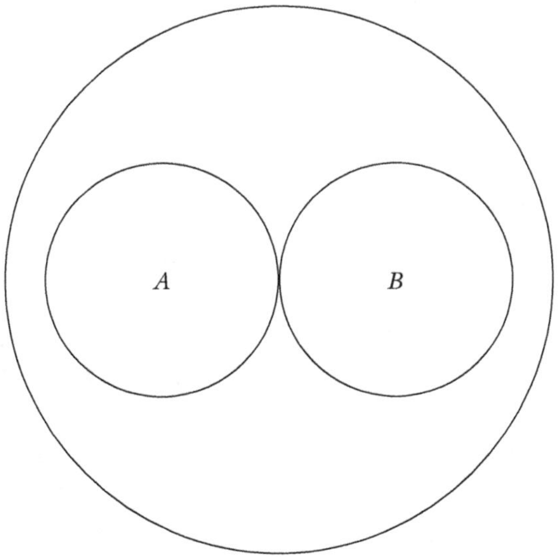

Figure 15: Contradictories of coextensive terms (for §27)

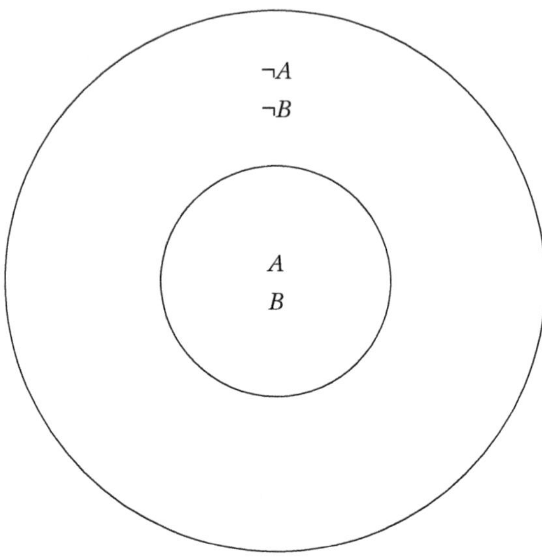


Figure 16: Contradictories of terms, one included in the other (for §27)

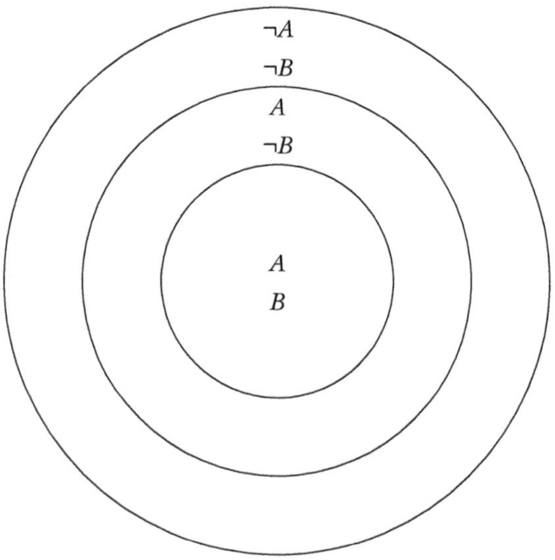

Figure 17: Contradictories of overlapping terms (for §27)

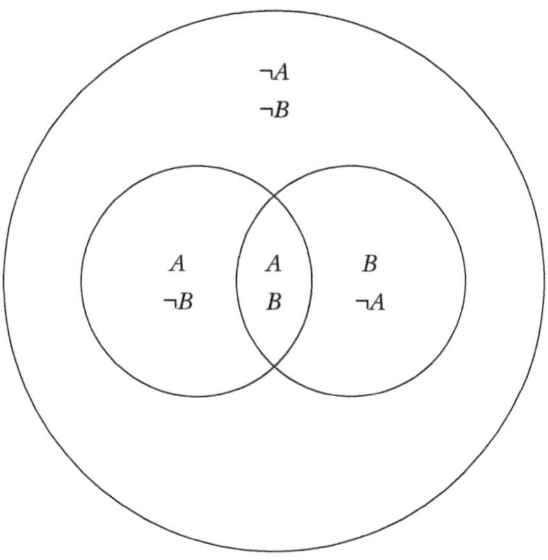


Figure 18: Contradictories of two disjoined terms, case 1 (for §27)

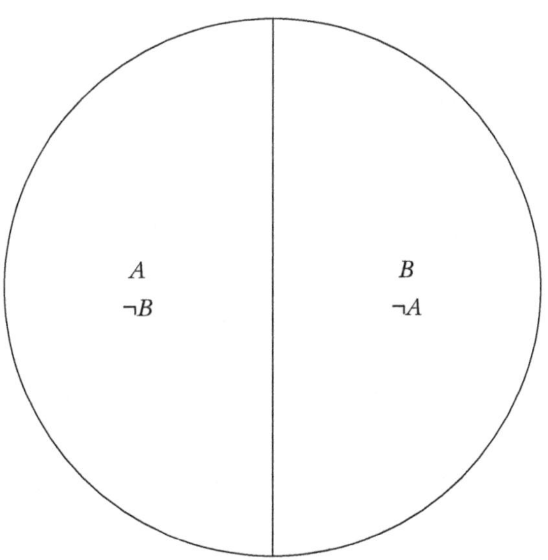

## Figure 19: Contradictories of two disjoined terms, case 2 (for §27)

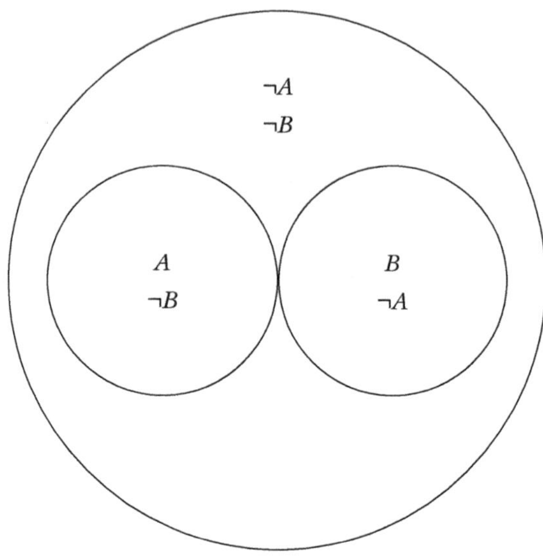


## Figure 20: Al-Kātibī on definitions and delineations (for §36)

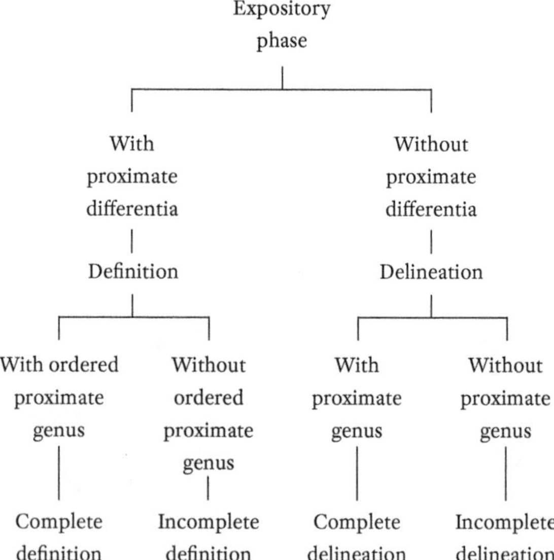

FIGURE 21: SPECIES OF PROPOSITIONS

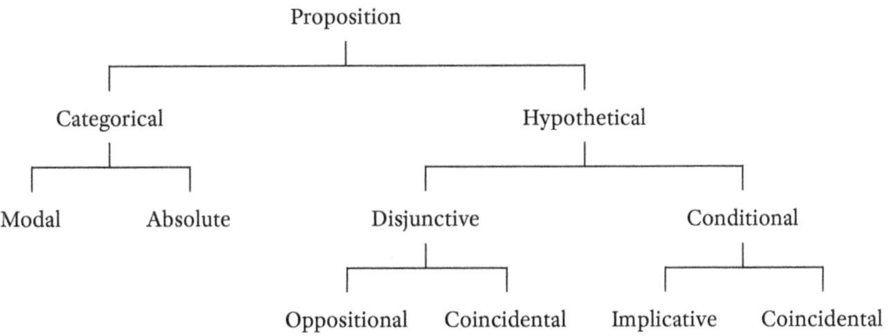


FIGURE 22: RELATIONS AMONG EXTERNALIST AND ESSENTIALIST AFFIRMATIVES (FOR §47)

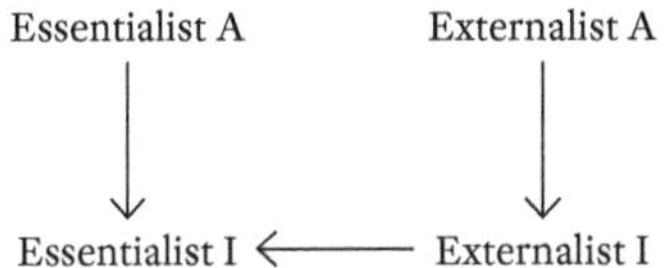


FIGURE 23: RELATIONS AMONG EXTERNALIST AND ESSENTIALIST NEGATIVES (FOR §47)

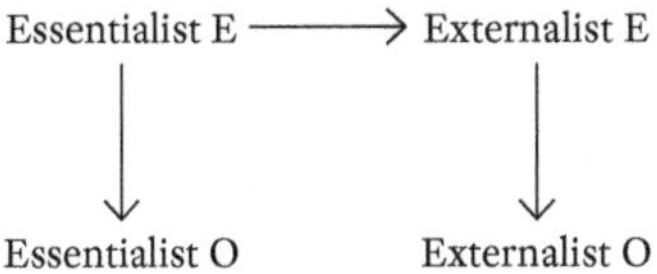

## Figure 24: Implicational relations among simple propositions

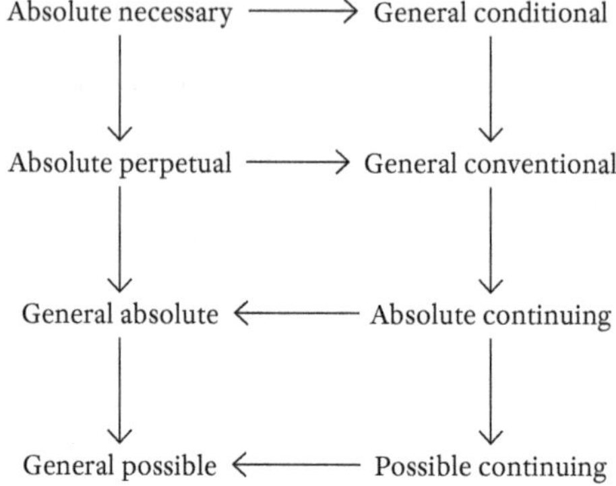


## Figure 25: Implicational relations among subset of propositions first mentioned in §74

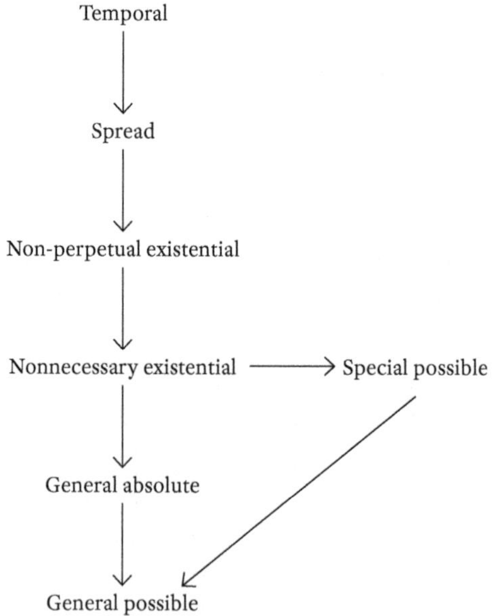

## Figure 26: Square of opposition: referential necessity and possibility (for §69.1)

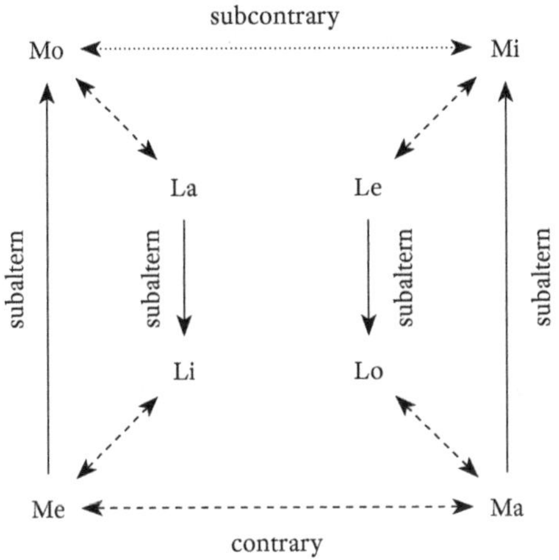


## Figure 27: Square of opposition: descriptional necessity and possibility (for §69.4)

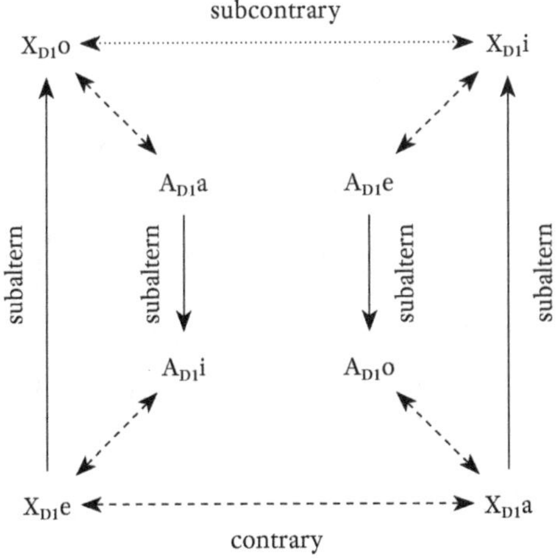

## Figure 28: Referential L, A, X, and M: entailment and contradiction

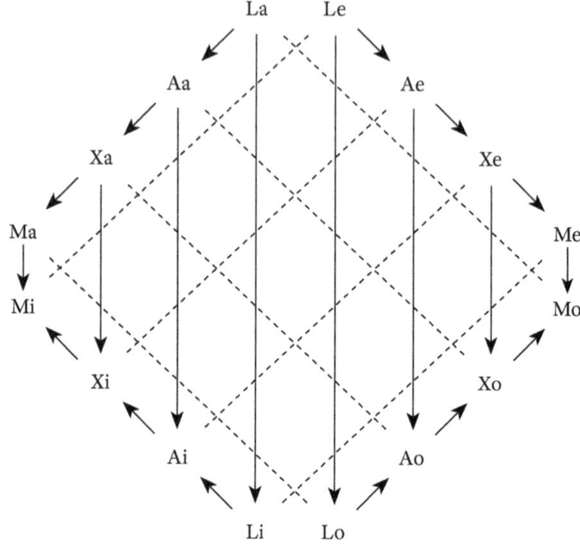


## Figure 29: Descriptional L, A, X, and M: entailment and contradiction

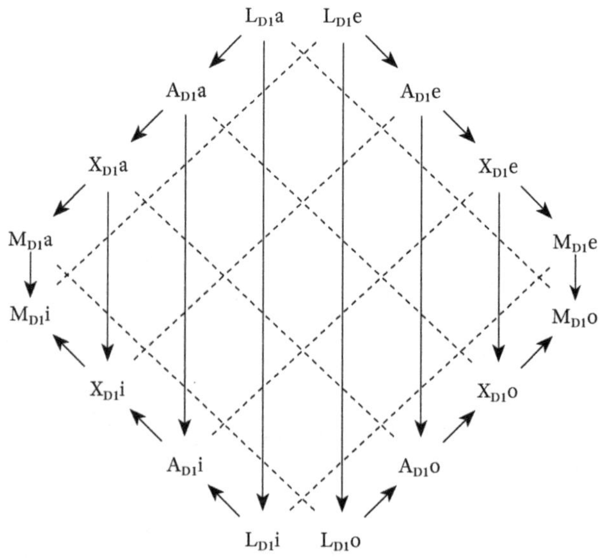

## Figure 30: Square of opposition: conditionals (for §72)

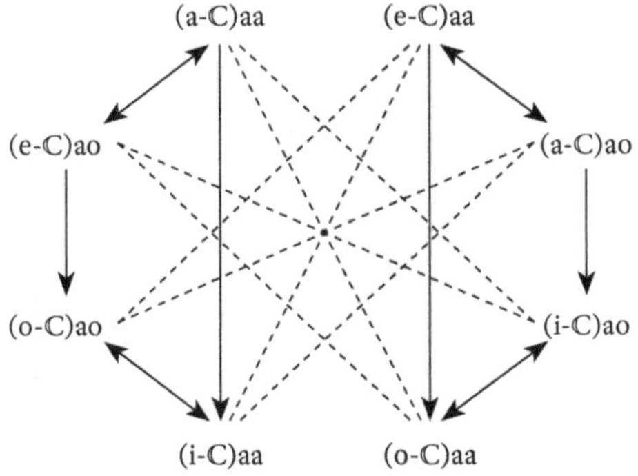


## Figure 31: Implicational relations among hypothetical propositions claimed or implicit in §87.1

$(\text{a-}\mathbb{C})pq \longleftrightarrow (\text{e-}\mathbb{D}^2)p \neg q$

$(\text{a-}\mathbb{C})pq \longleftrightarrow (\text{a-}\mathbb{D}^3)\neg pq$

$(\text{e-}\mathbb{D}^2)p \neg q \longleftrightarrow (\text{a-}\mathbb{D}^3)\neg pq$

## Figure 32: Conditionals entailed by exclusive disjunction as claimed in §87.2

$(\text{a-}\mathbb{C})\neg pq \longleftrightarrow (\text{a-}\mathbb{D}^1)pq \longleftrightarrow (\text{a-}\mathbb{C})p \neg q$

$(\text{a-}\mathbb{D}^1)pq \longleftrightarrow (\text{a-}\mathbb{C})\neg qp$

$(\text{a-}\mathbb{D}^1)pq \longleftrightarrow (\text{a-}\mathbb{C})q \neg p$

## Figure 33: Mutual entailment between alternative denial ($\mathbb{D}$2) and inclusive disjunction ($\mathbb{D}$3) as claimed in §87.3

$(\text{a-}\mathbb{D}^2)pq \longleftrightarrow (\text{e-}\mathbb{D}^3)\neg p \neg q$

FIGURE 34: AL-KĀTIBĪ'S PRIMARY DIVISION OF THE FALLACIES, *JĀMIʿ AL-DAQĀʾIQ* (LEAVING ASIDE FALLACIES FROM BOTH FORM AND MATTER TOGETHER)

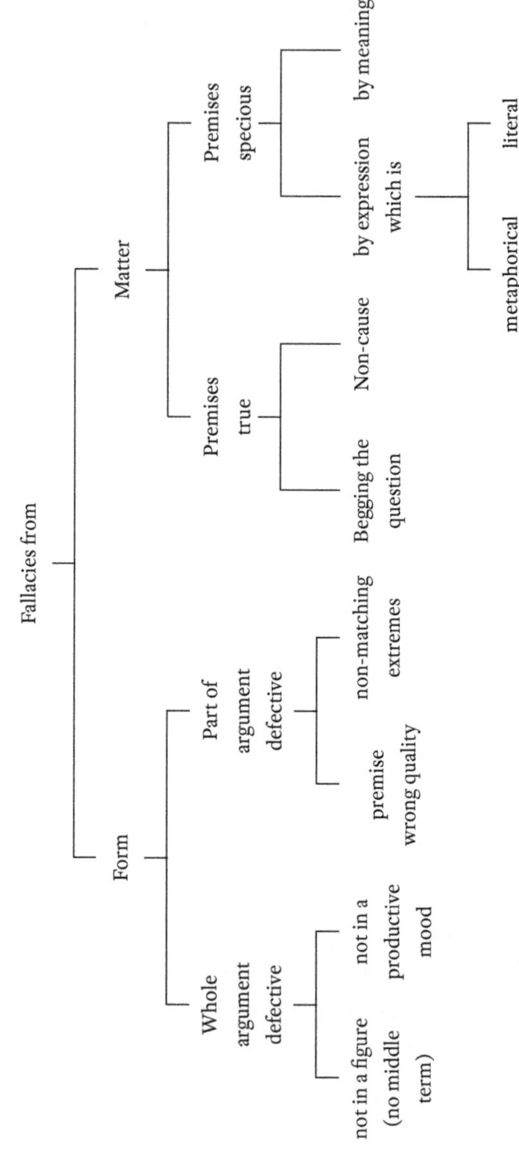

# Appendix 1: Names of Propositions

I list here the translations of the names of the propositions as proposed by Rescher and Strobino, along with the symbols they use. I list the Rescher symbol and translation of the proposition's name, then Strobino's translation and symbol. I give my modification of the Strobino symbol in brackets at the end.

| | |
|---|---|
| □E | absolute necessary (*ḍarūriyyah muṭlaqah*); referential necessity: **L**. |
| ∀E | absolute perpetual (*dā'imah muṭlaqah*); referential perpetuity: **A**. |
| □C | general conditional (*mashrūṭah ʿāmmah*); descriptional unrestricted necessity: $\mathbf{L_{D1}}$. |
| ∀C | general conventional (*ʿurfiyyah ʿāmmah*); descriptional unrestricted perpetuity: $\mathbf{A_{D1}}$. |
| ∃E | general absolute (*muṭlaqah ʿāmmah*); referential one-sided absoluteness: $\mathbf{X_1}$. |
| ◇E | general possibility (*mumkinah ʿāmmah*); referential one-sided possibility: $\mathbf{M_1}$. |
| □C&~∀E | special conditional (*mashrūṭah khāṣṣah*); descriptional restricted necessity: $\mathbf{L_{D2}}$. |
| ∀C&~∀E | special conventional (*ʿurfiyyah khāṣṣah*); descriptional restricted perpetuity: $\mathbf{A_{D2}}$. |
| ∃E&~□E | nonnecessary existential (*wujūdiyyah lā-ḍarūriyyah*); referential nonnecessary absoluteness: $\mathbf{X_3}$ ($\mathbf{X_{\sim L}}$). |

∃E&~∀E non-perpetual existential (*wujūdiyyah lā-dā'imah*); referential two-sided absoluteness: $\mathbf{X_2}$.

□T&~∀E temporal (*waqtiyyah*); referential temporal determinate: **T** ($\mathbf{L_{T2}}$).

□S&~∀E spread (*muntashirah*); referential temporal indeterminate: **U** ($\mathbf{L_{X2}}$).

◇E&~□E special possibility (*mumkinah khāṣṣah*); referential two-sided possibility: $\mathbf{M_2}$.

# Appendix 2: Propositional Forms

A: Every C is B (universal affirmative, *mūjibah kulliyyah*);
E: No C is B (universal negative, *sālibah kulliyyah*);
I: Some C is B (particular affirmative, *mūjibah juz'iyyah*);
O: Some C is not B (particular negative, *sālibah juz'iyyah*).

Modal propositions are given below in all four forms, first in Arabic with dummy variables (often there is no example in the *Rules*, and—caveat lector—I have set down what I believe would be al-Kātibī's phrasing), then in a close English translation, then in a translation in English that strikes me as natural, and that hopefully conveys the meaning of the proposition. I set out first the simple and then the compound propositions that are customarily investigated; I then go on to give only those further propositions that al-Kātibī refers to for the squares of opposition or in inferences.

## *The simple propositions customarily investigated*

1. **L**: absolute necessity proposition (*ḍarūriyyah muṭlaqah*); referential necessity.

   **L** a-proposition: *bi-l-ḍarūrah kull jīm bā'*
   Necessarily, every C is B.
   Every C is necessarily B.

   **L** e-proposition: *bi-l-ḍarūrah lā shay' min jīm bā'*
   Necessarily, no C is B.
   No C is possibly B.

**L** i-proposition: *bi-l-ḍarūrah baʿḍ jīm bāʾ*
Necessarily, some C is B.
Some C is necessarily B.

**L** o-proposition: *bi-l-ḍarūrah baʿḍ jīm laysa bāʾ*
Necessarily, some C is not B.
Some C is not possibly B.

2. **A**: absolute perpetuity proposition (*dāʾimah muṭlaqah*); referential perpetuity.

   **A** a-proposition: *dāʾiman kull jīm bāʾ*
   Always, every C is B.
   Every C is always B.

   **A** e-proposition: *dāʾiman lā shayʾ min jīm bāʾ*
   Always, no C is B.
   No C is ever B.

   **A** i-proposition: *dāʾiman baʿḍ jīm bāʾ*
   Always, some C is B.
   Some C is always B.

   **A** o-proposition: *dāʾiman baʿḍ jīm laysa bāʾ*
   Always, some C is not B.
   Some C is never B.

3. **L$_{D1}$**: general conditional (*mashrūṭah ʿāmmah*); descriptional unrestricted necessity.

   **L$_{D1}$** a-proposition: *bi-l-ḍarūrah kull jīm bāʾ mā dāma jīm*
   Necessarily, every C is B as long as it is C.
   Every C is necessarily B as long as it is C.

   **L$_{D1}$** e-proposition: *bi-l-ḍarūrah lā shayʾ min jīm bāʾ mā dāma jīm*
   Necessarily, no C is B as long as it is C.
   No C is possibly B as long as it is C.

**$L_{D1}$** i-proposition: *bi-l-ḍarūrah baʿḍ jīm bāʾ mā dāma jīm*
Necessarily, some C is B as long as it is C.
Some C is necessarily B as long as it is C.

**$L_{D1}$** o-proposition: *bi-l-ḍarūrah baʿḍ jīm laysa bāʾ mā dāma jīm*
Necessarily, some C is not B as long as it is C.
Some C is not possibly B as long as it is C.

4. **$A_{D1}$**: general conventional (*ʿurfiyyah ʿāmmah*); descriptional unrestricted perpetuity.

**$A_{D1}$** a-proposition: *dāʾiman kull jīm bāʾ mā dāma jīm*
Always, every C is B as long as it is C.
Every C is always B as long as it is C.

**$A_{D1}$** e-proposition: *dāʾiman lā shayʾ min jīm bāʾ mā dāma jīm*
Always, no C is B as long as it is C.
No C is ever B as long as it is C.

**$A_{D1}$** i-proposition: *dāʾiman baʿḍ jīm bāʾ mā dāma jīm*
Always, some C is B as long as it is C.
Some C is always B as long as it is C.

**$A_{D1}$** o-proposition: *dāʾiman baʿḍ jīm laysa bāʾ mā dāma jīm*
Always, some C is not B as long as it is C.
Some C is not ever B as long as it is C.

5. **$X_1$**: general absolute proposition (*muṭlaqah ʿāmmah*); referential one-sided absolute.

**$X_1$** a-proposition: *bi-l-iṭlāq al-ʿāmm kull jīm bāʾ*
By general absoluteness, every C is B.
Every C is at least once B.

**$X_1$** e-proposition: *bi-l-iṭlāq al-ʿāmm lā shayʾ min jīm bāʾ*
By general absoluteness, no C is B.
No C is always B.

$\mathbf{X_1}$ i-proposition: *bi-l-iṭlāq al-ʿāmm baʿḍ jīm bāʾ*
By general absoluteness, some C is B.
Some C is at least once B.

$\mathbf{X_1}$ o-proposition: *bi-l-iṭlāq al-ʿāmm baʿḍ jīm laysa bāʾ*
By general absoluteness, some C is not B.
Some C is not always B.

6. $\mathbf{M_1}$: general possible proposition (*mumkinah ʿāmmah*); referential one-sided possibility.

$\mathbf{M_1}$ a-proposition: *bi-l-imkān al-ʿāmm kull jīm bāʾ*
By general possibility, every C is B.
Every C is possibly B.

$\mathbf{M_1}$ e-proposition: *bi-l-imkān al-ʿāmm lā shayʾ min jīm bāʾ*
By general possibility, no C is B.
No C is necessarily B.

$\mathbf{M_1}$ i-proposition: *bi-l-imkān al-ʿāmm baʿḍ jīm bāʾ*
By general possibility, some C is B.
Some C is possibly B.

$\mathbf{M_1}$ o-proposition: *bi-l-imkān al-ʿāmm baʿḍ jīm laysa bāʾ*
By general possibility, some C is not B.
Some C is not necessarily B.

*The compound propositions customarily investigated*

7. $\mathbf{L_{D2}}$: special conditional (*mashrūṭah khāṣṣah*); descriptional restricted necessity.

$\mathbf{L_{D2}}$ a-proposition: *bi-l-ḍarūrah kull jīm bāʾ mā dāma jīm lā dāʾiman*
Necessarily, every C is B as long as it is C, not always.
Every C is necessarily B as long as it is C, and no C is always B.

$L_{D2}$ e-proposition: *bi-l-ḍarūrah lā shay᾽ min jīm bā᾽ mā dāma jīm lā dā᾽iman*
Necessarily, no C is B as long as it is C, not always.
No C is possibly B as long as it is C, and every C is at least once B.

$L_{D2}$ i-proposition: *bi-l-ḍarūrah baʿḍ jīm bā᾽ mā dāma jīm lā dā᾽iman*
Necessarily, some C is B as long as it is C, not always.
Some C is necessarily B as long as it is C, and those Cs are at least once not B.

$L_{D2}$ o-proposition: *bi-l-ḍarūrah baʿḍ jīm laysa bā᾽ mā dāma jīm lā dā᾽iman*
Necessarily, some C is not B as long as it is C, not always.
Some C is not possibly B as long as it is C, and those Cs are at least once B.

8. $A_{D2}$: special conventional (*ʿurfiyyah khāṣṣah*); descriptional restricted perpetuity.

$A_{D2}$ a-proposition: *dā᾽iman kull jīm bā᾽ mā dāma jīm lā dā᾽iman*
Always, every C is B as long as it is C, not always.
Every C is always B as long as it is C, and no C is always B.

$A_{D2}$ e-proposition: *dā᾽iman lā shay᾽ min jīm bā᾽ mā dāma jīm lā dā᾽iman*
Always, no C is B as long as it is C, not always.
No C is ever B as long as it is C, and every C is at least once B.

$A_{D2}$ i-proposition: *dā᾽iman baʿḍ jīm bā᾽ mā dāma jīm lā dā᾽iman*
Always, some C is B as long as it is C, not always.
Some C is always B as long as it is C, and those Cs are at least once not B.

$A_{D2}$ o-proposition: *dā᾽iman baʿḍ jīm laysa bā᾽ mā dāma jīm lā dā᾽iman*
Always, some C is not B as long as it is C, not always.
Some C is not ever B as long as it is C, and those Cs are at least once B.

9. **$X_{\sim L}$**: nonnecessary existential (*wujūdiyyah lā-ḍarūriyyah*); referential nonnecessary absoluteness.

**$X_{\sim L}$** a-proposition: *kull jīm bā' bi-l-fi'l lā bi-l-ḍarūrah*
Actually, every C is B, not necessarily.
Every C is at least once B, and no C is necessarily B.

**$X_{\sim L}$** e-proposition: *lā shay' min jīm bā' bi-l-fi'l lā bi-l-ḍarūrah*
Actually, no C is B, not necessarily.
No C is always B, and every C is possibly B.

**$X_{\sim L}$** i-proposition: *ba'ḍ jīm bā' bi-l-fi'l lā bi-l-ḍarūrah*
Actually, some C is B, not necessarily.
Some C is at least once B, and those Cs are possibly not B.

**$X_{\sim L}$** o-proposition: *ba'ḍ jīm laysa bā' bi-l-fi'l lā bi-l-ḍarūrah*
Actually, some C is not B, not necessarily.
Some C is not always B, and those Cs are possibly B.

10. **$X_2$**: non-perpetual existential (*wujūdiyyah lā-dā'imah*); referential two-sided absoluteness.

**$X_2$** a-proposition: *kull jīm bā' bi-l-fi'l lā dā'iman*
Actually, every C is B, not always.
Every C is at least once B, and no C is always B.

**$X_2$** e-proposition: *lā shay' min jīm bā' bi-l-fi'l lā dā'iman*
Actually, no C is B, not always.
No C is always B, and every C is at least once B.

**$X_2$** i-proposition: *ba'ḍ jīm bā' bi-l-fi'l lā dā'iman*
Actually, some C is B, not always.
Some C is at least once B, and those Cs are not always B.

**$X_2$** o-proposition: *ba'ḍ jīm laysa bā' bi-l-fi'l lā dā'iman*
Actually, some C is not B, not always.
Some C is not always B, and those Cs are at least once B.

11. $\mathbf{L_{T2}}$: temporal (*waqtiyyah*); referential temporal determinate.

See Appendix 4.

$\mathbf{L_{T2}}$ a-proposition: *bi-l-ḍarūrah kull qamar munkhasif waqt ḥaylūlat al-arḍ baynahu wa-bayna l-shams lā dā'iman*
Necessarily, every moon is eclipsed on the earth's coming between it and the sun, not always.
Necessarily, every C is B at time T, not always.
Every C is necessarily B at time T, and no C is always B.

$\mathbf{L_{T2}}$ e-proposition: *bi-l-ḍarūrah lā shay' min al-qamar bi-munkhasif waqt al-tarbīʿ lā dā'iman*
Necessarily, no moon is eclipsed at the moment of quadrature, not always.
Necessarily, no C is B at time T, not always.
No C is possibly B at time T, and every C is at least once B.

$\mathbf{L_{T2}}$ i-proposition: *bi-l-ḍarūrah baʿḍ qamar munkhasif waqt ḥaylūlat al-arḍ baynahu wa-bayna l-shams lā dā'iman*
Necessarily, some moon is eclipsed on the earth's coming between it and the sun, not always.
Necessarily, some C is B at time T, not always.
Some C is necessarily B at time T, and those Cs are not always B.

$\mathbf{L_{T2}}$ o-proposition: *bi-l-ḍarūrah baʿḍ qamar laysa bi-munkhasif waqt al-tarbīʿ lā dā'iman*
Necessarily, some moon is not eclipsed at the moment of quadrature, not always.
Necessarily, some C is not B at time T, not always.
Some C is not possibly B at time T, and those Cs are at least once B.

12. **$L_{X2}$**: spread (*muntashirah*); referential temporal indeterminate.

See Appendix 4.

**$L_{X2}$** a-proposition: *bi-l-ḍarūrah kull insān mutanaffis fī waqt mā lā dā'iman*
Necessarily, every man breathes at a given time, not always.
Necessarily, every C is B at some time, not always.
Every C is necessarily B at some time, and no C is always B.

**$L_{X2}$** e-proposition: *bi-l-ḍarūrah lā shay' min al-insān bi-mutanaffis fī waqt mā lā dā'iman*
Necessarily, no man breathes at a given time, not always.
Necessarily, no C is B at some time, not always.
No C is possibly B at some time, and every C is at least once B.

**$L_{X2}$** i-proposition: *bi-l-ḍarūrah ba'ḍ jīm bā' fī waqt mā lā dā'iman*
Necessarily, some C is B at some time, not always.
Some C is necessarily B at some time, and those Cs are not always B.

**$L_{X2}$** o-proposition: *bi-l-ḍarūrah ba'ḍ jīm laysa bā' fī waqt mā lā dā'iman*
Necessarily, some C is not B at some time, not always.
Some C is not possibly B at some time, and those Cs are at least once B.

13. **$M_2$**: special possible (*mumkinah khāṣṣah*); referential two-sided possibility.

**$M_2$** a-proposition: *kull jīm bā' bi-l-imkān lā bi-l-ḍarūrah*
Possibly, every C is B, not necessarily.
Every C is possibly B, and no C is necessarily B.

**$M_2$** e-proposition: *lā shay' min jīm bā' bi-l-imkān lā bi-l-ḍarūrah*
Possibly, no C is B, not necessarily.
No C is necessarily B, and every C is possibly B.

**$M_2$** i-proposition: *baʿḍ jīm bāʾ bi-l-imkān lā bi-l-ḍarūrah*
Possibly, some C is B, not necessarily.
Some C is possibly B, and those Cs are not necessarily B.

**$M_2$** o-proposition: *baʿḍ jīm laysa bāʾ bi-l-imkān lā bi-l-ḍarūrah*
Possibly, some C is not B, not necessarily.
Some C is not necessarily B, and those Cs are possibly B.

*Unlisted simple propositions called on by al-Kātibī*

14. **$L_{T1}$**: absolute temporal (*al-waqtiyyah al-muṭlaqah*); assumed in working out the contradictories for **$L_{T2}$** as one of its component propositions; conclusion to some first-figure syllogistic mixes; see Appendix 4.

**$L_{T1}$** a-proposition: *kull jīm bāʾ bi-l-ḍarūrah fī waqt muʿayyan*
Necessarily, every C is B at time T.
Every C is necessarily B at time T.

**$L_{T1}$** e-proposition: *lā shayʾ min jīm bāʾ bi-l-ḍarūrah fī waqt muʿayyan*
Necessarily, no C is B at time T.
No C is possibly B at time T.

**$L_{T1}$** i-proposition: *baʿḍ jīm bāʾ bi-l-ḍarūrah fī waqt muʿayyan*
Necessarily, some C is B at time T.
Some C is necessarily B at time T.

**$L_{T1}$** o-proposition: *baʿḍ jīm laysa bāʾ bi-l-ḍarūrah fī waqt muʿayyan*
Necessarily, some C is not B at time T.
Some C is not possibly B at time T.

15. **$L_{X1}$**: absolute spread (*al-muntashirah al-muṭlaqah*); assumed in working out the contradictories for **$L_{X2}$** as one of its component propositions; conclusion to some first-figure syllogistic mixes.

**$L_{X1}$** a-proposition: *kull jīm bāʾ bi-l-ḍarūrah fī waqt mā*
Necessarily, every C is B at some time.
Every C is necessarily B at some time.

**L**$_{X1}$ e-proposition: *lā shayʾ min jīm bāʾ bi-l-ḍarūrah fī waqt mā*
Necessarily, no C is B at time T.
No C is possibly B at time T.

**L**$_{X1}$ i-proposition: *baʿḍ jīm bāʾ bi-l-ḍarūrah fī waqt mā*
Necessarily, some C is B at some time.
Some C is necessarily B at some time.

**L**$_{X1}$ o-proposition: *baʿḍ jīm laysa bāʾ bi-l-ḍarūrah fī waqt mā*
Necessarily, some C is not B at some time.
Some C is not possibly B at some time.

16. **X**$_{T1}$: temporal absolute (*al-muṭlaqah al-waqtiyyah*); conclusion in some first- and second-figure mixes.

 I don't think I've ever seen **X**$_{T1}$ written out as a proposition in full, whether with dummy letters or concrete terms; see **M**$_{T1}$ in Appendix 4.

 **X**$_{T1}$ a-proposition: *kull jīm bāʾ bi-l-fiʿl fī waqt muʿayyan*
 By general absoluteness, every C is B at time T.
 Every C is actually B at time T.

 **X**$_{T1}$ e-proposition: *lā shayʾ min jīm bāʾ bi-l-fiʿl fī waqt muʿayyan*
 By general absoluteness, no C is B at time T.
 No C is actually B at time T.

 **X**$_{T1}$ i-proposition: *baʿḍ jīm bāʾ bi-l-fiʿl fī waqt muʿayyan*
 By general absoluteness, some C is B at time T.
 Some C is actually B at time T.

 **X**$_{T1}$ o-proposition: *baʿḍ jīm laysa bāʾ bi-l-fiʿl fī waqt muʿayyan*
 By general absoluteness, some C is not B at time T.
 Some C is not actually B at time T.

17. **X**$_{X1}$: spread absolute (*al-muṭlaqah al-muntashirah*); again, a conclusion in some first- and second-figure mixes.

 I don't think I've ever seen **X**$_{X1}$ written out as a proposition in full, whether with dummy letters or concrete terms; this is my best guess.

$\mathbf{X}_{X1}$ a-proposition: *kull jīm bāʾ bi-l-fiʿl fī waqt mā*
By general absoluteness, every C is B at some time.
Every C is actually B at some time.

$\mathbf{X}_{X1}$ e-proposition: *lā shayʾ min jīm bāʾ bi-l-fiʿl fī waqt mā*
By general absoluteness, no C is B at some time.
No C is actually B at some time.

$\mathbf{X}_{X1}$ i-proposition: *baʿḍ jīm bāʾ bi-l-fiʿl fī waqt mā*
By general absoluteness, some C is B at some time.
Some C is actually B at some time.

$\mathbf{X}_{X1}$ o-proposition: *baʿḍ jīm laysa bāʾ bi-l-fiʿl fī waqt mā*
By general absoluteness, some C is not B at some time.
Some C is not actually B at some time.

18. $\mathbf{M}_{T1}$: temporal possible (*al-mumkinah al-waqtiyyah*); given as contradictory of $\mathbf{L}_{T1}$, a component of $\mathbf{L}_{T2}$.

See Appendix 4, though note al-Ḥillī gives *fī dhālika l-waqt* for *fī waqt muʿayyan* (*ḤQ* 296.12–14).

$\mathbf{M}_{T1}$ a-proposition: *kull jīm bāʾ bi-l-imkān fī waqt muʿayyan*
Possibly, every C is B at time T.
Every C is possibly B at time T.

$\mathbf{M}_{T1}$ e-proposition: *lā shayʾ min jīm bāʾ bi-l-imkān fī waqt muʿayyan*
Possibly, no C is B at time T.
No C is necessarily B at time T.

$\mathbf{M}_{T1}$ i-proposition: *baʿḍ jīm bāʾ bi-l-imkān fī waqt muʿayyan*
Possibly, some C is B at time T.
Some C is possibly B at time T.

$\mathbf{M}_{T1}$ o-proposition: *baʿḍ jīm laysa bāʾ bi-l-imkān fī waqt muʿayyan*
Possibly, some C is not B at time T.
Some C is not necessarily B at time T.

19. $\mathbf{M_A}$: perpetual possible (*al-mumkinah al-dā'imah*); given as contradictory of $\mathbf{L_{X1}}$, a component of $\mathbf{L_{X2}}$.

See Appendix 4; I adopt the name for this proposition given in *Ḫ K* 126.11, and Rescher and vander Nat, "Theory of Modal Syllogistic," 25.

$\mathbf{M_A}$ a-proposition: *kull jīm bā' bi-l-imkān dā'iman*
Always, every C is possibly B.

$\mathbf{M_A}$ e-proposition: *lā shay' min jīm bā' bi-l-imkān dā'iman*
Always, no C is necessarily B.

$\mathbf{M_A}$ i-proposition: *ba'ḍ jīm bā' bi-l-imkān dā'iman*
Always, some C is possibly B.

$\mathbf{M_A}$ o-proposition: *ba'ḍ jīm laysa bā' bi-l-imkān dā'iman*
Always, some C is not necessarily B.

20. $\mathbf{X_{D1}}$: absolute continuing (*al-ḥīniyyah al-muṭlaqah*); given as contradictory of $\mathbf{A_{D1}}$, and as conclusion to a number of third- and fourth-figure syllogistic mixes.

The *ḥīna*-clause is given in some examples as *fī ba'ḍ awqāt kawnihi jīm*, for example in §69.3: "Everyone afflicted with pleurisy may cough at times while afflicted" (*kull man bi-hi dhāt al-janb yumkinu an yas'ala fī ba'ḍ awqāt kawnihi majnūban*). *Bi-l-iṭlāq al-'āmm* could be put at the beginning or end of the proposition.

$\mathbf{X_{D1}}$ a-proposition: *kull jīm bā' ḥīna huwa jīm*
Every C is [at least once] B while it is C.
Every C is at least once B while C.

$\mathbf{X_{D1}}$ e-proposition: *lā shay' min jīm bā' ḥīna huwa jīm*
No C is [always] B while it is C.
No C is always B while C.

**X**$_{D1}$ i-proposition: *ba'ḍ jīm bā' ḥīna huwa jīm*
Some C is [at least once] B while it is C.
Some C is at least once B while C.

**X**$_{D1}$ o-proposition: *ba'ḍ jīm laysa bā' ḥīna huwa jīm*
Some C is not B [at least once] while it is C.
Some C is not always B while C.

21. **M**$_{D1}$: possible continuing (*al-ḥīniyyah al-mumkinah*); given as contradictory of **L**$_{D1}$.

As with **X**$_{D1}$. The *ḥīna*-clause can be replaced with *fī ba'ḍ awqāt kawnihi jīm*; *bi-l-imkān al-'āmm* can be replaced as in the example given for 20, which is to say, by the modalized copula, *yumkinu an yakūna*.

**M**$_{D1}$ a-proposition: *bi-l-imkān al-'āmm kull jīm bā' ḥīna huwa jīm*
Possibly, every C is B while C.
Every C is possibly B while C.

**M**$_{D1}$ e-proposition: *bi-l-imkān al-'āmm lā shay' min jīm bā' ḥīna huwa jīm*
Possibly, no C is B while C.
No C is necessarily B while C.

**M**$_{D1}$ i-proposition: *bi-l-imkān al-'āmm ba'ḍ jīm bā' ḥīna huwa jīm*
Possibly, some C is B while C.
Some C is possibly B while C.

**M**$_{D1}$ o-proposition: *bi-l-imkān al-'āmm ba'ḍ jīm laysa bā' ḥīna huwa jīm*
Possibly, some C is not B while C.
Some C is not necessarily B while C.

*Unlisted compound propositions called on by al-Kātibī*

Al-Kātibī mentions six more compound propositions as conclusions to inferences.

22. **L2**: non-perpetual necessary (impossible proposition) (*al-ḍarūriyyah al-lā-dā'imah*), given as conclusion to a first-figure mix.

    **L2** a-proposition: *bi-l-ḍarūrah kull jīm bā' lā dā'iman*
    Every C is necessarily B, not always.
    Every C is necessarily B, and no C is always B.

    **L2** e-proposition: *bi-l-ḍarūrah lā shay' min jīm bā' lā dā'iman*
    Necessarily, no C is B, not always.
    No C is possibly B, and every C is at least once B.

    **L2** i-proposition: *bi-l-ḍarūrah ba'ḍ jīm bā' lā dā'iman*
    Necessarily, some C is B, not always.
    Some Cs are necessarily B, and those Cs are at least once not B.

    **L2** o-proposition: *bi-l-ḍarūrah ba'ḍ jīm laysa bā' lā dā'iman*
    Necessarily, some C is not B, not always.
    Some Cs are not possibly B, and those Cs are at least once B.

23. **A2**: non-perpetual perpetual (impossible proposition) (*al-dā'imah al-lā-dā'imah*), given as conclusion to some first-figure mixes.

    **A2** a-proposition: *dā'iman kull jīm bā' lā dā'iman*
    Always, every C is B, not always.
    Every C is always B, and no C is always B.

    **A2** e-proposition: *dā'iman lā shay' min jīm bā' lā dā'iman*
    Always, no C is B, not always.
    No C is ever B, and every C is at least once B.

    **A2** i-proposition: *dā'iman ba'ḍ jīm bā' lā dā'iman*
    Always, some C is B, not always.
    Some Cs are always B, and those Cs are at least once not B.

$\mathbf{A_2}$ o-proposition: *dā'iman baʿḍ jīm laysa bā' lā dā'iman*
Always, some C is not B, not always.
Some Cs are not ever B, and those Cs are at least once B.

24. $\mathbf{A_{D(2)}}$: non-perpetual-for-some conventional (*al-ʿurfiyyah lā dā'imah li-l-baʿḍ*), given as converse of certain propositions, and as conclusion for some fourth-figure mixes.

$\mathbf{A_{D(2)}}$ a-proposition: *dā'iman kull jīm bā' mā dāma jīm lā dā'iman li-l-baʿḍ*
Always, every C is B as long as it is C, not always for some.
Every C is always B as long as it is C, and some C is not always B.

$\mathbf{A_{D2}}$ e-proposition: *dā'iman lā shay' min jīm bā' mā dāma jīm lā dā'iman li-l-baʿḍ*
Always, no C is B as long as it is C, not always for some.
No C is ever B as long as it is C, and some C is at least once B.

$\mathbf{A_{D2}}$ i-proposition: *dā'iman baʿḍ jīm bā' mā dāma jīm lā dā'iman li-l-baʿḍ*
Always, some C is B as long as it is C, not always for some.
Some C is always B as long as it is C, and some of those Cs are not always B.

$\mathbf{A_{D2}}$ o-proposition: *dā'iman baʿḍ jīm laysa bā' mā dāma jīm lā dā'iman li-l-baʿḍ*
Always, some C is not B as long as it is C, not always for some.
Some C is not ever B as long as it is C, and some of those Cs are at least once B.

25. $\mathbf{X_{T2}}$: non-perpetual temporal absolute (*al-muṭlaqah al-waqtiyyah al-lā-dā'imah*); conclusion for a first-figure mix.

$\mathbf{X_{T2}}$ a-proposition: *kull jīm bā' fī waqt muʿayyan lā dā'iman*
Every C is B at time T, not always.
Every C is B at time T, and no C is always B.

$\mathbf{X}_{T2}$ e-proposition: *lā shay' min jīm bā' fī waqt muʿayyan lā dā'iman*
No C is B at time T, not always.
No C is B at time T, and every C is at least once B.

$\mathbf{X}_{T2}$ i-proposition: *baʿḍ jīm bā' fī waqt muʿayyan lā dā'iman*
Some C is B at time T, not always.
Some C is B at time T, and those Cs are not always B.

$\mathbf{X}_{T2}$ o-proposition: *baʿḍ jīm laysa bā' fī waqt muʿayyan lā dā'iman*
Some C is not B at time T, not always.
Some C is not B at time T, and those Cs are at least once B.

26. $\mathbf{X}_{X2}$: non-perpetual spread absolute (*al-muṭlaqah al-muntashirah al-lā-dā'imah*); conclusion for a first-figure mix.

$\mathbf{X}_{X2}$ a-proposition: *kull jīm bā' fī waqt mā lā dā'iman*
Every C is B at some time, not always.
Every C is B at some time, and no C is always B.

$\mathbf{X}_{X2}$ e-proposition: *lā shay' min jīm bā' fī waqt mā lā dā'iman*
No C is B at some time, not always.
No C is B at some time, and every C is at least once B.

$\mathbf{X}_{X2}$ i-proposition: *baʿḍ jīm bā' fī waqt mā lā dā'iman*
Some C is B at some time, not always.
Some C is B at some time, and those Cs are not always B.

$\mathbf{X}_{X2}$ o-proposition: *baʿḍ jīm laysa bā' fī waqt mā lā dā'iman*
Some C is not B at some time, not always.
Some C is not B at some time, and those Cs are at least once B.

27. $\mathbf{X}_{D2}$: non-perpetual absolute continuing (*al-ḥīniyyah al-muṭlaqah al-lā-dā'imah*)

$\mathbf{X}_{D2}$ a-proposition: *kull jīm bā' ḥīna huwa jīm lā dā'iman*
Every C is [at least once] B while it is C, not always.
Every C is at least once B while C, and no C is always B.

$\mathbf{X}_{D2}$ e-proposition: *lā shay' min jīm bā' ḥīna huwa jīm lā dā'iman*
No C is [always] B while it is C, not always.
No C is always B while C, and every C is at least once B.

$\mathbf{X}_{D2}$ i-proposition: *ba'ḍ jīm bā' ḥīna huwa jīm lā dā'iman*
Some C is [at least once] B while it is C, not always.
Some C is at least once B while C, and those Cs are not always B.

$\mathbf{X}_{D2}$ o-proposition: *ba'ḍ jīm laysa bā' ḥīna huwa jīm lā dā'iman*
Some C is not B [at least once] while it is C, not always.
Some C is not always B while C, and those Cs are at least once B.

# Appendix 3: Examples of Quantified Hypothetical Propositions

The following examples are taken from *ḤQ* 285–86.

Conditionals:

A-conditional: (a-ℂ)aa. Whenever the sun is up, then it is day (*kullamā kānat al-shams ṭāliʿah fa-l-nahār mawjūd*; alternatives to *kullamā*: *mahmā*, *matā*);

E-conditional: (e-ℂ)aa. Never, if the sun is up, then it is night (*laysa al-battata idhā kānat al-shams ṭāliʿah fa-l-layl mawjūd*);

I-conditional: (i-ℂ)aa. Sometimes, if the sun is up, then it is day (*qad yakūnu idhā kānat al-shams ṭāliʿah fa-l-nahār mawjūd*);

O-proposition: (o-ℂ)aa. Two forms (no examples given): (1) Sometimes not, if P then Q (*qad lā yakūnu*); (2) Not always, if P then Q (*laysa kullamā*, or *laysa mahmā*, or *laysa matā*).

Disjunctives:

A-proposition: (a-𝔻)aa. Always, either the sun is up, or it is not (*dāʾiman immā an takūna l-shams ṭāliʿah aw lā takūna*);

E-proposition: (e-𝔻)aa. Never, either the sun is up, or it is day (*laysa al-battata immā an takūna l-shams ṭāliʿah wa-immā an yakūna l-nahār mawjūdan*);

I-proposition: (i-D)aa. Sometimes, either the sun is up, or it is night (*qad yakūnu immā an takūna l-shams ṭāliʿah wa-immā an yakūna l-layl mawjūdan*);

O-proposition: (o-D)aa. Two forms (no examples given): (1) Sometimes not, either P or Q (*qad lā yakūnu*); (2) Not always, either P or Q (*laysa dā'iman*).

# Appendix 4: Contradictories for Modalized Propositions

Here is a summary of the a- and o-proposition contradictories:

**L/M** The absolute necessity proposition has as its contradictory the general possibility proposition: "every A is necessarily B" contradicts "some A is not necessarily B" (or "some A is possibly not B").

**A/X** The absolute perpetual has the general absolute: "every A is always B" contradicts "some A is not always B" (or "some A is sometimes not B").

**$L_{D1}$/$M_{D1}$** The general conditional has the continuing possibility (*ḥīniyyah mumkinah*): "every A is necessarily B as long as it is A" contradicts "some A is possibly not B while A" (or "some A is not necessarily B while A").

**$A_{D1}$/$X_{D1}$** The general conventional has the continuing absolute (*ḥīniyyah muṭlaqah*): "every A is always B as long as it is A" contradicts "some A is sometimes not B while A" (or "some A is not always B while A").

## Compounds (read subject to §71; taken from *ḤQ* 295–96):

**$L_{D2}$** a-proposition contradicts **$M_{D1}$** o-proposition or **A** i-proposition: the contradictory of "every C is necessarily B as long as it is C, not always" is "either some C is not necessarily B while C, or some C is always B" (*naqīḍ kull jīm bi-l-ḍarūrah bā' mā dāma jīm lā dā'iman immā ba'ḍ jīm laysa bā' bi-l-imkān ḥīna huwa jīm aw ba'ḍ jīm bā' dā'iman*);

**$A_{D2}$** a-proposition contradicts **$X_{D1}$** o-proposition or **A** i-proposition: the contradictory of "every C is always B as long as it is C, not always" is "either some C is not always B while C, or some C is always B" (*naqīḍ kull jīm bā' mā dāma jīm lā dā'iman immā ba'ḍ jīm laysa bā' ḥīna huwa jīm aw ba'ḍ jīm bā' dā'iman*);

**X**$_2$ a-proposition contradicts **A** i-proposition or **A** o-proposition: the contradictory of "every C is B, not always" is "either some C is always B, or some C is never B" (*naqīḍ kull jīm bā' lā dā'iman immā ba'ḍ jīm bā' dā'iman aw ba'ḍ jīm laysa bā' dā'iman*);

**X**$_{\sim L}$ a-proposition contradicts **A** o-proposition or **L** i-proposition: the contradictory of "every C is B, not necessarily" is "either some C is never B, or some C is necessarily B" (*naqīḍ kullu jīm bā' lā bi-l-ḍarūrah immā ba'ḍ jīm laysa bā' dā'iman aw ba'ḍ jīm bā' bi-l-ḍarūrah*);

**L**$_{T2}$ a-proposition contradicts **M**$_T$ o-proposition or **A** i-proposition: the temporal is a compound of an absolute temporal (*waqtiyyah muṭlaqah*) and a general absolute, so its contradictory is either a possibility temporal or a perpetuity; so the contradictory of "every C is B necessarily at a specified time, not always" is "either possibly at that time some C is not B, or some C is always B" (*naqīḍ kull jīm bā' lā bi-l-ḍarūrah fī waqt mu'ayyan lā dā'iman immā ba'ḍ jīm laysa bā' bi-l-imkān fī dhālika l-waqt aw ba'ḍ jīm bā' dā'iman*);

**L**$_{X2}$ a-proposition contradicts **M**$_A$ o-proposition or **A** i-proposition: the spread is a compound of an absolute spread (*muntashirah muṭlaqah*) and a general absolute, so its contradictory is either a perpetual possible or a perpetual; so the contradictory of "every C is B necessarily at some time, not always" is "either always some C is not necessarily B, or some C is always B" (*naqīḍ kull jīm bā' lā bi-l-ḍarūrah fī waqt mā lā dā'iman immā ba'ḍ jīm laysa bā' bi-l-imkān dā'iman aw ba'ḍ jīm bā' dā'iman*);

**M**$_2$ a-proposition contradicts **L** o-proposition or **L** i-proposition: the contradictory of "every C is B by a special possibility" is "either some C is not possibly B or some C is necessarily B" (*naqīḍ kull jīm bā' bi-l-imkān al-khāṣṣ immā ba'ḍ jīm laysa bā' bi-l-ḍarūrah aw ba'ḍ jīm bā' bi-l-ḍarūrah*).

# Appendix 5: List of Translated Texts in Commentary

| | | |
|---|---|---|
| §0 | Text 0.1 | *TŠ* 93.1–2 |
| §1 | Text 1.a | *TT* 62.pu–63.2 |
| | Text 1.1 | *ḤQ* 183.1–5 |
| | Text 1.2 | *ḤQ* 183.12–184.4 |
| | Text 1.3 | *TŠ* 100.7–12 |
| §2 | Text 2.1 | *ḤQ* 184.u–185.8 |
| | Text 2.2 | *ḤQ* 184.8–pu |
| §4 | Text 4.1 | *ṬḤ* 118.18–apu |
| §5 | Text 5.1 | *ḤQ* 189.7–11 |
| | Text 5.2 | *RM* 10.1–10.8 |
| §6 | Text 6.1 | *TT* 23.pu–25.1 |
| §7 | Text 7.1 | *TŠ* 121.4–12 |
| §8 | Text 8.1 | *Ḫ̮K* 13.1–5 |
| §9 | Text 9.1 | *RM* 19.pu–20.3 |
| | Text 9.2 | *Ḫ̮K* 13.8–10 |
| | Text 9.3 | *TŠ* 124.11–125.8 |
| §10 | Text 10.1 | *ḤQ* 200.3–8 |
| | Text 10.2 | *Ḫ̮K* 11.9–pu |
| §12 | Text 12.1 | *ḤQ* 202.6–203.12, 204.7–10 |
| §13 | Text 13.1 | *ḤQ* 205.1–6 |
| §15 | Text 15.a | *TŠ* 142.u–143.1 |
| | Text 15.1 | *TT* 129.pu–130.2 |
| §16 | Text 16.1 | *TŠ* 141.10–16 |
| | Text 16.2 | *ḤQ* 209.pu–210.2 |
| §17 | Text 17.1 | *ḤQ* 210.7–211.3 |
| | Text 17.2 | *ḤQ* 211.4–8 |
| | Text 17.3 | *TŠ* 143.15–u |
| | Text 17.4 | *TŠ* 145.9–u |
| §19 | Text 19.1 | *ḤQ* 214.11–pu |
| | Text 19.2 | *ṬḤ* 193.1–8 |
| §20 | Text 20.1 | *ḤQ* 215.7–apu |
| | Text 20.2 | *TŠ* 150.apu–u |
| | Text 20.3 | *Ḫ̮K* 45.14–u |
| | Text 20.4 | *TT* 150n1 |
| §23 | Text 23.1 | *ḤQ* 220.5–11 |
| | Text 23.2 | *ḤQ* 220.14–apu |

|  |  |  |
|---|---|---|
| §24 | Text 24.1 | *TŠ* 163.3–4 |
| | Text 24.2 | *TŠ* 163.u–164.2 |
| §25 | Text 25.1 | *TT* 168.1–169.u |
| | Text 25.2 | *ḪK* 35.15–36.2 |
| | Text 25.3 | *ḤQ* 221.u–222.3 |
| §25 | Text 25.4 | *ḤQ* 222.12–15 |
| §28 | Text 28.1 | *ḪK* 36.3–4 |
| §30 | Text 30.1 | *ḤQ* 230.7–14 |
| §31 | Text 31.1 | *TŠ* 183.10–12 |
| | Text 31.2 | *TŠ* 183.apu–184.2 |
| §32 | Text 32.1 | *ḤQ* 232.11–13, 232.pu–233.2 |
| §33 | Text 33.1 | *TŠ* 186.7–188.1 |
| §34 | Text 34.1 | *ḤQ* 235.apu–pu |
| | Text 34.2 | *ḤQ* 236.7–8 |
| §35 | Text 35.1 | *ḤQ* 237.8–10 |
| | Text 35.2 | *ḤQ* 237.12–u |
| §36 | Text 36.1 | *ḤQ* 238.5–u |
| | Text 36.2 | *ḤQ* 239.1–9 |
| | Text 36.3 | *ḤQ* 239.12–16 |
| §37 | Text 37.1 | *ḤQ* 240.9–u |
| | Text 37.2 | *ḤQ* 241.1–3 |
| | Text 37.3 | *ḤQ* 241.4–12 |
| | Text 37.4 | *ḤQ* 241.pu–u |
| §38 | Text 38.a | *TŠ* 201.3–7 |
| | Text 38.1 | *AI* 22.2–4 |
| | Text 38.2 | *TT* 221.6–u |
| | Text 38.3 | *TŠ* 202.1–3 |
| | Text 38.4 | *ḤQ* 242.8–apu |
| | Text 38.5 | *TŠ* 202.6–11 |
| | Text 38.6 | *TŠ* 202.12–apu, 203.1–3 |
| §39 | Text 39.1 | *ḤQ* 245.15–apu |
| §40 | Text 40.1 | *ṬḤ* 142.7–u |
| | Text 40.2 | *TŠ* 209.9–12 |
| | Text 40.3 | *ḤQ* 247.12–u |
| | Text 40.4 | *ḤA* 56.20–apu |
| | Text 40.5 | *ḤQ* 247.10–11 |
| | Text 40.6 | *TŠ* 210.8–10 |
| | Text 40.7 | *TT* 234.3–6 |
| | Text 40.8 | *TT* 236.6–8 |
| | Text 40.9 | *TŠ* 204.15–pu |
| §42 | Text 42.1 | *ḤQ* 250.6–13 |
| §43 | Text 43.1 | *ḤQ* 251.u–252.2 |
| | Text 43.2 | *TT* 243.7–u |
| §45 | Text 45.a | *ḪK* 109.5–apu |
| | Text 45.1 | *TT* 246.pu–247.pu |
| | Text 45.2 | *TT* 250.7–251.4 |
| | Text 45.3 | *TT* 253.3–7 |
| | Text 45.4 | *TT* 253.8–9 |
| | Text 45.5 | *TT* 253.10–13 |
| | Text 45.6 | *TT* 253.14–254.2 |
| | Text 45.7 | *TT* 256.1–257.9 |
| | Text 45.8 | *TT* 257.16–258.pu |
| | Text 45.9 | *TT* 258.u–260.1 |
| | Text 45.10 | *ḪK* 145.11–pu |
| | Text 45.11 | *ḤQ* 254.16–pu |
| | Text 45.12 | *ḤQ* 254.u–255.9 |

| | | |
|---|---|---|
| §46 | Text 46.1 | *ḤQ* 255.14–256.8 |
| §47 | Text 47.1 | *ḤQ* 256.9–15 |
| | Text 47.2 | *TŠ* 224.9–pu |
| §48 | Text 48.1 | *TT* 263.pu–264.2 |
| §49 | Text 49.1 | *TT* 265.5–6 |
| §50 | Text 50.1 | *TT* 267.5–12 |
| | Text 50.2 | *TT* 268.8–10 |
| | Text 50.3 | *TT* 270.11–14 |
| | Text 50.4 | *ḤQ* 258.14–16 |
| §51 | Text 51.1 | *ḤQ* 259.apu–260.7 |
| | Text 51.2 | *TŠ* 233.12–234.1 |
| §52 | Text 52.1 | *ṬḤ* 265.5–266.3 |
| | Text 52.2 | *Ḫ K* 104.7–11 |
| | Text 52.3 | *RM* 272.4–apu |
| §60 | Text 60.1 | *ḤQ* 276.6–277.2 |
| | Text 60.2 | *ḤQ* 277.apu–278.6 |
| | Text 60.3 | *ḤQ* 278.10–u |
| | Text 60.4 | *ḤA* 79.12 |
| §62 | Text 62.1 | *ḤQ* 280.5–6 |
| §63 | Text 63.1 | *ḤQ* 281.1–10 |
| | Text 63.2 | *ḤQ* 282.2–6 |
| | Text 63.3 | *ḤQ* 282.7–8 |
| §64 | Text 64.1 | *ḤQ* 282.9–10 |
| | Text 64.2 | *ḤQ* 283.2–15 |
| §65 | Text 65.1 | *ḤQ* 284.6–285.6 |
| §67 | Text 67.a | *TŠ* 274.9 |
| | Text 67.1 | *ḤQ* 289.9–290.2 |
| §68 | Text 68.1 | *RM* 177.10–apu |
| | Text 68.2 | *ḤQ* 291.14–pu |
| | Text 68.3 | *ḤQ* 292.6–12 |
| | Text 68.4 | *ḤQ* 292.13–pu |
| §69 | Text 69.1 | *ḤQ* 294.6–7 |
| §70 | | *ḤQ* 295.7–296.u (paraphrase) |
| §71 | Text 71.1 | *ḤQ* 297.10–15 |
| §72 | Text 72.1 | *ḤQ* 298.3–5 |
| §73 | Text 73.a | *ḤQ* 299.17–apu |
| | Text 73.1 | *AI* 51.1–3 |
| | Text 73.2 | *ḤQ* 299.1–9 |
| | Text 73.3 | *TT* 344.11–u |
| | Text 73.4 | *TŠ* 290.9–12 |
| §74 | Text 74.1 | *ḤQ* 299.pu–300.8 |
| §76 | Text 76.1 | *ḤQ* 303.1–7 |
| | Text 76.2 | *ḤQ* 356.5–8 |
| | Text 76.3 | *ḤQ* 303.8–12 |
| | Text 76.4 | *Ḫ K* 135.4–apu |
| | Text 76.5 | *ḤQ* 303.apu–u |
| §77 | Text 77.1 | *ḤQ* 306.2–4 |
| §78 | Text 78.1 | *ḤQ* 311.6–7 |
| | Text 78.2 | *ḤQ* 310.apu–311.5 |
| §79 | Text 79.1 | *ḤQ* 312.1–6 |
| §80 | Text 80.1 | *ḤQ* 312.pu–313.15 |
| §81 | Text 81.1 | *ḤQ* 315.1–3 |

| | | |
|---|---|---|
| §82 | Text 82.1 | *Ḫ̮K* 147.2–3; quoting *AQ* 93.11–13 |
| | Text 82.2 | *Ḫ̮K* 147.6–12 |
| §82 | Text 82.3 | *ḤQ* 315.9–apu |
| | Text 82.4 | *TT* 364n1 |
| §83 | Text 83.1 | *ḤQ* 316.2–5 |
| | Text 83.2 | *ḤQ* 316.14–apu |
| | Text 83.3 | *ḤQ* 317.14–318.9 |
| | Text 83.4 | *ḤQ* 319.3–9 |
| | Text 83.5 | *ḤQ* 320.12–15 |
| §85 | Text 85.1 | *ḤQ* 322.u–323.4 |
| | Text 85.2 | *ḤQ* 323.13–pu |
| §86 | Text 86.1 | *ḤQ* 325.4–13 |
| | Text 86.2 | *ḤQ* 325.14–326.8 |
| | Text 86.3 | *TT* 375.7–u |
| | Text 86.4 | *TT* 377.5–6 |
| | Text 86.5 | *TŠ* 310.14–16 |
| §87 | Text 87.1 | *TŠ* 311.8–16 |
| | Text 87.2 | *ḤQ* 327.9–14 |
| | Text 87.3 | *TŠ* 311.17–312.2 |
| | Text 87.4 | *TŠ* 312.2–u |
| | Text 87.5 | *ḤQ* 329.11–13 |
| §88 | Text 88.1 | *RM* 244.u–245.2 |
| | Text 88.2 | *Ḫ̮K* 239.11–pu |
| §89 | Text 89.1 | *ḤQ* 334.6–10 |
| | Text 89.2 | *ḤQ* 334.pu–335.1 |
| | Text 89.3 | *TT* 386.13–apu |
| | Text 89.4 | *TT* 387.6–9 |
| §90 | Text 90.1 | *TT* 388.13–14 |
| | Text 90.2 | *TT* 391.apu–pu |
| §92 | Text 92.1 | *TT* 396.10–12 |
| | Text 92.2 | *TT* 395.14–u |
| §92 | Text 92.3 | *TT* 396.4–9 |
| §93 | Text 93.1 | *ḤQ* 343.5–11 |
| §94 | Text 94.1 | *TT* 401.12–16 |
| §95 | Text 95.1 | *TT* 405.15–17 |
| §97 | Text 97.1 | *TT* 412.1–413.u |
| §98 | Text 98.1 | *ḤQ* 356.5–357.4 |
| | Text 98.2 | *TŠ* 335.8–14 |
| §99 | Text 99.1 | *ṬḤ* 394.10–395.5 |
| | Text 99.2 | *AI* 70.5–7 |
| | Text 99.3 | *TŠ* 338.6–8 |
| §100 | Text 100.1 | *TŠ* 339.9–11 |
| | Text 100.2 | *TŠ* 340.6–11 |
| §101 | Text 101.1 | *TŠ* 341.1–3 |
| | Text 101.2 | *AI* 74.4–11 |
| | Text 101.3 | *TŠ* 341.6–11 |
| §102 | Text 102.1 | *TŠ* 343.5–11 |
| | Text 102.2 | *ḤQ* 363.pu–364.4 |
| | Text 102.3 | *TŠ* 344.4–u |
| §103 | Text 103.1 | *ḤQ* 365.7–u |
| | Text 103.2 | *ḤQ* 366.pu–367.7 |
| | Text 103.3 | *TŠ* 350.5–9 |

§104 Text 104.1 *TŠ* 352.3
Text 104.2 *TŠ* 352.4–7

§105 Text 105.a *TŠ* 352.13–353.9
Text 105.1 *TŠ* 353.12–354.2

§105 Text 105.2 *TŠ* 354.7–11

§106 Text 106.1 *ḤQ* 374.9–375.1
Text 106.2 *TŠ* 355.8–apu

§107 Text 107.1 *ḤQ* 376.11–14

§108 Text 108.1 *TŠ* 358.apu–u

§109 Text 109.1 *ḤQ* 380.3–13
Text 109.2 *TŠ* 359.11–14
Text 109.3 *TŠ* 359.15–360.2
Text 109.4 *TŠ* 360.7–11

§110 Text 110.1 *TT* 448.9–u

§112 Text 112.1 *TT* 451.13–u

§113 Text 113.1 *TŠ* 364.3–7
Text 113.2 *TŠ* 364.8–apu
Text 113.3 *TŠ* 364.pu–u

§114 Text 114.1 *TŠ* 365.apu–366.2

§115 Text 115.1 *TŠ* 366.7–apu
Text 115.2 *TŠ* 368.7

§116 Text 116.a *TŠ* 368.13–u
Text 116.1 *TŠ* 370.1–7
Text 116.2 *TŠ* 370.10–13
Text 116.3 *TŠ* 370.pu–371.4
Text 116.4 *TŠ* 372.4–10
Text 116.5 *TŠ* 372.13–15

§117 Text 117.1 *TŠ* 372.pu–373.5
Text 117.2 *TŠ* 373.6–11
Text 117.3 *TŠ* 374.1–4

§118 Text 118.1 *TŠ* 375.4–10
Text 118.2 *TŠ* 375.apu–u
Text 118.3 *TŠ* 376.14–15
Text 118.4 *TŠ* 377.1–10

§119 Text 119.1 *ḤQ* 408.9–12
Text 119.2 *ḤQ* 409.1–2
Text 119.3 *ḤQ* 409.6–8
Text 119.4 *TŠ* 379.1–6
Text 119.5 *TŠ* 379.14–u
Text 119.6 Chester Beatty 3577, 78a.1–78a.14

§120 Text 120.1 *TŠ* 381.1–8
Text 120.2 *TŠ* 386.8–387.10

# Bibliography


Ahmed, Asad Q., trans. *Avicenna's Deliverance: Logic*. Karachi: Oxford University Press, 2011.

Aristotle. *Manṭiq Arisṭū*. Edited by ʿAbd al-Raḥmān Badawī. 2 vols. Cairo: Maṭbaʿat Dār al-Kutub al-Miṣriyyah, 1948.

Averroes. *Le philosophe et la loi: Édition, traduction et commentaire de l'abrégé du Mustaṣfā*. Edited, translated, and commented by Ziad Bou Akl. Scientia Graeco-Arabica, vol. 14. Berlin: De Gruyter, 2015.

Avicenna. *Fontes Sapientiae* (*ʿUyūn al-ḥikmah*). Edited by ʿAbdurraḥmān Badawi. Cairo: Publications de l'Institut Français d'Archéologie Orientale du Caire, 1954.

———. *Kitāb al-Ishārāt wa-l-tanbīhāt: Le livre des théorèmes et des avertissements* [= *AI*]. Vol. 1. Translated by J. Forget. Leiden, Netherlands: Brill, 1892.

———. *Manṭiq al-mashriqiyyīn (Oriental Logic)*. Edited by M. D. al-Khaṭīb and ʿA. F. al-Qatlān. Cairo: al-Maktabah al-Salafiyyah, 1910.

———. *The Metaphysics of The Healing: A Parallel English–Arabic Text*. Translated by Michael E. Marmura. Provo, Utah: Brigham Young University Press, 2005.

———. *Al-Najāt min al-gharaq fī baḥr al-ḍalālāt* [=*AN*]. Edited by M. Dānishpazhūh. Tehran: Enteshārāt-e Dāneshgāh, 1985.

———. *Al-Shifāʾ: al-Ilāhiyyāt. See* Avicenna, *The Metaphysics of the Healing.*

———. *Al-Shifāʾ: al-Manṭiq: al-Burhān*. Edited by A. A. ʿAfīfī. Cairo: al-Maṭbaʿah al-Amīrīyah, 1956.

———. *Al-Shifāʾ: al-Manṭiq: al-ʿIbārah* [=*AʿI*]. Edited by M. M. al-Khuḍayrī. Cairo: al-Hayʾah al-Miṣrīyyah al-ʿĀmmah li-l-Taʿlīf wa-l-Nashr, 1970.

———. *Al-Shifāʾ: al-Manṭiq: al-Madkhal* [=*AM*]. *See* Di Vincenzo, *Avicenna, The Healing, Logic: Isagoge.*

———. *Al-Shifāʾ: al-Manṭiq: al-Maqūlāt*. Edited by I. Madkour, A. Ahwānī, G. Anawati, M. M. al-Khuḍayrī, and S. Zāyid. Cairo: al-Hayʾah al-ʿĀmmah li-Shuʾūn al-Maṭābiʿ al-Amīriyyah, 1959.

———. *Al-Shifāʾ: al-Manṭiq: al-Qiyās* [=*AQ*]. Edited by S. Zāyid. Cairo: al-Hayʾah al-ʿĀmmah li-Shuʾūn al-Maṭābiʿ al-Amīriyyah, 1964.

Al-Baghdādī, Abū l-Barakāt. *Al-Kitāb al-muʿtabar fī l-ḥikmah*. Edited by Zayn al-ʿĀbidīn al-Mūsawī, ʿAbdallāh ibn Aḥmad al-ʿAlawī, Aḥmad ibn Muḥammad al-Yamānī, and Muḥammad ʿĀdil al-Quddīsī. Hyderabad, India: Jamʿiyyat Dāʾirat al-Maʿārif al-ʿUthmāniyyah, 1939.

Barhebraeus. *Specimen Historiae Arabum, Sive, Gregorii Abul Farajii Malatiensis de Origine & Moribus Arabum Succincta Narratio, in Linguam Latinam Conversa, Notisque e Probatissimis apud Ipsos Authoribus, Fusius Illustrata*. Translated by Edward Pococke. Oxford: H. Hall, 1663.

Barnes, Jonathan. *Porphyry: Introduction*. New York: Oxford University Press, 2003.

Al-Bayḍāwī, ʿAbdallāh. *Nature, Man and God in Medieval Islam: ʿAbd Allah Baydawi's Text, Tawaliʿ al-Anwar min Mataliʿ al-Anzar, along with Mahmud Isfahani's Commentary, Mataliʿ al-Anzar, Sharh Tawaliʿ al-Anwar*. Islamic Philosophy, Theology and Science. Texts and Studies, vol. 47. Edited and translated by Edwin E. Calverley and James W. Pollock. Leiden, Netherlands: Brill, 2002.

Benevich, Fedor. "Scepticism and Semantics in Twelfth-Century Arabic Philosophy." *Theoria* 88 (2022): 72–108.

Black, Deborah L. *Logic and Aristotle's Rhetoric and Poetics in Medieval Arabic Philosophy*. Islamic Philosophy, Theology and Science. Texts and Studies, vol. 7. Leiden, Netherlands: Brill, 1990.

Buridan, John. *Summulae de Dialectica*. *See* Klima, *John Buridan, Summulae de Dialectica.*

Copenhaver, Brian P., Calvin G. Normore, and Terence Parsons, trans. *Peter of Spain: Summaries of Logic; Text, Translation, Introduction, and Notes*. Oxford: Oxford University Press, 2014.

Davidson, Herbert A. *Alfarabi, Avicenna, and Averroes on Intellect: Their Cosmologies, Theories of the Active Intellect, and Theories of Human Intellect*. New York: Oxford University Press, 1992.

Di Vincenzo, Silvia. *Avicenna, The Healing, Logic: Isagoge: A New Edition, English Translation and Commentary of the Kitāb al-Madḫal of Avicenna's Kitāb al-Šifāʾ*. Scientia Graeco-Arabica, vol. 31. Berlin: De Gruyter, 2021.

Eichner, Heidrun. "The Post-Avicennian Philosophical Tradition and Islamic Orthodoxy: Philosophical and Theological Summae in Context." PhD diss., MLU Halle-Wittenberg, 2009.

El-Rouayheb, Khaled. *The Development of Arabic Logic (1200–1800)*. Basel: Schwabe, 2019.

———. "Does a Proposition Have Three Parts or Four? A Debate in Later Arabic Logic." *Oriens* 44 (2016): 301–31.

———. "Impossible Antecedents and Their Consequences: Some Thirteenth-Century Arabic Discussions." *History and Philosophy of Logic* 30 (2009): 209–25.

———. "Al-Kātibī al-Qazwīnī." In *Encyclopaedia of Islam*, 3rd ed.

———. "Post-Avicennan Logicians on the Subject Matter of Logic: Some Thirteenth- and Fourteenth-Century Discussions." *Arabic Sciences and Philosophy* 22 (2012): 69–90.

———. *Relational Syllogisms and the History of Arabic Logic, 900–1900*. Islamic Philosophy, Theology and Science. Texts and Studies, vol. 80. Leiden, Netherlands: Brill, 2010.

———. "Sunni Muslim Scholars on the Status of Logic, 1500–1800." *Islamic Law and Society* 2 (2004): 213–32.

———. "*Takmīl al-Manṭiq*: A Sixteenth-Century Arabic Manual on Logic." In *Illuminationist Texts and Textual Studies: Essays in Memory of Hossein Ziai*, edited by Ahmed Alwishah, Ali Gheissari, and John Walbridge, 197–256. Leiden, Netherlands: Brill, 2018.

———. "Two Fourteenth-Century Islamic Philosophers: Ibn Mubārakshāh al-Bukhārī and Mullāzāde al-Kharziyānī." *Oriens* 48, 3–4 (2020): 345–66.

Fallahi, Asad. "Fārābī and Avicenna on Contraposition." *History and Philosophy of Logic* 40 (2019): 22-41.

Al-Fārābī, Abū Naṣr. *Kitāb al-Ḥurūf.* Edited by M. Mahdī. Beirut: Dār al-Mashriq, 1990.

———. *Sharḥ al-ʿIbārah. See* Zimmermann, *Al-Fārābī's Commentary and Short Treatise on Aristotle's De Interpretatione.*

Al-Ghazālī, Abū Ḥāmid. *Al-Mustaṣfā min ʿilm al-uṣūl.* Būlāq, Egypt: al-Maṭbaʿah al-Amīriyyah, 1324/1906.

Gutas, Dimitri. "Aspects of Literary Form and Genre in Arabic Logical Works." In *Glosses and Commentaries on Aristotelian Logical Texts: The Syriac, Arabic and Medieval Latin Traditions*, edited by Charles Burnett, 29–64. London: Warburg Institute, 1993.

Gutas, Dimitri. *Avicenna and the Aristotelian Tradition: Introduction to Reading Avicenna's Philosophical Works.* 2nd edition. Islamic Philosophy, Theology and Science. Texts and Studies, vol. 89. Leiden, Netherlands: Brill, 2014.

———. "The Empiricism of Avicenna." *Oriens* 40 (2012): 391–436.

Hermans, Erik. "A Persian Origin of the Arabic Aristotle? The Debate on the Circumstantial Evidence of the Manteq Revisited." *Journal of Persianate Studies* 11 (2018): 72–88.

Al-Ḥillī, al-Ḥasan ibn Yūsuf ibn al-Muṭahhar. *Al-Asrār al-khafīyyah fī l-ʿulūm al-ʿaqlīyyah* [=*ḤA*]. Qom, Iran: Markaz al-Abḥāth wa-l-Dirāsāt al-Islāmiyyah, Qism Iḥyāʾ al-Turāth al-Islāmī, 2000.

———. *Al-Qawāʿid al-jaliyyah fī sharḥ al-Risālah al-Shamsiyyah* [=*ḤQ*]. Edited by F. Ḥ. Tabrīziyān. Qom, Iran: Muʾassasat al-Nashr al-Islāmī, 1432/2012.

Hodgson, Marshall G. S. *The Expansion of Islam in the Middle Periods.* Vol. 2 of *The Venture of Islam: Conscience and History in a World Civilization.* Chicago: University of Chicago Press, 2004.

Ibn Khaldun, Abu Zayd. *The Muqaddimah: An Introduction to History.* Translated by Franz Rosenthal. Vol. 3. London: Routledge, 1958.

Ibn Mubārakshāh. *Sharḥ al-Shamsiyyah.* MS 616, fols. ob–122a. Zeytinoğlu Halk Kütüphanesi, Kütahya, Turkey.

Joseph, Horace W. B. *An Introduction to Logic.* 2nd ed. Oxford: Clarendon Press, 1906.

Kalbarczyk, Alexander. *Predication and Ontology: Studies and Texts on Avicennian and Post-Avicennian Readings of Aristotle's Categories.* Scientia Graeco-Arabica, vol. 22. Berlin: De Gruyter, 2018.

Kalbarczyk, Nora. *Sprachphilosophie in der Islamischen Rechtstheorie.* Islamic Philosophy, Theology and Science. Texts and Studies, vol. 103. Leiden, Netherlands: Brill, 2019.

Al-Kāshī, Afḍal al-Dīn. *Al-Minhāj al-mubīn.* MS Browne D.19(10) ff. 13r–75v. Cambridge University Library. Persian text is published in M. Minuvi and Y. Mahdavi, *Muṣannafāt Afḍal al-Dīn Muḥammad Marqī Kāshānī* (Tehran: Chāpkhāne Duwlatiye Īrān, 1337 HŠ/1959, logic vol. 2, 477–582).

Al-Kātibī, Najm al-Dīn. *Al-Mufaṣṣal fī sharḥ al-Muḥaṣṣal.* Edited by ʿAbd al-Jabbār Abū Sanīnah. 2 vols. Jordan: al-Aṣlayn li-l-Dirāsāt wa-l-Nashr: Kalām al-Buḥūth wa-l-Iʿlām, 2018.

———. *Al-Risālah al-Shamsiyyah fī l-qawāʿid al-manṭiqiyyah.* Edited by M. Faḍlallāh. Casablanca: al-Markaz al-Thaqāfī, 1998.

———. *Sharḥ Kashf al-asrār.* Enver Şahin, "Kâtibî'nin Şerhu Keşfi'l-Esrâr Adlı Eserinin Tahkîki ve Değerlendirmesi (Critical Edition and Analysis of Kātibī's Sharh Kashf al-asrâr)," PhD diss., Recep Tayip Erdoğan Üniversitesi, Rize, Turkey, 2019.

Keynes, John Neville. *Studies and Exercises in Formal Logic: Including a Generalisation of Logical Processes in Their Application to Complex Inferences.* 4th ed. London: Macmillan, 1906.

Al-Khūnajī, Afḍal al-Dīn. *Kashf al-asrār ʿan ghawāmiḍ al-afkār* [=*ḪK*]. Edited by K. El-Rouayheb. Tehran: Iranian Institute of Philosophy and the Institute of Islamic Studies, Free University of Berlin, 2010.

Kilwardby, Robert. *Notule libri priorum.* Edited and translated by Paul Thom and John Scott. Auctores Britannici medii aevi, 23–24. Oxford: Oxford University Press for the British Academy, 2015.

Klima, Gyula. *John Buridan, Summulae de Dialectica: An Annotated Translation, with a Philosophical Introduction*. New Haven, CT: Yale University Press, 2001.

Klinger, Dustin. "Language and Logic in the Graeco-Arabic Tradition: A History of Propositional Analysis from the Hellenic Commentators on Aristotle to Theories of the Proposition in Arabic Philosophy, 900–1350." PhD diss., Harvard University, Boston, 2021.

Lameer, Joep. *The Arabic Version of Ṭūsī's Nasirean Ethics*. Islamic Philosophy, Theology and Science. Texts and Studies, vol. 96. Leiden, Netherlands: Brill, 2015.

———. *Al-Fārābī and Aristotelian Syllogistics: Greek Theory and Islamic Practice*. Islamic Philosophy, Theology and Science. Texts and Studies, vol. 20. Leiden, Netherlands: Brill, 1994.

———. "Aristotelian Rhetoric and Poetics as Logical Arts in Medieval Islamic Philosophy." *Bibliotheca Orientalis* 50 nos. 5/6 (1993): 563–82.

———. *Conception and Belief in Ṣadr al-Dīn al-Shīrāzī: Introduction, Translation and Commentary*. Tehran: Iranian Institute of Philosophy, 2006.

Łukasiewicz, Jan. *Aristotle's Syllogistic from the Standpoint of Modern Formal Logic*. 2nd edition. Oxford: Oxford University Press, 1957.

Marmura, Michael E. "Avicenna's Chapter on Universals in the *Isagoge* of His *Shifā'*." In *Islam: Past Influence and Present Challenge*, edited by A. Welch and P. Cachia, 34–56. Edinburgh: Edinburgh University Press, 1979.

Michot, Yahya. *Ibn Sīnā: Lettre au Vizir Abū Sa'd. Editio Princeps*. Beirut: Dar al-Bouraq, 2000.

Palmer, E. H. *A Descriptive Catalogue of the Arabic, Persian, and Turkish Manuscripts in the Library of Trinity College, Cambridge, with an Appendix, Containing a Catalogue of the Hebrew and Samaritan Mss. in the Same Library*. Cambridge: Deighton, Bell, 1870.

Peter of Spain. *Summaries of Logic. See* Copenhaver et al., *Peter of Spain: Summaries of Logic*.

Philoponus. *On Aristotle Categories 1–5*. Translated by Riin Sirkel, Martin Tweedale, and John Harris. Ancient Commentators on Aristotle. London: Bloomsbury Academic, 2016.

Porphyry. *Introduction. See* Barnes, *Porphyry: Introduction.*

Pourjavady, Reza, and Sabine Schmidtke. *Critical Remarks by Najm al-Dīn al-Kātibī on the Kitāb al-Maʿālim by Fakhr al-Dīn al-Rāzī, Together with the Commentaries by ʿIzz al-Dawla Ibn Kammūna.* Series on Islamic Philosophy and Theology Texts and Studies, vol. 5. Tehran: Iranian Institute of Philosophy and Institute of Islamic Studies, Free University of Berlin, 2007.

Al-Rahim, Ahmed H. *The Creation of Philosophical Tradition: Biography and the Reception of Avicenna's Philosophy from the Eleventh to the Fourteenth Centuries A.D.* Diskurse der Arabistik, vol. 21. Wiesbaden, Germany: Harrassowitz Verlag, 2018.

Al-Rāzī, Fakhr al-Dīn. *Mafātīḥ al-ghayb al-mushtahar bi-l-Tafsīr al-kabīr.* Cairo: al-Maṭbaʿah al-Bahiyyah al-Miṣriyyah, 1938.

———. *Manṭiq al-mulakhkhaṣ* [=*RM*]. Edited by A. F. Qarāmalikī and A. Aṣgharīnizhād. Tehran: Dāneshgāh-e Ṣāde, 2002.

———. *Muḥaṣṣal afkār al-mutaqaddimīn wa-l-muta'akhkhirīn min al-ʿulamā' wa-l-ḥukamā' wa-l-mutakallimīn.* Cairo: al-Maṭbaʿah al-Ḥusayniyyah al-Miṣriyyah, 1905.

———. *Sharḥ al-Ishārāt.* Edited by ʿA. R. Najafzādeh. Tehran: Anjuman Āthār wa-Mafākhir Ferhangi, 2005.

Rescher, Nicholas. "Avicenna on the Logic of 'Conditional' Propositions." In *Studies in the History of Arabic Logic*, edited by Nicholas Rescher, 76–86. Pittsburgh, PA: University of Pittsburgh Press, 1963.

———. *Al-Fārābi's Short Commentary on Aristotle's Prior Analytics.* Pittsburgh, PA: University of Pittsburgh Press, 1963.

———. *Temporal Modalities in Arabic Logic.* Dordrecht, Netherlands: D. Reidel, 1967.

Rescher, Nicholas, and Arnold vander Nat. "The Theory of Modal Syllogistic in Medieval Arabic Philosophy." In *Studies in Modality*, edited by Nicholas Rescher, Ruth Manor, Arnold vander Nat, and Zane Parks, 17–56. Oxford: Blackwells, 1974.

Sabra, Abdelhamid I. "Avicenna on the Subject Matter of Logic." *The Journal of Philosophy* 77 (1980): 746–64.

———. Review of Rescher's *Al-Fārābī's Short Commentary on Aristotle's Prior Analytics* (Pittsburgh 1963). *Journal of the American Oriental Society* 85:2 (1965): 241–43.

Al-Samarqandī, Shams al-Dīn. *Qisṭās al-afkār fī l-manṭiq* [=*SQ*]. Edited with notes by Asadallah Fallāḥī. Tehran: Mu'assasat Pizhuhishi Ḥikmat wa-Falsafah Īrān, 1441/2020.

Sayılı, Aydin. *The Observatory in Islam and Its Place in the General History of the Observatory*. Ankara: Turk Tarih Kurumu Basimevi, 1960.

Al-Shāfiʿī, Muḥammad ibn Idrīs. *The Epistle on Legal Theory*. Edited and translated by Joseph E. Lowry. Library of Arabic Literature. New York: New York University Press, 2013.

Schöck, Cornelia. "Name (*ism*), Derived Name (*mushtaqq*), and Description (*waṣf*) in Arabic Grammar, Muslim Dialectical Theology and Arabic Logic." In *The Unity of Science in the Arabic Tradition*, edited by Shahid Rahman, T. Street, and H. Tahiri, 329–60. Dordrecht, Netherlands: Springer, 2008.

Smith, R. *Aristotle: Prior Analytics*. Indianapolis, IN: Hackett, 1989.

Smyth, William. "Controversy in a Tradition of Commentary: The Academic Legacy of al-Sakkākī's *Miftāḥ al-ʿUlūm*." *Journal of the American Oriental Society* 112:4 (1992): 589–97.

Street, Tony. "Afḍal al-Dīn al-Khūnajī (d. 1248) on the Conversion of Modal Propositions." *Oriens* 42 (2014): 454–513.

———. "Al-ʿAllāma al-Ḥillī (d. 1325) and the Early Reception of Kātibī's *Shamsīya*: Notes towards a Study of the Dynamics of Post-Avicennan Logical Commentary." *Oriens* 44 (2016): 267–300.

———. "Avicenna's Twenty Questions on Logic: Preliminary Notes for Further Work." *Documenti e Studi Sulla Tradizione Filosofica Medievale* 21 (2010): 97–111.

———. "Kātibī (d. 1277), Taḥtānī (d. 1365), and the *Shamsiyya*." In *The Oxford Handbook of Islamic Philosophy*, edited by Khaled El-Rouayheb and Sabine Schmidtke, 348–74. New York: Oxford University Press, 2016.

———. "An Outline of Avicenna's Syllogistic." *Archiv für Geschichte der Philosophie* 84 (2002): 129–60.

———. “The Reception of *Pointers* 1.6 in Thirteenth-Century Logic: On the Expression’s Signification of Meaning.” In *Philosophy and Language in the Islamic World*, edited by Nadja Germann and Mostafa Najafi, 101–28. Berlin: De Gruyter, 2020.

Strobino, Riccardo. “Avicenna on the Indemonstrability of Definition.” *Documenti e Studi Sulla Tradizione Filosofica Medievale* 21 (2010): 113–63.

———. *Avicenna’s Theory of Science: Logic, Metaphysics, Epistemology.* Berkeley Series in Postclassical Islamic Scholarship. Berkeley: University of California Press, 2021.

———. “Ibn Sina’s Logic.” In *The Stanford Encyclopedia of Philosophy*, edited by Edward N. Zalta. https://plato.stanford.edu/archives/fall2018/entries/ibn-sina-logic/.

———. “Per Se, Inseparability, Containment and Implication: Bridging the Gap between Avicenna’s Theory of Demonstration and Logic of the Predicables.” *Oriens* 44 (2016): 181–266.

———. “Time and Necessity in Avicenna’s Theory of Demonstration.” *Oriens*, 43 (2015): 338–67.

———. “What If That (Is) Why? Avicenna’s Taxonomy of Scientific Inquiries.” In *Aristotle and the Arabic Tradition*, edited by A. Alwishah and J. Hayes, 50–75. Cambridge: Cambridge University Press, 2015.

Tabrīzī, Abū l-Majd Muḥammad ibn Masʿūd. *Ark of Tabrīz (Safīna-Yi Tabrīz)*. Tehran: Markaz Nashr-e Dāneshgāhī, 1423/2002.

Al-Taftāzānī, Saʿd al-Dīn. *Sharḥ al-Risālah al-Shamsiyyah* [=*TŠ*]. Edited by Jādallāh Bassām Ṣāliḥ. Qom, Iran: Dār Zayn al-ʿĀbidīn, 2012.

Al-Tahānawī, Muḥammad ibn ʿAlī et al. *A Dictionary of the Technical Terms Used in the Sciences of the Musalmans*. Calcutta: W. N. Lees, 1862.

Al-Taḥtānī, Muḥammad ibn Muḥammad Quṭb al-Dīn al-Rāzī. *Taḥrīr al-qawāʿid al-manṭiqiyyah fī sharḥ al-Risālah al-Shamsiyyah*. Edited by M. Bīdārfar. Qom, Iran: Intishārāt Bīdār, 2011.

———. *Taḥrīr al-qawāʿid al-manṭiqīyyah fī sharḥ al-Risālah al-Shamsīyyah*. Cairo: Ḥalabī and Sons, 1948.

Thom, Paul. “Al-Fārābī on Indefinite and Privative Names.” *Arabic Sciences and Philosophy* 18 (2008): 193–209.

———. "Avicenna's Mereology of the Predicables." In *Mereology in Medieval Logic and Metaphysics: Proceedings of the 21st European Symposium of Medieval Logic and Semantics*, edited by Farbizio Amerini, 55–74. Pisa, Italy: Scuola Normale Superiore, 2019.

———. "Logic and Metaphysics in Avicenna's Modal Syllogistic." In *The Unity of Science in the Arabic Tradition*, edited by Shahid Rahman, T. Street, and H. Tahiri, 361–76. Dordrecht, Netherlands: Springer, 2008.

———. *Medieval Modal Systems: Problems and Concepts*. Aldershot, UK: Ashgate, 2003.

———. *The Syllogism*. Munich: Philosophia, 1981.

Al-Ṭūsī, Naṣīr al-Dīn. *Ḥall mushkilāt al-ishārāt* [=*ṬḤ*]. Edited by S. Dunyā. 2nd ed. Cairo: Dār al-Maʿārif, 1971.

———. *Taʿdīl al-miʿyār fī naqd Tanzīl al-afkār*. In *Collected Texts and Papers on Logic and Language*, edited by M. Mohaghegh and T. Izutsu. Tehran: Tehran University Press, 1971.

———. *Akhlāq-Nāṣirī*. *See* Lameer, *The Arabic Version of Ṭūsī's Nasirean Ethics*.

Young, Walter Edward. "Concomitance to Causation: Arguing *Dawarān* in the Proto-Ādāb al-Baḥth." In *Philosophy and Jurisprudence in the Islamic World*, edited by Peter Adamson, 205–82. Berlin: De Gruyter, 2019.

Zimmermann, F. W., trans. *Al-Fārābī's Commentary and Short Treatise on Aristotle's De Interpretatione*. London: Oxford University Press for the British Academy, 1981.

# Further Reading


## The Tradition of Greek Philosophy in Arabic

Gutas, Dimitri. *Greek Thought, Arabic Culture*. London: Routledge, 1998.

———. *Avicenna and the Aristotelian Tradition: Introduction to Reading Avicenna's Philosophical Works*. 2nd edition. Islamic Philosophy, Theology and Science. Texts and Studies, vol. 89. Leiden, Netherlands: Brill, 2014.

Peters, Francis E. *Aristotle and the Arabs: The Aristotelian Tradition in Islam*. New York: New York University Press, 1968.

Al-Rahim, Ahmed H. *The Creation of Philosophical Tradition: Biography and the Reception of Avicenna's Philosophy from the Eleventh to the Fourteenth Centuries A.D.* Diskurse der Arabistik, vol. 21. Wiesbaden, Germany: Harrassowitz Verlag, 2018.

## Traditions of Learning

Berkey, Jonathan P. *The Transmission of Knowledge in Medieval Cairo: A Social History of Islamic Education*. Princeton Studies on the Near East. Princeton, NJ: Princeton University Press, 1992.

Brentjes, Sonia. "On the Location of the Ancient or 'Rational' Sciences in Muslim Educational Landscapes (AH 500–1100)." *Bulletin of the Royal Institute for Inter-Faith Studies* 4.1 (2002): 47–72.

Eichner, Heidrun. "The Post-Avicennian Philosophical Tradition and Islamic Orthodoxy: Philosophical and Theological Summae in Context." PhD diss., MLU Halle-Wittenberg, Germany, 2009.

Ibn Khaldun, Abū Zayd. *The Muqaddimah: An Introduction to History*. Translated by Franz Rosenthal. Vol. 3. London: Routledge, 1958.

Makdisi, George. *The Rise of Colleges: Institutions of Learning in Islam and the West*. Edinburgh: Edinburgh University Press, 1981.

Pfeiffer, Judith. "Confessional Ambiguity vs. Confessional Polarization: Politics and the Negotiation of Religious Boundaries in the Ilkhanate." In *Politics, Patronage and the Transmission of Knowledge in 13th–15th Century Tabriz*, edited by Judith Pfeiffer, 129–68. Iran Studies, vol. 8. Leiden, Netherlands: Brill, 2013.

## Texts from Post-Mongol Marāghah

Madelung, Wilferd. "Nasir al-Din Tusi's Ethics: Between Philosophy, Shi'ism and Sufism." In *Ethics in Islam*, edited by Richard Hovannisian, 85–101. Malibu, CA: Undena, 1983.

Morrison, Robert. "What Was the Purpose of Astronomy in Ījī's *Kitāb al-Mawāqif fī 'Ilm al-Kalām*?" In *Politics, Patronage and the Transmission of Knowledge in 13th–15th Century Tabriz*, edited by Judith Pfeiffer, 201–29. Iran Studies, vol. 8. Leiden, Netherlands: Brill, 2013.

Ragep, F. Jamil. *Naṣīr Al-Dīn al-Ṭūsī's Memoir on Astronomy (al-Tadhkira fī 'ilm al-hay'a)*. Vols. 1 and 2. Sources in the History of Mathematics and Physical Sciences, vol. 12. Berlin: Springer-Verlag, 1993.

Al-Ṭūsī, Naṣīr al-Dīn. *The Nasirean Ethics*. Translated by G. M. Wickens. Persian Heritage Series. London: Allen and Unwin, 1964.

## Studies on Arabic Logic

Chatti, Saloua. *Arabic Logic from Al-Fārābī to Averroes: A Study of the Early Arabic Categorical, Modal, and Hypothetical Syllogistics*. Cham, Switzerland: Springer Basel AG, 2020.

El-Rouayheb, Khaled. *The Development of Arabic Logic (1200–1800)*. Basel: Schwabe, 2019.

Kalbarczyk, Alexander. *Predication and Ontology: Studies and Texts on Avicennian and Post-Avicennian Readings of Aristotle's Categories*. Scientia Graeco-Arabica, vol. 22. Berlin: De Gruyter, 2018.

Rescher, Nicholas. *Temporal Modalities in Arabic Logic*. Dordrecht, Netherlands: D. Reidel, 1967.

———. "The Theory of Modal Syllogistic in Medieval Arabic Philosophy." In *Studies in Modality*, edited by Nicholas Rescher and Ruth Manor Rescher, 17–56. Oxford: Blackwells, 1974.

Strobino, Riccardo. *Avicenna's Theory of Science: Logic, Metaphysics, Epistemology*. Berkeley Series in Postclassical Islamic Scholarship. Berkeley: University of California Press, 2021.

Thom, Paul. *Medieval Modal Systems: Problems and Concepts*. Ashgate Studies in Medieval Philosophy. Aldershot, UK: Ashgate, 2003.

## Translations

Ahmed, Asad Q. *Avicenna's Deliverance: Logic*. Studies in Islamic Philosophy. Karachi: Oxford University Press, 2011.

Chatti, Saloua, and Wilfrid Hodges. *Al-Fārābī, Syllogism: An Abridgement of Aristotle's "Prior Analytics."* Ancient Commentators on Aristotle. New York: Bloomsbury Academic, 2020.

Di Vincenzo, Silvia. *Avicenna, "The Healing, Logic: Isagoge": A New Edition, English Translation and Commentary of the "Kitāb al-Madḫal" of Avicenna's "Kitāb al-Šifāʾ."* Scientia Graeco-Arabica, vol. 31. Berlin: De Gruyter, 2021.

Zimmermann, F. W. *Al-Farabi's Commentary and Short Treatise on Aristotle's "De Interpretatione."* Oxford: Oxford University Press for the British Academy, 1981.

# List of Technical Terms

| ARABIC TERM | ENGLISH TERM | FIRST OCCURRENCE IN TEXT |
|---|---|---|
| *adāh* | particle | §11 |
| *ʿadamī* | privative (of term) | §49 |
| *akbar* | major (term) | §90 |
| *ʿaks* | converse, conversion | §§5, 73 |
| *ʿaks al-naqīḍ* | contraposition | §82 |
| *ʿaks al-tartīb* | reversing the order of the premises (i.e. metathesis) | §95 |
| *ālah* | instrument | §3 |
| *ʿalam* | proper name | §12 |
| *amr* | command | §14 |
| *ʿaqliyyah* | mental | §25 |
| *ʿaraḍ* | accident | §5 |
| *ʿaraḍ ʿāmm* | general accident | §23 |
| *ʿaraḍ dhātī* | essential accident | §5 |
| *ʿaraḍī* | accidental | §5 |
| *ʿaraḍī mufāriq* | separable accidental | §22 |
| *aṣghar* | minor (term) | §90 |
| *awḍāʿ* | situations (for quantifying over in conditional) | §65 |
| *awsaṭ* | middle (term) | §90 |
| *awwaliyyah* | primary, primitive (of propositions) | §116 |
| *badīhī* | primitive (of knowledge) | §2 |
| *baʿīd* | remote (of genus or differentia) | §18 |

| ARABIC TERM | ENGLISH TERM | FIRST OCCURRENCE IN TEXT |
|---|---|---|
| *basīṭah* | simple (of meaning or proposition) | §48 |
| *bayyin* | evident (of implicate) | §22 |
| *bayyinah bi-dhātihā* | self-evident | §91 |
| *bi-l-ʿaraḍ* | per accidens/ accidentally | §15 |
| *bi-l-fiʿl* | in actuality, actually | §52 |
| *bi-ḥasab al-dhāt* | with respect to the essence | §53 |
| *bi-l-imkān* | by possibility, possibly | §52 |
| *bi-l-iṭlāq* | in actuality, by absoluteness, at least once | §52 |
| *burhān* | demonstration | §80 |
| *burhān annī* | demonstration of the fact | §117 |
| *burhān limmī* | demonstration of the reasoned fact | §117 |
| *ḍābiṭ* | guideline , rule | §59 |
| *dākhil fī jawāb mā huwa* | intrinsic to the answer to "what is it?" | §33 |
| *dalālah* | signification | §7 |
| *ḍarb* | mood (of syllogism) | §90 |
| *dawām* | perpetuity | §51 |
| *dawr* | circle (in reasoning), vicious circle | §2 |
| *dawrān* | concomitance | §115 |
| *dhāt* | essence | §5 |
| *dhihniyyah* | mental | §12 |
| *duʿāʾ* | petition | §14 |
| *fard* | individual, member, item | §12 |
| *faṣl* | differentia | §5 |
| *fī jawharihi* | in its substance , essentially | §20 |
| *fī l-khārij* | actual existence (in extramental reality) | §8 |
| *ḥadd* | (1) [real] definition | §36 |
| | (2) term | §90 |
| *ḥadd nāqiṣ* | incomplete or deficient definition | §36 |
| *ḥadd tāmm* | complete definition | §36 |
| *ḥaqīqah* | (1) literal | §12 |
| | (2) reality | §20 |
| *ḥaqīqah basīṭah* | simple reality | §32 |
| *ḥaqīqiyyah* | exclusive (of disjunctive) | §60 |

| ARABIC TERM | ENGLISH TERM | FIRST OCCURRENCE IN TEXT |
|---|---|---|
| *ḥaṣr* | exhaustiveness | §115 |
| *hay'ah* | form | §11 |
| *ḥujjah* | argument | §6 |
| *ḥukm* | judgment | §1 |
| *iḍāfah* | relation (as category) | §68 |
| *iftirāḍ* | ecthesis | §77 |
| *ījāb* | affirmation | §1 |
| *ikhtilāf mūjib li-ʿadam al-intāj* | discrepant conclusions, contrasted instances | §92 |
| *iktisāb* | acquiring , acquisition | §3 |
| *ʿilliyyah* | causality | §60 |
| *ʿilm* | knowledge, science | §1 |
| *iltimās* | request | §14 |
| *iltizām* | implication (kind of signification) | §7 |
| *imtināʿ* | impossibility | §6 |
| *ʿinādiyyah* | oppositional (of disjunctive ) | §61 |
| *infikāk* | separation | §22 |
| *inḥilāl* | analysis | §38 |
| *intāj* | production (of syllogistic conclusion) | §75 |
| *intiẓām* | organize (as a syllogism) | §81 |
| *iqtirān* | connection (between categorical premises) | §90 |
| *irtidād* | reduction (of second- or higher figure syllogism to first) | §93 |
| *irtifāʿ* | removing | §52 |
| *ism* | name | §11 |
| *isnād* | subordination | §1 |
| *istiḥālah* | impossibility | §9 |
| *istilzām* | entailment | §9 |
| *istiqrā'* | induction | §114 |
| *istithnā'* | repeating (as in affirming antecedent or denying consequent) | §111 |

| ARABIC TERM | ENGLISH TERM | FIRST OCCURRENCE IN TEXT |
|---|---|---|
| *ithbāt* | affirmation | §1 |
| *iʿtirāf* | acknowledgement | §118 |
| *ittiḥād* | unity, identity | §68 |
| *jadal* | dialectic | §118 |
| *jawhar* | substance | §20 |
| *jihah* | mode | §51 |
| *jins* | genus | §5 |
| *jins al-ajnās* | supreme genus | §31 |
| *jins ʿālin* | superior genus | §31 |
| *jins iḍāfī* | relative genus | §31 |
| *jins mufrad* | isolated genus | §31 |
| *jins mutawassiṭ* | intermediate genus | §31 |
| *jins sāfil* | inferior genus | §31 |
| *juzʾ ghayr tāmm* | incomplete part (of hypothetical proposition) | §106 |
| *juzʾ tāmm* | complete part (of hypothetical) | §105 |
| *juzʾ wa-kull* | part and whole | §5 |
| *juzʾī* | particular | §5 |
| *juzʾī ḥaqīqī* | real particular | §15 |
| *juzʾī iḍāfī* | relative particular | §28 |
| *kādhib* | false | §38 |
| *kāfin* | sufficient (of condition) | §22 |
| *kalimah* | verb | §11 |
| *kammiyyah* | quantity | §42 |
| *kayfiyyah* | quality | §42 |
| *khabar* | information | §14 |
| *khāṣṣah* | proprium | §23 |
| *khiṭābah* | rhetoric | §118 |
| *khulf* | absurd, impossibility, inconceivable | §76 |
| *khuṣūṣiyyah* | specificity | §16 |
| *kidhb* | falsity | §14 |
| *kubrā* | major (premise) | §90 |
| *kull* | whole (in part and whole) | §5 |

| ARABIC TERM | ENGLISH TERM | FIRST OCCURRENCE IN TEXT |
|---|---|---|
| *kullī* | universal | §15 |
| *kullī ʿaqlī* | mental universal | §25 |
| *kullī manṭiqī* | logical universal | §25 |
| *kullī ṭabīʿī* | natural universal | §25 |
| *lafẓ* | expression | §7 |
| *lāzim* | implicate | §22 |
| *luzūm* | implication (of meaning) | §22 |
| *mabdaʾ* | principle (of science) | §120 |
| *māddah* | matter (of proposition, syllogism) | §51, §116 |
| *maʿdūlah* | metathetic (of categorical with indefinite terms) | §48 |
| *mafhūm* | concept | §15 |
| *māhiyyah* | quiddity | §9 |
| *maḥmūl* | predicate | §5 |
| *maḥṣūrah* | quantified (with respect to meaning) | §42 |
| *majāz* | figurative | §12 |
| *majhūl* | unknown | §3 |
| *majmūʿ* | aggregate | §1 |
| *makhṣūṣah* | singular | §42 |
| *malzūm* | implicant | §22 |
| *maʿnan* | meaning | §7 |
| *māniʿat al-jamʿ* | alternative denial (kind of disjunction) | §60 |
| *māniʿat al-khuluww* | inclusive disjunction | §60 |
| *manqūl* | transferred (of expression's signification) | §12 |
| *manqūl iṣṭilāḥī* | technically transferred | §12 |
| *manqūl sharʿī* | legislatively transferred | §12 |
| *manqūl ʿurfī* | conventionally transferred | §12 |
| *maqbūlah* | received proposition | §118 |
| *maqīs* | derivative analogue | §115 |
| *maqīs ʿalayhi* | principal analogue | §115 |
| *al-maqūl fī jawāb mā huwa* | what is said in answer to "what is it?" | §16 |

| ARABIC TERM | ENGLISH TERM | FIRST OCCURRENCE IN TEXT |
|---|---|---|
| *maʿrūḍ* | substrate | §22 |
| *masāʾil* | questions (or theorems of science) | §120 |
| *mashhūrah* | endoxic proposition | §118 |
| *matbūʿ* | antecedent (of conditional) | §9 |
| *maṭbūʿ* | norm (as natural inference of a given schema) | §105 |
| *maṭlūb* | what is sought, the question | §77 |
| *mawḍūʿ* | (1) imposed (said of expression imposed on meaning) | §12 |
| | (2) subject (of a categorical proposition) | §40 |
| | (3) subject (of a science) | §120 |
| *min jihat al-lafẓ* | with respect to expression | §119 |
| *min jihat al-maʿnā* | with respect to meaning | §119 |
| *muʿānid* | opposed | §65 |
| *muʿarrāh* | stripped, abstract | §28 |
| *muʿarrif* | that which defines a thing (i.e., definiens) | §35 |
| *mutabāyin* | disjunct | §27 |
| *mubāyin* | distinct (of terms, also heteronymous) | §13 |
| *mufrad* | term (specifically, simple term) | §10 |
| *mughālaṭah* | fallacy | §119 |
| *muḥāl* | absurd, impossibility, inconceivable | §27 |
| *muḥaṣṣalah* | determinate (of categorical proposition with positive terms) | §48 |
| *muhmalah* | indefinite proposition | §43 |
| *mujarrabah* | proposition based on experience | §116 |
| *mūjibah* | affirmative proposition | §41 |
| *mukhayyilah* | image-eliciting proposition | §118 |
| *mukhtaliṭah* | mix (of modalized premises) | §98 |
| *mulāzamah* | implication (of meaning) | §8 |
| *mumkin* | contingent, two-sided possible | §12 |
| *munfaṣilah* | disjunctive | §39 |
| *munfaṣilah ittifāqiyyah* | coincidental disjunctive | §61 |
| *muntij* | productive (of syllogism) | §81 |

| ARABIC TERM | ENGLISH TERM | FIRST OCCURRENCE IN TEXT |
|---|---|---|
| *muqaddamah* | premise | §90 |
| *muqaddam* | antecedent (of conditional) | §60 |
| *murādif* | synonymous (of expressions) | §13 |
| *murakkab* | compound (of term or proposition) | §10 |
| *musallamah* | conceded proposition | §118 |
| *musāwin* | coextensive | §5 |
| *musawwarah* | quantified (with respect to expression) | §42 |
| *mushāghibī* | eristic | §119 |
| *mushāhadah* | observational proposition | §116 |
| *mushakhkhiṣ* | individuating | §28 |
| *mushakkik* | systematically ambiguous | §12 |
| *mushtarak* | equivocal | §12 |
| *mustawin* | straight (in conversion) | §73 |
| *muṭābaqah* | correspondence (kind of signification) | §7 |
| *mutawāṭi'* | univocal | §12 |
| *mutawātirah* | proposition based on sequential testimony | §116 |
| *muttaṣilah ittifāqiyyah* | coincidental conditional | §60 |
| *muttaṣilah luzūmiyyah* | implicative conditional | §60 |
| *naqīḍ* | contradictory (of terms or propositions) | §5 |
| *natījah* | conclusion | §89 |
| *nātijah* | productive (of syllogism) | §91 |
| *naw'* | species | §16 |
| *naw' al-anwā'* | lowest species (i.e. infima species) | §30 |
| *naw' ḥaqīqī* | real species | §29 |
| *naw' iḍāfī* | relative species | §29 |
| *naw' mufrad* | isolated species | §30 |
| *naw' mutawassiṭ* | intermediate species | §30 |
| *naw' sāfil* | lowest species (i.e. infima species) | §30 |
| *naẓarī* | inferred | §2 |
| *nisbah* | relation (between terms in proposition) | §40 |
| *qaḍiyyah* | proposition | §5 |
| *qaḍiyyah dā'imah* | perpetual proposition | §52 |

| ARABIC TERM | ENGLISH TERM | FIRST OCCURRENCE IN TEXT |
|---|---|---|
| *qaḍiyyah ḍarūriyyah* | necessary proposition | §3 |
| *qaḍiyyag fiʿliyyah* | actuality proposition | §98 |
| *qaḍiyyah ḥadsiyyah* | intuited proposition | §116 |
| *qaḍiyyah ḥamliyyah* | categorical proposition | §38 |
| *qaḍiyyah ḥīniyyah mumkinah* | possible continuing proposition | §69 |
| *qaḍiyyah ḥīniyyah muṭlaqah* | absolute continuing proposition | §69 |
| *qaḍiyyah juzʾiyyah sālibah* | particular negative, o-proposition | §42 |
| *qaḍiyyah mashrūṭah* | conditional (categorical) proposition | §52 |
| *qaḍiyyah mashrūṭah khāṣṣah* | special conditional (categorical) proposition | §53 |
| *qaḍiyyah maẓnūnah* | suppositional proposition | §118 |
| *qaḍiyyah mūjibah juzʾiyyah* | particular affirmative, i-proposition | §42 |
| *qaḍiyyah mūjibah kulliyyah* | universal affirmative, a-proposition | §42 |
| *qaḍiyyah mumkinah* | possible proposition | §52 |
| *qaḍiyyah mumkinah khāṣṣah* | special possible proposition | §59 |
| *qaḍiyyah munʿakisah* | convertible proposition | §100 |
| *qaḍiyyah muntashirah* | spread proposition | §58 |
| *qaḍiyyah muntashirah muṭlaqah* | absolute spread proposition | §58 |
| *qaḍiyyah muwajjahah* | modal proposition | §51 |
| *qaḍiyyah muṭlaqah* | absolute proposition | §52 |
| *qaḍiyyah muttaṣilah* | conditional (hypothetical) proposition | §39 |
| *qaḍiyyah qiyāsuhā maʿahā* | implicitly syllogistic propositions | §116 |
| *qaḍiyyah sālibah kulliyyah* | universal negative, e-proposition | §42 |

| ARABIC TERM | ENGLISH TERM | FIRST OCCURRENCE IN TEXT |
|---|---|---|
| *qaḍiyyah ṭabīʿiyyah* | natural proposition | §43 |
| *qaḍiyyah ʿurfiyyah* | conventional proposition | §52 |
| *qaḍiyyah ʿurfiyyah khāṣṣah* | special conventional proposition | §54 |
| *qaḍiyyah waqtiyyah* | temporal proposition | §57 |
| *qaḍiyyah waqtiyyah muṭlaqah* | absolute temporal proposition | §57 |
| *qaḍiyyah wujūdiyyah lā-dāʾimah* | non-perpetual existential proposition | §56 |
| *qaḍiyyah wujūdiyyah lā-ḍarūriyyah* | nonnecessary existential proposition | §55 |
| *qāʿidah* | rule | §59 |
| *qānūn* | canon | §3 |
| *qarīb* | proximate (of genus or differentia) | §5 |
| *qarīnah* | mood (of syllogism) | §90 |
| *qawl shāriḥ* | explanatory phrase | §6 |
| *qayd al-lā-darūrah* | restriction of nonnecessity | §55 |
| *qayd al-lā-dawām* | restriction of non-perpetuity | §53 |
| *qism* | division | §38 |
| *qiyās* | syllogism | §81 |
| *qiyās iqtirānī* | connective syllogism | §89 |
| *qiyās istithnāʾī* | repetitive syllogism | §89 |
| *qiyās al-khalf* | reductio | §93 |
| *qiyās murakkab* | compound syllogism | §112 |
| *rābiṭah* | copula | §40 |
| *radd* | reduction (of second- or higher figure syllogism to first) | §94 |
| *rafʿ* | denying (the consequent) | §110 |
| *rasm* | delineation | §36 |
| *rasm nāqiṣ* | incomplete delineation | §36 |
| *rasm tāmm* | complete delineation | §36 |
| *rujūʿ* | reduction (of second- or higher figure syllogism to first) | §93 |

| ARABIC TERM | ENGLISH TERM | FIRST OCCURRENCE IN TEXT |
|---|---|---|
| *ṣādiq* | true | §6 |
| *safsaṭah* | sophistry | §118 |
| *salb* | negation | §50 |
| *sālibah* | negative | §41 |
| *shahādah* | testimony | §116 |
| *shakhṣ* | individual | §16 |
| *shakhṣiyyah* | singular | §42 |
| *shakl* | figure (of syllogism) | §80 |
| *sharṭ* | condition | §68 |
| *sharṭiyyah* | hypothetical | §38 |
| *shiʿr* | poetry | §118 |
| *ṣidq* | truth | §14 |
| *ṣughrā* | minor (premise) | §90 |
| *sūr* | quantifier | §42 |
| *ṣurah* | form | §1 |
| *tabāyun juzʾī* | partial disjunction | §27 |
| *tabāyun kullī* | complete disjunction | §27 |
| *tābiʿ* | consequent (of conditional) | §9 |
| *taḍammun* | containment (kind of signification) | §7 |
| *taḍāyuf* | correlation | §60 |
| *taḥqīq* | verification | §27 |
| *takhalluf* | counterexample | §115 |
| *talāzum* | coimplication | §50 |
| *tālin* | consequent (of conditional) | §60 |
| *tāmm* | complete (of expression) | §14 |
| *tamthīl* | example | §115 |
| *al-tanāfī* | incompatibility | §39 |
| *tanāquḍ* | contradiction (of propositions) | §67 |
| *tanbīh* | notification | §14 |
| *taqdīr* | supposition | §60 |
| *taqyīdī* | restrictive (of expression) | §14 |
| *ṭaraf* | extreme (of proposition) | §38 |
| *tardīd* | setting out as disjuncts | §71 |

| ARABIC TERM | ENGLISH TERM | FIRST OCCURRENCE IN TEXT |
|---|---|---|
| *targhīb* | exhortation | §118 |
| *taʿrīf* | definition (weak sense) | §35 |
| *tartīb* | ordering | §3 |
| *tasalsul* | regress | §2 |
| *taṣawwur* | conception | §1 |
| *taṣdīq* | assertion | §1 |
| *taslīm* | concession | §88 |
| *taʾthīr* | influencing | §118 |
| *thubūt* | affirmation | §1 |
| *thulāthiyyah* | three-part (of proposition) | §40 |
| *thunāʾiyyah* | two-part (of proposition) | §40 |
| *ʿumūm muṭlaq* | inclusion | §26 |
| *ʿumūm min wajh* | overlap | §26 |
| *waḍʿ* | (1) imposition | §7 |
| | (2) affirming the antecedent | §110 |
| *wahmiyyah* | estimative proposition | §118 |
| *wāqiʿ fī ṭarīq mā huwa* | what arises on the way to "what is it?" | §33 |
| *waqt muʿayyan* | specified moment | §57 |
| *waṣf* | description | §52 |
| *wujūdī* | positive (of term) | §49 |
| *yaqīn* | certainty | §116 |
| *yaqīniyyah* | proposition of certainty | §116 |
| *zaman* | time, tense | §68 |

# Index

# About the NYU Abu Dhabi Research Institute

The Library of Arabic Literature is a research center affiliated with NYU Abu Dhabi and is supported by a grant from the NYU Abu Dhabi Research Institute.

The NYU Abu Dhabi Research Institute is a world-class center of cutting-edge and innovative research, scholarship, and cultural activity. It supports centers that address questions of global significance and local relevance and allows leading faculty members from across the disciplines to carry out creative scholarship and high-level research on a range of complex issues with depth, scale, and longevity that otherwise would not be possible.

From genomics and climate science to the humanities and Arabic literature, Research Institute centers make significant contributions to scholarship, scientific understanding, and artistic creativity. Centers strengthen cross-disciplinary engagement and innovation among the faculty, build critical mass in infrastructure and research talent at NYU Abu Dhabi, and have helped make the university a magnet for outstanding faculty, scholars, students, and international collaborations.

## About the Translator

Tony Street is a Fellow of Clare Hall at the University of Cambridge. He works on medieval Islamic intellectual history, focusing on Arabic logical texts written in the thirteenth century. He has held visiting positions at Paris 7, Berkeley, Oxford, and the Israel Institute of Advanced Studies. He is currently translating a commentary on the logic of Avicenna's *Pointers and Reminders* by Najm al-Dīn al-Kātibī's colleague and rival, Naṣīr al-Dīn al-Ṭūsī.

# The Library of Arabic Literature

For more details on individual titles, visit www.libraryofarabicliterature.org

*Classical Arabic Literature: A Library of Arabic Literature Anthology*
Selected and translated by Geert Jan van Gelder (2012)

*A Treasury of Virtues: Sayings, Sermons, and Teachings of ʿAlī*, by al-Qāḍī al-Quḍāʿī, with the *One Hundred Proverbs* attributed to al-Jāḥiẓ
Edited and translated by Tahera Qutbuddin (2013)

*The Epistle on Legal Theory*, by al-Shāfiʿī
Edited and translated by Joseph E. Lowry (2013)

*Leg over Leg*, by Aḥmad Fāris al-Shidyāq
Edited and translated by Humphrey Davies (4 volumes; 2013–14)

*Virtues of the Imām Aḥmad ibn Ḥanbal*, by Ibn al-Jawzī
Edited and translated by Michael Cooperson (2 volumes; 2013–15)

*The Epistle of Forgiveness*, by Abū l-ʿAlāʾ al-Maʿarrī
Edited and translated by Geert Jan van Gelder and Gregor Schoeler (2 volumes; 2013–14)

*The Principles of Sufism*, by ʿĀʾishah al-Bāʿūniyyah
Edited and translated by Th. Emil Homerin (2014)

*The Expeditions: An Early Biography of Muḥammad*, by Maʿmar ibn Rāshid
Edited and translated by Sean W. Anthony (2014)

*Two Arabic Travel Books*
*Accounts of China and India*, by Abū Zayd al-Sīrāfī
Edited and translated by Tim Mackintosh-Smith (2014)
*Mission to the Volga*, by Aḥmad ibn Faḍlān
Edited and translated by James Montgomery (2014)

*Disagreements of the Jurists: A Manual of Islamic Legal Theory*, by al-Qāḍī al-Nuʿmān
Edited and translated by Devin J. Stewart (2015)

*Consorts of the Caliphs: Women and the Court of Baghdad*, by Ibn al-Sāʿī
Edited by Shawkat M. Toorawa and translated by the Editors of the Library of Arabic Literature (2015)

*What ʿĪsā ibn Hishām Told Us*, by Muḥammad al-Muwayliḥī
Edited and translated by Roger Allen (2 volumes; 2015)

*The Life and Times of Abū Tammām*, by Abū Bakr Muḥammad ibn Yaḥyā al-Ṣūlī
Edited and translated by Beatrice Gruendler (2015)

*The Sword of Ambition: Bureaucratic Rivalry in Medieval Egypt*, by ʿUthmān ibn Ibrāhīm al-Nābulusī
Edited and translated by Luke Yarbrough (2016)

*Brains Confounded by the Ode of Abū Shādūf Expounded*, by Yūsuf al-Shirbīnī
Edited and translated by Humphrey Davies (2 volumes; 2016)

*Light in the Heavens: Sayings of the Prophet Muḥammad*, by al-Qāḍī al-Quḍāʿī
Edited and translated by Tahera Qutbuddin (2016)

*Risible Rhymes*, by Muḥammad ibn Maḥfūẓ al-Sanhūrī
Edited and translated by Humphrey Davies (2016)

*A Hundred and One Nights*
Edited and translated by Bruce Fudge (2016)

*The Excellence of the Arabs*, by Ibn Qutaybah
Edited by James E. Montgomery and Peter Webb
Translated by Sarah Bowen Savant and Peter Webb (2017)

*Scents and Flavors: A Syrian Cookbook*
Edited and translated by Charles Perry (2017)

*Arabian Satire: Poetry from 18th-Century Najd*, by Ḥmēdān al-Shwēʿir
Edited and translated by Marcel Kurpershoek (2017)

*In Darfur: An Account of the Sultanate and Its People*, by Muḥammad ibn ʿUmar al-Tūnisī
Edited and translated by Humphrey Davies (2 volumes; 2018)

*War Songs*, by ʿAntarah ibn Shaddād
Edited by James E. Montgomery
Translated by James E. Montgomery with Richard Sieburth (2018)

*Arabian Romantic: Poems on Bedouin Life and Love*, by ʿAbdallah ibn Sbayyil
Edited and translated by Marcel Kurpershoek (2018)

*Dīwān ʿAntarah ibn Shaddād: A Literary-Historical Study*, by James E. Montgomery (2018)

*Stories of Piety and Prayer: Deliverance Follows Adversity*, by al-Muḥassin ibn ʿAlī al-Tanūkhī
Edited and translated by Julia Bray (2019)

*Tajrīd sayf al-himmah li-stikhrāj mā fī dhimmat al-dhimmah: A Scholarly Edition of ʿUthmān ibn Ibrāhīm al-Nābulusī's Text*, by Luke Yarbrough (2019)

*The Philosopher Responds: An Intellectual Correspondence from the Tenth Century*, by Abū Ḥayyān al-Tawḥīdī and Abū ʿAlī Miskawayh
Edited by Bilal Orfali and Maurice A. Pomerantz
Translated by Sophia Vasalou and James E. Montgomery (2 volumes; 2019)

*The Discourses: Reflections on History, Sufism, Theology, and Literature—* Volume One, by al-Ḥasan al-Yūsī
Edited and translated by Justin Stearns (2020)

*Impostures*, by al-Ḥarīrī
Translated by Michael Cooperson (2020)

*Maqāmāt Abī Zayd al-Sarūjī*, by al-Ḥarīrī
Edited by Michael Cooperson (2020)

*The Yoga Sutras of Patañjali*, by Abū Rayḥān al-Bīrūnī
Edited and translated by Mario Kozah (2020)

*The Book of Charlatans*, by Jamāl al-Dīn ʿAbd al-Raḥīm al-Jawbarī
Edited by Manuela Dengler
Translated by Humphrey Davies (2020)

*A Physician on the Nile: A Description of Egypt and Journal of the Famine Years*, by ʿAbd al-Laṭīf al-Baghdādī
Edited and translated by Tim Mackintosh-Smith (2021)

*The Book of Travels*, by Ḥannā Diyāb
Edited by Johannes Stephan
Translated by Elias Muhanna (2 volumes; 2021)

*Kalīlah and Dimnah: Fables of Virtue and Vice*, by Ibn al-Muqaffaʿ
Edited by Michael Fishbein
Translated by Michael Fishbein and James E. Montgomery (2021)

*Love, Death, Fame: Poetry and Lore from the Emirati Oral Tradition*, by al-Māyidī ibn Ẓāhir
Edited and translated by Marcel Kurpershoek (2022)

*The Essence of Reality: A Defense of Philosophical Sufism*, by ʿAyn al-Quḍāt
Edited and translated by Mohammed Rustom (2022)

*The Requirements of the Sufi Path: A Defense of the Mystical Tradition*, by Ibn Khaldūn
Edited and translated by Carolyn Baugh (2022)

*The Doctors' Dinner Party*, by Ibn Buṭlān
Edited and translated by Philip F. Kennedy and Jeremy Farrell (2023)

*Fate the Hunter: Early Arabic Hunting Poems*
Edited and translated by James E. Montgomery (2023)

*The Book of Monasteries*, by al-Shābushtī
Edited and translated by Hilary Kilpatrick (2023)

*In Deadly Embrace: Arabic Hunting Poems*, by Ibn al-Muʿtazz
Edited and translated by James E. Montgomery (2023)

*The Divine Names*, by ʿAfīf al-Dīn al-Tilimsānī
Edited and translated by Yousef Casewit (2023)

*Bedouin Poets of the Nafūd Desert*, by Khalaf Abū Zwayyid, ʿAdwān al-Hirbīd, and ʿAjlān ibn Rmāl
Edited and translated by Marcel Kurpershoek (2024)

*The Rules of Logic*, by Najm al-Dīn al-Kātibī
Edited and translated by Tony Street (2024)

*Najm al-dīn al-Kātibī's al-Risālah al-Shamsiyyah: An Edition and Translation with Commentary*, by Tony Street (2024)

*A Demon Spirit: Arabic Hunting Poems*, by Abū Nuwās
Edited and translated by James E. Montgomery (2024)

*Arabian Hero: Oral Poetry and Narrative Lore from Northern Arabia*, by Shāyiʿ al-Amsaḥ
Edited and translated by Marcel Kurpershoek (2024)

*The Genius of Invective: Ibn Zaydūn's Letter Explained*, by Ibn Nubātah
Edited and translated by Peter Webb (2025)

*The Turks and the Caliphal Army*, by al-Jāḥiẓ
Edited and translated by Robert G. Hoyland (2025)

English-only Paperbacks

*Leg over Leg*, by Aḥmad Fāris al-Shidyāq (2 volumes; 2015)

*The Expeditions: An Early Biography of Muḥammad*, by Maʿmar ibn Rāshid (2015)

*The Epistle on Legal Theory: A Translation of al-Shāfiʿī's Risālah*, by al-Shāfiʿī (2015)

*The Epistle of Forgiveness*, by Abū l-ʿAlāʾ al-Maʿarrī (2016)

*The Principles of Sufism*, by ʿĀʾishah al-Bāʿūniyyah (2016)

*A Treasury of Virtues: Sayings, Sermons, and Teachings of ʿAlī*, by al-Qāḍī al-Quḍāʿī with the *One Hundred Proverbs* attributed to al-Jāḥiẓ (2016)

*The Life of Ibn Ḥanbal*, by Ibn al-Jawzī (2016)

*Mission to the Volga*, by Ibn Faḍlān (2017)

*Accounts of China and India*, by Abū Zayd al-Sīrāfī (2017)

*Consorts of the Caliphs: Women and the Court of Baghdad*, by Ibn al-Sāʿī (2017)

*A Hundred and One Nights* (2017)

*Disagreements of the Jurists: A Manual of Islamic Legal Theory*, by al-Qāḍī al-Nuʿmān (2017)

*What ʿĪsā ibn Hishām Told Us*, by Muḥammad al-Muwayliḥī (2018)

*War Songs*, by ʿAntarah ibn Shaddād (2018)

*The Life and Times of Abū Tammām*, by Abū Bakr Muḥammad ibn Yaḥyā al-Ṣūlī (2018)

*The Sword of Ambition*, by ʿUthmān ibn Ibrāhīm al-Nābulusī (2019)

*Brains Confounded by the Ode of Abū Shādūf Expounded: Volume One*, by Yūsuf al-Shirbīnī (2019)

*Brains Confounded by the Ode of Abū Shādūf Expounded: Volume Two*, by Yūsuf al-Shirbīnī and *Risible Rhymes*, by Muḥammad ibn Maḥfūẓ al-Sanhūrī (2019)

*The Excellence of the Arabs*, by Ibn Qutaybah (2019)

*Light in the Heavens: Sayings of the Prophet Muḥammad*, by al-Qāḍī al-Quḍāʿī (2019)

*Scents and Flavors: A Syrian Cookbook* (2020)

*Arabian Satire: Poetry from 18th-Century Najd*, by Ḥmēdān al-Shwēʿir (2020)

*In Darfur: An Account of the Sultanate and Its People*, by Muḥammad al-Tūnisī (2020)

*Arabian Romantic: Poems on Bedouin Life and Love*, by Ibn Sbayyil (2020)

*The Philosopher Responds: An Intellectual Correspondence from the Tenth Century*, by Abū Ḥayyān al-Tawḥīdī and Abū ʿAlī Miskawayh (2021)

*Impostures*, by al-Ḥarīrī (2021)

*The Discourses: Reflections on History, Sufism, Theology, and Literature—Volume One*, by al-Ḥasan al-Yūsī (2021)

*The Yoga Sutras of Patañjali*, by Abū Rayḥān al-Bīrūnī (2022)

*The Book of Charlatans*, by Jamāl al-Dīn ʿAbd al-Raḥīm al-Jawbarī (2022)

*The Book of Travels*, by Ḥannā Diyāb (2022)

*A Physician on the Nile: A Description of Egypt and Journal of the Famine Years*, by ʿAbd al-Laṭīf al-Baghdādī (2022)

*Kalīlah and Dimnah: Fables of Virtue and Vice*, by Ibn al-Muqaffaʿ (2023)

*Love, Death, Fame: Poetry and Lore from the Emirati Oral Tradition*, by al-Māyidī ibn Ẓāhir (2023)

*The Essence of Reality: A Defense of Philosophical Sufism*, by ʿAyn al-Quḍāt (2023)

*The Doctors' Dinner Party*, by Ibn Buṭlān (2024)

*The Requirements of the Sufi Path: A Defense of the Mystical Tradition*, by Ibn Khaldūn (2024)

*Fate the Hunter: Early Arabic Hunting Poems* (2024)

*The Book of Monasteries*, by al-Shābushtī (2025)

*In Deadly Embrace: Arabic Hunting Poems*, by Ibn al-Muʿtazz (2025)

*The Divine Names: A Mystical Theology of the Names of God in the Qurʾan*, by ʿAfīf al-Dīn al-Tilimsānī (2025)

*The Rules of Logic*, by Najm al-Dīn al-Kātibī (2025)

*Bedouin Poets of the Nafūd Desert*, by Khalaf Abū Zwayyid, ʿAdwān al-Hirbīd, and ʿAjlān ibn Rmāl (2025)

www.ingramcontent.com/pod-product-compliance
Lightning Source LLC
Jackson TN
JSHW020245060825
88299JS00001B/1

* 9 7 8 1 4 7 9 8 4 0 6 8 7 *